JANE M.
GU

CHAMPAGNE

AND
SPARKLING WINES

JANE MacQUITTY'S
GUIDE TO
CHAMPAGNE
AND
SPARKLING WINES

Mitchell Beazley

Published in Great Britain in 1993
by Mitchell Beazley International,
an imprint of Reed Consumer Books Limited,
Michelin House, 81 Fulham Road
London SW3 6RB
and Auckland, Melbourne, Singapore and Toronto

First published 1986 as *Jane MacQuitty's Pocket Guide to Champagne and Sparkling Wines*. This edition revised, updated and expanded, published 1993.

ISBN 1857329481

A CIP catalogue record for this book is available from the British Library

Editor: Anthea Snow
Art Editor: Paul Tilby
Data Inputting: Alison Franks
Illustrations: Madeleine David
Maps: Sue Sharples
Production: Fiona Wright

Executive Editor: Anne Ryland
Art Director: Tim Foster

Typeset in Bembo
Produced by Mandarin Offset, Hong Kong
Printed and bound in China

Contents

How to Use this Book

This book is a country-by-country guide to champagne and the world's sparkling wines.

The Introduction on pages 8–26 explains how champagne and sparkling wines are made, the grapes they are made from, their different styles, and how to buy, store, serve and enjoy them.

Throughout the book, 'champagne' refers to sparkling wine from the Champagne region, while 'sparkling wine' refers to wine from outside that region. Each country has an introduction that provides a background to the wines produced including, where necessary, a 'Labels and the Law' section that deciphers the confusing jungle of sparkling wine terminology. This is followed by a directory of the producers in that country, listed alphabetically, which offers a profile of each firm and an assessment of its wines.

As the method by which a sparkling wine is made is an important indication of quality, the method (or methods) used by each producer is shown by a code:

MC *Méthode champenoise*
CC *Cuve close*, also known as the Charmat, bulk or tank method
TM Transfer method
CM Continuous, or Russian continuous flow method
IM Injection or carbonated method
MR *Méthode rurale*
MD *Méthode dioise*
MG *Méthode gaillaçoise*

These methods are explained on pages 10–16.

In addition, there is a star rating for the wines:
  →★ Basic, usually mass produced
  ★ Acceptable everyday fizz
  ★★ Recommended; definitely above average
  ★★★ Highly recommended; excellent quality
  ★★★★ Finest; rare, prestigious and, alas, expensive
  ★→★★ Producer whose range includes both ordinary
        and superior, recommended wine
  ☆ Indicates the predicted future quality of a wine that
        has not yet been released.

Producers cross-referenced within the directories appear in small caps. Other symbols in the directory sections include:

'76, '82 Recommended vintages that have been especially successful for producers appear, where appropriate, between the method and the star rating. Most occur in the section on champagne, where the staying power and supremacy of vintages are well established. A general guide to champagne vintages is on pages 33–36.

Star buys Most countries feature several producers with specific 'star buys'. These represent exceptional quality and value for money.

The following abbreviations are used in the book:

g/l	grams per litre	**kg**	kilograms
ha	hectares	**M**	million
km	kilometres		

All figures are the latest available. The Glossary at the end of the book explains the various terms used in connection with champagne and sparkling wine. Choosing any wine is a matter of personal taste and style. The views in this book are entirely those of the author.

Acknowledgments

This book could never have been written without the help of friends and family all over the world. In particular I would like to thank the following for their invaluable assistance: David Balls, Penny Bool, Pierre Bouard, Matthew Boucher, Christine Campbell, Nicholas Clarke MW, Judy Coleman, Eileen Crane, Brian Croser, Cecilia Daniels, Terry Dunleavy, Ronald Emler, André Enders, Sam Folsom, Sarah Fraser, Richard and Jenny Freeman, Toni Gill, Richard Goodman, Jean Gordon, Philip Hedges, João Henriques, Michael Hill-Smith, Nancy Jarratt, Fritz and Maureen Joubert, Margaret Le Roy, John Lipitch, Catherine Manac'h, Malcom McIntyre, Valera Nibbio, John Page, Rupert Ponsonby, Jan Read, Max Ringrow, Michaela Rodeno, Errol Slyfield, Charles Sydney, Alan Tenscher, Dip Ing Traxler, Jean Valentine, John Walter, Jeremy Watson, Simon Watson and Robin Young.

Introduction

Every year we drink some 1,400M bottles of champagne and sparkling wine. This means that throughout the world more than 46 bottles of 'fizz' are opened every second. Over 30 different countries now produce sparkling wine, and the latest surprising arrivals in the sparkling wine stakes, China and India, endorse this worldwide passion for fizz.

Europe still produces 80 percent of the world's sparkling wines, but the USA and, to a lesser extent, Australia are rapidly gaining ground. Just 300M bottles are produced outside Europe. Champagne's share, more than 240M bottles, is not huge either. Nor is *méthode champenoise* the most common method of putting bubbles in a bottle — that distinction goes to Monsieur Charmat's swift, economical tank method.

But whether it be Charmat or champagne, sparkling wine continues to be the world's favourite festive drink. And as with every style of wine, there are good, bad and ugly examples. This book aims to sort one from the other. Never again should you have to suffer what one early Victorian toast so aptly described as: 'Champagne to our real friends and real pain to our sham friends'.

The Wines

The world's winemakers are an imaginative lot. There can be few grape varieties, or other fruits for that matter, that somebody somewhere has not tried to turn into a sparkling wine. Some of the more bizarre attempts have included *méthode champenoise* sparklers made from fruit such as pineapples, pears or apples. No less extraordinary perhaps to taste are those white sparkling wines that have used, say, the tart gooseberry-green charms of the Sauvignon Blanc grape as their base (as in many South African wines), or even decolourized red wines.

Flavoured fizz seems to have caught the imagination of modern winemakers, who use everything from almonds to strawberries to titillate the tastebuds! All these sparkling wine flavour fancies are unlikely to last forever. What most of us are looking for, wittingly or unwittingly, in the perfect glass of fizz is something that approaches the finesse and flavour of champagne. It could well be that there are more magical combinations of grape varieties out there than champagne's classic Pinot Noir, Chardonnay and Pinot Meunier mix. But, if so, they have yet to be discovered.

The Grapes

Champagne is made from a blend of white and black grapes, the latter gently pressed to yield only white juice. Pinot Noir and Pinot Meunier are the black grapes used and Chardonnay the white. Champagnes in which the black grapes dominate usually have a deep golden, occasionally pinky glow to them. The Chardonnay-dominated wines are a paler, often green-tinged, straw-yellow colour.

When the *chef de cave* in Champagne comes to put the blend together in the spring after the vintage, he is looking for a balanced collection of full-flavoured (but not overwhelming) base wines with high acidity and low alcohol. Pinot Noir will give him the backbone, strength and depth of flavour he wants, while the Chardonnay imparts elegance, freshness, lightness and finesse. This leaves Pinot Meunier with its aromatic nose and soft, subtle, quick-maturing style to marry the other two and tone down any overtly flavoured edges they may have had. Pinot Meunier, however, should not be dismissed as a second-class sparkling wine grape variety: it isn't (see pages 27–28).

So far the most successful *méthode champenoise* wines made outside Champagne are those that contain a fair proportion of Chardonnay or Pinot Noir, or both. Even within France, whose wine-producing regions remain fiercely parochial and independent of one another, the merits of the Chardonnay grape for one, as a sparkling wine base, have been recognized outside Champagne. Both Crémant d'Alsace and Blanquette de Limoux winemakers include the Chardonnay grape in their finest and most expensive blends, and are convinced that it has raised the quality of their sparkling wines. However, regional traditions and the choice of grapes still remain sacrosanct in some areas. The newest French sparkling wine appellation, Crémant de Bordeaux, created in 1990, sticks resolutely to the region's already well-established white grape trio of Sémillon, Sauvignon and Muscadelle, (although rumoured experimental Chardonnay plantings in the area have been successful).

Outside France the superiority of Chardonnay and Pinot Noir has been acknowledged. California, as usual, appears to be leading the field, with Chardonnay widely planted and, to a lesser extent, Pinot Noir, with plenty of new plantings in the Carneros district. Australia, New Zealand, South Africa and Spain, among others, are increasingly following suit. Once all these new plantings come on stream, and many have already done so, their sparkling wines will certainly be even tougher competition for the *champenois*. To date, Chardonnay and Pinot Noir planted outside cool-climate Champagne, in hot-climate areas such as Australia and California, have a tendency if left unchecked to take on overly hefty, big, fat fruity flavours. Toning down this hot country exuberance in favour of cool country-style finesse is a current preoccupation of many of the world's sparkling winemakers. How great this New World competition becomes will be intriguing to observe.

The Methods

Méthode champenoise Despite the efforts of modern technology, the costly, time-consuming and labour-intensive *méthode champenoise* is still the best way to make sparkling wine.

In Champagne the grapes are picked by hand to minimize spoilage and the possibility of staining the juice with bruised black grape skins, and taken directly to a nearby press house. Each firm owns numerous such *vendangeoirs*, which are scattered throughout the region, again to minimize spoilage. Interestingly, several New World producers with large vineyards now follow Champagne's lead by hand picking.

The grapes are pressed swiftly and gently, either in the traditional, vertical wooden presses or in modern, automated, horizontal presses, of which the best and most frequently used version is the bladder press. Each press is loaded with 4,000kg of grapes, but only the first 2,550 litres pressed from these can be sold as champagne. The advantage of the old-fashioned champagne presses and the reason why many of the big firms, including Moët & Chandon, still use them is that these shallow presses reduce the time the juice spends in contact with the skins, minimizing staining. In addition, a natural filtering effect takes place as the juice runs quickly down through the mass of grapes and out through the wooden slats. The first 2,050 litres-worth of 'free-run juice' literally flows from the press with little or no pressing. This is the *vin de cuvée*, the finest quality juice. The next best quality juice is the *vin de taille*, or second pressing, and this adds up to 500 litres. The final pressing, once known as the *deuxième taille*, producing a darker and inferior base wine, was officially abolished in Champagne following new regulations in 1992. All three champagne grapes are pressed and fermented separately.

The first fermentation takes place in the cellars of the various champagne houses to which the must or juice has been transported. This slow, cool fermentation takes 3–4 weeks. Today, houses such as Krug and Alfred Gratien use oak casks in which to ferment their wine, but large, stainless steel fermenters are much more common. After first fermentation the wine is racked into a clean cask or tank. Cold settling and clarification of the must prior to fermentation to prevent any possible spoiling and to give cleaner, clearer juice a is standard practice now in hot countries for *méthode champenoise* wines.

In the January after the harvest the *chef de cave* starts to put the various blends of still wines or *cuvées* together. Apart from base wines made from Chardonnay, Pinot Noir and Pinot Meunier, the champagne blender also has at his disposal wines from different vintages (including considerably older reserve wines) and from different villages. At any one time he might have a hefty, musk melon-like Pinot Noir from Ay, a fruity, aromatic Pinot Meunier from Leuvrigny and a light, racy, flowery Chardonnay from Cramant, plus a host of other wines.

In theory, non-vintage wines could contain 70 different wines or more. In practice, it is usually half that number or less. Champagne, like many of the finest *méthode champenoise* wines from elsewhere, acquires much of its majesty from the harmonious combinations of many different wines. The end result is far greater than any of the individual components. The permutations are endless, but all the elements must be orchestrated into one perfectly polished piece. No wonder the *champenois* are keen on musical analogies

By April the complex and highly skilled task of tasting, analysing and blending is completed on a small scale and the next step is to ensure that the wines in the vast tanks in the cellar are blended in exactly the same proportions. The blended still wine is then bottled with the *liqueur de tirage*, a sugar and wine solution with a little of a selected yeast strain, and the bottle is given a temporary seal – a crown cap in most cases, not unlike the cap that seals beer bottles. Some houses still use a proper cork instead of a crown cap at this stage, but this is usually only for their finest champagnes. Any bottle that has been sealed with a crown cap has a curvaceous crown ring at the neck of the bottle, just as beer bottles do. Those champagnes that have been stoppered with a proper cork have a straight-sided or square-edged ring at the neck.

Once the wine is sealed in thick, heavy-duty, glass bottles, made to withstand pressure, the second fermentation begins and the yeast gradually converts the sugar into alcohol. At the same time carbon dioxide (CO_2) bubbles are given off and dissolve in the wine. Once the fermentation has stopped, a yeasty sediment falls to the underside of the bottle. It is vital that the wine remains in contact with this sediment during the ageing period which now follows, because it gives the wine the intriguing, complex flavours that are one of the hallmarks of champagne.

Removing the sediment is the next stage. Before Veuve Clicquot came up with the idea of *remuage*, or riddling, in 1816, getting rid of the sediment was rather a clumsy affair. Today, the process is much as Madame Clicquot developed it. The bottles are placed horizontally in *pupitres* (wooden racks with holes) and gradually shaken and twisted in the racks by the *remueur* until they are upended and the sediment has collected at the neck and is resting on the cork.

Remuage carried out manually is both time-consuming and

labour-intensive, a fact which led, in the early 1970s, to the introduction of automatic *remuage*. Riddling machines known as *gyropalettes*, bottle-filled square cages, imitate the movements of the *remueur* by shaking and twisting on a timed programme. Automatic or partially automatic *remuage* is now being used by many producers, reducing the time taken for this process from at least two months to just one week. However, not everyone in Champagne is convinced of the suitability of these machines, and many *champenois* insist on hand riddling for their top *cuvées*.

A new, experimental *remuage* technique uses *micro-billes*. Bottles are seeded with these porous yeast capsules and, after the second fermentation and ageing process has taken place, the bottles are upended and the sediment, trapped inside the *micro-billes*, falls at once onto the cork. Moët & Chandon are likely to be the first to release wines made by this method, possibly by the late 1990s. The very latest high tech preoccupation however, replacing *micro-billes*, is flocculating yeasts, which could reduce the *remuage* process to as little as one day.

Once the riddling and ageing period is over the champagne is ready for disgorging or *dégorgement*. The traditional method of disgorgement by hand, known as *dégorgement à la volée*, allows the cork dangerously to shoot out of the bottle and can easily waste more wine than is necessary. Most firms use the *dégorgement à la glace* process in which the neck of the upended bottle is dipped into a freezing brine solution. The sediment is frozen into a soft pellet of ice which shoots out of the bottle when the crown cap or cork is removed. A little wine escapes at the same time and the bottle is then topped up with a blend of wine and sugar known as the *dosage*. The amount of sugar used determines whether the wine will be dry (*brut*) or one of the sweeter styles (*see* page xx). The second, or final, cork, the one customers remove themselves, is then inserted and fixed firmly with a wire muzzle.

Méthode rurale This was the first method devised to give still wines bubbles, and was practised mainly in regions where the wines had a natural tendency to sparkle. The Benedictine monks of St-Hilaire at Limoux, in southwest France, no doubt used this method, perhaps as early as 1531, to make their sparkling wines. Before the wine bottle was introduced, in the late 17th century, these naturally sparkling wines would develop a pleasing *pétillance* in cask in the spring after the vintage, when the warmer weather would encourage a secondary or malolactic fermentation. By leaving the wine in cask in contact with the yeasty sediment, a cloudy, rustic, slightly sparkling wine was produced. Few of these simple wines can be found today but one true, French, *méthode rurale* sparkler does still exist: Vin de Blanquette. Since it is neither filtered nor riddled, the resulting wine, like those very early versions, is cloudy. It is difficult to obtain outside the Limoux region.

Méthode dioise Clairette de Die, from Die in the Rhône, is the only wine made by this technique in France, a refined version of the *méthode rurale*. Made mostly by the Cave Coopérative at Die it involves fermentation prolonged (3–4 months) by refrigeration, and regular filtration. The wine is then transferred to sealed bottles where fermentation continues and the bubbles given off are trapped in the wine. Once the wine has finished its bubble-inducing fermentation, it is given a final filtration to remove sediment and put into clean bottles. The chief advantage of the *méthode dioise* is that the fresh, floral, fruity charm of the Muscat grape is kept and, unlike most *méthode rurale* wines, Clairette de Die Tradition is star-bright, not slightly cloudy.

Méthode gaillaçoise Another variation on the *méthode rurale*, which is perhaps a little less sophisticated than the *méthode dioise*. *Méthode gaillaçoise* wines come from Gaillac in southwest France and are seldom found outside the region. Like all *méthode rurale* wines, they have a spontaneous second fermentation in bottle without the aid of sugar and yeast. In practice this second fermentation is a continuation of the first. The wine does not receive a *dosage*.

Transfer A compromise between *cuve close* and *méthode champenoise*, giving some of the latter's finesse for far less work. The second fermentation takes place in bottle, as in the *méthode* *champenoise*, and the wines are aged for a short period. However, there is no expensive riddling and disgorgement. Instead, the wine is transferred under pressure from the bottles into a tank. The sediment sinks to the bottom, the wine is drawn off, given its *dosage* and a final filtration and then bottled, still under pressure. Transfer method wines are now produced mainly in the USA. Their quality is indeed finer than *cuve close* but still not on a par with *méthode champenoise* wines. Kriter is a famous French transfer method wine.

Cuve close, Charmat, bulk or tank Perfected by Eugène Charmat in 1907, following on from his father's work and based on the theory that if, as in the *méthode champenoise*, a second bubble-inducing fermentation worked well in a bottle, it could also take place in a tank. Still wine is pumped into a giant, stainless steel pressure tank and yeast and sugar are injected, starting the second fermentation. The wine is then left to settle, transferred off its sediment and filtered into a holding tank where it receives a *dosage* prior to bottling. As all these processes take place under pressure, the bubbles given off during the second fermentation remain trapped in the wine. Given the speed and ease of production – it can take just three weeks from start to finish – it is not surprising that this is now one of the most popular methods of producing sparkling wine. The quality, although a noticeable step up from that of carbonated fizz, will never equal that of *méthode champenoise* wines. Once again, the bubbles are larger than the pin-head variety of champagne and disappear fairly rapidly.

Russian continuous flow This ingenious system, in which bubbles are introduced via a second fermentation in tank, allows the Russians to produce vast quantities of ordinary sparkling wine for what must be the minimum possible outlay and manpower. A continuous supply of base wine is fed under pressure through a row of fermentation tanks. This row is joined by others. A continuous flow of sugar and yeast solution is fed into one set of tanks and *dosage* into another, while, in between, is a series of tanks for filtering, pasteurizing and cold stabilization. The whole process takes three weeks from start to finish and, true to its name, a continuous supply of sparkling wine is ready to be bottled from the final tank. The Russians calculate that these sparkling wines are 20 percent cheaper than those produced by the *cuve close* method. Outside the USSR few firms admit to using this process – one that does is Lancers in Portugal.

Carbonated or injection The cheapest, quickest and least lovely way of putting bubbles into wine. Still wine is placed in a large, closed tank and chilled. Carbon dioxide is pumped into the wine, which is then bottled under pressure. Fizzy lemonade or cola is made in the same way. Carbonated wines have large bubbles that disappear quickly and an off-putting frothy, soda–pop character in the mouth.

Use of the Term Méthode Champenoise/Méthode Traditionnelle

Brussels is to blame. For four years, EC ministers deliberated over the difficult problem as to exactly what constituted a *méthode champenoise* wine. They failed to come up with a precise EC definition and a typical bureaucratic decision was reached: if the committee could not agree then the solution was to ban the description entirely from sparkling wines.

An eight-year transition period, ending on 31 August 1994, precedes the ruling that the term *méthode champenoise* technically should not appear on any new sparkling wines made by this method, coming from or exported to any EC country. Those producers who had already used this phrase on their labels for some time could continue to use the term, but they too must gradually phase it out, and completely remove it by 31 August 1994. This ruling accounted for the surprisingly large quantities of *méthode champenoise* wine produced in France during the 1993 vintage.

Perhaps typically, the French claim that banning the phrase will put an end to the confusion that exists in wine drinkers' minds, who, while the term persists, might mistakenly think that any *méthode champenoise* wine is champagne. More cynical observers believe that it is the important markets for non-French *méthode champenoise*, such as in the UK or USA, that have prompted this decision. The EC would perhaps be better advised to turn its attention to preventing the Australians and Americans from using the term 'champagne' itself to describe their sparkling wines, much of which has not even been made by the *méthode champenoise*.

So far, the term '*crémant*' is a widely adopted new title for French *méthode champenoise* wine, and, as a result, usually refers to fully sparkling or mousseux wine rather than, as before, to softly sparkling styles. The original French *appellation contrôlée crémants* are, in return, becomming fully sparkling wines, although this varies from region to region and between producers. Expect to see other regions' *crémant* bottles soon. For the purposes of this book, the term *crémant* is being used in its traditional sense (*see* page 19). The New World and regions in France other than Champagne have also been fighting back with the title '*méthode traditionnelle*', which is at present the most frequently used and accepted alternative to the words '*méthode champenoise*'. At the time of writing, however, all such terminology is very much in a state of flux. Discerning sparkling wine drinkers, I feel, deserve a better deal.

The Styles

Non-vintage Start your appreciation of sparkling wines with the non-vintage versions, which are widely available and, indeed, account for the vast majority of sales. These reflect the typical taste and style of each house and are blended every year to show a consistent 'house style', particularly in Champagne. By law all non-vintage champagne must now be aged for a minimum of one year in bottle before it is sold, and no champagne is allowed to be bottled in the year of its harvest, although this age limit may rise to 15 or even 18 months if the quality-minded *champenois* have their way. Thus, the youngest non-vintage champagne available today will be at least 15 months old. Most non-vintage champagne from the better houses is a blend of two or three recent vintages and has at least three years' bottle-age. The average non-vintage *cuvée* is a blend of about two-thirds black grapes to one-third white.

Vintage Finer, older and more expensive than non-vintage wines, these are wines or blends of wines from a single year, and as such they reflect both the character of the house *and* the year. In Champagne, again by law, they cannot be sold until three years after the harvest, but better producers try to give them at least five years' bottle-age. Not every year in Champagne is declared a vintage year (*see* pages 33–36 for a guide to champagne vintages). Vintage wines used to be the most popular of all the champagne styles; now, sadly, only small amounts are sold every year. Apart from labels bearing the vintage date, usually much too discreetly, the year will also be stamped on the cork of vintage champagne and other vintage fizz.

Rosé Pink or rosé sparkling wine and champagne should not be dismissed as simply a light-hearted little drink. It can be superb and sometimes eclipses its less rosy relations. There are two methods of making rosé sparkling wine and champagne. The quickest and least costly is simply to add a touch of the region's still red wine to the basic white-wine blend. This has the advantage of guaranteeing a consistent colour. A few champagne houses adhere to the traditional method, in which black grape skins are left in contact with the juice for a day or two, staining it a pretty pale pink. Laurent Perrier is one of the very few houses still to practise this method.

Prestige or deluxe Moët & Chandon was the first house to produce a deluxe champagne or *cuvée de prestige*, in 1921. The wine, known as Dom Pérignon, was blended initially only for friends and family. Others wines followed, and today almost every sparkling wine house makes a prestige offering, usually sold in an ornate bottle at a very high price. Whether they are all worth the money is another question. The *champenois* point out that theirs are usually made from the finest wines of the finest years and as such are *la crème de la crème*. After Dom Pérignon, Roederer's Cristal is probably the most famous example. Krug, incidentally, claims that all its champagnes are prestige *cuvées*, including its Grande Cuvée. Prestige wines may be made from the finest vintages, or from a blend of wines from the best years.

Crémant Once a term used only to describe softly sparkling wines, in advance of new EC regulations it has come to refer (in France) to quality French *méthode champenoise* wines usually of full pressure made outside the Champagne region (*see* page 17). Traditionally, though, these softly sparkling or 'creaming' wines are with roughly 3.5 atmospheres of pressure behind the cork instead of the usual 5 or 6 for fully sparkling, or *mousseux* wines. Some people prefer their gentle fizz as a partner for food to the fully sparkling styles. Crémant d'Alsace is slightly more sparkling, with about 4 atmospheres of pressure.

The new regulations (effective from 31 August 1994) will forbid the *champenois* from using the term *crémant* on their bottles. This means, sadly, that consumers will have no way of knowing whether their champagne is a *crémant* wine or not, unless there is a back label. Krug once produced a *crémant* champagne as, more recently, did Mumm. They will also ban the description '*méthode champenoise*' from any wine not champagne. This has encouraged Bordeaux's *méthode champenoise* producers to improve the quality of their sparkling wine and to rename it Crémant de Bordeaux. Regrettably, given champagne's obvious superiority and the *champenois*' determination not to lower the magical image of their product, this probably means the end of *crémant* champagne.

Blanc de blancs This ultra-fashionable term now crops up on numerous labels – perhaps rather more often than it should. A true *blanc de blancs* champagne or sparkling wine is a white wine made exclusively from white grapes. In Champagne this is therefore a 100 percent Chardonnay wine and, as such, should have a fine, light, fresh and fruity character. Some find *blanc de blancs* champagnes rather too shy and delicate, and for these people it is better to keep to the other vintage and non-vintage blends, which will have a fair proportion of big, full-bodied black grapes blended in with the white.

Blanc de noirs A rarity, at least in that the term hardly ever appears on a label. *Blancs de noirs* are white wines made, in most cases, in Champagne and from either or both of the black Champagne grapes, Pinot Noir and Pinot Meunier.

Blancs de noirs from other parts of the world may be produced from different black grapes. Rich, ripe and full-bodied, these wines are especially delicious with food. Bollinger's costly Vieilles Vignes Françaises is one example. Outside the Champagne region, and especially in the New World, these pale pink or pinky-orange wines are more common, but are usually not of first class quality.

Single-vineyard A rarity in the Champagne region but rather more common elsewhere. Purists will argue that these lack the harmony and balance of champagnes made from a blend of grapes from different vineyards, but they present a unique opportunity to taste an unblended wine and for that reason alone are worth experiencing. Do not expect them to be cheap. Krug's Clos du Mesnil and Philipponat's Clos des Goisses, both from walled vineyards, are two examples.

Coteaux Champenois The still red or white wines of the Champagne region, not widely available but worth seeking out. When the harvest is small, only a few still wines are made as most of the crop is needed to make champagne. The *blanc de blancs*, or Chardonnay, Coteaux Champenois can be tart and lean, but Moët & Chandon's version, named after its Château Saran property, is good. There are others. Lovers of red burgundy will not find it easy to recognize red Coteaux Champenois because, although made from the same grape, Pinot Noir, it is very different in style. Bollinger's La Côte aux Enfants is the best example.

Buyer's Own Brand or BOB These are champagnes or sparkling wines bottled not, as is usual, under the label of the producer but under that of the seller. It is therefore quite possible to be served a champagne marked with the name of a restaurant, wine merchant or supermarket which will have done nothing more than select a blend from the producer. New laws now mean that the producer's name will have to appear on the label, or at least appear in code. Given the appalling quality of some Buyer's Own Brand champagnes, this is long overdue. (*See also* How to Read a Champagne Label, pages 31–33.)

Ratafia, fine and marc Much admired by locals and knowledge-able champagne lovers, these unusual drinks from the Champagne region take a little getting used to. *Ratafia* is made from fresh champagne grape juice mixed with brandy or sometimes cognac. The result is rich, strong, sweet and alcoholic. Serve it ice-cold as an aperitif or *digestif*. *Fine* and *marc* are much stronger, with about 40 percent alcohol, about twice the strength of *ratafia*. *Fine*, a brandy distilled from the still wine of the region, is the better of the two but is difficult to find outside Champagne. *Marc* is distilled from the skins, pips and stalks left behind after the last pressing. It is a fiery, rustic tipple that not everyone appreciates. Again, it is rarely found outside Champagne.

Pétillant These are slightly sparkling wines whose sparkle, or *pétil-lance*, is either a natural attribute or has been introduced. Most *pétillant* wines have roughly two atmospheres of pressure behind the cork, unlike the fully sparkling, or *mousseux*, wines that have 5–6. The word '*pétiller*' means to crackle as well as to sparkle, which is why some countries and companies describe these as 'crackling' wines. *Perlant* wines have the least sparkle of all, with just over one atmosphere of pressure.

Dry or Sweet

Champagne and other sparkling wines from EC countries are among the few that specify exactly how dry or sweet they are. The levels set out below apply from April 1993.

Extra brut	(*Extra Herb*, very dry) 0–6 g/l
Brut	(*bruto*, *Herb*, dry) less than 15 g/l
Extra dry	(*Extra Trocken*) 12–20 g/l
Sec	(*seco*, *asciutto*, *secco*, *Trocken*, dry) 17–35 g/l
Demi-sec	(*semi-seco*, *meio-seco*, *abboccato*, *Halbtrocken*, *Halbsüss*, medium-dry) 33–50 g/l
Doux/riche	(*dulce*, *doce*, *dolce*, *Mild*, sweet, rich) more than 50 g/l

It is mandatory for every EC producer, including champagne producers, to include one of the above terms on their labels. Of them all it is the *brut* styles that are most widely available, followed by extra dry, *sec* and *demi-sec*. The *ultra brut*, *brut zéro* and *brut sauvage* non-*dosage* styles of champagne now fit into the new *extra brut* category as do many of the low *dosage* wines produced by houses such as Bollinger and Krug whose styles have always been dry.

The exact amount of residual sugar used in the categories listed above does, however, vary from firm to firm and from country to country. Even in Champagne, one company's extra dry could well be drier than another's *brut*. Sweetness can be a useful ally for any *chef de cave* for it can mask any defects that the base wine might have. Certainly it is noticeable that the less distinguished champagnes from the smaller houses do all have higher *dosage* levels than those of the first division firms. Popular non-vintage *brut* wines from mediocre years always carry far higher *dosage* levels too than those that are a product of first class harvests. Top champagne producers use sweetness as sparingly as possible, preferring simply to polish off their blends with a touch of *dosage*, if any, plus a little older reserve wine. Both Krug and Bollinger have produced champagnes with no *dosage* at all.

The History of Champagne and Sparkling Wine

No one knows quite who discovered champagne, or, indeed, whether it was 'discovered' at all. As is usual in the wine world, the early vinous achievements in sparkling wine were rarely recorded and all that is left is mostly opinion and rumour, rather than fact.

The Benedictine monks of St-Hilaire at Limoux in southwest France claim that they were the first to produce a sparkling wine, as early as 1531, probably by the *méthode rurale* (*see* pages 13–14). This could well have been the forerunner of Blanquette de Limoux.

Others maintain that the first person to discover fizz was another Benedictine monk, Dom Pierre Pérignon, the blind cellarmaster at the Abbey of Hautvilliers from 1668 to 1715. But still others argue that all Dom Pérignon can be credited with is the idea of blending grapes from different vineyards to make a more harmonious wine.

The English certainly did their bit to help the birth of champagne for they were the first to make glass wine bottles, in 1660, and were also using corks to seal them at about that time. Still wines from Champagne were being shipped in cask to England during this period, but by 1676 the English had learnt the secret of champagne itself. They shipped still wine to England in the spring, bottled it before the malolactic fermentation was complete and were rewarded with a slightly sparkling bottle of wine. The English also knew that adding sugar to the wine prior to bottling produced a stronger sparkle, although the French, it appears, took until 1700 to work this out. Rustic, cloudy, slightly sparkling wines from other parts of France, again whose fermentation was incomplete, served straight from the cask, probably predated this. But it was the introduction of the glass wine bottle that marked the true birth date of champagne and sparkling wine.

Buying, Storing, Serving and Enjoying Sparkling Wines

Champagne and sparkling wines are the most sensitive of all wines. Light and heat are arch-enemies. Champagne deteriorates alarmingly quickly in hot, bright surroundings, and 24 hours is often all it takes to 'kill' a bottle. Similarly, bottles left upright rather than horizontal (with the wet cork making an airtight seal) can deteriorate in a matter of days. It is therefore vital not only that champagne or sparkling wine is stored horizontally in a cool (10°C/ 50°F), dark place but also that it is bought from someone who has kept it in similar conditions. If in doubt, demand that your bottle comes direct from a new packing case that you can see has been stored on its side.

It is worth storing even non-vintage champagne (as opposed to sparkling wine) for at least six months to a year before drinking it. Given this extra touch of maturity it takes on a richer, fuller, more complex flavour. Vintage champagne should be cellared for 5–10 years, depending on the style of the vintage and your own personal taste. If you like the flavour of old, rich, nutty champagne, then by all means keep it for longer. A guide to champagne vintages is given on pages 33–36.

Opening a bottle of champagne or sparkling wine looks more difficult than it is. Provided you keep your thumb firmly on the cork throughout and point the bottle away from people and windows there should be no problem. Impressive though it may be to watch racing drivers shower their fans with foam or waiters pop corks with abandon, at home the idea is to get this expensive wine into a glass, rather than over the ceiling. The first step is to remove the lead foil and then with thumb on cork to remove the wire muzzle. Still holding onto the cork with your right hand (if you are right-handed) gently turn the bottle with your left. As soon as the cork starts to move, tighten your grip so that the gas gradually escapes and the wine remains in the bottle, rather than foaming everywhere. Tight corks can usually be eased off with a pair of champagne pliers or, better still, Screwpull's Champagne Star (most good wine merchants stock them). Failing that, hold the neck of the bottle under the hot tap for a few seconds and this will increase the pressure.

All champagne and sparkling wine should be served cool, not frozen. The optimum temperature is about 7.5°C (45°F). This can be reached by placing the bottle inside the fridge door for an hour or in a bucket of water and ice for ten minutes or so. Those who prefer their bubbly colder should simply put the bottle back in the bucket for another five minutes – much longer and the wine will be robbed of its bouquet and the cold will numb the palate.

Glasses also affect the pleasure of drinking sparkling wine. Avoid the saucer-shaped variety: they flatten the bubbles and the bouquet, and even when filled to the brim give only a small measure. Tall, thin, plain, tulip-shaped glasses or champagne *flûtes* are perfect. With these, the bouquet is concentrated and the bubbles should rise in an appealing, vigorous, steady stream to the surface. At all costs avoid swizzle sticks – you have paid for the bubbles so why not enjoy them! Make certain too that your glasses are perfectly clean. Even the slightest speck of detergent or dust, or a drop of water will leave you with a flat, disappointing glassful. It is hard to imagine the household that regularly has half-finished bottles of champagne or sparkling wine about but, for those that do, a champagne stopper is essential. This nifty little device clamps over the neck of the bottle and keeps the bubbles lively and the wine fresh for several days provided the bottle is kept in the fridge.

Bargain bottles of sparkling wine or champagne that turn out to be more acidic and less enjoyable than you hoped can be cheered up. Fizz mixed fifty-fifty with fresh orange juice creates a Buck's Fizz and fifty–fifty with Guinness produces a Black Velvet. Increase the proportions to two-thirds fizz and one-third orange juice or Guinness for a more alcoholic mix. Champagne cocktails are horrid, give you a headache and are a waste of good champagne. Instead, serve a Kir Royale or Framboise Royale, for which a teaspoon of *crème de cassis* or *framboise* (blackcurrant or raspberry liqueur is poured into a tulip glass and topped up with champagne).

Judging the amount of champagne or sparkling wine needed for a wedding or any other event where it is the only wine to be served is not difficult. Most people drink about half a bottle per head at these functions. (A bottle usually contains about six full glasses.) If you like the thought of a big bottle to serve at a party, the following are available although the largest are now very difficult to find: Magnum, 2 bottles; Jeroboam, 4 bottles; Rehoboam, 6 bottles; Methuselah, 8 bottles; Salmanazar, 12 bottles; Balthazar, 16 bottles; Nebuchadnezzar, 20 bottles.

Champagne and Sparkling Wine with Food

Champagne, or indeed a good sparkling wine, is everyone's favourite aperitif and restorative. The champagne effect is not simply a fanciful wine notion, for those innocent looking bubbles at the same time as they refresh the taste buds are actually pumping the wine's 12° or so of alcohol straight into the bloodstream. As a general rule, a dry, light *blanc de blancs* is the wine to choose before a meal, if you are to serve sparkling wines throughout, with the bigger, richer, more full-bodied wine being saved to drink with the food. In terms of champagne, this means a non-vintage Chardonnay-dominated (or indeed exclusively *blanc de blancs*) aperitif followed by a vintage Pinot Noir-dominated, or certainly Pinot Noir-influenced, wine with the meal.

If some palates find these rather too bubbly to accompany food, try the softly sparkling *crémant* wines whose gentle bubbles and mousse are roughly half that of the fully sparkling or *mousseux* wines. If even *crémant* disagrees with your digestion, try a still white or red Coteaux Champenois. It may lack the delightful effervescence of champagne but it has much of this region's majestic finesse and flavour.

A *doux* or *riche* style is the one to opt for as a dessert wine, but if you dislike sweet wine try a slightly sweet *demi-sec*.

Demi-sec or even *doux* champagnes, although now (unfairly) rather unfashionable, are worth considering for a wedding reception – not as the bubbly to be served throughout the event, because most palates would prefer a non-cloying brut or dry sparkling wine, but a glass with the wedding cake and for the toasts would be ideal. Finally, if you are worried about when to serve champagne, or sparkling wine, there is really no need. Fine fizz is welcome at any hour of the day or night...

Champagne

Le champagne, the wine, takes its name from La Champagne, the old province of France where it is made. Champagne, 90 miles (145 km) northeast of Paris, still produces the Rolls-Royce of sparkling wines. Other *méthode champenoise* wines from both inside and outside France have equalled and even surpassed those produced by some of the lesser-known houses, but so far no sparkling wine produced outside the region has been able to reach the heights achieved by the great names of Champagne and their top wines. It is doubtful whether they ever will. However, great strides forward in quality have been made since the first edition of this book, especially in the Antipodes and in California.

Champagne is not as pretty a place to visit as other French wine-producing regions. Indeed there are parts of it, such as the flat scenery viewed on the road into Reims from the airport, that can be spectacularly dull. But, if the low, rolling hills crowned with woods that overlook the neat carpet of vines, occasionally broken up by the odd church steeple and sleepy village, fail to impress, the soil should. It is the special, deep, chalky sub-soil (*belimnita quadrata*, unique to Champagne), covered by a thin layer of topsoil, that gives the wines from this region much of their quality. Conveniently the galleries carved out of this soft chalk and the early Gallo-Roman chalk pits also make ideal cellars in which to mature champagne.

The cool climate is another Champagne quality factor. It is easy to forget that this is the most northerly wine producing region in France and that its average annual temperature is just 10°C (50°F).

The region consists of some 35,000 ha (86,000 acres) of which only about 28,000 ha (69,000 acres) have been planted to vine. Pinot Meunier and Pinot Noir each account for more than a third of the planted vineyard area, leaving Chardonnay with around 7,000 ha (17,000 acres). Intriguingly, the proportion of the region planted to Chardonnay has decreased slightly in recent years, down one percent since 1984. The proportion of Pinot Meunier is always glossed over by the *champenois* but it has in the past accounted for the largest share of the total and is used in many blends. Today it accounts for 37 percent as does Pinot Noir, with Chardonnay amounting to 26 percent. With great houses such as

Krug using about 25 percent Pinot Meunier, it is clear that this grape, rather than being a poor relation of Chardonnay and Pinot Noir, is a useful champagne grape in its own right.

There are 250 different *crus* or villages within the Champagne region. Conveniently, these can be divided into four main areas: the compact Montagne de Reims, south of Reims and the River Vesle, the meandering Vallée de la Marne, which stretches from just before Château-Thierry to just after Epernay, the Côte des Blancs, which lies to the south of Epernay and ends just below Vertus, and the lesser-quality Aube district to the southeast of Vertus. In addition to these four there is the less distinguished Sézanne district that stretches south of Vertus. Part of the Vallée de la Marne, known as the Aisne, that lies south of the River Marne and Château-Thierry, also fits into this less distinguished category.

The Chardonnay grape's stronghold is the Côte des Blancs, while the Pinot Noir reigns in the Montagne de Reims, and Pinots Noir and Meunier both do well in the warmer, sunnier Vallée de la Marne. The outlying areas of the Aisne and the Aube grow considerably more Pinot Meunier than either of the other grapes.

Every year, just before the harvest, the price per kilo of grapes is worked out. This is no longer fixed by a committee consisting of growers and merchants, as it was before 1990. The authorities now announce a reference price prior to the vintage and the new free market in Champagne uses this as a basis for its deliberations. In practice this reference price is usually accepted by the free market and the previous percentage scale system continues to work. So grapes from the first class villages, known as *grands crus*, are paid 100 percent of the price. The *premiers crus*, the 43 villages on the next level down, are paid 90–99 percent (the top two, at 99 percent, are Mareuil-sur-Ay and Tauxières), and the scale then continues, down to the outlying villages rated at 80 percent, which receive 80 percent of the price. To date there are 17 *grands crus*: Ambonnay, Avize, Ay, Beaumont-sur-Vesle, Bouzy, Chouilly (for Chardonnay only), Cramant, Louvois, Mailly, Le Mesnil-sur-Oger, Oger, Oiry, Puisieulx, Sillery, Tours-sur-Marne (black grapes only), Verzenay and Verzy. The leading Chardonnay villages are Avize, Chouilly, Cramant, Le Mesnil-sur-Oger and Oger. The rest grow mainly Pinot Noir, although the odd Chardonnay vineyard can be found.

With the elevation of more villages to the 100 percent category

The Champagne Region

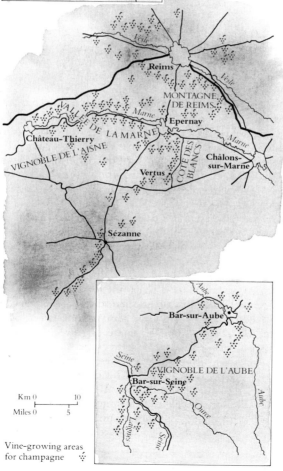

and others being assigned to a higher quality level as well, these ratings are perhaps less important than they used to be. Certainly it is impressive to find a house or blend that uses 100 percent-rated grapes exclusively. But those who grandly claim that their wines are all rated at an average of 97 percent or whatever are not necessarily proving anything in terms of quality. It is the delicate art of blending villages, vineyards, varieties and vintages that makes a great champagne, not simply the quality-rating of the grapes.

Champagne Quality

Great wines, it should go without saying, need to fix their sights firmly on quality. Champagne, as the past decade of increasingly bad press has certainly proved, is no exception. Indeed, with every winemaker in the world trying to challenge Champagne, and plenty succeeding in Australia and California, it is probably more important than ever before for the *champenois* to concentrate on quality. Sadly, many greedy, shortsighted *champenois* have not understood this. A steady stream of thin, green, miserable champagnes, even from important *grandes marques* houses, and certainly from the cut-price cooperatives and producers, flowed from the region throughout the 1980s and into 1990s. The magic word 'champagne' on a bottle of fizz is alas no longer a guarantee of quality. None of us should be seduced into believing that our bottle of bubbly is one of the greatest bottles of sparkling wine in the world. It may not be, and that is where this book comes in.

The good news is that at long last the industry has introduced stricter controls, which took effect from the 1992 vintage. These limited the yield per hectare from a maximum of 12,600 kg in the 1990 and 1991 harvests to a maximum of 11,960 kg in 1992 and hopefully a similar limit will be kept to in all future vintages. In addition, the yield from the presses has been reduced from one hectolitre of juice from every 150 kg of grapes to one hectolitre from every 160 kg. Thankfully this has so far put an end to the notorious, third pressing, whose lacklustre wines have given champagne such a bad name. In addition, the *champenois* must now distil or destroy the 50 litres of lees and juice solids left over from each pressing. Bumper crops, such as those of the 1982, 1983, 1986 and 1992 champagne vintages, are now having a sizeable proportion of their production set aside as reserve wines to help regulate champagne stocks and hopefully, in turn, quality.

Not content with the new, tougher controls, several champagne houses have now introduced their own, most notably Bollinger with its Charter of Quality. Bollinger's superior code of practice chiefly concerns the finer provenance of its grapes and this house's insistence on the long ageing of its wines on lees prior to sale. Moët & Chandon has also implemented similar, additional quality controls. Rumours that the Champagne authorities are upping the statutory minimum of 12 months' bottle age for non-vintage champagnes to 15 or even 18 months augur well too for the future quality of champagne.

With luck, despite the increase in Champagne's acreage since the war – up from 12,000 ha to almost 30,000 ha today – these lower yields of finer wine will account for a giant step forward in the quality of champagne sold in the 1990s. If not, the gap between well-made New World *méthode champenoise* wines and champagne will cease to exist.

How to Read a Champagne Label

It is easy to pick out a genuine French champagne on a shop shelf crowded with sparkling wines. True champagne will simply bear the word 'champagne' in large letters on the label plus the brand name of the producer, with the word 'France' and the name of the producer's town or village in much smaller letters underneath. The label will not bear the words '*méthode champenoise*' – if it does, then your bottle of bubbly has come from elsewhere.

Unlike all other French wines, champagne does not have to state its *appellation contrôlée* status. The word 'champagne' is enough. Champagne bottles also declare their degree of dryness or sweetness, from *extra brut* to *doux*, and, if applicable, the style, such as *blanc de blancs* or rosé. Vintage wines will bear the appropriate date.

The most important and revealing item of information on a champagne label is the CIVC (Comité Interprofessionnel du Vin de

Champagne) registration code, which is printed in minute lettering. The first two letters are the key to the champagne's origin:

NM are the most common and stand for *négociant-manipulant*.
These indicate wine from a merchant or *négociant*, someone who is
entitled to buy in grapes or wine from elsewhere in the
Champagne region to use in his own blends, which may or may
not contain wines from his own vineyards. All the big houses produce NM champagnes and the quality should be the most reliable
in the region. As with everything in life there are exceptions.

RM stands for *récoltant-manipulant*. Champagnes with this code are
produced by small growers who must use their own grapes to
make their wines. However they are allowed to buy in up to 5 percent from other sources. The quality varies tremendously. Watch
for the words '*grand cru*' on these labels since they indicate that the
champagne has been made from grapes rated at 100 percent on the
Champagne village quality scale. '*Premier cru*' indicates that the
grapes used have been rated at more than 90 percent. RM producers frequently omit these words from their labels, so those without
are not necessarily of lower quality than the others.

SR is a new code and denotes a wine from a Société de Récoltant,
or a company of wine growers who belong to the same family.
The code is simply a practical means of allowing a family to work
together, where the son, say, owns a press and the daughter a vineyard, to produce one family-made champagne.

R stands for a *récoltant*, or grower, who is neither a producer nor a
cooperative member but sells his grapes on to be processed elsewhere with other growers' grapes. A little champagne is returned
to him for his personal or family use, bearing his own label.

MA or '*marque d'acheteur*' means 'mark of the buyer' and refers to
the fact that the wine with this on its label is a Buyer's Own Brand
champagne. Wine merchant X or supermarket Y has visited a
champagne producer and requested that its own label and not that
of the producer be put on the bottle. In the past there have been
rumours that BOB producers were tired of their buyers receiving

all the accolades (or otherwise!) for wines they themselves had made. So a new ruling stipulates that either the producer's name must appear in full on the label, or, if it is still given anonymously in code, that the distributor's name and address must appear in full, thus allowing consumers, for the first time, to know something of their wine's provenance.

ND refers to a *négociant-distributeur*, someone who buys in finished champagne and distributes it under his own name, usually in Champagne or elsewhere in France. These champagnes are almost always only found in France and are not to be confused therefore with BOB champagnes and those on the export market.

CM or '*coopérative-manipulante*' indicates a wine that has been made by a cooperative. These wines are not to be sneered at, since their quality can be good.

RC, another new code, indicates a *récoltant-coopérateur*, a small grower who, lacking the wherewithal to make champagne himself, sends his grapes to one or more cooperatives to be processed and in return bottles are sent back to him to sell. As his grapes are likely to be blended with others, in effect what the consumer is getting is not a grower's wine but a cooperative's wine. RC wines are not to be confused with RM wines, which are true grower's champagnes.

More information about the various styles of champagne that are available can be found in the Introduction on pages 17–21.

Champagne Vintages

1992 *Less impressive than the '91s, let down by rain and rot and with only reasonable levels of acidity and alcohol. 'Entirely satisfactory' in Champagnespeak means than 1992 is unlikely to be a vintage year. 280M bottles.*

1991 *Champagne's previous three years were a hard act to follow and the good, ordinary '91s obviously did not try. By no means a bad* vintage, it was not a great one either, with uneven flowering, a late harvest and some rot. 274M bottles.

1990 As elsewhere in Europe, 1990 was an exceptional year in Champagne, the best it seems among the top quality trio of '88, '89 and '90. Despite an uneven start, the region's hot, dry summer resulted in vintage wines with good acidity and sugar levels and an above average yield. Much is expected of the '90s. This was the first year in which the 'free market' operated for pricing the region's grapes. 288M bottles.

1989 Despite hiccoughs in winter and spring weather, including frosts and uneven flowering, 1989's long, hot summer saved the day and produced top quality vintage wines that are almost on a par with the decade's best. 275M bottles.

1988 A record, early flowering and an average harvest date produced a lower yield of healthy grapes and some good wines that will mostly sell as vintage champagne. 224M bottles.

1987 A difficult, uneven year: a grim June followed by a late harvest with different start dates, produced high yields as in 1986 and mostly ordinary wines. The Chardonnay was less successful than the black grapes. 264M bottles.

1986 Sunny weather during the flowering ensured a high yield, which was reduced slightly by late rains in August and September and also by rot. Most houses have released, or are about to release, an '86. Quality is good – in some cases excellent. 259M bottles.

1985 A last-minute miracle vintage. Spring frosts killed 2,000 ha (5,000 acres) of vines, some 8 percent of the total area, and were followed by a cold, early summer, but a heatwave throughout September and October saved the day and 1985 for some has proved to be an exceptionally fine year. The crop, however, is small. 152M bottles.

1984 An indifferent year. A late flowering and an equally late harvest. The quality was mixed. 199M bottles.

1983 The second record breaker in a row after the '82. Happily quantity again went hand in hand with quality and most houses view the 1983 wines as very good vintage material. The '82s are thought just to have the edge, but higher acidity has meant that the '83s have lived longer. 302M bottles.

1982 An excellent year with abundant quantities of classic vintage wines, although some of these may show a slight lack of acidity. 295M bottles.

1981 A good year but a tiny crop which with the small 1980 and 1978 harvests gave the champenois supply problems. Most 1981 wines went into non-vintage blends. 92M bottles.

1980 The vintage that most champenois would prefer to forget. Average quality. Smallish crop. 113M bottles.

1979 A puzzler. The vintage was declared by most houses and many consider this an excellent year whose austere wines simply need time to reveal their true glory. Blind tastings in 1986 including all the big names proved disappointing with rot a noticeable feature of several wines. Time has turned many '79s into first class wines, rich and full and more attractive than when they were young. But dull '79s can still be tasted, so be careful with purchases of this vintage. 228M bottles.

1978 A small crop but a fairly good year. High acidity is a feature which some houses have attempted to tone down with a high dosage. 79M bottles.

1977 A difficult year. September sunshine helped but overall the quality was mediocre. 187M bottles.

1976 The year of the sun. Almost overpoweringly rich, ripe, full-bodied wines. The best, which can be superb, are those with sufficient acidity to balance the fruit. 203M bottles.

1975 A classic year. Magnificent, balanced, harmonious wines full of fruit and flavour. 168M bottles.

1974 *Unripe, disappointing wines. 163M bottles.*

1973 *An early vintage with wines that many feel are balanced and appealing, but even the best are now showing their age and should be drunk. 202M bottles.*

1972 *Thin, mean wines strictly for blending. 149M bottles.*

1971 *A wonderful year with fine, full-flavoured, balanced wines that have grown old gracefully and are still drinking well, but only a small crop. 81M bottles.*

1970 *A large vintage of good quality. Many of the round, fruity '70s are still going strong. 210M bottles.*

Older Fine Vintages

Not everyone enjoys the taste of old champagne with its soft, honeyed, hazelnut-like charms and gentle sparkle. But risky though it may be to hang on to a good vintage for 15 years or more, it is an experience that should be tried at least once. One exceptionally good year was 1969. Similarly the '66s from leading houses are still rich, elegant wines. Anything much older, or from lesser producers, means the odds start to work the other way, but try the great '61s or '59s, or even the '55s, '53s or '52s from the top champagne houses. Recently '53 Krug was the colour of old gold with hints of hazelnuts, biscuits and butterscotch, but little mousse.

Producers

Henri Abelé   MC   '76 '82 ★
50 rue de Sillery, 51100 Reims
Now owned by the all-powerful Freixenet sparkling wine group of Spain, the firm of Henri Abelé does not own any vineyards but produces about 42,000 cases annually. Two-thirds of this appears under the labels of its buyers. Among wines carrying the Abelé

name are Soirées Parisiennes Brut plus the non-vintage and vintage
Marque Impériale and a rosé. Half of production here is via automatic *remuage*. Henri Abelé champagne is only available in France
and is of simple, straightforward quality. One of the Abelé ancestors invented *dégorgement à la glace*; the firm was founded in 1757.

Ayala   MC   '59 '70 ★
2 boulevard du Nord, 51160 Ay
One of the great old-fashioned champagne names. Ayala champagne was apparently much admired by Queen Victoria's son
Edward, when Prince of Wales. Ayala has a colourful history: it
was founded by Edmond Ayala, the son of a Colombian diplomat,
in 1860. Vicomte de Mareuil, a friend of Edmond's father, introduced the young man to Champagne society and sensibly he
married one of the Vicomte's nieces — Gabrielle d'Albrecht. Mlle
Albrecht's dowry included an important vineyard or two and
Edmond promptly founded a champagne house on the strength of
this. Today Ayala, despite its illustrious past, is a somewhat forgot-
ten name, although some 70,000 cases are produced annually. A
little of this comes from the firm's own 99 percent-rated Pinot
Noir vineyards at Mareuil-sur-Ay. A typical Ayala blend would be
roughly 50 percent Pinot Noir, 20 percent Pinot Meunier and 30
percent Chardonnay. Ayala champagne is available in vintage and
non-vintage Brut, Brut Rosé, Demi-Sec and the vintage Blanc de
Blancs. The last of these is only released in very good years. About
half of the firm's total sales is exported, mainly to the UK, the
USA, Germany and Belgium. The quality of Ayala champagne is
simple and straightforward without being very exciting. The light,
biscuity Brut has a curious, almost metallic nose. The green, disappointing '79 is not recommended.

Barancourt   MC   '85 ★→
Place André Tritant, Bouzy, 51150 Tours-sur-Marne
Three growers, Brice, Martin and Tritant, joined together in 1966
to make and sell champagne under the single label of Barancourt.
Together they own 95 ha of vines and produce around 58,000
cases annually. Barancourt offers a wide range of champagnes but
its still red Coteaux Champenois wine, Bouzy Rouge, is their *pièce
de résistance*. Apart from a vintage and non-vintage champagne

made from Bouzy grapes, Barancourt also make Brut Réserve champagne from the three partners' scattered vineyards.

E Barnaut   MC   ★
51150 Bouzy

Philippe Secondé, André Secondé-Prevoteau's cousin (qv) runs this small house and as a trained oenologist is as well-placed as any in Champagne to get the best from his Bouzy vines. The speciality here is E Barnaut's Grand Reserve, a blend of Pinot Noir and Chardonnay from the family's own vines. It is also made from a decently-matured *cuvée* containing reserve wines dating from 1914.

Beaumet   MC   '81 '85 ★
3 rue Malakoff, 51207 Epernay

Beaumet is a name well known in the USA, the UK, Sweden and Belgium – its main export markets – but not in France. Since 1977 Jacques Trouillard has been the force behind Beaumet and in 1980 the firm moved to an old house with splendid cellars in the Parc Malakoff. The company originally belonged to the Beaumet family, who established the house in 1878. A certain percentage of Beaumet's own grapes, most of which are from the Côte des Blancs, go into its *cuvées* but most of the firm's needs are bought in and Pinot Noir is in fact the dominant grape in most of the blends. The vast majority of its 30,000-case sales is taken up by the non-vintage Brut made from two-thirds Pinot Noir and Pinot Meunier to one-third Chardonnay. Other labels include the Extra Dry, Demi-Sec, vintage and non-vintage Blanc de Blancs, vintage-dated Blanc de Noirs, Rosé and a raw, pear-drop-like Brut. *Ratafia*, *marc* and *fine* are also made here. Beaumet's finest champagne is its Cuvée Malakoff Blanc de Blancs. The firm has a high regard for both the '81 and the '85 vintage wines. Beaumet is closely associated with JEANMAIRE and OUDINOT.

Besserat de Bellefon   MC   '71 '75 ★→
Allée du Vignoble, 51061 Reims

Bought recently by MARNE & CHAMPAGNE, Besserat de Bellefon is a big champagne house that used to specialize in *crémants*, which accounted for about 40 percent of its sales. Founded in 1843 in Ay, Besserat moved in 1970 to rather showy, ultra-modern premises which cover 14 ha (34 acres) at Reims, complete with two large cellars that can be hired out for conferences and parties. Besserat de Bellefon's style is light, lean and not very exciting, but its *crémant*-style champagnes, both white and rosé, are made from a blend of 50 different wines and are well distributed. Besserat owns almost 10 ha (24 acres) of Ay Pinot Noir vines and buys in another 250 ha-worth of grapes to produce its 167,000 cases of champagne annually. Apart from the *crémant*-style wines, Besserat makes a Pinot Noir-dominant vintage and non-vintage *brut* plus its recently launched non-vintage B de B prestige *cuvée*. Besserat exports a great deal, principally to Switzerland and Belgium as well as to the UK. It is one of the few houses to make a rosé with less pressure, and suggests it should be drunk as an aperitif as well as with meats and cheeses. The firm's non-vintage *brut* is not recommended.

Billecart–Salmon   MC   '76 '86 ★→★★
40 rue Carnot, 51160 Mareuil–sur–Ay

Billecart-Salmon, currently directed by Jean Roland-Billecart, the fifth generation of his family, likes to be thought of as one of France's best-kept secrets. Certainly this small *grande marque* house founded in 1818 is only just stepping into the limelight. Its close to 40,000-case production is at present made almost entirely from bought-in grapes. The five percent that comes from its own Mareuil-sur-Ay Pinot Noir vineyards is used exclusively in its flowery, salmon-pink, strawberry-scented Rosé. Other Billecart wines include a lemony, flowery, non-vintage and vintage *brut*, a *demi-sec* and a *blanc de blancs*. The vintage Brut and Rosé are both Pinot Noir/Chardonnay blends and the Blanc de Blancs is pure Chardonnay from the three *grand cru* villages of Cramant, Avize and Mesnil-sur-Oger. The Billecart-Salmon style is lean, lively, flavoursome and Chardonnay-influenced, without being particularly special. However, the quality behind Billecart's distinctive 18th century-style bottles and labels has taken a noticeable step up of late, and the wines have filled out. Its best wine is the '86 Cuvée NF, with its rich, full, yeasty-musky style: a 60 percent Pinot Noir, 40 percent Chardonnay blend. The '78 Billecart Brut has an intense, green, almost asparagus-like character and the '79 is an acceptable, light, lean wine. France is the most important market, followed by the USA and the UK.

Binet
See H Germain & Fils

Boizel   MC   '82 ★→
14 rue de Bernon, 51200 Epernay

Boizel does not have any vineyards of its own and in most years produces more than 160,000 cases. The firm has been in family ownership since its foundation in 1834. It was one Auguste Boizel who founded this house, but unlike many similarly-sized champagne concerns which have now been swallowed up by larger companies, Boizel is still an independent, family-run business. Boizel Brut non-vintage accounts for the majority of sales here but this wine is also available in *sec* and *demi-sec* versions. The Blanc de Blancs, Rich, Rosé, Grand Vintage Brut and their *tête de cuvée* Joyau de France complete the range; the firm also produces a *ratafia*. All bar 20 percent of its wines are riddled automatically. The Blanc de Blancs was re-launched with a fancy 19th century label to commemorate Boizel's 150th anniversary. Today Evelyne Roques-Boizel, of the family's fifth generation, directs the firm. Boizel is a keen exporter, with more than half its annual sales achieved overseas. The main consumers of Boizel champagne are, principally, the UK plus, to a lesser extent, Switzerland and the USA. Krémer is another Boizel brand, from the firm it took over in 1912. Boizel produces a fair number of BOB champagnes. Boizel Rosé is a frothy, deep red-pink wine and the Brut Réserve is an appealingly soft, musky-lemony wine. Both are Pinot Noir-dominated, as is the Boizel Grand Vintage and Joyau de France.

Bollinger   MC   '70 '75 '76 '82 '85 ★→★★★★
16 rue Jules Lobet, 51160 Ay

In 1829, some years before Johann Joseph KRUG arrived in Champagne, his countryman Jacques Joseph Bollinger from Württemberg in Germany founded Bollinger. In the early days, Paul Renaudin was Bollinger's partner. The original nucleus of the firm was the vineyards owned by Joseph Bollinger's father-in-law, the Comte de Villermont. Monsieur le Comte did not wish to sully his name with any trade connections and thus the champagne produced was labelled Renaudin, Bollinger & Co, a name that appeared on bottles of Bollinger until the 1960s. Determined

Bollinger's stately headquarters at Ay

Mme Lily Bollinger, who steered her firm through the difficult years of German occupation, was the last of the Bollinger family and today the house is run by her nephew – wise, patrician, Christian Bizot – who, worried by the poor image and low quality of some of the Champagne region's wine, launched a Charter of Quality in 1991 (*see* page 31). Bollinger's Special Cuvée back label gives details of the charter and wine, including a statement that the champagne has been aged for three years in Ay prior to its release.

Bollinger is a traditionalist and its big, biscuity, dry, almost beefy style of champagne has always reflected this. To achieve this style Bollinger still vinifies its vintage champagnes partly in oak and for all its blends uses a noticeable proportion of reserve wines and Pinot Noir wines. Specifically, Ay Pinot Noir accounts for 35 per-cent of this variety used by Bollinger. Unlike other houses, Bollinger keeps its reserve wines in magnums and at any one time these account for about ten percent of its stock – about five years' worth in total. In particular, Bollinger's three year-old non-vintage champagne Special Cuvée contains a high proportion of reserve wines and is a blend of 60 percent Pinot Noir, 25 percent Chardonnay and 15 percent Pinot Meunier, whilst its vintage wines are 62 percent Pinot Noir to 35 percent Chardonnay and three percent Pinot Meunier. Bollinger is also a traditionalist when it comes to its vineyards, with only the first pressing used. It owns 144 ha (356 acres), which provide it with roughly 70 percent of its needs. As the full-bodied Bollinger taste indicates, almost all the vineyards are planted to Pinot Noir, the most important holdings being in Ay, Verzenay, Bouzy, Louvois, Tauxières, Avenay and Bisseuil. Bollinger also owns Chardonnay plots in Cuis and Grauves plus a little Pinot Meunier in Champvoisy. The latter is used only in the Special Cuvée.

Perhaps the most traditional wine that Bollinger makes is its extraordinarily fine Vieilles Vignes Françaises made from old ungrafted pre-phylloxera vines. The elegant musky, truffley '85 vintage of this classic *blanc de noirs* champagne is young as yet and noticeably different in style from other Bollinger vintages. But nonetheless it has a tremendous depth of flavour and fruit that will mature to make a most distinguished champagne.

At the other end of the Bollinger price scale is the Special Cuvée, which accounts for about 70 percent of the firm's total annual production of 125,000 cases. Clearly there is great demand for this non-vintage wine. In the past, and especially in the UK in the 1980s, there have been some alarming variations in the quality of Special Cuvée. At its best it is a superb, rich, smoky-biscuity, powerful champagne, at its worst it has been a thoroughly disappointing, young, green glassful. During the bad decades of the 1970s and 1980s, when demand far outstripped supply, Bollinger probably suffered from this variability problem more than any other *grande marque* house. However, Christian Bizot is the first notable *champenois* to admit publicly that quality was not all it should be: 'I took the decision to sell wine too young. Neither I nor my successors will take that risk again'.

The seductive RD '75 (disgorged in November 1985) is a wonderful example of textbook vintage Bollinger, with a glorious buttercup-gold colour and a rich, flowery, biscuity nose backed up by a similarly fine, full-bodied yet balanced palate. The RD stands for 'recently disgorged'. In other words, the champagne was matured on its lees or yeast until, in this case, November 1985. Bollinger believes strongly that this extra time in contact with the yeast (which varies from seven to ten years) gives the wine additional body and flavour. Certainly anyone who has tasted the '75 or the rich, smoky, hazelnut-like '70 would find it hard to disagree. The musky RD '73 is not as good and the RD '82 with its toasty-smoky scent and full, herbaceous palate needs time yet, but will be great. Bollinger also sells a five-year-old vintage-dated Grande Année Rosé (the racy, green '81 is the latest), plus the Grande Année Brut, whose '85 is rich, flavourful, creamy, musky wine.

Bollinger has bought a share in a leading Australian winery, Petaluma, which has released several *méthode champenoise* wines under the Croser label, named after its winemaker Brian Croser. Bollinger also owns Langlois-Château in the Loire. More than 70 percent of its champagne is exported, chiefly to the UK, the USA and Australia. It also makes a delicious, still red wine, La Côte aux Enfants – big, full, ripe, juicy, oaky '85 is well worth tasting.

Bonnaire MC '85 ★→★★
105 rue du Carouge, Cramant, 51200 Epernay
The *brut* non-vintage Champagne de Cramant, with its clean, fresh, lively, flowery taste, is a good example of the Bonnaire family's expertise. Bonnaire owns 21 ha (52 acres) and production remains below 17,000 cases. Half of Bonnaire's grapes, and no doubt some bought-in grapes too, go into the three-grape Bonnaire Brut with their own Chardonnay grapes responsible for the vintage Bonnaire Cramant and non-vintage Blanc de Blancs.

F Bonnet MC '64 ★→
Rue du Mesnil, Oger, 51190 Avize
F Bonnet, founded by *vigneron* Ferdinand Bonnet in 1922, is an old family firm, although not a well-known Champagne name. It is now owned by PIPER-HEIDSIECK and CHARLES HEIDSIECK, who in turn are owned by the Rémy Cointreau group. Mlle Nicole Bonnet is the current manager. The family's own vines, including 10 ha (24 acres) or so in the top Chardonnay villages of Oger and Avize and in the slightly less distinguished neighbouring village of Vertus, plus a little Pinot Noir and some other grapes from Bergères, supply almost all its needs. With an annual production of slightly more than 11,000 cases, made in Charles Heidsieck's cellars in Reims, F Bonnet is a small house but has a good reputation for its fine, aged, Chardonnay-dominant *cuvées*, most of which are now sold under Buyer's Own Brand labels. Chardonnay-only

champagnes include the Blanc de Blancs Reserve Carte Or Brut and the vintage-dated Selection. The one-third Pinot Noir wines include F Bonnet's Carte Blanche. Bonnet exports 20 percent of its wines, principally to the UK.

Bricout & Koch   MC   '69 ★→
7 route de Cramant, 51190 Avize

Owned by Kupferberg, the giant German sparkling wine concern, Bricout & Koch is one of the newer champagne houses. But the firm and its handsome cellars date back to 1820, when Charles Koch first sold champagne under his name. With annual production of more than 200,000 cases (aided by automatic *remuage*) B&K is a large house whose champagne is popular in Germany. The firm uses a blend of all three Champagne grapes to make its big, rich, musky-biscuity Bricout Carte Noire, light, fruity Carte Or, Rosé and Pol Varême; production is mainly divided between Carte Noire and Pol Varême. The vintage-dated Cuvée Charles Koch (currently the '81) is Bricout's finest wine. Bricout consider its '69 vintage to be its best offering so far.

Albert le Brun   MC   '80 '83 '85 ★★→
93 avenue de Paris, 51000 Châlons-sur-Marne
Star buy Blanc de Blancs Brut, Cuvée Réservée Brut

Founded by Léon le Brun in 1860 in Avize, this firm later moved to Châlons, where it has handsome cellars. Albert le Brun champagnes are definitely worth seeking out as several wines in the range are excellent and the others are often bargain buys – a considerable achievement for this medium-sized family firm that produces around 20,000 cases annually. The most notable in the le Brun range is the non-vintage Blanc de Blancs Brut, a three-star wine made from Avize Chardonnay, including the produce of the family's own 3 ha (7 acres) of Chardonnay vines there. This wine's fine, smoky bouquet and big, rich, gutsy taste in many ways seems more reminiscent of a *blanc de noirs* and is highly recommended. Le Brun's full-bodied, biscuity, smoky, non-vintage Pinot Noir-dominant Cuvée Réservée Brut is another good buy, as is their big, ripe '76. Albert le Brun also makes a Carte Blanche Brut and Demi-Sec plus a Rosé Brut, besides very small quantities of Bouzy Rouge and a white Coteaux Champenois. Le Brun considers its '79

Vieille France Brut, in its curious dumpy bottle, to be its best wine, but it lacks both balance and charm. Try the others instead! Over half the production is exported, mainly to Europe and the USA.

René Brun   MC   ★→
4 place de la Libération, 51160 Ay

René Brun founded this firm in 1942. Today his descendants run the company and produce some 20,000 cases annually. Most of this comes from their own vineyards at Ay. The Pinot Noir-dominated vintage and non-vintage Brut are well made and easy to drink.

Canard-Duchêne   MC   '83 '85 ★→★★
1 rue Edmond Canard, Ludes, 51500 Rilly-la-Montagne

Somewhat unfairly this house trails along in VEUVE CLICQUOT's wake, for the two belong to the same group, which is now part of LVMH (Louis Vuitton Moët Hennessy). Canard-Duchêne is however a worthy champagne firm in its own right. Its light, fruity, biscuity, albeit ordinary, non-vintage Brut is usually a good buy in most years, despite its lowly provenance. Canard-Duchêne, which was founded in 1868, owns 18 ha (45 acres) at Ludes on the Montagne de Reims but these vineyards only supply five percent of its grape needs. Production here tops 250,000 cases in almost every year.

This means that another 400 ha-worth (988 acres) of Pinot Noir and Pinot Meunier (probably, given Canard's low prices, from the Aube), plus a smaller amount of Chardonnay, are bought in. 200,000 cases of the inexpensive black grape-dominated Canard-Duchêne Brut are sold annually but the firm also makes tiny amounts of a *demi-sec*, a *rosé* and a vintage-dated *brut* – the '85 is a big, rich, nutty, but basic, bubbly – as well as its prestige Cuvée Charles VII, a 61 percent Pinot Noir to 39 percent Chardonnay blend. France consumes most of the wine, but about ten percent is exported to the UK and Europe. Visitors must arrange an appointment to see the modern Canard-Duchêne buildings above ground and the 3 miles (2 km) of cellars below.

De Castellane   MC   '70 '76 '82 ★→
57 rue de Verdun, 51204 Epernay

Dominating the mostly traditional Epernay skyline is de Castellane's crazy, crenellated tower now housing a 'champagne traditions' museum, which together with a butterfly garden attracts almost 80,000 visitors each year. This edifice, as well as the firm's famous red cross label, indicate that de Castellane has an important past. Vicomte Florens de Castellane founded this house, giving it his name and choosing its trademark. Production boomed and up until the 1960s much of the 250,000 cases of de Castellane champagne made annually was exported all around the world. Since then de Castellane has gone through a difficult time but is now determined to retrieve its old reputation – aided by LAURENT-PERRIER which now owns a large part of the firm. De Castellane however, enjoys the ninth largest sales of champagne in France, no doubt due to its connection with Maxim's.

Half of the firm's champagne undergoes automatic *remuage*. De Castellane does not own any vineyards and almost 70 percent of its total production is taken up by the black grapes–dominated Brut with its red cross label. Other de Castellane champagnes include the vintage Blanc de Blancs, a Brut Rosé plus the top of the line, vintage-dated Cuvée Commodore, Florens de Castellane and Ettore Bugatti in their pot-bellied bottles. De Castellane has recently introduced a sweet *liqueur de la Champagne*, which it says can be drunk either before or after a meal, or used as a base for cocktails, much like MOET's Petite Licorelle. The firm also produces Maxim's champagne, with its distinctive label, made in a range of styles. Maxim's Brut offers pleasant, soft, easy-to-drink flavours contrasting with an unusual, tea-leaf like aspect on the nose. The vanilla-pod-scented de Castellane Brut is equally quaffable.

Cattier   MC   ★
6–11 rue Dom Pérignon, 51500 Chigny-les-Roses

This small family firm, still owned by the Cattiers, was founded in 1920 and now produces around 34,000 cases annually. With 18 ha (44 acres) of vines in the Montagne de Reims, planted almost equally between the three Champagne grapes, Cattier's own vines supply it with almost all they need. The firm's black grapes–dominated 1er Cru non-vintage accounts for more than half its production, with a *demi-sec*, a rosé and the vintage and prestige Cuvée Renaissance completing the range. Cattier's Clos du Moulin, a 50 percent Pinot Noir, 50 percent Chardonnay, *premier cru*, single-vineyard, non-vintage bubbly, is of interest, for as the name suggests, it comes from an old, walled vineyard of which there are only a handful in the region.

Charles de Cazanove   MC   '73 '85 ★
1 rue des Cotelles, 51200 Epernay

Charles Gabriel de Cazanove founded the firm in 1811, but today the Lombard family, which controls SAME, is the major owner of de Cazanove champagne. The firm does not own any vineyards but buys in grapes during the harvest from various *vignerons* throughout the major champagne regions. It does however make the wines entirely itself. With an annual production of around 150,000 cases de Cazanove is a large firm, and, with de Castellane, is the tenth most popular champagne in France. Five different wines are made here: the Pinot Noir-dominated Brut Classique, the Chardonnay-dominated Brut Azur, plus a rosé and the vintage wines, of which the latest is the '85, and the firm's top *cuvée*, '85 Stradivarius, a 60 percent Chardonnay, 40 percent Pinot Noir wine. The main export markets are the UK and Switzerland.

A Charbaut & Fils   MC   '85 ★→
17 avenue de Champagne, 51205 Epernay

It is difficult to know quite what to make of Charbaut. On the one hand it is a highly-successful champagne firm that now has some magnificent revamped cellars in Epernay's equivalent of the Champs Elysées – the Avenue de Champagne. Clearly its own-label business for wine merchants, supermarkets and the like is thriving. On the other hand, the quality of its once-stylish blends regularly has its ups and downs. Perhaps this is the price of success.

André Charbaut founded the family firm in 1948, at Mareuil-sur-Ay, and his two sons René and Guy now run the company. Charbaut's annual production is almost 100,000 cases and the 54 ha (133 acres) of family-owned vines at Mareuil-sur-Ay, at the neighbouring village of Bisseuil and at Viviers-sur-Artaut in the Aube no longer supply all it needs. An additional 120 ha-worth (296 acres) of grapes is bought in. The Charbaut range consists of the non-vintage Pinot Meunier-dominated Brut, Rosé and Blanc de Blancs, plus the vintage-dated Brut and Blanc de Blancs. Charbaut also makes a still white, red and rosé Coteaux Champenois, plus *marc, ratafia* and *fine*. The '79 Cuvée de Reserve has a smoky, fruity palate – it is good but not great. Similarly the '76 Charbaut Certificate has a soft, vanilla-like and easy to quaff style. At its best the non-vintage Brut has been a lovely, warm, toasty, flavoury champagne with a good mousse, and the Rosé has been an equally delightful, fruity, pale pink *fraises de bois*-scented wine. All bar 20 percent of production undergoes automatic *remuage*. A new, shattered, crystallized, fancy bottle houses the Chardonnay-dominated Grand Cadeau, or Grand Evénement, which has just been released.

Chaudron & Fils   MC   '76 ★
Route de Billy-le-Grand, Vaudemanges, 51380 Verzy
The Chaudron family has a long history in both Vaudemanges and Verzenay on the Montagne de Reims. The company however did not start to sell its wines on a large scale until 15 years ago. Today it owns 15 ha (37 acres) of mostly Chardonnay vines on the eastern edge of the Montagne de Reims at Vaudemanges and at the delightful-sounding Billy-le-Grand. Its Pinot Noir vines are concentrated in Verzenay, Verzy and Beaumont. Together these supply only a third of Chaudron's needs and the balance needed for its annual 12,500-case production is bought in. Chaudron champagnes are available in *brut*, *rosé*, *demi-sec* and *sec*. Most are a blend of 60 percent Chardonnay and 40 percent Pinot Noir and Pinot Meunier. Brut Selection is the firm's latest *cuvée* – a blend of the first pressing of the family's own 100 percent quality-rated vines, aged for four years. It should be worth trying. France is the major market for Chaudron champagnes, but they are also exported to the UK, the USA and Germany.

A Chauvet   MC   ★
11 avenue de Champagne, 51150 Tours-sur-Marne
This small family concern owns 10 ha (25 acres) or so of vineyards, which account for almost all its needs. Production is slightly in excess of 4,000 cases annually, divided between a fruity *blanc de blancs* and a non-vintage Pinot Noir-dominant *brut* and rosé.

Clérambault   MC   ★
122 Grande Rue, 10250 Neuville
The Coopérative Vinicole de Neuville-Buxeuil, founded in 1951,

is the organization behind this label, launched in 1989. With about 132 ha (326 acres) at its members' disposal, providing some 50 percent of its needs, just over 40,000 cases of Clérambault are produced annually. Most of this is the 100 percent Pinot Noir Cuvée Tradition. Clérambault also produces a three grape-based Carte Noire, a rosé and vintage fizz including a *blanc de blancs*.

Collery
See H Germain & Fils

Dehours   MC   ★→
1/2 rue de la Chapelle, 02220 Cerseuil, Braine
This is a firm of growers, with around 30 ha (74 acres) of vines, including sizeable plantings of Pinot Meunier. Dehours' splendid, keenly-priced, Pinot Meunier-dominated non-vintage Brut, with a little less than one-third each of Pinot Noir and Chardonnay, went down well under an important BOB label recently in the UK.

Delamotte Père & Fils   MC   '70 '76 '85 ★★
5 rue de la Brèche d'Oger, 51190 Le Mesnil-sur-Oger
One of the oldest houses in Champagne, the sixth oldest to be precise, Delamotte was founded by François Delamotte in 1760. Since then, the heirs of Delamotte and Lanson have, at various times, controlled this house. Today, Delamotte is in the safe hands of the de Nonancourt family which also owns DE CASTELLANE, LAURENT-PERRIER, LEMOINE and SALON. Although Delamotte produces just 25,000 cases annually and is based in small premises at Le Mesnil-sur-Oger, the wines have a big reputation and are much admired by the *cognoscenti*. Laurent-Perrier's winemaker keeps a close eye on the firm's champagnes, which no doubt partly accounts for their finesse. Other contributory factors include the 5 ha (12 acres) of Chardonnay vines Delamotte owns at Le Mesnil-sur-Oger, which supply 20 percent of its needs. The remainder of Delamotte's grapes, from vineyards which cover a further 20 ha (49 acres) and are planted to 50 percent Chardonnay, 30 percent Pinot Noir and 20 percent Pinot Meunier are bought in. Delamotte's style is thus a Chardonnay-dominant one, and even its Brut is made of the above proportions of grapes. Other champagnes here include a *blanc de blancs* and a prestige cuvée, Nicolas

Louis Delamotte, both made exclusively from Chardonnay, plus a Pinot Noir rosé. A little Bouzy Rouge is also made. Two-thirds of Delamotte's wines is exported.

Delbeck   MC   ★★→
8 rue Piper, 51067 Reims

Delbeck is an old Champagne name, dating from 1832 but dormant for the past three decades until François d'Aulan, the owner, and Jacques Gauthier, who puts the delicious Delbeck blends together, resurrected it in 1991. Having previously run PIPER-HEIDSIECK, d'Aulan and Gauthier left to start up Delbeck, an old Piper brand, when Rémy Cointreau bought Piper.

Delbeck's immediate and early excellence clearly stems from the partners' long years of experience and knowledge gleaned from Piper-Heidsieck. However, the house style is a distinctive one and has nothing in common Piper's. Delbeck has six years' stock in its renovated Reims cellars, which partly accounts for the superiority of the champagnes. The other deciding factor is 30 ha (74 acres) of vines at Verzenay and Chenay, which give the firm three-quarters of its grape needs to help create just 25,000 cases of Delbeck champagne. Only three wines are made, and all are heavily influenced by Pinot Noir, with about 30 percent Chardonnay used to balance the blends. Non-vintage Brut Heritage is the big seller, and besides a vintage version Delbeck also makes a firm, lemony rosé.

The firm plans to open a small museum next door to its cellars, which will no doubt reveal how Delbeck was once the court champagne of King Louis Philippe, and also describe the founder, Frédéric-Désiré Delbeck's entry into the champagne business and his useful marriage to a niece of VEUVE CLICQUOT.

A Desmoulins   MC   ★
44 avenue Foch, 51201 Epernay

With just 12,500 cases produced annually, A Desmoulins is a small company, in family hands since 1908. Several different champagnes are made and all apart from the Blanc de Blancs are a blend of the three Champagne grapes. The Cuvée de Réserve Brut and Cuvée Prestige Brut are the mainstay of the firm, followed by Brut Royal, Grand Rosé Brut, a *demi-sec* and the '79 Blanc de Blancs Brut. The firm's full-bodied, fruity Cuvée Prestige is well thought of.

Germany and Belgium are the two export markets. Visitors are welcome by appointment.

Deutz   MC   '75 '82 '85 '88 ★→★★
16 rue Jeanson, 51160 Ay

William Deutz and Pierre Geldermann, both born in French Aix-la-Chapelle, now German Aachen, in the early 19th century, founded this firm in 1838. Today the Lallier family, the fifth generation descendants of William Deutz, run the company. Dynamic André Lallier clearly believes in international connections for, to date, the company has sparkling wine interests in five overseas countries (as well as a wine firm in Touraine and another in the Rhône). The Deutz & Geldermann Sektkellerei in Germany, with its 208,000-case output is by far the largest of these offshoots. In 1983 Deutz joined forces with Ste-Navarro Correas in Argentina and with DAE SUN in South Korea. The Maison Deutz winery in California is both owned and run by Deutz, whilst the firm's newest and most impressive overseas concern, in New Zealand, Deutz Marlborough Cuvée, is a joint venture with Montana. It will be interesting to see where Deutz goes next.

The Deutz style is a traditional one, using hand *remuage*. About 40 percent of its grape needs come from its own 42 ha (104 acres) of vineyards, most of which are situated in prime Pinot Noir country at Ay, Mareuil-sur-Ay and Bisseuil. But Deutz also has a sizeable holding of Chardonnay at Mesnil-sur-Oger, plus a little Pinot Meunier at Moussy and Pierry, just south of Epernay. All these grapes are turned into about 80,000 cases of well-made, pleasing, soft, fruity champagne which may not thrill the taste buds but does not disappoint them either. Most of this takes the form of an attractive, lemony-flowery, gentle non-vintage *brut*, a blend of 45 percent Pinot Noir, 30 percent Pinot Meunier and 25 percent Chardonnay. A vintage-dated *brut* (try the young, as yet lean, toasted *brioche*-like '86), rosé and *blanc de blancs* are also available. The painter Georges Mathieu has designed a special bottle for Deutz, and the house launched a handsome Pinot Noir–dominated 150th anniversary champagne in an equally handsome, star-encrusted, 19th century-style bottle. But the jewel in the Deutz crown is its prestige Cuvée William Deutz. The elegant, intense, flowery '85 is worth tasting, although it is only produced in limited quantities and there is even less of the rosé version. The straight '82 Deutz is a light, stylish, flowery-fruity wine. Deutz exports nearly half its production, mostly to the USA, Germany, Switzerland and the UK. Visitors can admire the ornate reception rooms painstakingly restored to 1860s style by André Lallier.

Veuve A Devaux
See Union Auboise

Dom Pérignon
See Moët & Chandon

André Drappier   MC   ★★
10200 Urville
The Drappier family has cultivated vines at Urville in the Aube for many generations; Remy Drappier, born in 1604 in the Haute-Marne, is believed to have been the first of the family to do so. Today, Drappier is one of the most important grower-*négociants* in the Aube region, with 70 percent of its holdings planted to Pinot Noir, and 15 percent each to Pinot Meunier and Chardonnay. The Aube is a Pinot Noir-dominant area and its wines in many respects have more in common with the warmer-climate wines of Chablis and Burgundy than they do with those of Champagne.

This is certainly true of Drappier, for its 12th century cellars, built by Cistercian monks from Clairvaux, produce an impressive array of distinctly Aubesque wines. André Drappier's splendid Pinot Noir-dominated Carte d'Or Brut is likely to be the most popular of these – with its rich, ripe, perfumed, smoky-fruity style it is definitely worth trying. Look out too for Drappier's Chardonnay-dominated, truffly Grande Sendrée prestige *cuvée* in its pot-bellied, 18th century-style bottle. Drappier's 'Signature' bottle Blanc de Blancs is less successful, but it is still a fresh, light and zippy champagne.

Duval Leroy   MC   '73 '86 ★→★★
69 avenue de Bammental, 51130 Vertus
Star buy Fleur de Champagne
Jules Duval merged his firm with that of Edouard Leroy in 1859. Duval Leroy is today one of those go-getting *négociant* houses,

selling an impressive 325,000 cases of champagne every year. Even more impressive perhaps is that the Duval-Leroy *brut*, generally under an own-label guise and usually in the better 'Fleur' quality, which is two-thirds Chardonnay, regularly comes top in blind non-vintage champagne tastings that include all the famous *grandes marques*. To attain both quantity and quality in champagne is a tremendous achievement, one which Duval succeeds in, although its quality does slip from time to time. Under its own label the firm offers a Carte Blanche Brut and Demi-Sec, the (superior) Fleur de Champagne Brut and Demi-Sec, a Cuvée des Roys Brut, plus vintage and rosé champagnes. Together these champagnes, which tend to be Chardonnay-styled, account for about a quarter of the firm's sales, and the remainder is sold as Buyer's Own Brand *brut* and *demi-sec*. Given such a vast output, it is understandable that Duval's own 140 ha (346 acres) of vines on the Côte des Blancs, plus others at Loisy, Sézanne and Bligny, account for only a fifth of its needs, with the rest bought in. At a recent tasting the straight Brut was excellent: elegant, rich, big, biscuity and fruity. The firm however considers that its fresh, flowery Fleur de Champagne Brut is the best ambassador for the house. Duval Leroy makes a red and white Coteaux Champenois and an old *marc*. By far its biggest export markets are the UK and Germany.

Nicolas Feuillatte   MC   ★
Chouilly, 51206 Epernay

The Brobdignagian-sized Centre Vinicole de la Champagne at Chouilly, founded in 1972, is the cooperative organization behind this name. Yet M Nicolas Feuillatte, a champagne grower, does exist and it was he who started to promote his champagne in New York, Paris and London two decades ago, just as he does today with the new Chouilly wine. About 4,000 growers bring their juice to this coop from 1,250 ha (3,088 acres) of vines, which has been pressed at any one of the 160 different pressing centres throughout the region, but in most cases in the Aube and Aisne. In theory, this massive hectarage should mean that the 125,000 cases of Nicolas Feuillatte, of the 1M cases plus produced here each year, are the cream of the crop. But, sadly, the quality is only average to ordinary. Perhaps it will improve. The Reserve Particulière Brut is Nicolas Feuillate's biggest seller. There is also a *blanc de blancs*, a rosé and vintage fizz plus the new Palmes d'Or *cuvée*, a blend of 40 percent Chardonnay, 40 percent Pinot Noir and 20 percent Pinot Meunier, which comes in a strange, dimpled bottle.

Roland Fliniaux   MC   ★★→
1 rue Léon Bourgeois, 51160 Ay
Star buy Fliniaux Rosé

Roland Fliniaux and his wife head this family firm, with their son Regis running it. The firm was founded in 1938 but inherited local winemaking traditions that date back to 1905. The Fliniaux style is wholeheartedly and uncompromisingly that of Ay. Although the family owns just 3 ha (7 acres) of vines at Ay, which supply a third of its needs, the other two-thirds also come from this important *grand cru* champagne village. Newcomers to the Fliniaux range will probably find the overwhelming, ripe musk melon scent and taste almost too much to cope with. Certainly the enormously powerful Carte Noire Brut has this character in abundance, wrapped up with other ripe fruit flavours such as pineapple and banana. Fliniaux also makes Carte Bleue, Rouge and vintage-dated Noire in addition to its Cuvée Prestige Tradition. The real star however is the splendid Rosé. This full-flavoured Ay rosé is one of the very few *rosé de noirs* available in Champagne. Its pretty, salmon-pink colour and attractive *fraises de bois* bouquet are backed up by a wonderfully rich and gutsy, fruity flavour. Definitely the pink'un to choose if you are fed up with pale, insipid rosé champagne.

The old champagne traditions are still much in evidence at this firm and disgorging is still *à la volée*, that is to say, done by hand without the use of ice. Fliniaux is a very small firm, producing just over 6,000 cases annually so you will have to hunt hard to find these champagnes. The firm exports its wines to the UK, Germany and Switzerland.

H Germain & Fils   MC   '85 ★
36 rue de Reims, 51500 Rilly-la-Montagne

About 100,000 cases of Germain champagne are made in most years; about half that amount is made of its baby brother Binet, and just 8,000 cases of Collery, another champagne label belonging to the same group. Germain is sold in supermarkets and the like – America in particular drinks large quantities – whereas Binet goes to small, specialist outlets. A Pinot Noir-dominated H Germain vintage and non-vintage *brut* and a Chardonnay-dominated rosé are produced. The firm owns 80 ha (198 acres), which provide H Germain and its associated labels, Binet and Collery, with about 40 percent of their needs.

Paul Gobillard   MC   '76 ★
Château de Pierry, Pierry, 51200 Epernay
Mme Paul Gobillard and her son Jean-Paul run this firm, which dates back to 1858 in Pierry but has only been a company since 1972. A small plot of Pierry's Pinot Meunier comprises this family's own vineyard holding but it also buys in some 30ha-worth (74 acres) of Pinot Meunier and Chardonnay, plus a little Pinot Noir. The firm makes 12,500 cases annually of its fruity Pinot Meunier-dominated non-vintage Carte Blanche and Brut Réserve plus four other Gobillard wines: a rosé, a *blanc de blancs*, the Cuvée Régence and Chardonnay-dominated vintage sparklers. Cuvée Régence is a fifty-fifty blend of Chardonnay and the two black Pinot champagne grapes. Most Gobillard champagne is sold in France but a little is exported to Switzerland. *Ratafia* and *marc* are also made. The grand, 18th century Château de Pierry is available for receptions and other gatherings. Paul Gobillard will receive visitors by prior appointment.

Paul Goerg   MC   '82 '85 ★→
4 place du Mont Chenil, 51130 Vertus
Not a well-known champagne name, but a respected one nonetheless, having carried off a silver medal at the Paris Concours and a gold at Vinexpo. Paul Goerg is the brand name of a small cooperative called Coopérative Agricole et Vinicole 'La Goutte d'Or', founded in 1950. With 111 members and some 120 ha (296 acres) at their disposal, sited at Le Mesnil-sur-Oger, Vertus and Bergères-les-Vertus, Paul Goerg's holdings are important. Some 40 percent of the cooperative's needs is bought in and although only 8,000 cases of Paul Goerg champagne are made annually, the coop produces a further 37,000 cases for its members' own use. Paul Goerg's vintage champagnes are much admired and the Brut Tradition has its followers too. The coop's latest edition is the non-*dosage* Brut Absolu, made from Chardonnay.

Gosset   MC   '76 '82 ★ →
69 rue Jules Blondeau, 51160 Ay

Somewhat unfairly perhaps, Gosset is one of those champagne houses that tends to be overlooked. Yet the traditions and history of this firm, dating back to 1584, make it the oldest winemaker – as opposed to champagne maker – in the region. Today Gosset is run by the 14th generation descendants of the founder Pierre Gosset. About ten percent of the grapes needed come from the firm's own 12 ha (30 acres) of Montagne de Reims Pinot Noir vineyards. In addition it buys in grapes from 30 different Côte des Blancs villages. All this adds up to some 40 ha (99 acres) of vines which, with an annual production of almost 60,000 cases, makes Gosset a medium-sized house. The firm believes in giving its champagnes a lengthy sojourn in the cellar before releasing them, and at any one time the cellars will contain more than five years' stock. Gosset has no wish to expand, preferring to remain a modest-sized, family-run quality-conscious house.

With four centuries under its belt, Gosset released a special Cuvée Quatrième Centenaire. The range now includes the non-vintage Brut Réserve (55 percent Chardonnay, 38 percent Pinot Noir, 7 percent Pinot Meunier), whose musky sweetness will not be appreciated by all. Also, the newer Grande Réserve, a rosé and the vintage-dated Grand Millésime Brut, currently the '83 (a blend of 53 percent Pinot Noir, 47 percent Chardonnay), and Rosé. The full-flavoured Gosset style will not be admired by everyone. However, the pungent, truffley, musky Pinot Noir-dominant Grande Réserve, the equally but more classy, lemony Chardonnay-influenced '83 Grande Millésime Brut and the sweet, cherry-like Rosé form an unusual range. The '79 Grande Millésime Brut with its fresh, green, lively, flavoury palate is recommended. The UK, the USA and Germany are the major export markets.

George Goulet   MC   ★ →
1 avenue de Paris, 5100 Reims

Part of the ABEL LEPITRE group, George Goulet, owned by Lionel Chaudron, deserves an entry of its own due to its superior quality. François Goulet was the first of his family to become involved with champagne but it was his son George, who joined the firm in 1867, who made Goulet such an important house – and gave his name to the champagne to boot. It was this George incidentally who dropped the 's' from his christian name, in order to help sales in the, then as now, vital UK market. Two-thirds of Goulet's champagnes are exported. Five different examples are made, including the Pinot Noir-dominated Brut Réserve, a *blanc de blanc* and a rosé, plus Goulet's top blend, the vintage-dated Cuvée du Centenaire, a 55 percent Pinot Noir, 45 percent Chardonnay wine.

Alfred Gratien   MC   '76 '79 '83 ★★→★★★
30 rue Maurice-Cerveaux, 51201 Epernay
Star buy '76 Alfred Gratien
The Seydoux family owns this champagne house in addition to its Gratien & Meyer Saumur operation, the full title of the company being Gratien, Meyer, Seydoux. The Epernay branch was opened in 1864. For a small house, producing just 10,000 cases annually, Alfred Gratien has a big reputation, which is entirely justified if its delicious, big, green herbaceous '76 and full-bodied nutty non-vintage Brut (a blend of about 49 percent Pinot Meunier, 44 percent Chardonnay and the rest Pinot Noir), are anything to go by. Alfred Gratien buys in all the Chardonnay, Pinot Noir and Pinot Meunier needed to create its vintage Brut, currently the '83 (a 61 percent Chardonnay, 33 percent Pinot Noir, 6 percent Pinot Meunier wine), its Rosé Brut and the non-vintage Brut.

Traditional methods are used here, including first fermentation in oak casks for all the wines and second fermentation in bottles stoppered with corks, not crown caps. The English greatly enjoy the mature, nutty, slightly oxidized style that is the hallmark of all Gratien's champagnes except the fruity, grapey Rosé Brut, and the extra ageing this house gives its wines is always noticeable. Cuvée Paradis Brut and Rosé, two new non-vintage Alfred Gratien champagnes are the product of better years – 1985 for the Brut and 1988 for the Rosé. The UK is a big export market, followed by the USA and Japan, besides others. Visitors are welcome at Alfred Gratien during working hours by appointment to visit the small museum and tour the cellars.

Emile Hamm & Fils   MC   '75 ★→
16 rue Nicolas Philipponnat, 51160 Ay
Hardly the most celebrated name in Champagne, yet Emile Hamm

produces a respectable 20,000 cases annually. With only slightly more than 3 ha (7 acres) of vines at Ay, this firm buys in the vast majority of its grapes. The family has been running the firm since 1943 and today makes five different *cuvées* plus still white Coteaux Champenois. The backbone of the blends is supplied by 15 complementary villages, whose wines are turned into the Signature Hamm, Sélection, Réserve 1er Cru and Rosé Brut, as well as the vintage-dated Brut (the family has high hopes for its '85). Hamm's straight 1er Cru Brut is a pleasant, light, waxy-appley, two-star champagne. Most of the champagne is drunk in France but a little is exported, mainly to EC countries and Switzerland. The firm receives visitors during office hours, preferably by appointment.

Charles Heidsieck   MC   '82 '83 '85 ★→★★
4 boulevard Henry Vasnier, 51100 Reims

Charles-Camille Heidsieck, or Champagne Charlie as his American clients nicknamed him, founded this firm in 1851. Like the other Heidsiecks of Reims, Charles-Camille was a relative of Florens-Louis and broke away from the main firm to set up on his own. It must have been hard for the 29 year-old to compete with the other two already well-established champagne Heidsiecks, but success in the USA saved the day. Since then six generations of Heidsiecks have run the house. From 1976 HENRIOT briefly held a majority shareholding, but in late 1985 Rémy, the Cointreau group (which also owns KRUG), bought Charles Heidsieck. It is unlikely that this will mean dramatic changes for there are still numerous Heidsieck family shareholders.

Charles Heidsieck owns 25 ha (62 acres) but buys in 90 percent of what it needs to create about 250,000 cases annually. Most of this is taken up by the Brut Réserve non-vintage, re-blended in the mid-1980s from finer grapes and with a much-increased use of reserve wines (40 percent the firm claims) to make a very pleasant, golden, rich, biscuity bubbly – unfortunately at a much increased price. Brut Réserve is made from a blend of 37.5 percent each of Pinots Noir and Meunier to 25 percent Chardonnay. In addition, the vintage range includes a *brut*, a rosé, the Blancs de Millénaires and a *blanc de blancs*, all usually made from three-quarters Pinot Noir to one-quarter Chardonnay. The Charles Heidsieck style has deepened and much improved of late and, unusually for any *grande marque* house, more than 60 percent is exported. Its new prestige champagne, the '81 Cuvée Champagne Charlie, made from a blend of Pinot Noir and Chardonnay, is also a step forward in the direction of quality. A *marc* and a Coteaux Champenois, the Cuvée des Augustins, are also available. Visitors may admire the giant, modern, stainless steel fermenters and the 2,000-year-old chalk cellars, but only by appointment.

Heidsieck & Co Monopole MC ★→
83 rue Coquebert, 51054 Reims

Sorting one Heidsieck from another is a confusing business – but then everyone in Champagne is related to or associated with everyone else in some way. German-born Florenz-Ludwig Heidsieck set up his champagne firm in 1785 and became Florens-Louis. He had no children, so his German nephews came to Reims to help run the business. The descendants of the first nephew, Louis Walbaum-Heidsieck, are still connected with this firm. Other nephews eventually broke away to set up on their own, hence PIPER-HEIDSIECK and CHARLES HEIDSIECK.

Heidsieck & Co did not officially acquire the Monopole tag until 1923. The firm in fact introduced its famous Dry Monopole brand in 1860 and customers were already referring to the company as Heidsieck Monopole (to distinguish it no doubt from the other Heidsiecks) not long after that. Like MUMM and PERRIER-JOUET, Heidsieck is now part of Seagram's mighty champagne empire. More than 150,000 cases are made here in most years.

Heidsieck owns about 100 ha (247 acres) of vineyards, supplying roughly one-third of its needs. The most famous of these is at Verzenay, dominated by a huge old windmill that Heidsieck bought in 1923 and which has served as both observation point and entertainment venue, and is increasingly being used by Mumm. The Heidsieck range, made in Mumm's cellars, now includes the red-top Sec and a green-top Demi-Sec, plus a rosé and a vintage wine. The Heidsieck Dry Monopole non-vintage Brut is currently a dull and disappointing glassful, with some curious nuances of flavour. But the amazingly strong, overripe, exotic fruit smell and taste of Heidsieck's '76 Diamant Bleu prestige *cuvée* has its loyal followers. This wine is fifty-fifty Pinot Noir and Chardonnay, but other wines in the Heidsieck range tend to be

Pinot Noir-dominated. The straight '79 Heidsieck Dry Monopole vintage has some of Diamant Bleu's full-blown character.

Henriot   MC   '66 '73 '82 ★→★★
3 place des Droits de l'Homme, 51100 Reims

Keeping up with the champagne trade is almost a full-time occupation. Suffice it to say that Henriot, which had an impressively ancient champagne history as a firm of growers, and was once connected with CHARLES HEIDSIECK, is now owned by VEUVE CLIC-QUOT, which is part of the giant LVMH group (Louis Vuiton Moët Hennessy). Quite what changes this has brought is difficult to judge. The Henriot family first became involved in champagne in 1808. Today, run by the clever Joseph Henriot, who clearly aims for quality, it is one of the very few houses which is almost self-sufficient in grapes, and insists on using only Pinot Noir and Chardonnay. With 110 ha (272 acres) providing 90 percent of its needs, and the remaining grapes coming from Henriot workers' own vineyards, this house is fortunate indeed. Henriot's own vineyards are spread throughout the three main regions but two-thirds are planted to Chardonnay, primarily on the Côte des Blancs, and all its champagnes are heavily Chardonnay influenced. Together the grapes yield almost 100,000 cases annually, most of which consists of the unusual, beefy, fruity non-vintage Souverain Brut. A *blanc de blancs* and the vintage-dated Henriot Brut and Rosé complete the standard range. Both the vintage and non-vintage wines are 60 percent Pinot Noir to 40 percent Chardonnay blends.

Henriot however had two prestige *cuvées*, which are now, alas, no more: the vintage-dated Chardonnay-dominated Cuvée Baccarat and the fearfully expensive but rather delicious Réserve Baron Philippe de Rothschild, both aged for about five years. The '79 Baron Philippe de Rothschild Réserve, with its elegant, flowery-toasty taste is a wonderful champagne. Henriot features prominently in three-star restaurants and hotels in France and on the direct mail-order market there, which together take 60 percent of production. In general the style is light and fairly invigorating.

Ivernel   MC   '71 ★→
4 rue Jules Lobet, 51100 Ay

Ivernels have been in Ay since 1500 and, although this firm only

dates from 1963, an earlier Ivernel champagne house was founded
in 1889. Bernard Ivernel learned the champagne business from his
father Henri (a *chef de cave* at ROEDERER and KRUG) and revived the
family firm in the early 1960s. It is now owned by GOSSET, and by
all accounts is winding down. With only 2 ha (5 acres) of Ay Pinot
Noir and Pinot Meunier, a further 25 ha (62 acres) is bought in.
Almost 16,000 cases of Ivernel Brut, Rosé, Cuvée du Roi François
1er, Blanc de Blancs and a vintage champagne are made here annually. Cuvée Vincent Ivernel is the latest addition to the range.
Ivernel is highly regarded in France; the chief export markets are
the UK, Switzerland, Belgium and Holland. Red and white still
Coteaux Champenois are also produced in very small quantities.

Jacquart   MC   '85 ★→
5 rue Gosset, 51066 Reims
The CRVC cooperative, which produces this brand, is one of several in the region now to sell champagne direct to the public,
although most cooperatives usually stick to the own-label business.
CRVC is obviously determined that its Jacquart brand should be a
rip-roaring success and it is now the eighth most popular champagne in France. Since its introduction in 1981 its flying horse
trademark has been aggressively marketed in France and is now
being introduced elsewhere. The cooperative's members own
1,000 ha (2,470 acres) between them and produce some 830,000
cases of champagne annually. Almost all of this is now sold as
Jacquart, but there are still 50,000 cases of Buyer's Own Brand
wines. Jacquart champagne is available as both the non-vintage,
nutty, flowery Brut Tradition and as the classier, Chardonnay-
dominated, perfumed, easy-drinking Brut Sélection. In addition,
there is the non-vintage Rosé and a vintage champagne usually
made from 60 percent Pinot Noir to 40 percent Chardonnay. The
'86 was a waxy, glacé fruit-style wine with a rough finish.
Jacquart's prestige vintage *cuvée* rejoices in the cumbersome title of
La Grande Cuvée Nominée Rosé; there is also a Nominée Blanc
version. *Ratafia* and Bouzy Rouge are also made.

Jacquesson & Fils   MC   '75 '76 '85 ★→★★
68 rue du Colonel Fabien, 51530 Dizy, Epernay
Jacquesson champagne is heavily billed as 'originally supplied to

Napoléon the Great'. Bonaparte even went so far as to present the house with a gold medal in 1810 'for the beauty and richness of its cellars'. Latter-day Wellington admirers should not be put off by this historical trifle. Jacquesson champagnes are worth getting to know, especially the Cuvée de Prestige, which is big, bold and delightfully rich, and the full-bodied, musky-oaky '83 Signature Brut, fermented in oak. Founded in 1798, this firm today owns 33 ha (82 acres) of vines of an average 96 percent quality rating. Most of these Chardonnay and Pinot Noir vineyards are to the north and south of Epernay. Jacquesson also owns Pinot Meunier vineyards at Lagery and buys in some 20 ha-worth (49 acres) of Pinot Meunier, mainly from elsewhere. The firm's own vineyards provide 60 percent of its needs, and annual production is around 34,000 cases. Apart from the fifty–fifty Chardonnay and Pinot Noir Signature, aged in wood and vintage-dated, Jacquesson produces a *blanc de blancs* plus the Pinot Meunier-dominated non-vintage Perfection Brut and Rosé Brut. The vintage-dated Perfection Brut and Millésime Ancien are made from a blend of all three champagne grapes. Jacquesson feels that the hallmark of its champagnes is suppleness – in other words they are soft, attractive and easy to drink. It would be hard to disagree. Jacquesson is exported chiefly to Switzerland, Germany and the UK.

Jeanmaire MC '81 ★
12 rue Godart-Roger, 51207 Epernay
Owned by OUDINOT and sharing the same address, Jeanmaire is now run by the Trouillard family. Exactly the same policies rule here as at Oudinot, and Jeanmaire shares the Oudinot facilities. Eight different champagnes are made here, including a vintage and non-vintage *brut*, extra dry, *demi-sec*, rosé, *blanc de blancs* and *blanc de noirs* wines, and a deluxe *cuvée* sold as Cuvée Elysée. The '88 Blanc de Blancs was zesty, floral and nothing special. Jeanmaire also makes *ratafia*, *marc* and *fine*. Jeanmaire champagnes are Pinot Noir-dominated. Jeanmaire is also associated with BEAUMET.

Krug MC '53 '69 '73 '76 '81 '82 ★★★→★★★★
5 rue Coquebert, 51100 Reims
Star buy Grande Cuvée
Krug is quite simply the king of champagne. Private Cuvée

devotees may have had some worrying moments when this robust and much-prized Krug was replaced by the lighter more Chardonnay-influenced Grande Cuvée. (It did take time to get used to the new Krug, with its noticeably higher proportion of Chardonnay.) But now the non-vintage Grande Cuvée blend, with its rich, seductive, biscuity smell, fruity, full-bodied taste and long, firm finish is so mouthwateringly delicious that all doubts have long gone. Grande Cuvée accounts for 80 percent of the firm's sales.

Johann Joseph Krug from Mainz in Germany founded the firm in 1843, after working for JACQUESSON for nine years. Today the fifth generation of Krugs – Henri and Rémi – is in charge and as always it is the Krugs who put the blends together. The sixth generation, in the shape of Olivier, Henri's son, and Caroline, Rémi's daughter, started work at Krug in 1993, its 150th anniversary year.

The Krugs are perfectionists. Often as many as 50 different wines from 25 villages and ten separate vintages go into their Grande Cuvée blend, which is roughly 45 percent Pinot Noir, 23 percent Pinot Meunier and 32 percent Chardonnay. Similarly their latest vintage, the '82 (30 percent Chardonnay, 54 percent Pinot Noir, 16 percent Pinot Meunier) – a delicious, bold, buttery, classic Krug vintage year – is a blend of 19 different *crus*, or villages. Krug Rosé, launched in 1983 (52 percent Pinot Noir, 24 percent Pinot Meunier, 24 percent Chardonnay), is a less burdensome blend of 11 different *crus* from four vintages. There is however no set recipe – each spring the various blends are painstakingly put together and the proportions therefore differ slightly from year to year.

About 20 percent of Krug's grapes come from its own 20 ha plus (49 acres) of vines principally at Ay, Le Mesnil-sur-Oger and the four new hectares at Trépail. Other important sources of supply include Mareuil-sur-Ay and Ambonnay for Pinot Noir, Oger and Avize for Chardonnay, and Leuvrigny for Pinot Meunier. Krug considers the Meunier grape to be an important part of any fine champagne. It insists on fermenting all its wines in traditional 205-litre wooden casks, firmly believing that much of the distinctive Krug style stems directly from this process. Krug also uses only the first pressings for its wines. The champagnes are aged for an exceptionally long time before sale and the house holds an unparalleled six years' stock in its handsome, old cellars. All this adds up to just 41,000 cases per annum, all deemed by the Krugs to be prestige *cuvées* and certainly fetching prestige prices.

The Krug style is extraordinarily fine, characterized by a deep, golden colour, an intense, biscuity, almost hazelnut-like nose, a rich, harmonious, complex palate and a long, firm, lingering finish. It is as majestic and magnificent as any champagne drinker could crave. But vintage Krug in particular embodies all these characteristics and more. Its powerful charms need time to be seen at their best, but hold on to any Krug vintage for ten years or more and you will be rewarded with all these flavours. Certainly anyone who has been lucky enough to taste the sensational '69, with its incredibly strong, rich, mouthfilling, biscuity-buttery finesse and flavour, or the rich, flavoury, still-going-strong '53, or the smoky, almost Yquem-like '28, will have tasted Krug at its greatest. Minor Krug disappointments have included the lemony, walnuty Rosé plus the earlier vintages of Clos du Mesnil from Krug's own 1.87 ha (5-acre) walled vineyard of Chardonnay vines. Now that these vines have more age, later vintages, such as the '82, are not unlike a Côte d'Or white burgundy in style, with lots of nutty, lemony-gold Chardonnay fruit. Italy, the UK and the USA are the major export markets. Sales are almost always 'on allocation' – in other words, rationed. Rémy Cointreau took an interest in Krug in 1970 and became the major shareholder in 1977.

Lang Biémont   MC   '85 ★
Les Ormissets, Oiry, 51530 Epernay
With production at more than 41,000 cases a year, Lang Biémont is obviously not an unknown firm. The name of this house, established in 1875, is rarely seen abroad however, although the firm does export to the UK, Germany and elsewhere. Lang Biémont owns 30 ha (74 acres) of vines, which give it half of its needs, and uses grapes from the Côte des Blancs and Sézanne as well as from the less illustrious Aube and Aisne areas. Most of the light, lively Lang Biémont champagnes are 60 percent Chardonnay, 30 percent Pinot Noir, 10 percent Pinot Meunier. The range includes the Cuvée Réservée, a rosé and the Carte d'Or; Cuvée LB III, a Chardonnay-dominant vintage blend, and the 100 percent Chardonnay vintage Cuvée d'Exception are Lang Biémont's best wines. The firm intends to launch an organic *cuvée* in 1993.

Lanson   MC   '66 '71 ★→
12 boulevard Lundy, 51100 Reims

People either love or loathe Lanson's young, light, lively, lemony style, typified by the immensely successful Black Label Brut, the fourth most popular champagne in both France and the rest of the world and the biggest seller in Britain in 1992.

The house was founded in 1760 by François DELAMOTTE. A powerful concern, with annual sales adding up to over half a million cases, it is now owned two-thirds by MARNE & CHAMPAGNE and one-third by Allied Lyons. To fuel Lanson's prolific output all grapes are bought in, from up to 1,000 ha (2,470 acres) of vines scattered throughout the three champagne main regions, and then processed at six press houses. Most of these vineyards appear to be planted with Pinot Noir. Like all of the big champagne houses, Lanson is somewhat secretive about the exact blends of its brands, but Black Label, introduced in 1937 and accounting for about 80 percent of sales, is thought to be a blend of 35 percent Chardonnay, 50 percent Pinot Noir and 15 percent Pinot Meunier. Lanson's prestige *cuvée* is its Noble Cuvée de Lanson, a 60 percent Chardonnay to 40 percent Pinot Noir wine, whose beefy, musty character is not a good advertisement for the company. Other Lanson labels include a rosé, a vintage *brut* and a *blanc de blancs*, plus a Chardonnay-dominant 225th Anniversary Special Cuvée from the 1980 vintage. The frothy, full-flavoured, almost beefy '79 straight Brut is not recommended, but the flowery, elegant, toasty '76 is balanced and well made. If only all Lanson vintages had this class. The firm also makes a still red Coteaux Champenois plus a *ratafia* and *marc*. Besides the UK and France, Lanson also sells well in Switzerland, Germany, Italy and Japan.

Larmandier-Bernier   MC   ★→
43 rue du 28 août, 51130 Vertus

Jules Larmandier founded this house in 1930. His grandson's wife and two children now run the firm. Although Larmandier no longer exclusively uses its own vines to create its annual 7,000 or so cases, it has access to 10 ha (25 acres) of family vineyards at Cramant and others. Larmandier's Brut Tradition is their big seller but the non-vintage Cramant is a speciality of the house. With its fresh, green, racy style and lively finish it makes an excellent aperitif champagne.

Laurent–Perrier   MC   '70 '75 '79 '85 ★★→★★★★
Domaine de Tours-sur-Marne, 51150 Tours-sur-Marne
Star buy Cuvée Grande Siècle

Modern, well-equipped Laurent-Perrier lies some distance to the
east of Epernay at Tours-sur-Marne. Like many champagne
houses, Laurent-Perrier's name combines those of both husband
and wife. Eugène Laurent founded the firm in 1812 and when he
died, in 1887, his widow Mathilde Perrier took over and added her
name to his. In 1938 the firm passed to the Nonancourt family,
which owns it today. Laurent-Perrier is one of the biggest and
most powerful champagne houses. It now owns the other quality-
minded champagne concerns of DELAMOTTE, LEMOINE, SALON and
DE CASTELLANE, and has 105 ha (259 acres) of its own, which
provide about 12 percent of the firm's annual needs. Production is
now at almost 700,000 cases.

LP's sales place it fifth in all the important champagne markets
in the world, and its range is one of the most imaginative and var-
ied in the region. Mostly Chardonnay-dominated (from roughly
55 percent down to 45 percent for the straight *brut*), there is a style,
it seems, to suit every customer. The choice includes a well-made,
bone-dry non-*dosage* Ultra Brut, which, with its raw, flowery,
astringent style, is not dissimilar perhaps to the firm's 'Sugarless
1893 Grand Vin'. LP is one of the very few houses still making a
traditional rosé, whose coral pink colour and faint strawberry
flavour stem from Pinot Noir skins delicately staining the juice.
Riddling, incidentally, is still done by hand here. Other non-vintage wines include the unexciting but again well-made, fruity, appley Brut plus a *demi-sec*. The house's non-vintage *pièce de résistance*
is the wondrous prestige Grand Siècle La Cuvée, a four-star wine
whose classic, intense, toasty, flowery taste makes it one of the
most majestic champagnes available, on a level with, if not superior
to, MOET's Dom Pérignon and ROEDERER's Cristal. LP makes several vintage champagnes including a *brut* (try the vigorous, fruity
'79) and the intriguing Millésime Rare. The latter is old champagne, made from wine left over from fine vintages primarily
reserved for the Grand Siècle blend. The '73 had a deep gold
colour, a heady, herbaceous nose and a soft, buttery taste. In addition, there are now new vintage versions of Grand Siècle: the
Alexandra Brut Rosé and the Exceptionnellement Millésimé,

which, as the name suggests, is only made in truly great vintage years. The wonderful, fresh, flavoury '85 was the first edition of this ultra prestige *cuvée*, the '90 will be the next. Laurent's Coteaux Champenois wines are a speciality and worth trying, if you can find any, especially the fresh, fruity Blanc de Blancs Chardonnay on which the firm in many ways made its reputation.

Leclerc Briant MC '88 ★
67 rue de la Claude Ruelle, 51204 Epernay
Still a family firm, Leclerc Briant was founded in 1872. This Epernay-based house owns substantial vineyards (30 ha/74 acres) and produces some 25,000 cases annually, mostly from its own vines. Leclerc Briant's labels include a Cuvée de Réserve Brut plus a *demi-sec* and a rosé. The quality of these champagnes does vary but the Cuvée Special Club is well thought of.

R & L Legras MC '73 ★→★★
10 rue des Partelaines, Chouilly, 51200 Epernay
Not a well-known name, but Legras' *blanc de blancs* is the house fizz for several French Michelin-approved establishments. The superior prestige Cuvée St Vincent is well worth experiencing, especially the '73. Legras' Brut Intégral was the first non-*dosage* champagne. A rosé and a vintage-dated *blanc de blancs* are also made.

Lemoine MC ★→
Rue de Chigny, 51500 Rilly-la-Montagne
Part of the LAURENT-PERRIER empire together with SALON, DELAMOTTE and DE CASTELLANE. Whilst these other LP-owned houses tend, quite rightly, to overshadow Lemoine, its stylish, lively, classy, lemony champagnes are still worth seeking out.

Abel Lepitre MC ★
4 avenue de Général Giraud, 51055 Reims
Abel Lepitre is the best known of Les Grands Champagnes de Reims' offerings. The other two brands in this stable are GEORGE GOULET and St-Marçeaux. About 84,000 cases of all three champagnes are produced annually, of which Abel Lepitre accounts for about half, with the balance split equally between the other two firms. Outside France the most important consumers of these

champagnes are the UK, the USA and Switzerland. Abel Lepitre was once a celebrated champagne in Europe. It is available in both a *brut* and a *crémant blanc de blancs* version. The '79 Crémant, with its powerful, herbaceous, almost green cabbage-like taste will not appeal to everyone. The St-Marçeaux Extra Quality Brut has a similarly off-putting, grassy bouquet backed up by an aggressive lemony-smoky taste.

Mailly-Champagne   MC   '83 ★→
28 rue de la Libération, 51500 Mailly

This group of Mailly producers, founded in 1929, is one of the most celebrated cooperatives in the Champagne region. Today Mailly makes almost 34,000 cases a year, from about 70 ha (173 acres) of vines. Surprisingly for a cooperative, most of the wine is sold under its own label. The Mailly range is generally based on a blend of three-quarters Pinot Noir to one-quarter Chardonnay. It offers among others a *brut*, a rosé, a vintage *brut* and a deluxe *cuvée*, the Cuvée des Echansons. Mailly champagnes are sound if unexciting examples of the cooperative art; Cuvée des Echansons is the best of the range. Mailly also produces red and white Coteaux Champenois.

Marie Stuart   MC   ★
8 place de la République, 51059 Reims

Although it has an imposing building on the corner of the Place de la République, Marie Stuart is perhaps a little less impressive than it might appear. The house is run by the Comptoir Vinicole de Champagne, which in turn is owned by the Société Anonyme de Magenta (SAME). Founded in 1867, Marie Stuart now makes more than 100,000 cases of champagne each year, all of which is made from bought-in grapes or wine. The Marie Stuart Brut, made from 60 percent Pinot Noir to 40 percent Chardonnay, and bearing this ill-fated queen's likeness on the label, as all the wines do, accounts for most of the sales. Small amounts of a *demi-sec*, *blanc de blancs*, rosé, vintage *brut* and the Cuvée de la Reine are also produced. The style of Marie Stuart champagne is light and not particularly memorable. France consumes most of this bubbly, but a little is also sent abroad, mostly to Germany, Belgium, the UK and Switzerland.

Marne & Champagne   MC   ★→
22 rue Maurice-Cerveaux, 51205 Epernay

Even the most determined champagne sleuths may not find this
name on many champagne labels. Marne & Champagne is the second largest stockholder in Champagne and most of its energy is
devoted to being a 'bank' for other houses – if one of the big concerns runs out of a certain style of wine, Marne & Champagne can
step in to fill the gap. Apart from its sizeable involvement in stock-
holding, this house, owned by the hardworking but now elderly
Gaston Burtin, specializes in Buyer's Own Brand champagnes.
Many supermarkets and wine merchants in the UK and elsewhere
sell Marne & Champagne bubbly under their own labels, which
explains why the firm enjoys the third largest champagne sales in
the UK. Despite the company's large size, the quality of its BOB
wines has often been excellent, and many of its non-vintage efforts
have been well-made, lively, verdant, yeasty champagnes. However,
this house has also been known to turn out coarse and raspingly
green wines. Marne & Champagne has recently been taking more
interest in the wines it markets itself under the Giesler, Alfred
Rothschild and Eugène Clicquot labels. It lately acquired LANSON
and BESSERAT DE BELLEFON; Gauthier is another important brand.

Médot   MC   ★
30 rue Werlé, 51051 Reims

This tiny champagne house, producing slightly more than 6,000
cases annually, owns just 4 ha (10 acres) on the Montagne de
Reims, which supply only 15 percent of its needs, the rest being
bought in. Despite the small quantities made of the four Médot
champagnes (Cuvée Classique, Cuvée Réserve Direction, vintage
Brut and Blanc de Blancs), the firm still exports to Europe and the
USA. Médot is proud of its limited edition Clos des Chaulins
champagne. It is one of the few in the region to come from a
walled vineyard like KRUG's Clos du Mesnil.

Mercier   MC   '70 '75 ★→
75 avenue de Champagne, 51333 Epernay

Eugène Mercier thought big: when he founded his champagne
house in 1858 he rejected the traditional, convoluted, rabbit-
warren champagne cellars and chose long, straight galleries instead.

The end result was 47 wide galleries covering some 10 miles (18 km). Today visitors to Mercier are driven round in a small train to admire these galleries plus a collection of wine presses and, of course, to be shown the various stages in the making of champagne. First-time visitors to the region will find Mercier an enjoyable house to visit.

Mercier became associated with MOET & CHANDON in 1970 and a year later both houses became part of the giant Moët-Hennessy group, which is now part of LVMH. Inevitably, Mercier's role is now one that fits in with the group's plans rather than following any independent path. Thus, while Moët is the export champagne, Mercier is principally designed for the French market: of the 300,000-case production, some 241,000 cases are consumed by the enthusiastic French, making it the number two brand in France, after Moët. Mercier has 225 ha (556 acres) of its own vines, planted to 77 percent Pinot Meunier, 12 percent Pinot Noir and 11 percent Chardonnay, but 75 percent of its needs have to be bought in. Like many large champagne concerns Mercier is reluctant to reveal its blends, but it is highly likely that Mercier champagne is a Pinot Meunier-dominant wine. Its low price certainly indicates this, as do its own outlying holdings, three-quarters of which are planted to Pinot Meunier. Mercier champagnes will therefore never be in the first league. At their best they enjoy a golden colour and a rich, full-bodied taste that makes them good with food; at their worst they can be dull and somewhat metallic in style. Mercier's current, frothy, tutti-frutti, non-vintage Brut is no doubt the big seller here, but there is a non-vintage Demi-Sec and Rosé. Vintage wines include a Brut; the '86 is a Chardonnay-dominated, burnt toast-scented, lemony champagne. Mercier's latest *cuvée de prestige* is the non-vintage Bulle d'Or, made exclusively from Chardonnay and Pinot Noir. The UK is an important export market.

Moët & Chandon   MC '70 '73 '75 '78 '81 ★→★★★★
20 avenue de Champagne, 51200 Epernay
Star buy '78 and '81 Moët & Chandon

To be as enormous as Moët is and to produce the quality it does at its 250th anniversary must be a minor miracle. Its total yearly production is now almost 2M cases, which makes Moët, part of LVMH, the biggest selling champagne in France and the world. A very large chunk of this is probably taken up by its non–vintage Brut Impérial (sold as Première Cuvée in the UK). But Dom Pérignon, Moët's deluxe *cuvée*, first sold in 1936, must now account for some sizeable sales given the extraordinary demand for this liquid status symbol. The USA in particular just cannot get enough of DP, as they call it, or of DPR, as its pink sister is known. Other Moët wines include the white and rosé vintage–dated Brut Impérial plus an extra dry and a *crémant demi-sec* which is rarely seen. Moët also makes a fine Coteaux Champenois *blanc de blancs* named after its beautiful Château Saran near Epernay. *Ratafia, marc* and an aged *marc* complete the range.

Moët's size and premier position amongst the champagne houses did not happen by chance. There have been Moëts in Champagne since the early 15th century but the earliest reference to Claude Moët of Epernay as a champagne-maker is dated 1743. Mme de Pompadour was a devoted customer apparently, but it was Claude's son Jean–Rémy who made Moët the most famous and fashionable champagne of the time, not only in France but worldwide. The house still occupies this position today. In 1832 Claude's son-in-law, the Comte Chandon de Briailles, linked his name to that of Moët. The house has always owned vineyards and these now total 615 ha (1,519 acres), planted roughly equally to the three champagne grapes, scattered throughout the region, representing just 25 percent of its needs.

Moët's taste today is a very distinctive one. About a decade ago there were some alarming ups and downs in both quality and style, but even the Pinot Noir-dominated non–vintage Brut has now settled down to a rich, golden colour backed up by a warm, fruity taste with a firm backbone of flavour that has a little of the metallic aspect that MERCIER shares. Not a great glass of champagne, but an agreeable and drinkable one nonetheless. Vintage Moët varies dramatically in style from year to year: the '81 was made mainly from Pinot Noir, whilst the '73 was principally Chardonnay. These vintage wines have also much improved over the years – the '78s in particular were excellent. The white is a big, ripe, bouncy wine with a lot of fruitiness and a dramatic bouquet reminiscent of passion fruit. The rosé is, suitably, a pretty rose–pink colour and has a taste like crushed strawberries, as does the '86, although this wine has a hefty finish. The '86 Brut, mainly from Pinot Noir, is a smoky, perfumed, full-flavoured wine. Dom Pérignon is of course the firm's flagship, usually made from a blend of about 50 percent Pinot Noir to 50 percent Chardonnay (though this can vary by 10 percent for each grape, hence the '85's 60 percent Chardonnay, 40 percent Pinot Noir mix). The grapes come from Moët's best vine-yards and from vines averaging 40 years' of age. Its dark green 18th century-style bottle has been much imitated, but so far not the taste. The '85 was a big, rich, fruity wine with a steady stream of bubbles and a multi-layered, biscuity-smoky, perfumed style stem-ming from the 60 percent of Chardonnay in its mix. The '71 DPR, or Rosé, with its pinky-orange colour and slight taste was less impressive. This champagne is named after the blind Benedictine monk credited as the first to finalize the champagne process.

80 percent of production is exported. This house is one of the most technologically advanced in Champagne with the results of its research into instant *remuage* by *micro-billes* likely to hit the world's shelves soon. It has outposts in California (Domaine Chandon), Australia (Greenpoint Vineyards), Brazil (Provifin), Argentina (Proviar), Spain (Cava Chandon), Germany and Austria (Chandon Handelsgesellschaft). Moët & Chandon welcomes visitors and has a small Dom Pérignon museum.

Montaudon   MC   '76 ★
6 rue Ponsardin, 51100 Reims
It would be hard to miss the big, red 'M' emblazoned on all but one Montaudon champagne bottle. Yet even though Montaudon is exported to the USA, the UK, Australia, Belgium, Switzerland and Germany it is rare to see a bottle on sale. Perhaps the French keep most of the annual 75,000 cases for themselves? This medium-sized, lesser-known champagne firm, founded in 1891, is still owned by the Montaudon family. The most interesting wines in the range are the Montaudon Grande Rosé and the still, red Coteaux Rouge made from the family's own vines. In addition to using its owns grapes, Montaudon has to buy in roughly a further 70 ha-worth (173 acres), split equally between the three cham-pagne varieties. The range includes a *brut*, a *demi-sec*, a vintage-dated champagne and a *blanc de blancs*. The black grapes-dominated non-vintage Brut accounts for the vast majority of sales, although this wine's strong, herbaceous taste will not appeal to everyone.

G H Mumm MC '73 '82 ★→★★
34 rue du Champ-de-Mars, 51100 Reims

With the distinctive, bright-red sash on both foil and label it is easy to see when the next door table is drinking Mumm in either its vintage or non-vintage Brut guises – a sales point that probably did not escape Seagram, the giant wine and spirits group, when it bought Mumm in 1972. Equally eye-catching is Mumm's Demi-Sec bubbly, with its emerald green sash. Mumm's vintage Rosé, in its appropriately pale pink livery, looks positively introverted by comparison. All three are made predominantly from black grapes. The quality of these standard Mumm champagnes is however sometimes less impressive than their looks.

Launched in 1876, the non-vintage, Pinot Noir-dominated Mumm Cordon Rouge is a very big seller: a fresh enough, young, green, yeasty champagne albeit with a short finish. One step up from this is Mumm's de Cramant. This champagne, once a *crémant* wine, used to provide a wonderful, fresh, flowery, appley mouthful but in recent years, as its self-conscious, postage-stamp-sized label has got bigger, its flavour seems to have diminished. It is still however a great rarity for it is made entirely from Chardonnay grapes grown in the village of Cramant, and as such should not be missed. It still has less fizz than Cordon Rouge, in keeping with its *crémant* past. Mumm's finest champagne is the prestige René Lalou, whose '79 was a lovely, delicate, fragrant, flowery wine; definitely a three-star champagne. Grand Cordon is the firm's newest, astonishingly expensive, prestige *cuvée* and, like the Lalou, is a fifty-fifty blend of Pinot Noir and Chardonnay. Its perfumed, smoky, clean-cut style is pleasant. The firm's straight '79, with its raw, aggressive taste is not recommended.

Mumm sounds like, and is, a German name, for the original Herr Mumm came from Rüdesheim and founded his champagne firm in Reims in 1827. It remained a family business until 1914, but after the First World War it was taken over by French management with René Lalou as one of its first directors and eventually as chairman. Today Mumm owns 327 ha (808 acres) of vines, which give it about a quarter of its needs each year. Of these, its Pinot Noir holding at Bouzy and its Chardonnay holding at Cramant are the most important. Mumm Cuvée Napa is the firm's new California enterprise. The USA is the main export market and with sales topping almost 900,000 cases a year, Mumm champagnes are within the top three in France and the rest of the world.

Oudinot   MC   '81 ★→
12 rue Godart-Roger, 51207 Epernay

Jules Edouard Oudinot founded this firm in 1889, but Michel Trouillard, of the well-known Trouillard champagne family, took it over in 1981 and soon afterwards moved the business to Epernay. Oudinot owns vines in some important champagne villages and these represent half of its grape requirements, the rest being bought in. The Trouillards obviously try to cater for all tastes for their range offers eight different wines. The non-vintage Brut accounts for the majority of sales; Oudinot also makes an extra dry, a *demi-sec*, a non-vintage *blanc de blancs*, a vintage-dated *blanc de noirs*, *brut* and rosé, and finally the Cuvée Particulière BB Millés. *Ratafia*, *marc* and *fine* are also available. The Oudinot style is fruity and Pinot Noir-dominated. The firm's Blanc de Noirs is its newest idea. Oudinot is heavily involved in the export market, and the USA, the Low Countries, Switzerland and Italy are its most important markets. The company also controls the firm of JEANMAIRE and is closely associated with BEAUMET. Production of this group, which owns 80 ha (198 acres) of vines, is thought to be about 125,000 cases per annum.

Bruno Paillard   MC   '76 '85 ★→
Avenue de Champagne, 51100 Reims

Bruno Paillard obviously admired the late Baron Philippe de Rothschild, for his vintage champagne labels are, like the Rothschild labels the Baron introduced, illustrated with various artists' paintings, each one endeavouring to reflect that year's style: the '79 shows a lively, youthful village celebration, the '76 a sunny scene of bounteous prosperity. Young M Paillard comes from an old champagne family of both *vignerons* and brokers, and although he is still involved in broking, the champagne house that he founded in 1981 now takes up rather more of his time.

As yet only 25,000 cases of Champagne Bruno Paillard are produced annually (17,000 cases-worth are sold under other labels). More than 80 percent is exported to, among other countries, the USA, the UK, Belgium and Switzerland. But the energetic

M Paillard is keen to expand his small champagne house and to become a recognized name – his move to a swanky Avenue de Champagne address shows he is on his way. The top accolades could be some way off as yet since the crisp, streamlined Paillard champagnes are still rather too young and lean for most tastes, but M Paillard now ferments about 20 percent in wood, which should help to fill out their style. The firm does not own any vineyards.

Bruno Paillard is a firm believer in the low or non-*dosage* approach; he makes no *sec* or *demi-sec* wines and can produce a 'Dosage 0' (*brut zéro*) style if customers wish. Other Paillard champagnes include a Pinot Noir-dominated rosé, a smoky, oaky, but still somewhat lean *blanc de blancs*, a vintage *brut*, plus the non-vintage Première Cuvée Brut, with its ordinary, musky-oaky style, made predominantly from Pinot Noir followed by Chardonnay and Pinot Meunier. The vintage *cuvées* vary from year to year: '76 and '79 were Chardonnay-dominated, '81 was predominantly Pinot Noir. All Paillard labels carry disgorge dates. M Paillard considers his Chardonnay Réserve Privée, still a softly sparkling *crémant*-style wine, but no longer, due to a change in the law, displaying this term on the label, to be one of his most successful champagnes.

Palmer   MC   '82 ★
67 rue Jacquart, 51000 Reims
The Société Coopérative de Producteurs des Grands Terroirs de La Champagne is the illustrious-sounding cooperative behind the Palmer label. Founded in 1947, and with 310 ha (766 acres) under its control, Palmer produces some 167,000 cases annually, without having to buy in grapes or wine. With vineyards principally in the Montagne de Reims, planted to 50 percent Pinot Noir, 40 Chardonnay and 10 percent Pinot Meunier, this mix is clearly reflected in its blends. Palmer's Brut non-vintage is 60 percent Pinots Noir and Meunier to 40 Chardonnay, whilst its top Amazone de Palmer Brut prestige *cuvée* is an equal blend of Pinot Noir and Chardonnay. The UK, Belgium and Germany are the top export markets.

Pannier   MC   ★
23 rue Roger Catillon, 02400 Château Thierry
Pannier, based to the west of the Aisne region, produces almost

240,000 cases a year. Most is sold in France and about a third is BOB. Pannier is however keen to promote its own label, so we can expect to see these champagnes on sale increasingly in markets such as the UK, the USA and Germany. The champagnes have a noticeable proportion of Pinot Meunier in their blends. Pannier Brut is fresh and pear-drop-like. New Pannier champagnes include the Chardonnay-dominated swirly-labelled Egérie.

Joseph Perrier   MC   '73 '76 '85 ★→
69 avenue de Paris, 51016 Châlons-sur-Marne

Joseph Perrier, the son of a Châlons *négociant*, founded this firm in 1825. But the Perrier family ran out of heirs and in 1888 the house was taken over by Paul Pithois, whose family owns and runs it to this day. Of all the *grandes marques* houses, Joseph Perrier, situated in outlying Châlons, has one of the lowest profiles, probably because only 58,000 or so cases of champagne are made each year. The firm owns about 20 ha (49 acres) of vines situated at Cumières, Damery, Hautvillers and Verneuil in the Vallée de la Marne. Most supply Pinot Noir grapes but Verneuil supplies Pinot Meunier. A further two-thirds of this quantity is bought in to give this house the blending tools it needs, principally from the Montagne de Reims and the Côte des Blancs. The non-vintage Cuvée Royale Brut, which accounts for three-quarters of JP's sales, is made from Chardonnay, Pinot Noir and Pinot Meunier in equal parts. JP vintage wines have a higher proportion of Chardonnay, usually 50 percent.

The Joseph Perrier selection consists of a *demi-sec*, a *sec*, a *blanc de blancs*, a rosé and a vintage *brut*, besides a non-vintage *brut*. The '79 straight Brut both tasted and smelt of cheese straws. The firm's rarest and most expensive wine is a vintage prestige blend, Cuvée Jospehine. Unlike most prestige *cuvées*, it contains a high proportion of Pinot Noir (about 50 percent) with the remainder being Chardonnay. Cuvée Josephine is worthwhile. The non-vintage Joseph Perrier Brut has a somewhat chameleon character, one minute it is full-bodied and chocolatey, the next it is equally firm but toasty and almost woody in style. Joseph Perrier also makes *ratafia*, *marc* and white and red Coteaux Champenois wines. The UK, Belgium, Germany, Switzerland and Italy are its chief export markets.

Perrier-Jouët   MC   '82 '85 ★→★★
28 avenue de Champagne, 51201 Epernay

PJ, as the wine world refers to this house, has always had one of the most glamorous and fashionable reputations among champagne firms. This probably dates from the days of the pre-First World War belle époque era, when everyone from actress Sarah Bernhardt, who apparently bathed in it, to Queen Victoria, who no doubt merely drank it, was a Perrier-Jouët devotee. Pierre-Nicolas-Marie Perrier founded the company in 1811 and in order to distinguish it from other Perrier champagne concerns added his wife's maiden name, Jouët, to the firm's title. Perrier-Jouët's main 40 ha (100 acres) of vineyards surround Cramant and Avize on the Côte des Blancs and the house feels that it is these grapes above all that give the champagnes their clean-cut, light, flavoury style. A further 60 ha or so (148 acres) of Perrier-Jouët vines are situated at Dizy and Ay in the Vallée de la Marne and at Verzenay and Mailly on the Montagne de Reims. Vinay and Orbais are two other holdings. Another 250 ha (618 acres) of grapes are bought in to help produce some 250,000 PJ cases annually. The firm is now, like HEIDSIECK MONOPOLE and MUMM, part of Seagram's champagne interests.

PJ's most famous champagne and the one that sums up this firm's style is the Belle Epoque in Emile Gallé's pretty, art nouveau bottle, for which a garland of enamel anemones is fired directly onto the surface of the glass. The predominantly Chardonnay '78 Belle Epoque, with its rich, golden colour, persistent bubbles and full, warm, flowery smell and taste, albeit let down by a slightly aggressive finish, is a good example of Perrier-Jouët's art. Similarly, the non-vintage Grand Brut is usually a golden and agreeable, rich, biscuity wine with Chardonnay a noticeable proportion of its mix. Other champagnes here include a pink, faintly fruity version of Belle Epoque, which is not recommended, plus the ultra-prestige blend, Blason de France (also made in a rosé version), and a vintage PJ Brut (the rich, golden, biscuity '79 is recommended). All bar a third of Perrier-Jouët's production is exported, with the UK, Italy, Switzerland, Germany and the USA being the chief markets. The USA, in particular, is a major consumer of Belle Epoque. Perrier-Jouët was, in 1848, the first house to sell a dry champagne in the UK.

Philipponnat   MC   '75 ★
13 rue du Pont, Mareuil-sur-Ay, 51160 Ay

This small firm, dating from 1910, with 12 ha (30 acres) of vine-yards, supplying just a quarter of its needs, is now owned by the Marie Brizard group. Its most celebrated champagne is the robust, vintage-dated Clos des Goisses, a blend of 70 percent Pinot Noir to 30 percent Chardonnay made from the family's own vines. Le Reflet, a new wine, is made 50 percent from Clos des Goisses' grapes. The firm's non-vintage Brut is an agreeable and fruity, if unexciting, Pinot Noir-dominated champagne; its non-vintage Rosé, with its pale salmon-pink colour, is of a similar standard and has a fresh, green, almost fig-like taste. In most years Philipponnat produces about 50,000 cases of bubbly, of which roughly half is exported.

Jules Pierlot   MC   ★
15 rue Henri Martin, 51207 Epernay

France consumes 70 percent of Jules Pierlot's 10,000-case produc-tion, which explains why this house is little known elsewhere. The UK, Switzerland, the Low Countries and Belgium do however each import a small amount of Jules Pierlot champagne.

Founded in 1889, the firm does not own any vines and simply buys in whatever base wines it needs. Its Carte Rouge Brut and Demi-Sec and Casque d'Or Brut and Demi-Sec are a mix of both Pinot Noir and Pinot Meunier. The Cuvée Spéciale and Blanc de Blancs *bruts* are both made exclusively from Chardonnay. A rosé *brut* plus the Cuvée des Archers complete the range. Jules Pierlot wines are generally light, young and easy to drink.

Piper-Heidsieck   MC   '76 '79 '82 ★→★★
51 boulevard Henry Vashier, 51100 Reims

Everyone it seems from 17 royal or imperial courts to Marilyn Monroe has had a preference for Piper-Heidsieck. Christian Heidsieck, a nephew of the original Heidsieck (*see* Heidsieck Monopole), started trading on his own in 1834 but died within the year. His widow married M Piper in 1837, hence Piper-Heidsieck. More recently, the Marquis d'Aulan and his family were the major shareholders, an association that dates back to 1850. However, Piper-Heidsieck, like CHARLES HEIDSIECK, is now wholly owned by Rémy Cointreau. Piper only owns 22 ha (54 acres) in the Aube and thus has to buy in grapes from some 500 ha (1,235 acres) to make about 416,000 cases annually.

This house was the first in Champagne to use *gyropalettes* for *remuage* and by 1982 Piper's total production was riddled in this way. Piper's style is light, mostly without any special character or depth, and geared to consumers' tastes. The non-vintage Brut is dominated by black grapes, with Pinots Noir and Meunier making up 85 percent of the blend. The vintage range has higher proportions of Chardonnay. It is probably best to avoid the dull, anonymous non-vintage Brut and to go straight to the vintage wines. The pear-drop-like '79 had a good, frothy, foamy *mousse*. The splendid non-*dosage* Brut Sauvage, only recently vintage-dated, is one of the finest bone-dry bubblies available. Its handsome 18th century-style bottle contains a refreshing, flavoursome, zippy aperitif champagne (67 percent Pinot Noir, the rest Chardonnay), which is worth its premium price. Piper's most magnificent *cuvée*, the Chardonnay-dominated '76 Champagne Rare, is also worth seeking out, for its fine, frothy bubbles and light, elegant, chalky-flowery taste. Rare lives up to its name however for, like the Brut Sauvage, only 12,000 cases are made annually. The price reflects this.

Piper owns Piper Sonoma in California and has a joint venture in Argentina, known as Henri Piper, producing a fizz of the same name that is the second most popular Argentinian sparkling wine. Piper is also responsible for Vivency Crémant de Loire. It exports chiefly to the USA, the UK, Italy and Germany. The firm's vast cellars are open to the public throughout the year and visitors are driven around in a small passenger train to admire laser effects highlighting the history and production of champagne.

Ployez-Jacquemart   MC   ★
8 rue Astoin, Ludes, 51500 Rilly-la-Montagne

Four generations of growers have been involved in this firm, founded in 1930. Its 2 ha (5 acres) of vines provide only 15 percent of its needs for an annual production of slightly more than 5,000 cases of Extra Quality, Grande Réserve Sélection and Rosé, plus a vintage-dated champagne and a *cuvée de prestige*, the L d'Harbonville. Most are a fifty-fifty blend of Pinots Noir and Meunier. The UK, Belgium, Germany and the USA are the chief export markets.

Pol Roger MC '82 '85 '86 ★→★★★
1 rue Henri Lelarge, 51206 Epernay
Star buy '79 Pol Roger

'The world's most drinkable address' is how Sir Winston Churchill described his favourite champagne's Avenue de Champagne residence. When Sir Winston died, in 1965, Pol Roger returned the compliment by printing a black border of mourning on their labels. This was followed in 1984 with a new prestige champagne – Cuvée Sir Winston Churchill.

Pol Roger's style is a fine yet flowery, traditional one and every Pol Roger champagne is especially noted for its small, persistent bubbles and rich, creamy *mousse*. Founded in 1849 by M Pol Roger, today the firm is still family-owned. At present it is run by Christian Pol Roger and his cousin Christian de Billy, plus his son Hubert de Billy. Pol Roger owns some 82 ha (203 acres) of vines surrounding Epernay in both the Côte des Blancs and the Vallée de la Marne, which give it some 40 percent of its needs. The remainder required to produce an annual 125,000 cases is mostly Chardonnay and Pinot Meunier and is bought in. Pol Roger has always cultivated the English market and in the UK its pleasant, non-vintage, yeasty Extra Dry White Foil bears the words 'Reserved for Great Britain'. The firm also makes a Pinot Noir-dominant, clean, fruity, floral, creamy Extra Dry '86, plus a fine Rosé: the '79 (made from 60 percent Pinot Noir to 30 percent Chardonnay) had a deep pink colour and pleasant, flowery, cherry-like flavour – definitely one of the finest rosés. Pol's other brands include a vintage-dated Blanc de Chardonnay, which is not often seen, made from fine Côte des Blancs fruit. But its finest champagne is the robust, Pinot Noir-dominated Cuvée Sir Winston Churchill, a prestige *cuvée*, whose '85 is a full, deep-flavoured wine with the scent of lilies and, once again, those famous, creamy Pol Roger pinhead bubbles. About 55 percent of Pol Roger is exported, chiefly to the UK, the USA, and Germany. The firm's cellars may be visited during office hours by appointment.

Pommery MC '82 '85 ★→★★
5 place du Général Gouraud, 51100 Reims

Pommery & Greno, to use its full title is part of the giant LVMH group (*see* page 92), having been bought by the group in 1990.

Although the firm was founded in 1836, it was Mme Louise Pommery, one of the famous champagne widows, who really put this champagne house on the map. Her most enterprising move was to buy a large plot of land near Reims containing 120 Roman chalk pits. On the land above she built some bizarre baronial buildings, styled apparently after famous English country houses and surrounded by lawns. Below she connected the pits with an 11 mile (18 km) labyrinth of passages and galleries. Not content with this, Mme Pommery bought land opposite, where her daughter, who married the Comte de Polignac, built a grand property – the Château de Crayères. Nearby, a more recent, sports-loving Polignac gave up 32 ha (80 acres) of parkland to be turned into a vast sporting centre for the people of Reims, known as Parc Pommery. Today Château de Crayères is a three-star hotel and restaurant offering the finest food and accommodation in Champagne. Parc Pommery thrives and the cavernous cellars (Prince Alain de Polignac is Pommery's cellar master) with their ornate carved bas-reliefs are some of the region's most spectacular.

Pommery's 300 ha (741 acres), planted to 60 percent Pinot Noir and 40 percent Chardonnay, now account for 30 percent of its needs and its annual production adds up to over 500,000 cases. Unfortunately all this does not detract from the fact that most glasses of Pommery are not all they should be. Non-vintage Pommery Brut Royal has improved slightly over the years and now has a welcoming, smoky, barley sugar-like scent and taste but the *dosage* is too high for discerning palates. It accounts for at least 90 percent of sales and is made from equal portions of the region's three grape varieties. The other wines such as the Rosé and vintage Brut Pommery wines can also disappoint; the '80 Pommery was for instance an unusual, lime-juice like champagne. However, things are looking up at Pommery for its new '85 Louise Pommery champagne, made from 60 percent Avize and Cramant Chardonnay and 40 percent Ay Pinot Noir, is everything a *grande prestige cuvée* should be: rich, complex and delicious, with tremendous, deep, waxy, floral flavours. Madame Pommery herself would have heartily approved. Cuvée Louise Pommery Rosé is the firm's latest edition. Pommery's cellars are open to the public, even at weekends. Outside France, Pommery's main markets are Germany, Italy, Switzerland and the UK.

Rapeneau   MC   ★
69 avenue de Champagne, 51205 Epernay

Rapeneau is a big seller in France, where all except ten percent of its production is sold. The USA is its most successful export market. In most years Rapeneau makes 125,000 cases. Martel is a Rapeneau brand name.

Louis Roederer   MC   '75 '77 '81 '82 ★★→★★★★
21 boulevard Lundy, 51053 Reims

Roederer is truly one of *the* champagne greats. It says much for the sheer breed and distinction of the Roederer style that its great prestige champagne, Cristal, was still utterly delicious even in poor years such as '74 and '77. If Roederer's competitors complain that every vintage since '66 (with the exception of '68 '72 '80 '84 and '87) has appeared on a Cristal label, its customers certainly do not.

The firm was founded in 1776 but Louis Roederer did not become involved until more than half a century later. Young, energetic M Roederer soon boosted sales to more than 200,000 cases, with Russia a keen consumer. When Tsar Alexander II asked the makers of the Russian imperial court's favourite champagne to produce a superior bottle to the plebeian green variety, Roederer obliged with the chic Cristal bottle, made in crystal-clear glass. Today Roederer owns 180 ha (445 acres) of vines of which 75 ha (185 acres) are on the Côte des Blancs and the remainder in the black grape strongholds of the Montagne de Reims and Vallée de la Marne. These supply around 75 percent of Roederer's requirements, a unique situation for any leading champagne house and one which explains why Roederer's champagnes are so remarkably consistent. The remaining 20 percent is Pinot Noir which is bought in, as is a tiny percentage of Pinot Meunier.

Production is limited to 200,000 cases, on the small side for such a leading name, and yet another factor influencing Roederer's quality. Roederer's method of working is traditional and old-fashioned with noticeable use of reserve wines that have been both kept in wood and left to age in bottle on their yeasts, and with old wines used again in the final *dosage*. The result is a range of rich, honeyed, biscuity, full-bodied wines whose two-thirds Pinot Noir to one-third Chardonnay blend is deliciously apparent. Roederer's Extra Quality non-vintage blend – a delicious, rich and yeasty wine – was replaced some years ago by a superior, non-vintage wine with four years' ageing called Brut Premier, whose rich, fruity-biscuity style usually pleases, and which accounts for 125,000 cases in most years. Other non-vintage champagne here includes the Grand Vin Sec and the sweeter Carte Blanche Demi-Sec and Extra Dry.

The vintage range consists of a *brut*, rosé and a softly sparkling *crémant*-style *blanc de blancs*, which are finer still. But the glorious Cristal, golden in its protective Lucozade-yellow wrapping, is everything a great champagne should be. Perfection. The '77 has a steady *mousse*, warm, toasty smell and intense, biscuity, honeyed taste, and look out too for the '85, a rich, honeyed, lemony, nutty wine. A rosé Cristal is also made. Roederer has an operation in California (Roederer Estate) and another in Tasmania (Jansz). The firm exports 60 percent of its champagnes, chiefly to the USA, Germany, Italy, Switzerland, Belgium and the UK.

Packing grapes into a traditional, vertical champagne press

Théophile Roederer   MC   ★→
20 rue Andrieux, 51058 Reims

Théophile Roederer is entirely owned and run by Louis Roederer. Although the finest grapes and wines are kept for big brother Louis, Théophile's range, which includes a vintage and non-vintage *brut* plus a *demi-sec*, is admirable.

Ruinart   MC   '76 '75 ★★→★★★
4 rue des Crayères, 51100 Reims
Star buy '76 Dom Ruinart Blanc de Blancs

Ruinart, founded in 1729, is the oldest champagne house. GOSSET, which dates back to 1584, is the oldest firm of still winemakers in the region but it was Nicolas Ruinart, it appears, who first sold champagne. Nicolas' uncle, Dom Thierry Ruinart, was a Benedictine monk and a friend of Dom Pérignon, and it seems likely that he knew the secret of champagne and handed it down to his nephew. Successive generations of Ruinarts increased the family fortunes and by 1832 Ruinart was well regarded worldwide especially in Russia and the USA. In 1963 Ruinart became part of the large Moët-Hennessy group and thereby associated with MOET & CHANDON. Ruinart now belongs to LVMH (*see* page 92).

Today the 15 ha (37 acres) of Ruinart's own Chardonnay vines at Sillery supply only 20 percent of its needs. Total production adds up to a modest 100,000 cases per annum. Ruinart is usually overshadowed by its giant associates, Moët, VEUVE CLICQUOT, POMMERY and MERCIER. This is unfair, because the light, flowery-citrusy Ruinart style can – and does – stand on its own two feet. It has also been known to surpass that of its two big brothers, Mercier and Moët. Ruinart champagnes also represent extraordinarily good value for money, especially Dom Ruinart, the firm's prestige *cuvée*, which is half the price of Dom Pérignon. The '76 Dom Ruinart Blanc de Blancs was a lovely, racy, flowery champagne with intriguing citrussy undertones, and the '83 was an equally impressive, full, golden, hazelnut, biscuit wine. Both are elegant four-star champagnes. The '79, with its dull fruit and frothy palate is not recommended. The rosé version of Dom Ruinart, a predominantly Chardonnay wine, is rather faint-hearted by comparison. In addition, Ruinart has a vintage 'R' de Ruinart, a predominantly Pinot Noir wine, plus the non-vintage, musky, smoky 'R' de

Ruinart made from a blend of all three champagne grapes. There is also a first class and much admired white Coteaux Champenois. The USA, Germany and Switzerland are the main export markets.

Sacotte MC '76 '78 ★
13 rue de la Verrerie, Magenta, 51190 Epernay
Sacotte celebrated its centenary in 1987 and is now part of the Vranken-Lafitte group. It owns no vineyards but buys in grapes each vintage from different *vignerons* to make 25,000 cases annually of its vintage and non-vintage Brut, Rosé Brut and vintage-dated Blanc de Blancs champagne. A special Cuvée du Centenaire from the 1982 vintage is available.

Louis de Sacy MC '76 ★
6 rue de Verzenay, 51380 Verzy
This family firm was founded in the late 1960s. André Sacy runs the company but Louis de Sacy's name appears on most of the labels. The firm owns 30 ha (74 acres) of vines that, apart from a plot in Avize, are mostly in outlying areas. These supply it with 90 percent of its needs. Sacy is a medium-sized house producing about 25,000 cases annually. A *brut*, *demi-sec* and vintage rosé comprise the Sacy range. All three have a high proportion of Pinot Noir. Sacy exports to the UK, Germany and Switzerland.

Salon MC '66 '71 '79 ★★★
Le Mesnil-sur-Oger, 51190 Avize
So closely entwined with the top Chardonnay village of Le Mesnil-sur-Oger is this distinguished champagne house that everyone refers to it as Salon Le Mesnil. It would be difficult to have a more prestigious or rarefied approach to the creation of champagne than Salon. Only the first pressing of Mesnil Chardonnay is used and, more exclusive still, only from the finest vintage years. (On average this means one year out of three.) Since 1928, less than two dozen vintages of the one style of Salon have been released, and what is more, a maximum of only about 7,000 cases is now made of each. Salon has 12 years' stock currently maturing in its cellars.

Given the scarcity and impeccable credentials of Salon, its high price is justified. Champagne Salon was founded in 1921 by Eugene-Aimé Salon, whose family lived near Champagne. M Salon bought his own vineyard at Mesnil and made the first *blanc de blancs* Salon champagne for his friends. Demand increased, this '28 vintage champagne was sold at Maxim's, and Salon began to buy in the finest Chardonnay grapes from other Mesnil-sur-Oger growers, just as it does today. Salon currently owns 1 ha (2 acres) at Mesnil and buys in 6 ha-worth (15 acres). The most traditional champagne techniques are still employed here, including ageing the base wine in small wooden casks, using hand *remuage* and disgorging by hand. From the 1950s until 1984, talented champagne-maker Robert Billion created the Salon *cuvées* to the same exacting standards set by M Salon. The firm went through a worrying period under BESSERAT DE BELLEFON's ownership but is now owned by LAURENT-PERRIER, and things should therefore start to look up.

Since Robert Billion's death in 1984 there has been some doubt over future *cuvées*, which again no doubt Laurent-Perrier will put right. Noted for its walnut-like scent, Salon aficionados should buy up whatever they can of the rich, full and flowery '73, the glorious, intense, almost meaty '71 and the still surprisingly youthful and fresh '69. The latest vintage, the '82, has a deep, herbaceous style, but the '79, with its glorious, deep, toasty-biscuity palate, is finer.

SAME   MC   ★→
1 rue des Cotelles, 51200 Epernay
Société Anonyme de Magenta-Epernay, to use SAME's full title, goes back over 60 years. The Lombard family owns and manages this organization, whose entire output is almost exclusively geared towards Buyer's Own Brands, although the firm does have some labels of its own such as Marguerite Christel and Marcel Rouet. SAME tries to be as quality conscious as possible given its substantial annual production (about 167,000 cases), and releases wines with a minimum of three years' cellar age. Magenta is another SAME brand. The Magenta Carte Blanche Brut has a rich, buttery palate and solid fruit, let down by a slightly metallic finish. SAME also controls CHARLES DE CAZANOVE.

A Secondé-Prevoteau   MC   ★→★★
2 rue du Château, Ambonnay, 51150 Tours-sur-Marne
Star buy Princesses de France Brut
André Secondé-Prevoteau's grandfather founded this firm, but the

family was involved in making champagne long before that. M Secondé-Prevoteau owns 12 ha (30 acres) of top Ambonnay vines, predominantly Pinot Noir but also some Chardonnay. The Secondé-Prevoteau style is big, gutsy and full-bodied, one that goes well with food. The non-vintage Princesses de France Brut with its three-quarters Pinot Noir and one-quarter Chardonnay blend is a good introduction to this house. Its strong bouquet, flowery and perfumed, is backed up by a real mouthful of well-vinified Pinot Noir flavour, albeit a touch short and aggressive on the finish. Heftier still is the Fleuron de France Blanc de Noirs, again a non-vintage wine, whose big, beefy, biscuity taste definitely needs food to accompany it – and even then some palates may still find it too positive. Secondé also makes a big, firm, fruity, still Ambonnay Rouge Coteaux Champenois that has all sorts of attractive raspberry and beetroot-like flavours on the palate. The firm is now owned by CHARLES HEIDSIECK but André Secondé-Prevoteau still makes the wines.

Jacques Selosse   MC   '82 '86 ★→★★
22 rue Ernest Vallé, 51190 Avize
This small, traditional, family-run house owns vineyards at Avize and Cramant. Only the first class fruit from its own 6 ha (15 acres) of vines is used. This factor and the ultra-traditional Selosse techniques, such as fermentation in small oak casks and hand riddling and disgorging, make these champagnes so worthwhile. The firm also ages its wines for longer than normal before releasing them onto the market. Three years for the non-vintage champagne and four years or more for the vintage wines is usual. The non-vintage Blanc de Blancs is indeed a two-star-plus wine, with its elegant, green, herbaceous nose and zippy, streamlined palate – a great achievement from a small grower who produces under 4,000 cases annually. Anselme Selosse, Jacques' son, is now in charge and he also makes a vintage-dated *blanc de blancs*, the non-vintage Vieille Réserve and the vintage-dated Cuvée Club Special (the '79, with its strong, musty-perfumed smell and taste is not recommended).

Taittinger   MC '76 '78 '81 '85 '86 ★→★★★★
9 place Saint-Nicaise, 51100 Reims
Taittinger has the name, the wines and the reputation of one of the

grandest of *grandes marques* firms and indeed this still family-controlled house is within the world's top ten. Yet Pierre Taittinger did not found his celebrated champagne house until 1930. As a young French officer he had been stationed during the First World War at the impressive Château Marquetterie, just south of Epernay. After the War he bought both the château and its vineyards and started to make champagne. In addition, he bought two cellars in Reims, one under the 13th century Saint-Nicaise Abbey. Taittinger now owns 260 ha (642 acres) of vines, 35 percent Chardonnay, 40 percent Pinot Noir and 25 percent Pinot Meunier, which give Taittinger over half of its needs. Total production is over 300,000 cases.

The taste of Taittinger at its finest is an elegant, delicate, heavily Chardonnay-influenced style with a unique, flowery perfume all of its own. This does not always manifest itself with the non-vintage Brut, but is present in abundance with Taittinger's prestige *cuvée*, the glorious 100 percent Chardonnay, hand-riddled Comtes de Champagne, also available in a 100 percent Pinot Noir rosé version. Taittinger does not give too much away, but it seems likely that the unusual, perfumed, non-vintage Brut Reserve, that accounts for the lion's share of sales, contains a significant portion of Chardonnay, perhaps as much as 40 percent, with the two Pinots supplying the remainder in roughly equal amounts. Cuvée Prestige Rosé is the other non-vintage wine here. The rest of the range includes a vintage *brut* – the '80 was perfumed, flavoury and easy to drink – besides the Chardonnay Comtes de Champagne, whose '76 was a wonderful, stylish, flowery champagne. The '85 Comtes was again a very elegant, musky, perfumed wine.

Taittinger's latest idea is the de luxe, expensive Taittinger Collection, whose bottles are protected from harmful heat and light by a plastic coating. The Hungarian painter Victor Vasarely designed the first bottle – the gold-encased '78. Various artists' work has since decorated the bottles, with Roy Lichtenstein's 1985 edition looking the most stylish. Hans Hartung's memorable 1986 edition is the latest. The Pinot Noir-dominant '78 had a delicious, rich, warm, flowery character. Taittinger now owns the champagne house Irroy (destined to become a better known second label, as is another Taittinger *marque,* Saint Evrémond) and Bouvet-Ladubay in the Loire, and Domaine Carneros in the Napa Valley.

J de Telmont   MC   ★→
51480 Damery

These inexpensive champagnes are definitely worth tracking
down. Founded in 1920 and owned by the l'Hôpital family, only
small amounts are produced here every year. The non-vintage
Grande Réserve Brut is made partly from Pinot Noir grapes grown
in the firm's own 24 ha (59 acres) of vineyards at Damery in the
Marne Valley. This blend consists of 45 percent Pinot Noir, 45
percent Pinot Meunier and 10 percent Chardonnay. Its ripe, elder-
flower bouquet and flowery-biscuity, black grape character is recommended, although recent editions have become a shade
one-dimensional. The l'Hôpitals also make a *blanc de blancs* which,
with its fresh, soft, sweet taste and higher price, is less impressive.

Alain Thienot   MC   '82 ★
14 rue des Moissons, 51100 Reims

Alain Thienot, once a broker in the region, and with a foot in both
Champagne and Bordeaux, owns this house, dating from 1925,
and its 14 ha (35 acres) of vines. Although these vineyards provide
less than 20 percent of his needs, they are in such prestigious places
as Ay and Le Mesnil-sur-Oger. In most years, 44,000 cases are
made, with the Brut non-vintage, a blend of all three champagne
grapes, the big seller followed by a vintage version that also comes
as a rosé. Grand Cuvée Brut is the firm's most expensive wine.
Recent, rapid expansion has encouraged M Thienot to build a new
winemaking facility and cellar on the outskirts of Reims.

Union Auboise   MC   ★→
Domaine de Villeneuve, 10110 Bar-sur-Seine

Union Auboise des Producteurs de Vin de Champagne is just what
it sounds like – a group of Aube coops. It consists of 13 producers
with some 750 growers and 1,200 ha (2,964 acres) between them,
making over 150,000 cases annually. Abel Jeannin and Léonze
d'Albe are its two main labels. This pair are currently available only
in non-vintage versions but vintage and rosé styles are about to be
launched. Devaux is another important label and Grande Réserve
is the group's most popular wine. The Union currently exports to
Germany, the Low Countries and (a little) to the USA, but most is
taken by the UK. Production is likely to increase dramatically here.

Union Champagne   MC   ★→
7 rue Pasteur, 51190 Avize

This vast, modern cooperative with its ten smaller branches looks after 1,000 growers in total, whose vines are situated on the Côte des Blancs apart from 20 percent on the Montagne de Reims. It is an enormous concern, responsible for more than 800,000 cases annually. The '85 De Saint Gall Brut, made from one-third of each of the three champagne grapes, was fresh and fruity but not great. Like many champagne cooperatives, it produces own-label wines (80 percent of production is returned to its numerous growers to be sold under their own labels), but it also has several brand names of its own, including De Saint Gall. The De Saint Gall non-vintage Brut Rosé, with its curious pink colour complete with blue over-tones, has a fresh, fruity bouquet but an aggressive palate. The 1980 vintage-dated De Saint Gall was a cheesy, over-ripe champagne. The Union also has a well-made, fresh, crisp, clean vintage *blanc de blancs*, whose Chardonnay elegance shows. Pierre Vaudon, another Union label, is fresh, fruity and easy to drink. Orpale '83 the firm's new *blanc de blancs* prestige champagne and is priced accordingly.

De Venoge   MC   ★→
30 avenue de Champagne, 51204 Epernay

De Venoge has palatial premises on the Avenue de Champagne. Its wines are rather more prosaic. De Venoge is, however, an inventive marketeer, from its vintage-dated Champagne des Princes, sold in a reusable glass decanter, through to its champagne-cork-man logo complete with top hat and monocle. Founded in 1837, this firm has no vineyards of its own but buys in whatever it needs to create 100,000 cases of champagne each year. In addition to Champagne des Princes, de Venoge sells a Brut, the pleasant, fruity-peppery Cordon Bleu and Brut Rosé besides its vintage-dated Brut, Blanc de Blancs and Rosé. The firm is especially proud of its non-vintage Rosé. De Venoge is heavily involved in the own-label business and is associated with Trouillard, another Epernay champagne house.

Veuve Clicquot–Ponsardin   MC   '83 '85 ★→★★★
12 rue du Temple, 51054 Reims

Nicole-Barbe Ponsardin, who married François Clicquot in 1799, was the greatest of all the champagne widows. Tragically widowed, aged 27, in 1805 she took over the firm founded in 1772 (although her father-in-law wished to sell it) and renamed it Veuve Clicquot-Ponsardin.

This name still graces every bottle of 'the widow' to this day. By the time she died 61 years later, at the age of 89, she had founded a bank, invented a vital new stage in the *méthode champenoise* process called *remuage*, in 1816, (*see* pages 12–13) and made her champagne world famous. Other coups executed by this remarkable woman included the launch of this firm's famous yellow label (in practice more of a vivid orange) and the eventual export of three-quarters of its production. Russia was an important market. Today Clicquot champagnes reflect the traditions of the past with their fruity, full-bodied, almost peppery style that has noticeably improved in finesse in recent years, due in part no doubt to the input of tireless Joseph Henriot.

Clicquot now owns some 280 ha (692 acres) which supply almost a third of its needs. Another 600 ha-worth (1,482 acres) (two-thirds Pinot Noir to one-third Chardonnay) are bought in. All this adds up to 700,000 cases. Clicquot is reluctant to reveal its exact blends but it is clear that they are dominated by black grapes, no doubt by as much as two-thirds. The big, bouncy flavours of the Pinot Noir grape are an integral part of all Clicquot styles. The non-vintage yellow-label Clicquot Brut, made from almost two-thirds Pinot Noir to one-third Chardonnay, with a hefty dollop of Pinot Meunier (often as much as 16 percent) and a now-noticeable use of reserve wine, has had its ups and downs, as have other famous *grandes marques bruts*. Sales of this champagne top 458,000 cases in most years. Today's edition is deep, fruity and delicious. The gold-label vintage Brut, a two-thirds Pinot Noir to one-third Chardonnay wine, is better, of course, and the '85 was blessed with a big, rich, smoky, biscuity taste. The '80 was full, flowery and yeasty. Clicquot makes a little vintage rosé (the orangey-pink metallic '78 is not recommended).

Also in the range are a non-vintage *sec*, *demi-sec* and rich. Clicquot's finest champagne is the hand riddled La Grande Dame, whose generously curved bottle has slimmed down a little of late, but must surely still be reminiscent of the great lady herself. The '85's glorious, rich, full-bodied, peppery style is worth seeking out.

It is a two-thirds Pinot Noir, one-third Chardonnay blend. Veuve Clicquot, bought by Louis Vuitton, is now part of the giant LVMH group and has been since 1987 when Louis Vuitton and Moët Hennessy merged. Recently Clicquot took a 75 percent share in Cape Mentelle of Australia and Cloudy Bay of New Zealand. However, the latter's Pelorus is not a joint venture fizz and there has been no major input from Clicquot. Germany, Italy and France are the top three Veuve markets.

Vranken–Lafitte (C Lafitte)   MC   *
42 avenue de Champagne, 51200 Epernay

Clever marketeer and technician Paul-François Vranken set up his champagne business in 1976. At first the firm simply sold Buyer's Own Brand champagnes to outlets such as supermarkets, but M Vranken was soon selling his own Veuve Monnier and other brands such as Demoiselle and SACOTTE. Sales went well both in France and abroad and in 1983 a new bubbly was launched called Charles Lafitte. Not a shameless lift of the famous Bordeaux name as it happens, for there is a real Charles Lafitte sitting on the company's board. The Vranken-Lafitte group has a modern, automated winemaking plant at Vertus on the Côte des Blancs, plus a recently-acquired château nearby called des Castaignes. Vranken owns 49 ha (121 acres) which supply just 10 percent of its needs. It uses plenty of Chardonnay in its blends plus sizeable amounts of Pinot Meunier. Charles Lafitte labels include vintage and non-vintage *brut*. Veuve Monnier champagnes are available in a range of styles. Annual production of the group is now thought to top 300,000 cases. Charles Lafitte accounts for about half, Champagne Demoiselle for 50,000 cases, and a sizeable amount of own-label wines for much of the rest. Quality is average rather than special.

Other Champagne Producers

Doyen, Reims; Ellner & Fils, Epernay; Gardet & Co, Rilly-la-Montagne; Granier, Sézanne; Louis Kremer, Epernay; Charles A Prieur, Vertus; Trouillard, Epernay.

The Loire

The sparkling wines of the Loire are the chief French challengers to those of Champagne in terms of quantity – indeed some would say in quality too. The vineyards along the length of this attractive, winding river produce substantial amounts of sparklers, most of which come from its central regions of Anjou, Saumur and Touraine. Roughly 2M cases are produced annually, almost 1M coming from Saumur.

Loire sparkling wines at best are light, fruity and generally very easy to drink. Not perhaps the kind one wants to linger over and savour, but the majority do make useful aperitif and party wines. Unfortunately some large Saumur firms today seem keener on quantity than quality. Thankfully there are others such as Ackerman-Laurance where both walk hand in hand.

One of the most agreeable aspects of Loire sparkling wine is its low price. You may not get the distinction or grandeur of champagne, but you will get a pleasant, fresh, *méthode champenoise* alternative for less than half the cost. This has not escaped the *champenois*, and several champagne firms have Loire interests.

The grapes behind sparkling Saumur are principally the Chenin Blanc, or Pineau de la Loire as locals call it, plus a wide range of other white (including Chardonnay) and black Loire grapes. A lack of top sparkling wine grapes is the Loire's biggest problem, as well as laws stipulating that not more than 20 percent of varieties such as Chardonnay may go into the Saumur blend. Almost three-quarters of Saumur is *brut* and the rest is *demi-sec*. Both white and pink versions are made.

To the west of Saumur is the Anjou district, whose slightly sweet white and rosé wines play second fiddle to those of Saumur. Most lack the acidity and life necessary for a fine sparkling wine. To the east of Saumur is Touraine, whose white, red and rosé sparklers are not perhaps in the same class as Saumur but nonetheless have a place in the sparkling wine spectrum. Inexpensive *méthode champenoise* Touraine *mousseux* such as the popular Blanc Foussy may not be the best sparkling wine in the world but it is appreciated by cost-conscious customers.

In the heart of Touraine, on the north bank of the Loire, lies

Vouvray, where the finest Loire sparkling wines are produced, with distinctive, appley, waxy flavours. Sparkling Vouvray is made in two different styles: the fully-sparkling or *mousseux* variety and the slightly-sparkling *pétillant* style. The *pétillant* kind is much more difficult to make than *mousseux* and its gentle bubbles should stem from a slight second fermentation in bottle. Marc Brédif is one of the few remaining firms which specializes in genuine *pétillant* Vouvray. Only Chenin Blanc may be used to make Vouvray and over half the *appellation*'s yield is now turned into fizz.

On the opposite side of the Loire from Vouvray is Montlouis and its *pétillant* and *mousseux* wines (just like its still wines) are similar to, if not as good as, those of Vouvray. Sparkling Montlouis, however, is lighter and less intensely fruity.

The last category of Loire sparkling wine is Crémant de Loire, introduced in 1975. This can come from anywhere in the region but in terms of quality it should be finer than the others. (In practice most sparkling Vouvray is actually rather better.) Grapes for Crémant de Loire should be picked by hand and have a lower yield. Only the first juice of the gentler pressing should be used and the wine should have longer ageing than other Loire sparklers. About 167,000 cases of Crémant de Loire are produced annually.

Producers

Aimé Boucher   MC   ★→
Huisseau-sur-Cosson, 41350 Vineul, 37210 Vouvray
This large *négociant* firm selects wine from all over the Loire and has numerous cellars scattered throughout the region. An intense, ripe, fruity sparkling Vouvray and Crémant de Loire are two of its specialities. Quality is good for a firm of its size.

Ackerman-Laurance   MC   ★★
Rue L Palustre, St-Hilaire-St-Florent, 49426 Saumur
In 1811 M Ackerman married Mlle Laurance and thus the important Saumur house of Ackerman-Laurance was founded. Today Ackerman produces some 500,000 cases annually. Not all of this is taken up by Ackerman's own white and pink 1811, available in

both *brut* and *demi-sec* versions, and Crémant de Loire wines because this firm produces 'own label' sparkling wines for numerous outlets. Founder Jean Ackerman learnt the *méthode champenoise* process in Champagne and for 37 years his 4 miles (7 km) of Loire hillside cellars, once a stone quarry, were the only ones in Saumur to house wines made by this method. Ackerman–Laurance now uses bought-in Chenin Blanc, Chardonnay, Cabernet Franc and Groslot in addition to 40 ha-worth (99 acres) of its own. With such vast production it is surprising that Ackerman still performs some *remuage* by hand, although other equipment here is ultra-modern. The range consists of the big-selling 1811 Saumur and Brut Royal, plus the Louis Ackerman *crémant* range. For Ackerman's rosé sparklers the Cabernet is the major grape. The quality of Ackerman's sparkling wine is reliably consistent; the 1811 is fresh with a flowery-fruity character and the pink has a wonderful, strawberry scent. Look out too for its top Saumur sparkler the Cuvée Jean-Baptiste Ackerman, a *blanc de blancs* no doubt with an invigorating dash of Chardonnay in its mix. The firm is now owned by the family-run Rémy-Saumur group (nothing to do with Rémy-Cointreau), which also owns Laugel in Alsace and Rémy Pannier in Saumur. France takes half of Ackerman's production, the UK and Belgium much of the rest.

Le Cellier du Beaujardin   MC   ★
19 rue Nationale, 37150 Civray de Touraine

Jointly owned by the Caves Coopératives of Civray de Touraine and Bléré-Athée, this *cellier* makes several different sparkling wines. Case sales usually exceed 16,000 per annum. Non-vintage Touraine *méthode champenoise* wines in a straight and a *demi-sec* version are on offer as well as a not-dissimilar Chenin Blanc-based Pirettes brand in *brut* and *demi-sec*. Le Cellier's 42 ha (104 acres) of Chenin Blanc vines are mainly in the Touraine communes of Civray, Bléré and Athée. Automatic *remuage* aids production.

Blanc Foussy   MC   ★
95 quai de la Loire, Rochecorbon

Blanc Foussy, in its dumpy bottle, is, in terms of quantity, the biggest Touraine sparkler of them all. Annual production stands at about 167,000 cases for Blanc Foussy's Vin Vif de Touraine, in white *brut* and *demi-sec*, and pink *brut* versions. The makers are the Société des Vins de France, who use Chenin Blanc grapes partly from their own 60 ha (148 acres) of vineyard but mostly bought in from numerous growers all over the Touraine region. While the quality of Blanc Foussy is fairly consistent, the sweet, yeasty taste is not very exciting. However their up-market sparkler, the Cuvée des Comtes de Touraine, has a proportion of Chardonnay in its mix and should be worth trying. Société des Vins de France also produce Château Moncontour sparkling Vouvray in a wide range of styles, of which the Brut is a pleasant, appley, cheesy wine. Most is exported to the USA. The Crémant Extra Brut is an agreeable, ripe, and again cheesy wine; and try the Château Moncontour Crémant Extra Brut Blanc de Blancs. Veuve Oudinot is another sparkling wine produced by the same firm.

Bouvet-Ladubay   MC   ★→★★
Rue Ackerman, St-Hilaire-St-Florent, 49426 Saumur

Bouvet-Ladubay has been owned by Taittinger since 1974. After ACKERMAN-LAURANCE, it is the oldest Saumur house, having been founded in 1851 by Etienne Bouvet. Like Jean Ackerman, M Bouvet married a local girl, Mlle Ladubay – a canny move as she was the firm's accountant. Bouvet have recently launched the Mlle Ladubay trio in her honour, consisting of a rosé, *brut* and vintage-dated *brut* made from Chenin Blanc, Cabernet Franc and Chardonnay grapes. The '90 vintage Brut is a fresh, green, musky wine that is good not great. Financial problems forced the firm to sell out to the MONMOUSSEAU family in 1933 and since then three generations of Monmousseaux have guided Bouvet-Ladubay. Today 5 miles (8 km) of limestone cellars behind Bouvet's hand-some, turreted courtyard produce 142,000 cases of sparkling wine via automatic *remuage*. Bouvet is a keen export house with roughly a third of total production kept for the French market, the rest going principally to the USA and UK.

Bouvet tries to buy in only grapes or juice rather than base wine and this policy ensures that quality is kept up. Numerous different wines are made, including basic non-appellation red and white sparklers. The white Saumurs use Chenin Blanc, the rosés a mix of Cabernet Franc and Groslot. The sparkling Saumur range consists primarily of a Chenin Blanc-based *brut* plus the finer Excellence wines, the Cabernet- and Groslot-based Rosé and the red Cabernet- and Gamay-based Rubis. Better still is the vintage-dated, warm, peppery Brut Saphir sparkler which is no doubt where the ten percent of bought-in Bouvet Chardonnay goes. Both the Chenin Blanc *brut*, aged for 18 months, and the Saphir, only made in selected vintages and aged for two years, are worth trying, the *brut* having a reasonable, earthy flavour. Top of Bouvet's range is the new, non-vintage Cuvée Tresor one of the first Loire sparklers to undergo its first fermentation in oak barrels, adding an extra measure of complexity to the final wine. The result – deep, ripe and spicy-oaky – is impressive.

Caves de la Bouvraie   MCCC   ★
49123 Ingrandes–sur–Loire
Unravelling the various affiliated sparkling wine firms in the Loire could take a lifetime as everyone appears to be related in some way to everyone else. Suffice it to say that the Caves de la Bouvraie was founded by Henry Grandin in 1885 and is now owned by the Berger group – an important French wine and spirit organization. Berger produces vast quantities of *cuve close* sparklers that sell well within France. Caves de la Bouvraie buys in base wines made from the Chenin Blanc, Folle Blanche and Ugni Blanc grapes, plus a little Chardonnay recently, and turns them into 166,000 cases of sparkling wine in most years. Non-vintage *brut* versions of the Noblet Crémant de Loire and the non-appellation Grandin French sparkling wine account for most of its sales. The vast majority of Bouvraie's wines are sold in the USA.

Marc Brédif   MC   ★→★★
87 quai de la Loire, Rochecorbon, 37210 Vouvray
Marc Brédif's cavernous limestone cellars are among the most spectacular in Vouvray and culminate in a vast circular *cave* where tastings usually take place. The very old Brédif vintages may now all have been sold, but the newer sparkling Vouvrays are still impressive. Marc Brédif has long been associated with Vouvray *pétillant*, a slightly sparkling wine that gains its mild bubbles from the *méthode champenoise* but is tricky to make. Apart from the chalky, musty *pétillant* sparklers (*brut* and *sec*), Marc Brédif produces fully-sparkling or *mousseux* wines in full, appley *brut*, *sec* and *demi-sec*

versions. Brédif *pétillant* is kept for about five years before being sold. Drink any of these slightly sparkling or *mousseux* wines and you will find that the quality is good. Marc Brédif, founded in 1882, is now part of Patrick de Ladoucette's empire. With 20 ha (49 acres) of Vouvray vineyards supplying half of Brédif's needs, production totals about 17,000 cases in most years.

Le Clos Baudoin   MC   ★★→★★★
Vallée de Nouy, 37210 Vouvray

'Estate-bottled by Prince Poniatowski' proudly proclaims the Aigle d'Or sparkling Vouvray label. Prince Philippe Poniatowski became the sole proprietor of Le Clos Baudoin in 1971 but the estate had been in his family's hands for over 70 years. The prince has 21 ha (52 acres) of Chenin Blanc vines and, like most sparkling Vouvray producers, he says that it is the harvest that determines the proportion of still to sparkling wines produced every year. (No grapes or wine are bought in.) However, he calculates that during the last six years or so about one-third of the total production has been turned into *méthode champenoise* wine, commenting that very ripe years such as 1985, 1989 and 1990 are unsuitable vintages for sparkling wine. Apart from the Aigle d'Or sparkling Vouvray, Prince Poniatowski also makes very small quantities of a Touraine rosé from 2 ha (5 acres) of Cabernet Franc. Old-fashioned, traditional methods continue here: the *méthode champenoise* wines are disgorged by hand and the first fermentation takes place in oak. Aigle d'Or is delicious – a fragrant, flowery and elegant wine. The somewhat jammy rosé is less successful. Most of the Prince's wines are sold in France but the USA takes some as does the UK.

Daheuiller   MC   ★
28 rue du Ruau, 49400 Varrains

This small-scale producer makes just 1,500 cases annually of Crémant de Loire. The Daheuiller family uses its own 5 ha (12 acres) of Chenin Blanc grapes to form the base of this *cuvée*, adding a little of its own Chardonnay and Cabernet Franc too. All of the family's tiny production is riddled by hand. Some is exported to the UK. Five generations of *vignerons* have worked at this Domaine des Varinelles estate.

Domaine Dutertre   MC   ★
Place du Tertre, 20 rue d'Enfer, 37530 Limeray
This small Touraine house at the extreme east of the region makes almost 6,000 cases of sparkling wine annually. The quality here is mostly simple *mousseux* standard. Dutertre's wines are sold under Rosé and Blanc labels, besides the better quality white and pink Cuvée Saint Gilles Crémant de Loire wines. Chenin Blanc grapes from the family's 8 ha (20 acres) of vineyards plus Gamay, Cabernet Franc and Pinot Noir are used. The rosé is fifty–fifty Gamay and Pinot. Dutertre exports five percent of production.

A Foreau   MC   ★
Clos Naudin, 37210 Vouvray
One of the most respected names in Vouvray. The Foreau family's policy of giving its wines lengthy ageing prior to selling has been known to result in bottles of varying degrees of quality. The Foreaux own about 12 ha (30 acres) in total and produce tiny quantities each year. A bottle of their *brut* sparkling Vouvray was a mature, beefy wine.

Domaine de la Gabillière   MC   ★→
LEPA 13 route de Bléré, 37403 Amboise
Pascal Buron runs this viticultural lycée and no doubt employs his students to help him prepare what are regarded as excellent white and pink Crémant de Loire wines.

Gratien & Meyer   MC   ★→
Château de Beaulieu, Route de Montsoreau, 49401 Saumur
Gratien, Meyer, Seydoux is the official title of this firm, now owned by the Seydoux family, which also owns the champagne house of Alfred Gratien. With an annual production of about 167,000 cases, Gratien buys in its grapes from 200 growers. One of the larger Saumur houses, it is well known abroad due to its good distribution system and the fact that almost 50 percent of its wine is exported.

Founded in 1864 by Alfred Gratien, the firm now owns 22 ha (54 acres) of vineyards planted to Chenin Blanc and Cabernet Franc, plus 2 ha (5 acres) of Chardonnay. Together these supply just ten percent of the firm's needs. Automatic *remuage* and the old, hand–powered version are both used. Half a dozen different sparkling wines are made, of which the most popular must be the Gratien & Meyer Brut (a sweet, toasty *demi-sec* and an over–ripe, fruity rosé are also in this range). Then there are the dangerous-sounding Cuvée Flamme Brut and Rosé, a dry red non–appellation Rouge Cardinal Mousseux and a Crémant de Loire. A wine school is held here every summer.

Cave Coopérative du Haut–Poitou   MC   ★→
32 rue Alphonse Plault, 86170 Neuville de Poitou

This southern Loire VDQS outpost is increasingly admired by both the trade and the public for its constantly–improving range of inexpensive and well–made wines. Founded in 1948, the coopera-tive now has some 1,200 members with 911 ha (2,250 acres) between them. Producing wines of good quality on such a large scale is no mean feat and the cooperative hopes to acquire AC status in the near future. Two different sparkling wines are made here, the excellent, clean, fruity Diane de Poitiers Brut Rosé from Cabernet Franc, and the somewhat oily, Chardonnay–based Diane de Poitiers Blanc de Blancs Brut.

Huet   MC   ★★→
Domaine du Haut-Lieu, 37210 Vouvray

M Gaston Huet's sparkling wine production must be one of the most frustratingly variable in the world: in 1984 almost 9,000 cases, the next year nothing. But it is the harvest and only the harvest that dictates the eventual style of the Huet Vouvrays. Sparkling wine lovers will just have to hope that another green year like 1979 comes along, when almost no still Huet Vouvray was made at all. Of the 32 ha–estate (79 acres), divided into three plots, known as Clos du Bourg, Le Mont and Haut-Lieu, all is planted to Chenin Blanc except for 2 ha (5 acres) of Gamay. This is used for the Touraine Mousseux Rosé in both *brut* and *demi-sec* styles. Huet is widely acknowledged as being the finest estate in Vouvray, as any-one who tastes their non–vintage *brut*, *sec* or *demi-sec* will agree. The Brut Vouvray Pétillant is a rich, biscuity, toasty wine. Huet exports ten percent of production.

Langlois-Château   MC   ★→
Rue L Palustre, St-Hilaire-St-Florent, 49426 Saumur

Slightly more than a century old, Langlois-Château is another of
the Loire husband-and-wife enterprises. In this case M Edouard
Langlois married Jeanne Château. The family still owns about 15
percent of this firm but the rest now belongs to the champagne
house of Bollinger. Langlois makes still and sparkling wines, with
grapes from only 4 ha (10 acres) of its Chenin Blanc and
Chardonnay vineyards being used for the sparklers. As this quantity
only supplies 10 percent of its needs, Langlois buys in Chenin
Blanc from another 35 ha (86 acres). Just 25,000 cases per annum
of sparkling wine are made here – a fairly small total given the
mighty Bollinger connection. But Langlois-Château does make
numerous own-label sparkling wines for others and is hoping to
expand soon. No doubt its automatic *remuage* system has been
expanded greatly to deal with this. Only three different Crémant
de Loire Langlois wines are made now and the quality is reasonable. Top of the line is the vintage-dated Reserve; there is also a
non-vintage and rosé version. The non-vintage Brut is fresh and
waxy but not very exciting.

Les Caves de la Loire   MC   ★→
Routes de Vauchretien, 49320 Brissac

This cooperative, founded in 1951, now has 450 members whose
60 ha (148 acres) at Brissac, Beaulieu, Tigné and Thouarcé are
turned into fizz. Just 4,000 cases of sparklers are made and then
exported to the UK and elsewhere. Most is sold under the
Crémant de Loire Comte de Treillière label as both a pleasant,
yeasty *brut* and a fresh, fruity, pretty-hued rosé *brut* style. The
straight *brut* in recent years won a gold label at Mâcon. Basic
Saumur *brut* and rosé are also made, and look out for the superior
100 percent Diamant de Loire Crémant de Loire fizz. Philippe
Deval is one of the Caves' brand names.

J M Monmousseau   MC   ★
71 route de Vierzon, 41401 Montrichard

More than 80,000 cases of Touraine sparkling wine are made here
every year, most of which is sold under the Monmousseau Brut,
Cuvée JM93, JM Rosé and Crémant de Loire labels. The firm's

own 100 ha (247 acres) of vineyards at Azay-le-Rideau,
Montlouis, St-Georges-sur-Cher, Vouvray and St-Martin-le-Beau
supply 50 percent of its sparkling wine needs. A full range of
sparkling Vouvray wines is now made; the best wines of which are
still racked by hand. France takes 60 percent of this firm's fizz, with
the UK, Germany and USA also providing good markets. Once
run by the Monmousseau family and owned by Taittinger, the
firm has recently changed ownership.

Château de Montgueret MC   ★→
49560 Neuil-sur-Layon
André Lacheteau mostly makes sparkling Saumur at this property,
but he also makes a well thought of Crémant de Loire under the
Léon Leroi label. Watch out for the first release of his new
sparkling Saumur, from 1993.

Producteurs de Montlouis   MC   ★
2 route de St-Aignan, 37270 Montlouis-sur-Loire
The Cave Coopérative at Montlouis, founded in 1960 has 93 ha
(230 acres) of Chenin Blanc vines at Montlouis. This is all the
cooperative's members need to produce 67,000 cases of Montlouis
fizz annually, by the *méthode champenoise* using automatic *remuage*.
Quality is good not great.

De Neuville   MC   ★
31 rue Ackerman, St-Hilaire-St-Florent, 49400 Saumur
De Neuville, founded in 1856 and with an annual production of
some 250,000 cases, is not well known outside France, perhaps
because only 20 percent of its sparklers is exported. This firm buys
in grapes from about 100 ha (247 acres) of Chenin Blanc/Cabernet
Franc and, pleasingly, Chardonnay vineyards. Four sparkling wines
are made here: the fresh, minty sparkling Saumur de Neuville
Extra Quality Blanc and Rosé plus the superior Crémant de Loire
and Grand Crémant Cuvée Prodige.

Les Vignerons de la Noëlle   CC/MC   ★
BP 102, 44150 Ancenis
This group of vineyard owners, with some 30 ha (74 acres) of
Chenin Blanc and Chardonnay between them, was set up in 1955.

Situated in the eastern Loire, most of their annual production of 16,000 cases consists of a low-priced *cuve close vin mousseux* made from Folle Blanche, amongst other varieties. The *méthode champenoise* Prince de la Noëlle (from Folle Blanche and Chenin Blanc) and the superior Crémant de Loire (Chenin Blanc- and Chardonnay-based) are also made.

Domaine d'Orfeuilles MC ★→
La Croix Blanche Reugny, 37380 Monnaie
Bernard Hérivault enjoys a good local reputation for his *pétillant demi-sec* Vouvray but little of this is seen elsewhere.

James Paget MC ★→
Armentières, 37190 Azay-le-Rideau
Azay-le-Rideau can and does produce some fine Loire wines and James Paget's Tourraine fizz, especially the Demi-Sec Rosé, made from the same *assemblage* as the Azay *appellation*, goes down well.

Château de Passavant MC ★→
49560 Passavant-sur-Layon
Several generations of growers from the same family have tended vines here, which are overlooked by the handsome 12th century Passavant *château*. But the current incumbents, Jean and Noëlle David, did not found this family firm until 1975 and took until 1990 before releasing a Crémant de Loire. Considered by locals to be a good quality sparkler but on the expensive side, Château de Passavant is usually an 80 percent Chenin Blanc to 20 percent Chardonnay blend which puts it onto the top tier of Loire fizz. Not quite 5 ha (12 acres) of the property's own grapes are turned into just over 2,000 cases of fizz in most years, made entirely by the David family.

Rémy-Pannier MC ★
Rue L Palustre, St-Hilaire-St-Florent, 49400 Saumur
One of the largest sparkling Saumur firms, Rémy-Pannier thinks big whatever it does. This means that in addition to a wide range of still Loire wines it also makes vast quantities of sparkling Saumur as well as other sparklers. The Rémy family also owns most of ACKERMAN-LAURANCE.

Domaine St-Laurent   MC   ★→
30 rue Porte Nouvelle, 49260 Montreuil-Bellay
The Bertaud brothers make sparkling Saumur here; their Château
Piquot bubbly is particularly well thought of.

Cave Coopérative des Vignerons de Saumur   MC ★→
St-Cyr-en-Bourg, 49260 Montreuil-Bellay
This highly efficiently run cooperative has an excellent and thoroughly deserved reputation both for its still and for its sparkling
wines. With 260 members owning some 1,000 ha (2,470 acres)
between them, production of sparkling wine exceeds 87,000 cases
in most years, all of which is made from their own grapes.
Gyropalettes speed along production in the cooperative's 2 miles (4
km) of old limestone quarry cellars. The cooperative controls the
malolactic fermentation of its base wines destined for sparklers,
believing that this makes lighter and more supple sparkling wine. It
rates its Crémant de Loire, in both the *blanc brut* and rosé *brut* styles,
as its finest wine. The latter comes in both *sec* and *demi-sec* versions.
In addition, straight Saumur *brut* (vintage-dated) and *demi-sec* are
made, plus the firm's 'curiosity' – the Cuvée de la Chevalerie, a red
demi-sec mousseux.

Vallée Chartier   MC   ★→
37210 Vouvray
Philippe Brisebarre makes good sparkling Vouvray which is not
often seen outside the Loire.

Cave de la Vallée Coquette   MC   ★→
38 La Vallée Coquette, 37210 Vouvray
Philippe Thierry's cellars make some good *mousseux* Vouvrays
alongside more humdrum Touraine fizz. Look out for its top
Touraine and Vouvray sparkling wines, marked with their Cuvée
Reservée and Extra Réserve labels.

Claude Verdier   MC   ★
Boulevard Jean Moulin, 49400 Saumur
A little-known Saumur house producing 25,000 cases annually of
sparkling Saumur plus a little Crémant de Loire. Founded in 1962,
this family firm utilizes, as do most Saumur companies, the Chenin

Blanc, Cabernet Franc and Groslot grapes. Claude Verdier labels include Carte d'Or AJ Lecluse Blanc de Blancs, AJ Lecluse Saumur Brut, Claude Verdier Saumur and Nicholas Verdier Crémant de Loire. The last of these is the best wine.

Veuve Amiot   MC/CC   ★
Rue Jean Ackerman, St–Hilaire–St–Florent, 49400 Saumur

Named after the widow Elisa Amiot, who founded this firm in 1884, Veuve Amiot is now part of the internationally–minded Martini & Rossi group and its wines are made by CFVM, or Compagnie Française des Vins Mousseux, based in Tournan-en-Brie, which also produces Cadre Noir Brut Saumur. Like many Saumur houses, Veuve Amiot buys in all it needs to produce over 400,000 cases annually of reasonable–quality non-vintage sparkling wine. Gyropalettes are used here and encouragingly Chardonnay and Sauvignon grapes are beginning to appear in several of the firm's blends. Of the wide range of sparkling wines it produces, Veuve Amiot considers the earthy, perfumed Cuvée Haute Tradition to be its finest, followed by the Cuvée Réservée. The firm also makes Saumur *brut*, dry and *demi-sec* plus a Crémant de Loire Brut. Cheaper sparklers from the wider Anjou district include a rosé, a *pétillant blanc* and *rosé* and a *rouge mousseux* whose base wines come from outside the region. CFVM also makes the Vouvray Club brand and cheaper Muscat- or Ugni Blanc-based tank-method sparklers sold under the Muscador Opéra, Baron Charmeuil and Montparnasse labels, amongst others.

Les Vins Touchais   MC/CC   ★→
25 avenue du Maréchal Leclerc, 49700 Doué-la-Fontaine

The Touchais family is probably better known for its sweet dessert wines than for its range of sparkling wines. But in suitable years a proportion of the fruit from its 150 ha (370 acres) of vineyards (divided into four different estates) is turned into sparkling wine. Four sparklers are made: a sparkling Saumur known confusingly as Perles d'Anjou (*brut* and *demi-sec*) and a Vouvray *brut*, plus two non-appellation wines, the Cuvée Royale (*brut* and *demi-sec*) and a *cuve close* wine, the Duc des Nuits. Quality is ordinary.

Other Loire Sparkling Wine Producers

Albert Besombes, 'Moc Baril', Saumur; RE Dugast, Domaine des Moulins, Monnières; André Freslier, Vouvray; René Gouron, Chinon; Daniel Jarry, Vouvray.

Alsace

Alsace has been making sparkling wines for about a century. However, little was done to encourage production until 1976, when the *appellation contrôlée* Crémant d'Alsace was launched. Today, almost all sparkling wine produced in the region is *méthode champenoise* Crémant d'Alsace. This is slightly less sparkling than champagne or any other fully *mousseux* wine, but at four atmospheres of pressure it is slightly more sparkling than either Crémant de Loire or Crémant de Bourgogne.

Dopff 'Au Moulin' claim to have made the first sparkling Alsace wine around the beginning of this century. Before the First World War much of this wine, supposedly made from base wine or grapes from the Champagne region, was sold by Alsace merchants as 'champagne'. Thankfully, the Treaty of Versailles in 1919 put a

Alsace vines sheltered by the Vosges Mountains

stop to this practice, but unfortunately, those producers who were making a genuine Alsace sparkling wine also suffered and the industry did not fully recover until 1976.

Since then Crémant d'Alsace producers have rapidly made up for lost time. Where there was once only one producer there are now almost 500. Similarly, annual production is now about 14M bottles in an average year; prior to 1979 it was less than 1M. And it is not just the large cooperatives and grower-*négociants* who are making it: dozens of small independent growers are now also producing Crémant d'Alsace. With only a tiny proportion of this wine exported (just over 1M cases in 1991), it is clear that demand is coming from within France. Crémant d'Alsace is clearly in vogue and much is drunk in Alsace itself by the hoards of visitors who descend on this picture-postcard region whenever the sun shines.

Most Crémant d'Alsace is made from the light, fruity Pinot Blanc, often backed up by the less noble Auxerrois, but Riesling and the more full-bodied Pinot Noir and Pinot Gris may also be used. (Crémant d'Alsace rosé is a 100 percent Pinot Noir wine.) The classy Chardonnay is also grown increasingly in Alsace, specifically for the production of Crémant d'Alsace, and the quality of this wine should continue to increase as new plantings come on stream. In the meantime if you want to drink the finest Crémant d'Alsace it is worth paying extra for the premium sparklers, as most of these should contain a percentage of Chardonnay.

With such a range of grape varieties and flavours, the Crémant d'Alsace character is a chameleon one, changing according to producer and whether he or she intends to sell it cheaply to tourists merely wanting a taste of Alsace wine, or to a more discerning clientele. The cheapest Crémant d'Alsace need only be aged for nine months and can therefore be rushed onto shop shelves when it is scarcely a year old. This accounts for much of the mean, green wine sold under this *appellation*. One cooperative's Riesling-based sparkler could be intensely green and herbaceous whereas a small-scale grower's *crémant*, made exclusively from Pinot Blanc, could be a soft, mildly fruity wine. But, having found a wine you like, there is no guarantee that the next vintage will be of the same style. Crémant d'Alsace producers, given below-average Alsace harvests, are often forced to make do with the grapes or base wine that no one else wants. What point is there in sending your best Pinot

Blanc to be turned into fizz, when you can get a better price for it to be made into still wine? However, the appropriate and refreshingly high acidity levels necessary for good sparklers should not be a problem: all Crémant d'Alsace producers have to pick their grapes several days in advance of the general harvest date. If Crémant d'Alsace production is to continue at such a phenomenal rate it is clear that long-term contracts between *crémant* producers and growers will have to be made.

Currently most Crémant d'Alsace is of average to good quality and dry in style. It is rare to find an unacceptable or substandard bottle. However, it will be some years yet, if ever, before the sparkling wine producers of Alsace can challenge the *champenois*.

Producers

Cave Vinicole de Beblenheim   MC   ★
14 rue de Hoen, 68980 Beblenheim
One of the biggest producers of Crémant d'Alsace, Beblenheim has an impressive 220 or so members who own in the region of 220 ha (545 acres). The quality of the cooperative's wines however is only average. Caves de Hoen is one brand name, Lancelot de Hoen, a two-thirds Auxerrois to one-third Pinot Blanc two-year-old wine, is another.

Cave Coopérative de Bennwihr   MC   ★
3 rue du Général de Gaulle, 68630 Bennwihr
Another large Alsace coop that takes in growers' grapes not only from Bennwihr but also from the surrounding areas. It turns out good, ordinary, Crémant d'Alsace which is in no way extra special.

Maison Blanck   MC   ★★
32 Grande Rue, Kientzheim, 68420 Kaysersberg
Bernard and Marcel Blanck run Maison Blanck with their sons Frédéric and Philippe. Their Crémant d'Alsace in either the non-*dosage* Brut Sauvage or Extra Brut versions comes exclusively from their own 1.5 ha (3.7 acres) of vineyards at Kientzheim. The traditionalist Blancks are interested in quality, not quantity, and this

quest for the best shows in their wines, of which not quite 1,000 cases are made annually. The Extra Brut accounts for the majority of this and, like the Brut Sauvage, it is an unusual blend of two-thirds Pinot Blanc to one-third Riesling, Tokay and Pinot Gris. The Blancks first made sparkling wine in 1982 and so far consider their '86 vintage to be the finest they have made. Three-quarters of their fizz is sold in France and a new Chardonnay vineyard should increase quality here soon.

Paul Blanck   MC   ★→
32 Grand Rue, Kientzheim, 68240 Kaysersberg
There are many Blancks in Kientzheim. But this hard-working, knowledgeable family cares more than most about the contents of its bottles. In particular, the Blancks believe that each patch of their very variable Alsace soil produces wines with very different styles and flavours. Such a *terroir*-ist approach to life has paid of with their fine Crémant d'Alsace Brut.

Emile Boeckel   MC   ★→★★
2 rue de la Montagne, Mittelbergheim, 67140 Barr
'Over a hundred years of experience' boasts M Boeckel's sales lit-erature, but the firm has, like many Alsace wine producers, only been making *crémant* since 1980. Boeckel is the most important firm at Mittelbergheim but even so its *crémant* production barely tops 4,000 cases per annum. Boeckel's 5 ha (12 acres) of Crémant vineyards are partly planted to Chardonnay in addition to Auxerrois and Pinot Blanc. The small amount of Crémant d'Alsace Brut Extra, made entirely from Chardonnay, is definitely worth seeking out. Boeckel also produces a Crémant d'Alsace *brut* made from the other grape varieties. The firm exports 50 percent of its *crémant* and the rest is sold in France.

Cattin   MC   ★→
18 rue R Fremeaux, 68420 Voegtlinshoffen
The Cattin family has been associated with the unpronounceable village of Voegtlinshoffen for generations. Today Joseph Cattin produces a respectable amount of Crémant d'Alsace – just over 4,000 cases – from 6 ha (15 acres) of Voegtlinshoffen vines. Cattin believes in the traditional methods, including hand *remuage*, but

with controlled fermentation nevertheless. The firm's one sparkler, the Crémant d'Alsace Brut (made mostly from Pinot Blanc but with a little Pinot Gris and Riesling), is good rather than great.

Dopff 'Au Moulin'   MC   ★
68340 Riquewihr

With wine traditions that date back to 1574, Dopff 'Au Moulin' is one of the most important Crémant d'Alsace firms today and is still run by the family, with Pierre and Pierre-Etienne at the helm. Julien Dopff visited the Paris exhibition in 1900 and was so impressed with the *méthode champenoise* he saw demonstrated that he became determined to make a sparkling Alsace using the same process. After two years' study at Epernay, he launched the first ever Alsace sparkler just after the turn of the century. Originally known simply as Dopff, the firm added 'Au Moulin' to avoid confusion with DOPFF & IRION. Dopff 'Au Moulin' now owns some 20 ha (49 acres) of vines, mostly Pinot Blanc but with some Pinot Noir too, close to Colmar and Riquewihr. To meet its annual production of over 80,000 cases, grapes are bought in from another 50 ha (123 acres) planted to Pinot Blanc, Pinot Noir and Auxerrois.

To achieve such a healthy production figure (by Alsace standards) Dopff 'Au Moulin' uses gyropalettes for the *remuage* of most of its wine. Since 1982 the Dopff family has shared its equipment in a joint arrangement with both DOPFF & IRION and LAUGEL. Dopff make many different sparkling wines: the most popular are the beefy and somewhat aggressive Pinot Blanc- and Auxerrois-based Cuvée Julien Brut and the similarly-based alarming-sounding non-*dosage* Dopff Wild Brut. Other Dopff sparklers include the Blanc de Noirs and Au Moulin Rouge Rosé, both from Pinot Noir. The finest wines the firm makes, however, are the vintage-dated Cuvée Bartholdi, a 50 percent Pinot Blanc, 50 percent Pinot Noir wine specially bottled to commemorate the 100th anniversary of the Statute of Liberty, and the magnum bottle of Dopff Réserve Personnelle. About 30 percent of Dopff's *crémant* is exported.

Dopff & Irion   MC   ★
'Château de Riquewihr', 68340 Riquewihr

Riquewihr is the most enchanting village in Alsace. The half-timbered houses, cobbled streets and riot of colourful flowers look like the props for an opera set. Guy Dopff and Jean-Louis Irion joined forces after the Second World War but both families had previously made wine at Riquewihr for three centuries. Dopff & Irion makes wine on a vast scale and is the largest Alsace firm by far. It buys in Pinot Blanc and Auxerrois principally for its *crémant*, and just one hectare's worth of Pinot Noir. As is customary in Riquewihr, much of Dopff & Irion's wine is matured, bottled and made in the village; behind its window box and ancient doorway lies not a house but a modern cellar complete with stainless steel tanks and the latest wine equipment. The firm buys in many of its grapes and is a keen exporter. Its 12,500 cases of Crémant d'Alsace includes a green sparkler, slightly redolent of rubber but acceptable nonetheless. A rosé and a vintage-dated wine are also made. All three styles undergo automatic *remuage*.

Cave Vinicole d'Eguisheim   MC   ★→
6 Grande Rue, 68420 Eguisheim

The functional, tidy and well-equipped Eguisheim cooperative is one of the most important in France and certainly the largest in Alsace. Founded in 1902, it now boasts 800 members with 1,150 ha (2,842 acres) between them. In any one year an impressive 170-250 ha (420-617 acres) are given over to Crémant d'Alsace production, which often reaches 400,000 cases but can go down to half that in ripe years. It is therefore surprising to learn that part of its sparkling wine is still riddled by hand. This cooperative is one of the very few Alsace firms to offer a range of sparklers and there are five different Wolfbergers to choose from (the name the Cave markets its Crémant d'Alsace wines under). The Pinot Blanc-based Crémant Brut is the biggest seller, but other Alsace firms would be very happy to sell as much of the intense, green and herbaceous Crémant Riesling as is sold here. The Pinot Noir-based Crémant Rosé and the Crémant Prestige, made from Riesling and Pinot grapes, also sell well. In fact the only specialist, limited *crémant* line (4,000 cases) that Eguisheim produces is its aged, vintage-dated Wolfberger Millésime in its gaudy, enamelled bottle, made principally from Pinot Noir and Pinot Blanc.

Eguisheim is quick to point out the similarities between its Crémant d'Alsace and champagne but even tasting blind it is difficult to confuse the two. Wolfberger sparklers are of reasonable quality and during the past few years the cooperative has doubled its annual production. The coop saw the arrival in 1992 of Espace Wolfberger, a new, black-fronted, demonic-looking space age *crémant*-only winery. Inside are gyropalettes, automatic disgorging and packing lines, temperature-controlled stainless steel tanks and all the other high tech fizz weaponry that any bulk *méthode champenoise* producer could wish for. The first Wolfberger vintage in this new cellar was the '91. Wolfberger *crémant* is sold in France but a little is exported, mostly within Europe. Wolfberger now also sells two fruit flavoured fizzes whose *dosage* is replaced with a dollop of peach or blackberry liqueur. Clos de la Tourelle and Domaine Jux, single-vineyard *crémants*, are also made.

Geschickt   MC   ★
1 place de la Sinne, 68770 Ammerschwihr

The firm of Jérome Geschickt & Fils is 60 years old and has been handed down from father to son since its beginning. Geschickt's 2 ha (5 acres) of vines around Ammerschwihr produce 1,250 cases annually. Only one Crémant d'Alsace is produced, the vintage-dated Brut made from equal parts of Auxerrois, Pinot Blanc and Riesling. Hand riddling and limited production conspire to keep most of the Geschickt sparkling wine sales within Alsace and the rest of France, but a little is exported to Germany.

Louis Gisselbrecht   MC   ★
67650 Dambach-la-Ville

Not to be confused with the other Gisselbrecht in Dambach – WILLY GISSELBRECHT. This firm is also an important *négociant*, producing a wide range of Crémant d'Alsace wines including a well thought of Pinot Noir-based rosé.

W Gisselbrecht   MC   ★→
3A route du Vin, 67650 Dambach-la-Ville

For a firm as important as Willy Gisselbrecht it seems slightly incongruous that it should be situated at No 3A. However, Dambach's largest firm, founded in 1936, is a pleasant, modern establishment. The Gisselbrecht family has a tradition of buying in grapes in addition to using those from its own 3 ha (7 acres) of vines. Gisselbrecht's own Pinot Blanc and Auxerrois grapes account for 20 percent of its Crémant d'Alsace blends and it buys in the remainder from other producers of these varieties. Most of Gisselbrecht's 12,500-case annual production is taken up by its Pinot Blanc-based Crémant d'Alsace Brut, the Cuvée Prestige. The Crémant Rosé d'Alsace accounts for rather less of the total. *Remuage* is performed mostly by automatic means. Apart from the French market, Germany, the UK and Benelux buy Gisselbrecht.

Heim   MC   ★→
25 rue de la Liberté, 68250 Westhalten

An important firm of exporters, Heim has a good reputation both for its still and for its sparkling wines, which may even date back to 1765, when the firm was founded. Most of its Crémant d'Alsace is made using grapes from a group of small-scale growers who have some 90 ha (222 acres) between them. Heim insists on the very best quality from its growers (unlike some concerns) and this is obviously reflected in the wine. Heim's Crémant d'Alsace is called Imperial Brut, and 4,000 cases are now made for the firm by the Westhalten coop from Pinot Blanc and Auxerrois. A rosé and superior Pinot Blanc Cuvée Madame Sans-Gêre are also made.

Cave Vinicole de Hunawihr   MC   ★
48 route de Ribeauvillé, 68150 Hunawihr

Hunawihr was first mentioned in a papal bull of Pope Calixte II in 1123. This explains why the Hunawihr cooperative, founded in 1954, chose Cuvée Calixte as its sparkling wine brand name. The cooperative has 145 members, who own 13 ha (32 acres) between them for the production of Crémant d'Alsace. More than 13,000 cases of a non-vintage sparkler are made annually using mostly Pinot Blanc and Auxerrois, with a dash of Chardonnay. Given the relatively large production by Alsace standards it is not surprising that gyropalettes are in use. Quality is reasonable. Germany is the most important export market.

Kreydenweiss   MC   ★
Andlau, 67140 Barr

Marc Kreydenweiss of Domaine Fernand Gresser is well-known for the quality of his Alsace table wines. His Crémant d'Alsace, from a blend including Pinot Gris and Auxerrois, is above average too.

Laugel   MC   ★
102 rue de Gaulle, 67520 Marlenheim

This prosperous, well-equipped family firm was once run by Léon, Gérard, Jean-Michel and Philippe Laugel, but is now owned by the Rémy-Saumur group. Michel Laugel founded the firm in 1889 but there have been Laugels at Marlenheim since 1650. Exports are of prime importance here with about 40 percent of Laugel's *crémant* exported to Germany, Canada and the USA, amongst other countries. Laugel first made sparkling wine in 1982 − a non-vintage Pinot Blanc-based *blanc de blancs*. Today this wine still accounts for the lion's share of the firm's production − some 11,000 cases out of a total of some 12,000. In addition, Laugel makes a Pinot Noir-based *blanc de noirs* and rosé plus the vintage-dated Grand Millésime. Laugel shares *méthode champenoise* equipment (including automatic *remuage*) with DOPFF & IRION and DOPFF 'AU MOULIN'. There is also a Perles de Framboise aperitif − a blend of Crémant d'Alsace, raspberry liqueur and a dash of raspberry *eau de vie*.

Paul Mittnacht   MC   ★
35 rue du Nord, 68150 Hunawihr

The Vieille Cave de Cicogne is Paul Mittnacht's Crémant d'Alsace property and this grower-proprietor makes good, ordinary sparkling wine there.

Muhlberger   MC   ★
1 rue de Strasbourg, Wolxheim, 67120 Molsheim

François Muhlberger and his son Robert, like many of the Crémant d'Alsace producers, are heirs to ancient traditions; the first Muhlberger *vigneron* documented at Wolxheim was in 1777. However, it was more than two centuries before the family made its first sparkling wine, in 1982. Production has been growing steadily since then and the firm now produces in the region of 1,000 cases per annum of *crémant* − a *blanc de blancs brut* made from Auxerrois. *Remuage* is by hand and most of this wine is drunk by the French, although the Danes and Germans buy a little too.

Muré   MC   ★
Route du Vin, 68250 Rouffach

Reine-Thérèse Muré and her brother René run this attractive

place, overlooked by their important Clos St-Landelin, where the Murés have been growing vines since 1648. Old traditions are still much in evidence here and many wines are both fermented and aged in cask. Almost 6,000 cases of three different *crémant* wines are made here annually. Most of this is the Cuvée Prestige Muré Brut, made from a blend of Pinot Blanc, Auxerrois and Tokay, but a fair amount of Crémant d'Alsace de Riesling is also made in both a *brut* and a non-*dosage*, *brut zéro* style. The Murés' own 4 ha (10 acres) of mostly Riesling and some Pinot Blanc grapes, which provides only 50 percent of its sparkling wine needs; the rest is bought in. The sparkling wines produced here are of average quality and are automatically riddled.

Ostertag   MC   ★
87 rue Finkwiller, 67680 Epfig
Oenology school-trained André Ostertag makes a distinctive and somewhat unusual range of Alsace wines. His Riesling-, Pinot Blanc- and Auxerrois-based Crémant d'Alsace is no exception.

Cave Vinicole de Pfaffenheim   MC   ★
Pfaffenheim, 68250 Rouffach
This cooperative's full title is Cave Vinicole de Pfaffenheim, Gueberschwihr & Environs. Founded in 1957, it has 20 ha (49 acres), 200 members and says it is self-sufficient in Pinots Blanc and Gris, of which a small proportion is turned into 25,000 cases of sparkling wine annually. Hartenberger is the sparkling wine brand name and the best wine, the Brut, is made exclusively from Pinot Blanc. A Pinot Gris Hartenberger is also available, as is a rosé. Riddling is by way of automatic gyropalettes and quality is average.

Cave Coopérative de Ribeauvillé   MC   ★→★★
2 route de Colmar, 68150 Ribeauvillé
This important cooperative is a rare bird in the wine world for it manages to produce both quantity and respectable quality. It is also the oldest cooperative in France – founded in 1895. Today it has 90 members, who between them own 176 ha (435 acres) although only 12 ha (30 acres) are used for the coop's Crémant d'Alsace. This sparkling wine is sold under the brand name of Giersberger and only comes in a *brut* style. Unlike other Crémant d'Alsace

producers, Ribeauvillé makes its wine entirely from Pinot Blanc. Riddling is partly by hand and partly by the automatic method. Consequently, the annual 5,000-case production of the fresh, flowery Giersberger could increase.

Runner   MC   ★
1 rue de la Liberté, Pfaffenheim, 68250 Rouffach
Almost 4 ha (10 acres) of the commercially-minded M Runner's vines are set aside for Crémant d'Alsace. This family firm bases its sparkling wines principally on Pinot Blanc and Auxerrois, topped up with a little Tokay and Pinot Gris. The Runners use both hand riddling and gyropalettes and their *crémant* is made in a *brut* or *sec* style, according to demand. Germany is the only export market.

Schaller   MC   ★→
1 rue du Château, 68630 Mittelwihr
The firm of Schaller was founded in 1609 and Edward Schaller and his son Patrick (who studied in Champagne) have been making Crémant d'Alsace for more than a decade. With 2.5 ha (6 acres) of vines (and an additional 1 ha (2.5 acres) of Chardonnay bought in) the Schallers are currently producing 1,500 cases annually. An *extra brut* is the only Schaller sparkler and it is still riddled by hand. The Schallers feel that this blend has universal appeal. It is mostly Pinot Blanc which, they say, gives structure to the wine, plus Riesling, obviously giving the typical floral, fruity Alsace taste, and backed up with a little Pinot Gris to give the wine body.

Louis Sipp   MC   ★
68150 Ribeauvillé
Louis Sipp is one of the principal exporters of Crémant d'Alsace. A husband and wife team runs this firm and besides its own 30 ha (74 acres) of vines it also buys in grapes from numerous small growers. Do not expect the Sipp Crémant d'Alsace to be spectacular. It isn't.

Pierre Sparr   MC   ★→
2 rue de la 1ère Armée, 68240 Sigolsheim
Sigolsheim, as Pierre Sparr's address suggests, was entirely destroyed during the Second World War. But this firm, founded in 1892 and with winemaking traditions going back to 1680, is now

housed in a handsome new building and is one of the leading exporters of Alsace wine. René and his brother Charles direct operations and their sons, who represent the eighth generation of the family, also work in the firm. The base wine for their *crémant* is produced from 5 ha (12 acres) of their own Pinot Blanc and Auxerrois vines, and the Sparrs also buy in Pinot Blanc. Some 12,500 cases of their two sparkling wines, the Brut Reserve and the superior, vintage-dated Brut Dynastie, now with 15 percent Chardonnay to enliven the blend, are made in most years. The Sparrs, like most of the big Alsace houses, use automatic *remuage*. Their Crémant d'Alsace is always blended from a minimum of two different vintages to ensure continuity. The quality is good.

Thomann   MC   ★
11 Grand Rue, 68770 Ammerschwihr
Jean-Marie Thomann is now in charge of the Jean Baptiste Thomann firm and with his family makes a range of Crémant d'Alsace wines that are pleasing without being special.

Cave Vinicole de Traenheim   MC   ★→
67310 Traenheim
This little-known cooperative in the most northern part of Alsace controls 400 ha (988 acres), of which 10 ha (25 acres) of Pinot Blanc are used for its Crémant d'Alsace. More than 6,000 cases of the St-Eloi sparkler are made annually. The quality here is higher than that of most cooperatives.

Cave Coopérative de Turckheim   MC   ★→★★
16 rue des Tuileries, 68230 Turckheim
The impressive, modern Turckheim cooperative, founded in 1955 and now responsible for some of the finest Alsace wines, is the producer behind the Mayerling label. The coop's 230 members own 25 ha (62 acres) between them. Mayerling is made partly from their own grapes, and from a further 10 ha-worth (24 acres) which is bought-in. Just one sparkling wine is made — the non-vintage Mayerling Blanc de Blancs Brut, made from equal proportions of Pinot Blanc and Auxerrois; 25,000 cases are produced annually. Automatic *remuage* helps speed up production but as yet the coop does not export much sparkling wine. Mayerling is definitely

worth seeking out: with its elegant, flowery nose and racy, green palate it is one of the best *crémant* sparklers that Alsace produces.

Alfred Wantz   MC   ★
Mittelbergheim, 67140 Barr

As with most Alsace families, there are several branches of the Wantzs living in Mittelbergheim. However, Alfred Wantz makes the best Crémant d'Alsace.

Caves Vinicoles de Westhalten   MC   ★→
Route de Soultzmatt, 68111 Westhalten

There are 170 growers who belong to this cooperative, with 251 ha (620 acres) in Westhalten and various neighbouring villages. Like other Alsace cooperatives, it is amongst the largest producers of Crémant d'Alsace, which it makes from Pinot Blanc. Annual production of its strangely-titled Producteur Brut Blanc de Blancs now stands at about 13,000 cases. It is a soft and buttery wine, but nothing particularly special.

Wunsch & Mann   MC   ★
2 rue des Clefs, 68000 Wettolsheim

Just southwest of Colmar is Wettolsheim and the firm of Wunsch & Mann, founded in 1948. Originally the firm was run both by the Wunsch and the Mann families but today only the Manns are left. With 8 ha (20 acres) of their own Crémant d'Alsace Pinot Blanc and Auxerrois vines, the Manns now produce some 7,500 cases of just one sparkling wine annually – a *brut* – made via automatic *remuage*. The Manns use a little Chardonnay to lighten their some-what full-bodied, hearty style.

Other Crémant d'Alsace Producers

Lucien Albrecht, Orschwihr; Fréderic Berger & Fils, Riquewihr; Jean-Paul Ecklé, Katzenthal; Hering Fils, Barr; René Klein, St-Hippolyte; Landmann Ostholt, Soultzmatt; Charles Muller & Fils, Traenheim; André Wackenthaler, Ammerschwihr; Bernard Weber, Molsheim; Louis Wintzer, Soultz.

The Rest of France

Making sense of a row of French *vins mousseux* bottles takes both keen eyesight and determination. Any wine that simply carries the words *vin mousseux* without any regional or village designation will have been made from base wines that could come from anywhere in France. So don't be swayed by a famous producer's or company's name on a label if the words *vin mousseux* or French sparkling wine – and nothing else – accompany it. What you will be buying is not Monsieur X from the Loire's celebrated Loire sparkling wine, but his less distinguished *vin mousseux* made perhaps from the Charentes district's Ugni Blanc grape. Frustratingly, these *vins mousseux* can be made either by the *méthode champenoise* or the *cuve close* process, and the method will not always be printed on the label. Most of the wines are made by the *cuve close* system.

The next step up in the French sparkling wine hierarchy is the *vins mousseux de qualité*. These wines have to meet stricter regulations than ordinary *vins mousseux*, including longer ageing. They will have *Vin Mousseux Qualité* or the letters VMQ on the label. There are few wines in this category. Most will have been made by the *méthode champenoise*, which is now appearing increasingly on labels as *méthode traditionnelle*.

Another step up brings in those *appellation contrôlée* wines that come from a specific region or village. Most, again, are made by the *méthode champenoise*, and some by the *méthode dioise* or *méthode rurale*. The transfer method is very occasionally used. Annoyingly, here too the specific method does not always appear on the label; but the words *appellation contrôlée* plus the region or village name will appear.

The finest French sparklers of all, outside Champagne, are the softly sparkling or *crémant* wines. So far only six regions are producing *crémant*: Alsace (Crémant d'Alsace), the Loire (Crémant de Loire), Burgundy (Crémant de Bourgogne) and, with the latest arrivals, Bordeaux (the term Crémant de Bordeaux took effect from the '90 vintage), Limoux (Crémant de Limoux, again with effect from the '90 vintage) and the Rhône (Crémant de Die, with effect from the '93 vintage). Other regions such as Jura and Savoie may follow. Initially it seems contradictory that a regional *appellation* such as any of these should produce better wine than one confined to a specific area or village. But the *crémant* rules stipulate a lower yield per hectare, finer grapes, a longer ageing period and a gentler pressing with only the first pressings used. The quality shows.

Starting in northern France and working clockwise around the country, the nearest sparkling wine region to Champagne is Alsace. Next is Burgundy, with its Crémant de Bourgogne wines, introduced in 1975, of which about 4.5M bottles are produced annually from Pinot Noir, Pinot Blanc, Chardonnay and Aligoté. The quality of these can be excellent, especially if the producers (many of whom are members of cooperatives) use high proportions of either Chardonnay (the minimum allowed is 30 percent) or Pinot Noir (limited to 20 percent) in their blends. Burgundy also produces white, pink and red *vins mousseux*. These wines tend to rely heavily on the less worthy grape varieties such as Aligoté, Gamay and Sacy.

Farther south and east of Burgundy lie the mountainous Jura and Savoie districts. The sparkling wines from these regions, made from numerous different local grapes, are generally only available in the area of origin. This is no doubt partly due to the unquenchable thirsts of a never-ending stream of skiers. The various *appellations* include Arbois, L'Etoile and Seyssel besides the generic Vin de Savoie and Côtes du Jura. There is one VDQS wine, Vin du Bugey. The best known of these sparklers (and also the best quality) are the white, red and rosé Arbois wines and the white Seyssel *mousseux*. A *pétillant* Vin de Savoie is also made.

The Rhône region produces two sparkling wines: tiny amounts of the full-flavoured St-Péray from opposite Valence, and Clairette de Die which comes from a large area southeast of Valence around the town of Die. About 6.5M bottles of Clairette de Die are made every year in two totally different styles. The finest is the slightly sweet, grapey, flowery Clairette de Die Tradition made by the *méthode dioise*, predominantly from Muscat. Clairette de Die wines without the Tradition tag have, from the '93 vintage, been renamed Crémant de Die and will therefore have been made mostly from Clairette by the *méthode champenoise*. Surprisingly, the latter only accounts so far for 10,000 bottles annually, the remainder being taken up by Clairette de Die Tradition. The Mediterranean coast vineyards produce the occasional sparkling wine, the most important by far being Blanquette de Limoux from

Roussillon. The town of Limoux lies just south of Carcassonne. The region is a large one, producing some 8M bottles of sparkling wine annually. The grape varieties used are the robust local Mauzac, plus Chenin Blanc and the more recently-allowed Chardonnay. The quality of Blanquette de Limoux appears to have taken a slight dip in recent years but nonetheless it is still a fresh, yeasty and fruity sparkling wine. A new Crémant de Limoux *appellation*, covering the less traditional and probably classier Limoux sparkling wines made from greater quantities of Chenin Blanc and Chardonnay and less of the local Mauzac, was launched in 1990.

Southwest France provides the base wine for many sparklers, but most of these are bought by outside firms and receive their bubbles elsewhere. A few sparkling wines are made locally such as the Armagnac area's Vin Sauvage. One notable exception is Gaillac. The still wines of Gaillac have a tendency to sparkle naturally, due to a combination of soil, grape and climate. The Mauzac grape is the chief one here but other varieties are found, including Loin de l'Oeil ('far from view'). The best Gaillac sparklers are made by a variation of the *méthode rurale* known as the *méthode gaillaçoise* .

Farther north is the Bordeaux region, home, like Burgundy, to numerous sparkling wine firms. Most of these houses produce non-*appellation* sparklers, besides Bordeaux *mousseux* in white and pink versions. A new, superior, Crémant de Bordeaux *appellation* will now bring about a rise in the quality of this region's fizz, and the Bordelais expect to produce around 2M bottles annually. However, it is likely that the popular, non-*appellation*, cheap Bordeaux *mousseux* will continue be made.

Producers

Georges & Roger Antech   MC   ★→
Domaine de Flassian, 11300 Limoux

This little-known Blanquette de Limoux is owned by the Antech brothers, who run one of the larger family firms producing *blanquette*, making about 42,000 cases annually. Antech's own Mauzac, Chenin Blanc and Chardonnay grapes, some 60 ha (148 acres) in all, supply 40 percent of its needs, the balance being bought in.

Their superior Maistre Blanquetier with its tiny slip of a label and its dumpy flagon bottle has a good reputation, which augurs well for the firm's new Crémant de Limoux, with 20 percent Chardonnay in its mix. The white-and-black label wines are also well thought of, but Antech's top wine is the Carte Noire. Cuvée St-Laurent and the green label Prestige Antech are two other brands. A Crémant de Limoux has been made here since 1990. Considerable investment in both vini- and viticulture has paid off for the Antechs for their production has nearly doubled in recent years and quality is on the up.

Caves de Bailly   MC   ★★
89530 St-Bris-le-Vineux
Star buy Crémant de Bourgogne Meurgis
This modern cooperative, founded in 1972, lies just south of Auxerre close to the Chablis district, and has a reputation for its Crémant de Bourgogne. It has impressive 12th century cellars (carved out of limestone) and equipment which includes giant stainless steel vats that just scrape in under the cave's ceiling. There are 85 growers, with 250 ha (618 acres) between them, supplying the grapes. A winemaking staff of 20 turns the local Pinot Noir, Chardonnay and Aligoté into vintage-dated white and rosé Crémant de Bourgogne. These wines are made in a variety of different styles of which at total of 125,000 cases is made. The pale, almost blue-pink, rosé Brut has an intense, grassy, herbaceous character. Comte de Bailly, with its jagged label is the firm's newest sparkling wine. Meurgis is another brand name from Bailly that is especially worth seeking out, for its ripe, waxy, exotic '88 Blanc de Noirs Brut, which has been consistently good over the past five years. Bailly also makes a *vin mousseux* from grapes grown outside the region. Two-thirds of the wines are riddled by machine.

Producteurs de Blanquette de Limoux   MC/MR   ★→
Avenue du Mauzac, 11303 Limoux
No one will ever know whether it was the Benedictine monks of St-Hilaire who were truly the first to produce a sparkling wine, in 1531, or whether it was Dom Pérignon, almost two centuries later. However, this cooperative, founded in 1948, claims to produce 'the oldest *brut* in the world' and it would be difficult to prove it

wrong. The coop, with 500 members and 3,500 ha (8,648 acres), dominates the *appellation*, producing three bottles in every four.

Blanquette's above average quality is due to the region's chalky soil plus the trio of grape varieties: Mauzac, Chenin Blanc and Chardonnay. Two-thirds of the firm's grape needs come from these varieties. The distinctive, white, downy underside of the Mauzac leaf gives *blanquette* its name, and also much of its flavour, with the Chenin Blanc contributing fruitiness and the recently-allowed Chardonnay adding elegance and finesse. The cooperative is one of the biggest producers of sparkling wine in France. In 1993, its automatic gyropalettes yielded many millions of cases.

The range comprises a prestige vintage Sieur d'Arques Crémant de Limoux *cuvée*, its top wine, plus the lesser Vanel Crémant de Limoux sparklers and finally the highly popular Aimery range, made in both *blanquette* and *crémant* versions. Alderic and Blauers are two other brands. The firm's straight *brut* is a fresh, yeasty mouthful and the '79 Blanquette de Limoux is lively, fresh and appley. The coop also has tiny amounts of a cloudy *méthode rurale* Vin de Blanquette sparkler, most of which is consumed locally. Two-thirds of the cooperative's wines are sold in France. Belgium, Germany and the UK are the most important export markets.

Bouchard Aîné   CC/MC   ★
36 rue Ste-Marguerite, 21203 Beaune

Bouchard Aîné, as a serious burgundy house, really should know better, but it continues to sell Cold Duck, the ubiquitous, pink *cuve close* fizz, with the firm's name proudly on the label beneath a yellow baby duck floating in a saucer-shaped sparkling wine glass! Other *vins mousseux* here include the Cuvée Bouchard Aîné Blanc de Blancs in both *brut* and *demi-sec* versions. The only *méthode champenoise* wine sold is Blason de Bourgogne, a Crémant de Bourgogne. All this house's sparkling wines are made for it by other firms.

Louis Bouillot   MC   ★→
42 rue des Blés, 21700 Nuits-St-Georges

Maison Louis Bouillot turns out about 34,000 cases of sparkling wine every year, most of which is made from bought-in grapes or wine. Bouillot makes vintage and non-vintage Bourgogne Blanc and Rouge sparklers from a mix of Chardonnay/Pinot Noir and Aligoté, plus a small amount of Crémant de Bourgogne. Other Bouillot bubblies made from non-Burgundy base wines include Carte Noire and Monopole Blanc de Blancs. The Pinot Noir- and Chardonnay-based *crémant* wines are worth trying.

Café de Paris   CC   ★
Cubzac-les-Ponts, 33240 St-André-de-Cubzac
Café de Paris, made by the Caves at Cubzac, is a lot less exciting than it sounds. However, it is a vintage-dated *blanc de blancs* wine which is at least a step up in quality from its competitors. Like most of the cheap *cuve close* French sparklers it is made from various different base wines. The latest vintage is just acceptable: a slightly coarse, burnt toffee nosed wine.

G F Cavalier   CC   ★★→
67160 Wissembourg
Star buy GF Cavalier Brut
A recent name change from Chevalier to Cavalier was forced on this firm by E Chevalier of the Loire. No matter, for the Caves de Wissembourg's *cuve close* wines, sold under the brand name of G F Cavalier, are still of the same good quality and selling at the same low price. What seems remarkable about this highly efficiently run firm north of Strasbourg is that the *cuve close* wines (unlike their numerous competitors) are cheap, fresh, lively and drinkable. The firm is German owned and makes only *cuve close* wines, virtually all from wine bought in by the train-load from all over France. The majority probably comes from the Charentes region. G F Cavalier is available in Muscat Rosé, Sweet Red and Muscat Blanc versions as well as in the more desirable Brut and Blanc de Blancs styles, of which a *demi-sec* is also produced. Two prestige *cuvées* are sold under the Feist Belmont Blanc de Blancs and Pierre Larousse labels and Cavalier also produces own-label sparklers for big supermarket groups and the like. The firm's non-vintage Cavalier Brut is by no means a great wine but with its lively, clean, appley style it makes an excellent party fizz.

Charles de Fère Tradition MC ★★
02130 Fère en Tardenois

Extraordinary but true. Sixth-generation *champenois* Jean-Louis Denois has since the late 1980s made first class sparkling wines here that have much of the finesse and elegance of champagne. His training at Beaune oenology school, followed by a stint in the New World, has obviously given M Denois all the experience he needs to make superior *méthode champenoise* sparklers from Pinot Noir and Chardonnay grapes, taken initially from vineyards just outside the Champagne region. Today, Denois continues to use this source, but also uses Pinot Noir and Chardonnay from his own Aude estate of 20 hectares (49 acres), situated in southwest France. The end result, the non-*appellation méthode champenoise*, biscuity Brut Reserve and fruity Rosé, is impressive. Denois' joint venture in South African sparkling wine with Villiera Estate, that started off with the '84 vintage, sells its wine in the Cape as 'Charles de Fère Tradition, Product of South Africa'.

Chaverou CC →★
10 rue Galilée, 33200 Bordeaux

Chaverou is one of several Bordeaux-based sparkling wine firms who buy in base wine from all over the southwest to turn into low-price *cuve close* sparklers. The firm has a multiplicity of labels including Café de France, Henri Bontant, Galilée and M & P Chaverou. The quality is what you might expect: coarse, dull and not very nice.

Chevalier MC/CC ★
294 chemin des Tournons, 71850 Charnay-lès-Mâcon

This large Burgundian concern, founded in 1920, turns out 85,000 cases of bubbly annually (using 11 ha-worth (27 acres) of its own grapes). Half of this is made by the tank method and sold under the Chevalier Blanc de Blancs Brut Vin Mousseux label. Another very substantial proportion is turned into the Chevalier Monopole Blanc de Blancs, a *vin mousseux de qualité* made via the *méthode champenoise*. With 50 percent Chenin Blanc in its mix, its character is probably strongly reminiscent of Loire wines. This leaves just 12,000 cases of Crémant de Bourgogne bubbly, sold in a variety of styles including Prestige, a Pinot Noir- and Chardonnay-based wine. Usually, Aligoté features heavily in Chevalier's Crémant de Bourgogne. Germany and Greece are major export markets.

Hubert Clavelin   MC   ★→
Le Vernois, 39210 Voiteur

For once with a French regional sparkling wine it is immediately apparent from the label where it comes from: it is simply labelled by its *appellation* – Côtes du Jura. Four generations of Clavelins have run this traditional firm, which today produces about 12,500 cases of *méthode champenoise* wine a year. It owns 24 ha (59 acres) of vineyards, mostly Chardonnay, which provide two-thirds of its needs. More grapes, again mostly Chardonnay, are bought in. Most of the wine is drunk in France, but a little is exported to Germany and the USA. If you manage to find any, try it.

Caves des Coteaux de Gaillac   TM/MR   ★→
Labastide de Lévis, 81150 Marsac-sur-Tarn

Gaillac, in southwest France, has long had a reputation for its naturally-sparkling wines. The slightly sparkling wines made by the *méthode rurale*, known sometimes locally as the *méthode gaillaçoise*, are perhaps better than the fully-sparkling *mousseux* versions made by the *méthode champenoise* or transfer method. This cooperative, founded in 1951, uses mostly the transfer method to create its Gaillac *brut* and *demi-sec*, but uses the *méthode rurale* too. The coop's members have 70 ha (173 acres) of Mauzac grapes plus some of the local Loin de l'Oeil. Total annual production is 25,000 cases of lively, fruity sparkling wine. These traditional Gaillac wines are something of a curiosity within the sparkling wine world but are worth experiencing.

Les Coteaux de Gardie Coopérative   MC   ★
Gardie, 11250 St-Hilaire

This Blanquette de Limoux cooperative has 65 members and produces 40,000 cases annually of sparkling wine, sold mostly under the Blanche de Gardie label. Edouard de Clauzel is another brand name. The non-vintage Brut and Sec sparklers are based on the local Mauzac grapes while the vintage-dated Brut now has a large proportion of Chardonnay and a touch of Chenin Blanc in its blend. The cooperative's members own 200 ha (494 acres), so it is entirely self-supportive in grapes. The wine is exported to Belgium and Germany.

Bernard Delmas   MC   ★
Domaine La Batteuse, 11190 Antugnac

With 22 ha (54 acres), third-generation grower Bernard Delmas's organic wine property is one of the larger Blanquette de Limoux concerns, turning out 4,000 cases of fizz plus a straight *vin de pays*. Two styles of *blanquette* are made by Delmas: the Mauzac-domi-nated Tradition, with 20 percent Chardonnay, and the new wave Prestige, a blend of 30 percent Chardonnay, 20 percent Chenin Blanc and the remainder Mauzac. Half of the domaine's fizz is exported to the UK, and Germany also provides a large market.

André Delorme   MC/CC   ★→
Rue de la République, Rully, 71150 Chagny

More than 41,000 cases of sparkling wine are made here annually, making André Delorme a medium-sized firm. As is usual with most Crémant de Bourgogne producers, Jean-François Delorme uses a blend of different grapes. The Blanc de Noirs and Rosé are mainly Pinot Noir with a little Gamay; the Blanc de Blancs is mostly Chardonnay but now with a dash of Aligoté. Apart from these Crémants de Bourgogne (available in both *brut* and *demi-sec* versions), André Delorme makes *cuve close* method white and pink *vin mousseux brut*, both from grapes or wine from outside the region. The firm considers its new Crémant de Bourgogne Brut Cinquantenaire, a one-third each Pinot Noir, Chardonnay and Aligoté blend, to be its best wine. It was launched in 1992 to celebrate the firm's 50th anniversary. Delorme is very interested in the export market to countries such as the UK, Belgium, the USA and Germany. Just one-tenth of André Delorme's wines come from its own 7 ha (17 acres) Domaine de la Renarde estate and half of André Delorme's 41,000-case output is BOB bubbly.

Cave Coopérative de Die   MC/MD   ★→
Avenue de la Clairette, 26150 Die

Before this cooperative was founded in 1950 the Drôme region produced very little of the delightful, fresh Muscat Clairette de Die. Almost 40 years later this cooperative now produces half a million cases annually, which represents 80 percent of the total Clairette de Die production (the remainder is produced by small-scale, independent growers).

The slightly sweet Tradition is made by the rural *méthode dioise*, whose fermentation preserves all the fresh, lively fragrance of the Muscat grape. This fizz is usually a blend of 80 percent Muscat to 20 percent Clairette and is an excellent, flowery, grapey wine. The cooperative also makes a green apple like Clairette de Die Brut from Clairette grapes, using a second (*méthode champenoise*) fermentation in bottle. Voconces Brut, made from a blend of different grape varieties, is also made by the *méthode champenoise*. This large and impressively-equipped cooperative has 470 members with 1,000 ha (2,470 acres) between them scattered across the region's 32 communes. The cooperative's popular Clairdie is the second favourite sparkler in France after Kriter. Due to the gradual phasing out in France of the term *méthode champenoise* to describe any wine other than champagne, this cooperative will have no alternative but to market its Clairette de Die Brut, made from Clairette grapes, as a Crémant de Die, reserving the Clairette de Die *appellation* for its more traditional Muscat-based fizz.

Les Dryades   MC/CC   ★→
60 avenue des Pyrénées, 32800 Eauze
Expect to hear more of Les Dryades. This trio of Gascon cooperatives, founded in 1987, has produced three different sparkling wines to date: the superior *méthode champenoise* Soprane, the lesser quality, tank method Flutelle and the fruit-flavoured Les Mutines fizz. All three are made from the usual blend of Gascony grapes, including Ugni Blanc, Colombard and Gros Manseng. With good European distribution and a keen price, plus exports to the USA, Les Dryades should do well in the 1990s.

Compagnie Française des Grands Vins   CC/MC   ★
Rue Gustave Eiffel, 77220 Tournan-en-Brie
This large wine group, founded in 1909 and now situated just east of Paris, has outposts in both Burgundy and Saumur. It is now owned by Martini & Rossi, and its total production is enormous – nearly 5.5M cases a year. Most of this sea of wine comes from the Ugni Blanc grape from Charentes, plus Chenin Blanc from the

Loire and a little Chardonnay and Cabernet Franc from elsewhere. The majority is made by the *cuve close* method but the gyropalettes' *méthode champenoise* output is substantial too. The cheapest wine in the firm's range is the André Gallois, followed by the marginally classier *blanc de blancs* wines, Grand Impérial and Opéra Sec. One up again is the Muscat-based Pol Acker, which has a 100 percent Riesling relative, Pol Acker Riesling, and a Chardonnay version, which was launched in 1993. *Méthode champenoise* wines made here include Monopoles, Alfred Rothschild and Cadre Noir – the last is an earthy, musky, slightly atypical Saumur *brut* from the Loire. The group also produces a Crémant de Bourgogne, sold as Impériale Bourgogne, plus a new Loire-, Burgundy- and Alsace-based *crémant*, J de Villaret, and a sparkling Vouvray sold as Vouvray Club. Martin Laurent is its champagne brand. Compagnie Française des Grands Vins exports a third of its production and a quarter of all the *mousseux* (excluding champagne) that France makes.

Guinot   MC   ★
3 chemin de Ronde, 11304 Limoux
The Guinot family has been making sparkling wine since 1875 and now has 35 ha (86 acres) of vines at three different domaines. This gives Guinot only one-third of its needs to produce 18,000 cases annually, the rest being bought in. Apart from various styles of Blanquette de Limoux, Guinot makes a Crémant de Limoux.

Les Caves des Hautes Côtes et de la Côte   MC   ★→
Route de Pommard, 21200 Beaune
Onwards and upwards for the Hautes Côtes coop, which has now taken over the coop at Pommard too. Given the high quality of the still burgundies, the white Crémant de Bourgogne should definitely be worth trying. The standard blend (125,000 cases a year) is 40 percent each Pinot Noir and Chardonnay, 20 percent Aligoté.

Caves des Vignerons d'Igé   MC
71960 Igé
Igé, lying halfway between Mâcon and Cluny in the Mâconnais, is another Burgundy cooperative producing Crémant de Bourgogne, amongst other wines. With over 100 members, some of whom are

growers too, Igé devotes about 35 ha (86 acres) in most years to *crémant* production and produces some 15,000 bottles of fizz. Two different non-vintage *crémants* are made: the Brut, an 80 percent Chardonnay, 20 percent Pinot Noir blend, and the 100 percent Pinot Noir Rosé. France takes half of Igé's production, and the UK a quarter of its exports.

Kriter   TM   ★
5 rue du Collège, 21201 Beaune
Kriter is to Burgundy what Veuve du Vernay is to Bordeaux: a modestly-priced bulk method sparkler that the world drinks in vast quantities. It is sold in 96 countries, doing especially well in the USA and Germany, and is the biggest-selling sparkling wine in France. Anyone travelling on the autoroute through Burgundy cannot fail to notice Kriter's giant production plant, complete with fields of blackcurrant bushes whose fruit is turned into Kriter cassis. Unlike Veuve du Vernay, Kriter is apparently made by the transfer method – a process superior to the *cuve close*. Kriter's grapes are thought to include Burgundy's straightforward, fruity Aligoté, although the firm must also use grapes from outside the region. Kriter is available in Brut de Brut, Carte d'Or Demi-Sec and rosé styles, some of which are vintaged, some not. Two de luxe Kriter wines also made by the transfer method include the vintage Impérial and the sweet Délicatesse. More than 1M cases of Kriter are sold every year. The company is part of the Patriarche Père & Fils group.

Cave de Lugny   MC   ★→
71260 Lugny
This cooperative at Lugny, whose full title is the Groupement Lugny St-Gengoux, is in the heart of the Mâcon area. With its southerly, next door neighbour at Viré, it is the chief source of Crémant de Bourgogne. Opinions are divided as to which of these coops and Bailly produces the best *crémant*: it often varies from vintage to vintage. Founded in 1927 and with almost 500 members of which less than half are growers, Lugny has 60 ha (148 acres) of the region's Chardonnay and Pinot Noir vines at its disposal. This gives the cooperative all it needs to make 40,000 cases using gyropalettes. Most is sold as Crémant de Bourgogne Brut, a big, yeasty, almost chocolatey wine made from Pinot Noir and

Chardonnay. A *blanc de blancs* and a rosé are also made. All three are non-vintage wines.

Henri Mugnier   MC   ★→
1 rue du Perthuis, 71850 Charnay-lès-Mâcon
Henri and Pierre Mugnier make more than 18,000 cases of *méthode champenoise blanc de blancs mousseux* and Crémant de Bourgogne. The bought-in base wine is Chardonnay, and this fact, plus the traditional methods used in the 17th century Mugnier cellar suggest that quality should be better than most. Export markets include the USA and Italy.

Picamelot   MC   ★
Rully, 71150 Chagny
Established as recently as 1970 but with a history dating back to the 1920s, Picamelot has had a complicated ownership. The annual production of 25,000 cases is made entirely from bought-in base wine: Picamelot merely adds bubbles, via the *méthode champenoise*. *crémant* and other Bourgogne sparkling wines sadly account for a small percentage of the total. The majority is a straightforward *vin mousseux blanc* made apparently from the non-Burgundian Pinot de Tourenne grape. The Bourgogne wines are made principally from Aligoté and Pinot Blanc, the *crémant* wines from Chardonnay and Aligoté; all are non-vintage. Quality is no more than basic.

William Pitters   CC   →★
Rue de Banlin, 33310 Lormont
A hefty 583,000 cases of sparkling wine are made here annually. Club Prestige (*brut* and *demi-sec*) made from the southwest's ubiquitous Ugni Blanc grape, accounts for the lion's share of this. Other companies, however, would no doubt be very happy with yearly sales of 84,000 cases each of De Vaubrun (*brut* and *demi-sec*) and Muscat Rosé de Reinevald. (De Vaubrun has some Loire Chenin Blanc added to the Ugni Blanc.) All William Pitters sparklers are non-vintage *cuve close* wines and no stock is kept of any of them – thus they have no bottle-age. For this reason, do not expect too much from this firm.

Robert   MC   ★→
Domaine de Fourn, 11300 Pieusse

This estate has a good reputation for its Blanquette de Limoux wines, which it makes in all sorts of styles. Take your pick from the non-vintage Carte Ivoire and Carte Noire bubblies, plus the superior Maistre Blanquetier flask bottle. Dame Robert is the vintage-dated Blanquette de Limoux and the property also produces a new style Crémant de Limoux sparkler.

Caves les Vignerons de St-Péray   MC   ★→
07130 St-Péray

This tiny *appellation*, on the opposite bank from Valence in the heart of the Rhône, produces more sparkling than still wine. The quantities however are still minute, but with these wines' growing reputation, low-alcohol content, full-bodied flavour and rarity value they are worth trying. St-Péray is made mostly from the Marsanne plus a little of the other local Rhône grapes, the Rousanne and Roussette. The St-Péray Brut is a biscuity, slightly coarse wine.

Simonnet-Febvre & Fils   MC   ★→
9 avenue d'Oberwesel, 89800 Chablis

It is odd to discover that a firm so well-known for its Chablis also produces a decent quantity (some 10,000 cases per annum) of sparkling wine. The Simonnet family still owns this firm, founded in 1840, and uses the *méthode champenoise* to produce all its sparkling wines. Non-*appellation blanc de blancs* (mostly Ugni Blanc with a little Chardonnay to blend) plus a little of an exclusively Chardonnay-based fizz, accounts for most of the firm's output. In addition, there is a Crémant de Bourgogne white made from 50 percent Chardonnay to 50 percent Pinot Noir, and Pinot Noir-based rosé. The best of the bunch is undoubtedly this attractive, latter pair, both of which do well in the UK and Germany.

La Tête Noire   MC/CC   ★→
32 avenue de Verdun, 13340 Rognac

Not the ideal name for a sparkling wine firm perhaps. Grapes from 20 ha (49 acres) of the firm's own Aix-en-Provence Chardonnay are utilized here, plus the produce of 200 ha (494 acres) of less impressive grapes such as Chenin Blanc, Sémillon, Ugni Blanc, Grenache Blanc and Cabernet Sauvignon, which are bought in. Production given these quantities of grapes is understandably large – almost 200,000 cases a year. Automatic *remuage* and agglomerated yeast help to oil the wheels. Cuvée Clemente Blanc de Blancs is the big seller but Rosé d'une Nuit does reasonably well too. Edmond Thery, the firm's new 100 percent Chardonnay *méthode champenoise* fizz, should be worth trying, but less so the sparkling Pétillant de Chardonnay La Coste, which is also new. Recently, La Tête Noire has set up another Provence firm called Auran, whose brands include the Chardonnay-based Antonin Truffer. Other tank method fizz produced includes Paul de Coste, and there is fruit-flavoured fizz under the Alliance, Incartade and Albatros labels.

Jean Teysseire   MC   ★→
Avenue du 11 novembre, 07130 St-Péray
Jean Teysseire's father was a vine-grower in 1899 and the old traditions are certainly being continued with the next generation. M Teysseire owns only 2 ha (5 acres), of Roussette and Marsanne, but his *méthode champenoise* St-Péray Brut still has its own label.

Varichon & Clerc   MC/CC   ★→★★
Les Séchallets, 01420 Seyssel
Seyssel is another of those odd French regional sparkling wine specialities that few outsiders have ever heard of and even fewer tasted. It comes from mountainous skiing country on the road between Lyon and Geneva in the Savoie. Only tiny amounts are made usually but this family-owned *négociant* house cleverly has an arrangement with the local producers' *syndicat* to buy their harvest every year. In this way Varichon & Clerc, founded in 1900, manages to produce a handsome 200,000 cases plus of its *méthode champenoise* Seysell wine every year, half of which is still riddled by hand.

Sparkling Seyssel has a character all of its own due to the blend of local Savoie grapes – the Roussette (or Altesse) and the Molette. Another sparkler from local grapes is the VDQS Cerdon, made from a similar mix. In addition, Varichon & Clerc uses Jacquère, Clairette and Chenin Blanc grapes. It also sells *vins mousseux* from outside the region, without the *appellation* Seyssel tag at the bottom of the label. Of these, the firm's Carte Blanche, with its elegant, fresh, flowery style is excellent, and look out too for its Crémant de Bourgogne bubbly. Wines with the Seyssel distinction include Royal Seyssel, Seyssel Brut and Diner's Blanc de Blancs. The vintage-dated Royal Seyssel is considered to be the best Varichon & Clerc wine. A Pétillant de Savoie is also available, but not recommended. Tank method fizz is produced here too. The firm exports heavily to the USA, Italy, the UK and Japan, amongst others.

Vergnes   MC   ★
Domaine de Martinolles, 11250 St-Hilaire

The Vergnes are important Blanquette de Limoux *négociants*, with 65 ha (160 acres) of their own vines, from which they make 20,000 cases of fizz. Most of the vines are Mauzac and Chardonnay, but there is a little Chenin Blanc and Pinot Noir too. Just three different blends are made, of which the most traditional is the 100 percent Mauzac-based Blanquette Ancestrale, with just 6.5 percent alcohol. The finer Blanquette de Limoux has a good dollop of Chardonnay and Chenin Blanc to lift the blend, and the Crémant de Limoux, with 20 percent Chardonnay and 20 percent Chenin Blanc, is the top Vergnes fizz. Belgium, Germany and the UK are the top three Vergnes export markets.

Veuve Ambal   MC   ★→
BP 1, Rully, 71150 Chagny

Simplicity is everything, it seems, at Veuve Ambal. Unlike at other sparkling wine firms, the Veuve Ambal label is attached to only three different qualities of sparkling wine, of which 66,000 cases are sold annually. The lowest grade is the *méthode champenoise mousseux* that comes from outside the region (in *brut, demi-sec,* rosé *brut* and rosé *demi-sec*). The middle range, the Bourgogne *mousseux,* consists of a *blanc,* a rosé and a *rouge* (each available in *brut, sec* and *demi-sec*). The top category is the Rully Crémant de Bourgogne range, made mostly from Pinot Noir plus Chardonnay and a touch of Aligoté, is the one that will interest most palates. It is the wine that the firm will now be concentrating on. Today M Ambal's grandson runs the firm, founded by Marie Ambal in 1898, hence its name, and his wines are exported to Belgium and Italy, amongst other countries.

Veuve du Vernay   CC   →★
Société Remoise des Vins, Chemin de la Grange Noire, Merignac, 33700 Bordeaux

The name of this sparkling wine sounds as if it could be champagne – except it isn't. Veuve du Vernay is a simple *cuve close* wine with very successful sales figures; 2.5M cases were sold in 1992. The base wines come from Bordeaux, the Loire and Charentes with the Charentes' Ugni Blanc supplying the lion's share. Veuve is available in *brut, demi-sec* and rosé versions. The sweet, pink version is made from the Muscat of Alexandria grape, grown at Carcassonne near the Mediterranean coast. The Brut has a frothy mousse and an exotic, soapy, almost bananary nose and taste. In France this company sells a sweet, white sparkler called Muscabar, plus a sweet rosé called Rosabel. Paul Bur is an associated house. Veuve du Vernay, made in the unlovely, industrial outskirts of Bordeaux's Merignac airport area, is exported all over the world.

Vin Sauvage   MC   ★→
Sica Monluc, 32310 St-Puy

Vin Sauvage comes from deep in the heart of southwest France. Combined with a splash of the local Liqueur à l'Armagnac it makes a drink known as a Pousse Rapière. Blessed with a big, fat, fruity character it also happens to be very good on its own. Excellent value for money.

Cave de Viré   MC   ★★→
71260 Viré
Star buy '89 Crémant de Bourgogne Brut

The Viré cooperative, founded in 1928, lying just south of Mâcon in the heart of Burgundy's Mâconnais, produces only one sparkling wine. This Crémant de Bourgogne is made exclusively from the cooperative members' own Chardonnay – they have 50 ha (124 acres) between them. The quality, given the grapes, is well above the usual level of cooperative wine. At most, 40,000 cases are made each year and production is helped along by semi-automatic *remuage*. Its '89 Crémant de Bourgogne Brut is a lovely, rich, smoky, toasty wine with a good, creamy *mousse* and a fine, lemony, Chardonnay fruit finish. Viré is greatly interested in the export market especially Canada, Germany and the UK.

L Vitteau Alberti   MC   ★→★★
Rue du Pont d'Arrot, Rully, 71150 Chagny

Only 20 percent of the grapes used in the Vitteau Alberti *méthode champenoise* come from the Vitteau family's vineyards. However, the remainder, including Bourgogne Aligoté, Chardonnay, Pinot Noir and Gamay, are a definite notch up in quality from the usual. The range of sparkling wines includes a *méthode champenoise vin mousseux blanc de blancs brut* plus a Crémant de Bourgogne *blanc*. Tiny amounts of pink sparklers and a Bourgogne Rouge are also produced. *Remuage* is mostly by hand. Exports go mainly to the UK, Australia and Belgium. The Vitteaux are proud that several of those ultra-quality-conscious three-star French restaurants, including Taillevent in Paris and their own local Lameloise at Chagny, offer their Crémant de Bourgogne.

Other French Sparkling Wine Producers

Achard-Vincent, Die; Jean Bourdy, Arlay; A Clape, St-Péray; Domaines Viticoles des Salins du Midi, Montpellier; Pierre Sadoux, Sigoules.

Spain

Spanish sparkling wines have improved dramatically during the past decade. In the early 1980s most were clearly identifiable by their hot, sweet, earthy, peppery style. Today, although a slight peppery quality and lime–like sweetness is still detectable due to the ripeness of the grapes, most Spanish *méthode champenoise*, or Cava, sparkling wine is fresh, fruity and very easy to drink. Indeed, top producers such as Segura Viudas are making wine which has some of the class and elegance of champagne, for a fraction of the price. No wonder Cava exports have leapt from 3M bottles in 1974 to over 45M today. The Spanish too have increasingly enjoyed the fruits of their own vineyards and now down some 85M bottles of Cava bubbly annually.

This marked improvement has been due primarily to more advanced winemaking equipment and techniques, including stainless steel vats, cold fermentation and the latest Willmes or Vaslin presses. Rumasa, the now–defunct banking, wine and property group, certainly helped the industry by investing in its own sparkling wine operation at just the right time. Others soon followed. Spain's impressive average annual Cava production of some 130M bottles could not be achieved without the *girasol* (the Spanish word for 'sunflower'). This automatic, metal riddling frame invented in Spain holds about 500 bottles and enables two men to riddle five times as many bottles in one day as they were able to do by the old, *pupitre* method.

While Spanish winemaking techniques are getting better all the time, there are fewer changes taking place in the vineyards, although trained vines are now replacing the old system. Over 95 percent of Spanish Cava sparklers come from the Cataluña region, in northeast Spain, and the three traditional Cataluña grapes, Xarel-lo, Macabeo and Parellada, are still used everywhere. Xarel-lo gives firmness and acidity to the blend and Macabeo supplies the fruit and freshness, leaving the superior Parellada to donate softness as well as some fragrance and finesse. Several Cava houses have however been experimenting with Chardonnay. This classic variety can now officially be used by Cava producers and is beginning to appear in commercial blends. Those producers that are using the classy Chardonnay, such as Codorníu, have seen a marked improvement in the quality of their wines since its introduction. There are even some experimental plantings now of Pinot Noir. Expect another jump-up in Cava quality when wines made from the Chardonnay and Pinot Noir grape become more widely available. The *rosada* (rosé) style of Cava is usually made from Garnacha and Monastrell grapes. Many firms have now extended the time their Cava wines spend on yeast from the minimum of nine months to five years or more – again this has boosted quality.

Within Cataluña, southwest of Barcelona, is the Penedès region. Most of the Cava producers are based here, in the cooler, more mountainous Alt Penedès and Medio Penedès districts that fan out from San Sadurní de Noya, dominated by the extraordinary jagged teeth of the Montserrat Mountain. Wine estates have thrived in these areas since the early 16th century and Don José Raventós of Codorníu made the first Cava here in 1872.

To the north of Penedès is Alella, another Cava region and further north still is the Ampurdán-Costa Brava area, centred on Perelada in the province of Gerona. Still in Cataluña, but west of Barcelona, almost on the border with Aragón, is another Cava producer, Raimat at Lérida, which now produces a 100 percent Chardonnay Cava fizz. Other Cataluña Cava regions, to the south in Tarragona, include Alto Campo and Conca de Barberà. Over 200 Cava producers now exist and they can buy in grapes or wine from anywhere within this Cava region of 40,000 ha (98,840 acres) in northern Spain. Several Rioja *bodegas*, most notably Muga and Bilbaínas, also produce Cava sparklers, as does the occasional Navarra producer. The major difference between Catalan Cavas and those from outside this area is that the latter are made 100 percent from the Macabeo grape (known in Rioja as Viura). Other Spanish producers not necessarily using the Cava method are dotted throughout the country at places such as Ainzón near Zaragoza and Cariñena. There are also *méthode champenoise* producers in Valencia and Extremadura but they may only use the words *metodo tradicional*, indicating *méthode champenoise*, and not Cava for their wines.

Up to 91 percent of all sparkling wine produced in Spain is made by the Cava method (*méthode champenoise*) and although the odd advertisement and truck in Penedès still bears the world *champaña*, Spain is careful not to use the jealously-guarded French name. New EC regulations mean that from 1994 the phrase *metodo champenoise* will not be permitted to describe a wine made by the champagne method. Instead *metodo tradicional* will be used.

Spanish sparkling wine laws and labelling requirements are some of the toughest and most explicit in the world (*see* below). No Cava house for instance may have any *cuve close*, carbonated or transfer method equipment on the premises. It therefore seems both shortsighted and unfair for the French and the EC (backed by Italy, Germany and the UK) to insist that the term *méthode champenoise* can only be used to describe champagne. Still, though Spain is Europe's biggest *méthode champenoise* producer outside France and therefore has had the most to lose now that the legislation has been passed (*see* page OO), its Cava sales are, happily, still buoyant.

Apart from this irritating EC decision, Spain's sparkling wine industry appears to have few problems. The collapse of the Rumasa group in 1983 created considerable turmoil, but the Freixenet group, responsible, has absorbed the Rumasa Cava companies without any hiccups. With Freixenet's overseas interests in Champagne and California, plus Codorníu's in California's Napa Valley and Moët & Chandon's foundation of the Cava Chandon vineyard in Penedès in 1988 (where Chardonnay is planted in addition to the local trio), its own Cava sparklers are bound to improve and with them Spain's. The future looks good.

Spanish Sparkling Wine Labels and the Law

Spain has some of the most helpful, clear and concise sparkling wine label regulations in the world.

● 'Cava' (or 'cellar' in Spanish) comes from a demarcated wine region. The words '*Cava tradicional*', denote a wine that has been made by the *méthode champenoise* and must have spent a minimum of nine months in bottle on yeast before being disgorged. Vintage Cava wines must spend two years in bottle in contact with the yeast prior to disgorging and sale. All Cava wines must carry the word 'Cava' on the label and each cork is printed with a star symbol: ☆

- The words '*metodo tradicional*' and wines with the phrase '*fermentación en botella*' (second fermentation in this bottle) without the word '*cave*' indicate *méthode champenoise* sparklers made outside the Cava region.

- *Cuve close* or Charmat method sparkling wine is known as *granvas* or *grandes envases* in Spain. By law a minimum of 21 days must elapse between the addition of yeast and the actual bottling process. All such wine must have the word '*granvas*' printed on the label and carry this symbol on the cork: ○

- Transfer method sparklers in Spain are denoted by the words '*fermentación en botella*' (second fermentation in this bottle), which must appear on the label. The transfer method must continue for two months before bottling. *Fermentación en botella* sparkling wine carries this symbol on the cork: ▭

- Carbonated wine is denoted by the words '*vino gasificado*', which again must appear on the label. These wines carry a triangle symbol on the cork: △

- In Spain (and throughout this chapter) expect to see the following Spanish terms, given here with their French equivalent: 'brut de brut' for a non–*dosage* wine, '*brut natur*' or '*brut nature*' for a low- or non–*dosage* wine, '*brut*' for *brut*, '*seco*' for *sec*, '*semi-seco*' for *demi-sec*, '*semi-dulce*' and '*dulce*' for the sweeter or *doux* wines, and '*rosado*' for rosé.

Producers

L'Aixertell   CC   →★
Paseo del Urumea, 20014 San Sebastian, Guipuzcoa

L'Aixertell is jointly owned by Bodegas and Bebidas (Spain's vast wine firm) and FREIXENET, which bought the German firm Henkell's holding in this company some years ago. L'Aixertell produces 250,000 cases a year of sweet, inexpensive sparkling wine under Brut, Extra and Gran Cremant labels.

Cavas Albet i Noya   MC   ★
Can Vendrell, 08738 San Pau D'Ordal, Barcelona

Josep M Albet i Noya started his sparkling wine firm in 1979. Production of his *brut nature*, *brut*, *semi-seco* and *rosado* is limited to just over 3,000 cases per annum and the grapes (mostly Xarel-lo but with an increasing percentage of Parellada) come entirely from Señor Albet i Noya's own 20 ha (49 acres) of vineyard. The latest introduction is the Rosado, made from Tempranillo and Sumoll. The Brut Nature is the firm's finest sparkling wine. Encouragingly, future releases may well contain a proportion of Chardonnay.

Cavas del Ampurdán   CC   →★
Plaza del Carmen 1, 17491 Perelada, Gerona

This is the sister firm to Cavas del Castillo de Perelada but, according to Spanish law, because it produces still wines and sparklers made by the *cuve close* method, it must be housed in a different building from Cavas del Castillo, on the other side of the road. Muscantini is Ampurdán's Muscat-based sparkling wine and its Perelada *cuve close* wine is one of Spain's most popular sparklers. Ampurdán, formerly the Costa Brava Wine Company, is a name that the *champenois* will not forget: this firm was the defendant in the 1960 London court case in which the Spanish lost the right to call their sparkling wine 'champagne'.

Bodegas Bilbaínas   MC   ★→
Particular del Norte 2, 48003 Bilbão, La Rioja

This important Rioja house, founded in 1901, produces two types of sparkling wine: the superior Royal Carlton selection and the cheaper, sweeter and more luridly labelled Lumen range. Viura and a few Malvasia grapes from Bilbaínas' own 255 ha (630 acres) of vineyards supply the base wine that is turned into 50,000 cases of full-bodied Bilbaínas *méthode champenoise* every year. Royal Carlton accounts for most of the production, and *brut*, *seco* and *semi-seco* versions of both the Royal Carlton and the Lumen brands are made. Bilbaínas' most expensive sparkling wine is Royal Carlton's Brut Nature. The firm proudly reveals that after the Second World War, when many Champagne vineyards had been devastated, a 'prestigious champagne house' fulfilled its orders by buying Bilbaínas sparkling wine and selling it under its own label.

Cavas Bolet MC ★
Mas Lluet, 08732 Castellví de la Marca, Barcelona
This small, traditional Cava house, founded in 1982, produces *semi-seco*, *brut* and *brut natural* Bolet sparkling wines from the usual Penedès blend of Macabeo, Xarel-lo and Parellada. Lluet Brut and Brut Natural are made by the same house but spend 2–3 years ageing as opposed to Bolet's 1–2 years. The Bolet family owns 55 ha (136 acres) of Cava vines at its Mas Lluet property in the heart of Penedès. Just 2,500 cases are made each year; all are sold in Spain.

Bonaval MC ☆
Avenida Paz 19, 06200 Almendralejo, Badajóz
The family firm of Bonaval was founded in 1931, its full title being Industrias Vinícolas del Oeste, or Inviosa. The firm's first sparkling wine was released in 1987. The family produces just over 5,000 bottles of non-vintage *brut* and *seco* every year from its 32 ha-estate (80 acres) in Tierra de Barros, close to Almendralejo, which supplies two-thirds of the firm's 100 percent Macabeo grape needs. Bonaval claims it was the first Cava producer in Extremadura and exports to the UK and Portugal.

Bodegas Bordejé MC ★
Crta Borja-Rueda Km, 50570 Ainzon, Zaragoza
Bodegas Bordejé claims it was the first sparkling wine firm in Aragón. Established in 1770, it is situated in the mountainous Zaragoza region of Aragón. This family firm owns 80 ha (198 acres) of vines, half the crop being turned into 10,000 cases of sparkling wine sold under a *brut* label. Its sparklers are aged for many years on yeast. Bordejé is also experimenting with *rosado*.

Canals & Munné MC ★
Plaza Pau Casals 6, 08770 San Sadurní de Noya, Barcelona
The small family firm of José María Canals Casanovas was founded in 1930, though like many Cava concerns the estate dates from much earlier – 1890 in this case. No less than nine different Canals & Munné sparkling wines are produced in *seco*, *semi-seco* and *dulce* styles. Choose from Brut Nature, Brut, Rosado, Extra Especial, Extra, Cristal Dore, Gran Cremant, Carta Blanca and Reserva de l'Avi. The Gran Cru has 20 percent Chardonnay in its mix.

Castellblanch   MC/CC   ★→
Casetas Mir, 08770 San Sadurní de Noya, Barcelona

Castellblanch, once a Rumasa firm, is now owned by FREIXENET. The wines are however made at a different winery from those of Segura Viudas, also owned by Freixenet. Castellblanch was founded by Jerónimo Parera Figueras in 1908. Today its ugly, modern winery, although capable of storing and ageing 20M bottles, still has the air of a building site. Castellblanch only produces sparkling wine – almost 1M cases of it every year. Much of this is made from bought-in base wine but Castellblanch also owns 200 ha (494 acres) of vines. Castellblanch's Brut Zero (complete with red plastic seal) is good although not great – a mature, yeasty, slightly dull sparkling wine – whereas the Extra Brut has a similarly high alcohol level plus a pleasing, drinkable, citric, lime-juice-like taste. Also in the Castellblanch range are Gran Cremant and Cristal in various degrees of sweetness, plus Rosado, Lustros Brut, Gran Castell and Canals Nubiola. Of them all, Lustros and Gran Castell, both aged for two and a half years on yeast, are reckoned the best. Castellblanch is proud of having developed its own yeast strain.

Els Castellers   MC   ★
Bisbe Morgades, 08720 Vilafranca del Penedès, Barcelona

There are 397 members with 600 ha (1,482 acres) between them who belong to this cooperative, founded in 1933. Only 17,000 cases per annum of sparkling wine are produced here under Brut, Extra, Gran Cremant Brut Natural and Rosat labels. Els Castellers' blends use the usual trio of Cava grapes.

Castilla la Vieja   MC   ★→
Ctra Madrid-Coruña Km 170.6, 47490 Rueda, Vallodolid

The quality-minded Marqués de Grinon buys his Verdejo grapes here, which explains why the estate's *méthode champenoise* sparklers are so good. The Castilla la Vieja sparklers come in *brut* and *brut nature* styles and are worth seeking out.

Cavas del Castillo de Perelada   MC   ★→
P°de San Antonio 1, Perelada, Gerona

North of Barcelona and the Penedès region is the Ampurdán-Costa Brava area, whose winemaking activities are centred on

Perelada. The celebrated Cavas del Castillo here is definitely worth a detour. Admire the 14th century Castillo and church (with wine cellars below) plus the wine museum, library, glass and ceramic displays and the latest addition – a casino. Unlike other Ampurdán producers, Castillo makes only sparkling wine. The 50,000 cases of Castillo's sparklers include the well-regarded Gran Claustro, aged for 5–6 years in the firm's impressive Ampurdán cellars. The Brut Nature Castillo, with its flowery nose and pleasant, fruity taste is equally enjoyable. Other blends here include a *brut* and a *rosado extra seco*. The Castillo's newest wines include a 100 percent Chardonnay (labelled as such) and the Brut Nature. Quality is above average and Castillo puts this down to the correct balance of the very best in both new technology and traditional techniques.

Cava Chandon   MC   ☆→
08739 Subirats, Barcelona
Chandon España was founded in 1988, the same year that the first Chandon vines were planted here. With such a wealth of champagne knowledge from parent company Moët & Chandon, plus considerable expertise gleaned from Moët's overseas *méthode champenoise* sparkling wine ventures, Cava Chandon must be a rip-roaring success. So far, a stylish, modern winery complete with cool, underground Cava cellars has been built, and a 90 ha vineyard (222 acres) planted. Grapes are the usual Cava trio, but there is a little Chardonnay in the mix too. Cava Chandon has been on sale for several years in Spain, but the UK will not receive its first release until 1994. Quality is rumoured to be good, not yet great, but it is early days. About 254,000 cases were made in 1992.

Paul Cheneau   MC   ★→
Segura Viudas, 08770 San Sadurní de Noya, Barcelona
This delightfully-inexpensive Spanish sparkler, now part of the Rémy-Cointreau group, is made at Segura Viudas to leading wine writer and merchant Gerald Asher's own specifications. Mr Asher clearly understands the American palate. This soft, drinkable, predominantly Parellada *méthode champenoise* wine, aged for about three years, goes down well with the public and even with competitive California sparkling wine producers. Americans consume an impressive 200,000 cases every year.

Codorníu   MC   ★→
Afueras s/n, 08770 San Sadurní de Noya, Barcelona

Visiting Codorníu is an experience, not just for the gardens, lake and ancient oak tree, the century-old house with its tower, the museum and bizarre cathedral-like Puig-Cadafalch reception salon (now a national monument), but also for the cellars below. There are 11 miles (18 km) of man-made caves on five levels, containing 100 million bottles of sparkling wine, which must make Codorníu's cellars among the largest in the world. The firm sells 4M bottles annually. To become this big takes time. Codorníu dates back to 1551, but the year 1872 was perhaps an even more auspicious date, as that was when Don José Raventós made the first Spanish *méthode champenoise* wine in Codorníu's cellars.

Codorníu uses the first four gentle pressings of its Penedès grapes, most of which are bought in, with only 25 percent coming from its own vineyards. Codorníu, like its greatest competitor FREIXENET, has to use *girasols* for the *remuage*. Unidad 504, the Codorníu variety of *girasol*, looks like a rocking chair with 504 bottles of sparkling wine in the 'seat'. To ensure continuity and to improve quality, Codorníu keeps back mostly three-year-old reserve wines for blending, storing them in large stainless steel vats. The basic quality sparkling wines, the Première Cuvée and the Brut Clasico, a similar wine but with 20 percent Pinot Noir, have a musty nose and dull, yeasty-sulphury taste. Similarly the '80 Gran Codorníu, with five years or so on yeast, is a sour, vaguely biscuity wine. Codorníu's other brands, Non Plus Ultra (a 70 percent Pinot Noir, 15 percent Chardonnay, 15 percent Parellada blend), Rosado, Gran Cremant and the more recent Anna de Codorníu, with 90 percent Chardonnay in the blend, have improved in recent years. Even so, Anna de Codorníu is a light, vivacious, toasty Chardonnay fizz without great finesse.

Conde de Caralt   MC   ★
Ctra San Sadurní-Igualada, 08770 San Sadurní de Noya, Barcelona

Conde de Caralt wines are made at Segura Viudas's impressive headquarters and as with that other ex-Rumasa firm, René Barbier, this concern is now owned by the ever-expanding FREIXENET group. Like other Penedès wine firms, Conde de Caralt

Codorníu's fine *bodega* and grounds at San Sadurní de Noya

now has a range of table wines in addition to its sparklers – it made sparkling wine first, however. The wines are good rather than great. The non-vintage Brut is warm, rich, sunbaked and easy to drink, while the '80 Brut Nature is pleasing, intense, biscuity and yeasty, albeit with a strange, sour finish. A numbered *brut reservada*, *blanc de blancs*, *rosado extra seco* and *extra semi-seco* are also produced by de Caralt.

Delapierre   MC   ★
644 Avenida Gran Vía, Barcelona
Delapierre, owned by CODORNIU, produces a *blanc de blancs* as well as the partly Chardonnay-based Etiqueta Nera sparkling wine.

Anatole Dempierre   IM   →★
San Francisco 48, 44001 Teruel
Three brothers now run the Anatole Dempierre group, founded in 1929. About 125,000 cases of very ordinary fizz are made annually. The majority is sold under the Semi Seco Anatole Dempierre label,

a sweet, carbonated sparkler, although in most years about 17,000 cases are also made of the dryer Seco Château St Martori, another carbonated method wine. Any suggestions of a French connection here are illusory; the base wines for both bubblies come from the hot, arid plains of La Mancha. Africa and Russia are Dempierre's two major export markets.

Cavas Domecq   MC   ★→
Ctra Alto Penedès, 08770 San Sadurní de Noya, Barcelona
Domecq, like other large Spanish wine firms, has vinous outposts in several places including Mexico. Closer to home is its Cava concern, whose wines, no doubt due to the firm's superior wine-making knowledge, are much admired. The *rosado* version is made principally from the Garnacha grape. Occasionally, Domecq markets its wines under the Lembey name.

Duc de Foix   MC   ★
Rambla Ntra Señora 10, 08720 Vilafranca del Penedès, Barcelona
Covides is the large Penedès-based cooperative behind this Cava name. Founded in 1964, Covides has invested heavily in equipment over the past few years, which should help to give it the edge over its equally large and commercially-minded competitors.

Cavas Ferret   MC   ★
Avenida Cataluña, 08739 Guardiola de Font-Rubí, Barcelona
Parellada plays an important part in the manufacture of the sparkling wine produced at this small, renovated house. Cavas Ferret makes a *semi-seco*, *seco*, *brut* and *brut nature*. Ferret has 5 ha (12 acres) of its own vines and buys in the rest of its needs.

J Freixedas   MC   ★→
87-89 Calvo Sotelo, 08720 Vilafranca del Penedès, Barcelona
J Freixedas, almost 100 years old, is a respected name in the Penedès region. Despite its 69 ha (170 acres) San Cugat Sasgarrigues estate, this big producer still buys in grapes. Among its sparklers are Gran Cremant, Gran Brut Nature and the higher-quality Special Reserva Castilla La Torre.

Freixenet   MC   ★→★★

Joan Sala, 08770 San Sadurní de Noya, Barcelona

Star buy '81 Brut Nature

It is difficult to keep up with Freixenet. In 1983 a new winery at Ezequiel Montes in Mexico was completed. In 1984 it took over the Rumasa sparkling wines (Segura Viudas, Conde de Caralt, Castellblanch, René Barbier and Canals Nubiola). In 1985 it bought the French champagne house Henri Abelé. In 1986 the new Freixenet Gloria Ferrer winery opened in Sonoma, California. The Freixenet group is now one of the biggest sparkling wine producers in Spain, and indeed the world, with an annual total production of some 5M cases. This figure puts it alongside its greatest competitor, CODORNIU, and dwarfs that of any champagne house.

Freixenet, founded after Codorníu, in 1889, is still a family firm, run by the Ferrers. Its 100ha (247 acres) supply a tiny percentage of its total needs. The sparkling wine is riddled on *girasols* whose design – a cage of bottles on a pointed, octagonal base – differs from that of Codorníu, and the firm's recently much-expanded cellars also look distinctly different from those of Codorníu, with vast, stainless steel cold fermentation tanks et al housed in a vast, concrete edifice.

Freixenet's most popular sparkling wine is the clean, fruity and acceptable Carta Nevada Brut in its frosted yellow livery. More distinctive still is the black and gold Cordon Negro bottle, whose '81 is bland, fruity and a touch raw but nonetheless a reasonable sparkler. The '81 Brut Nature, now with about 30 percent Chardonnay in the blend, is finer and has a lovely freesia-like bouquet plus a good, clean, flowery taste. The '88 Brut Reserva is fresh, toasty and lime juice-scented without being special. The finest of all, made from the firm's best grapes and vinified in wood, is the Cuvée DS, named after courageous Dolores Sala who continued to run Freixenet after her husband (who founded the company) and son had been killed. Doña Sala had a fine palate and created the first vintage, the '69, herself and stipulated exactly what should go into the '77 *cuvée* before she died. The '88 vintage was an excellent, deep, rich, buttered toast of a wine.

Gramona MC ★→
Industria 36, 08770 San Sadurní de Noya, Barcelona

Another small Cava firm that produces *brut* and *nature* sparkling wine. Gramona sparklers, of which only 12,000 cases are made annually, spend a considerable length of time ageing on yeast, often as long as 7–8 years. The Gramona family owns 15 ha (37 acres) of vines and buys in the rest of its needs. Imperial is the basic Gramona blend, Tres Lustros the top wine.

Cavas Guilera MC ★
Ca l'Artigas, 08739 Lavern, Barcelona

This firm produces limited amounts of mostly four-year-old *extra seco*, *extra semi-seco*, *brut* and *nature* sparklers.

Cavas Hill MC ★
Bonavista 2, 08734 Mojá, Barcelona

Cavas Hill obviously believes in catering for each and every whim of its customers, for there are ten different sparklers to choose from. Mr Hill was an Englishman, as the name suggests, who set up his Mojá estate in 1660. A descendant built Cavas Hill's impressive underground cellars in 1918. The firm now owns 50 ha (123 acres) but buys in grapes too and is fond of describing its sparklers as 'masterpieces', which seems a trifle over-enthusiastic as its Gran Sec Brut Blanc de Blancs is a soft, ordinary, rhubarb-redolent sparkling wine and the '81 Brut Brutísimo is raw, green and not very nice at all. Other Cavas Hill sparklers are the Gran Reserva de Artesania (Brut de Brut), the Sant Manel (Brut, Extra Semi-seco, Extra Seco), the Oro Negro, the Garnacha-based Rosado and the Reserva Oro (Semi-seco and Seco).

Huguet MC ★→★★
Can Feixes 1, 08785 Cabrera de Noya

The Huguet family members are the folk behind this label and they produce just 4,000 cases of Cava wines annually. With 20 ha (50 acres) of vines, 15 percent of which is planted to Chardonnay, the Huguets are well-placed for quality wine production, particularly because they sell on most of their grapes and wines – much in demand due to the superior vineyard site – and keep only the best grapes for their own sparklers. With steep, poor, gravel vineyards situated at 1,600 feet above sea level in the Alt Penedès, at the base of the Montserrat Mountain, Huguet's best grapes must be the *crème de la crème* of the region. Only two Huguet Cavas are sold: the Brut Nature Gran Reserva and the Brut. Quality is considered to be first class. The pair are hand-riddled and spend at least three years on yeast prior to disgorgement. Excitingly, the Huguets are planting new Pinot Noir vineyards.

Jané Ventura   MC   ★→
Ctra de Calafell 2, 43700 El Vendrell, Tarragona
Close to Tarragona, Jané Ventura enjoys a good reputation for its Cavas made from the usual trio of grapes. Still a family-run firm, it produces amongst others a Brut Nature Gran Reserva plus a *rosado*.

Jaume Serra   MC   ★→
Finca El Padruel, 08800 Vilanova i la Geltrú, Barcelona
The first Jaume Serra started in Alella in the 1940s but moved to the El Padruell estate in the Penedès four decades later. An impressive 125,000 cases of Cava are made annually at this well-equipped property and the quality is good. Although Jaume Serra owns vineyards, bought-in grapes and wine are also used. The Jaume Serra range consists of a *brut nature*, *brut*, *seco* and *semi-seco*. Lesser Jaume Serra Cavas are sold under the Cristalino label.

Juvé y Camps   MC   →★
Sant Vernat 1, 08770 San Sadurní de Noya, Barcelona
Three different estates with 400 ha (988 acres) between them account for about one-third of Juvé y Camps' requirements. The rest of the grapes is supplied by local growers. Annual production is 148,000 cases of Reserva, Reserva de la Familia and fancy-bottled Gran Cru Juvé y Camps in various styles. Neither the sweet, overblown fruit character of the Reserva Brut, nor the marginally better but raw, beery and astringent '81 Reserva de la Familia are likely to win many fans.

Cavas Lavernoya   MC   ★→
San Pere 17, 08770 San Sadurní de Noya, Barcelona
This Cava house is owned by the Raventós Poch family with estates close to the Lavernó and Noya rivers. Lácrima Baccus is

Cavas Lavernoya's brand name and every year up to 84,000 cases of some seven different Lácrima sparklers are made. Lavernoya obviously specializes in inexpensive, bulk sales for it does not own any vineyards and most of its sparkling wine is made by the automatic *remuage* method. Lácrima's Brut Nature is disappointing. The Extra Reserve is drinkable but somewhat undistinguished – a warm, yeasty and vanilla-like wine. Other Lácrima sparkling wines include the Super Semi-seco, Gran Cremant Seco, Rosado and Primerisimo Grand Cru and Summun, the latter in strange, skittle-shaped bottles.

Lluet
See Bolet

Loxarel   MC   ★→
Masía Can Mayol, 08735 Vilobí del Penedès, Barcelona
Loxarel specializes in Cavas and indeed produces no other style of wine. Quality therefore at this well-equipped firm is better than most, especially as Loxarel only uses its own grapes. Loxarel makes many different styles of fizz, as most Cava houses do. Its basic range includes the Brut Daurat plus *seco* and *semi-seco*. One step up is its Reserva range, including the Reserva Brut Nature and the top blend, the Reserva Familiar.

Marqués de Monistrol   MC   ★→
Monistrol de Noya, 08770 San Sadurní de Noya, Barcelona
Founded in 1882 but bought out a century later, in 1980, by Martini & Rossi, Marqués de Monistrol owns 405 ha (1,000 acres) of vines and makes a wide range of sparklers. Monistrol sticks to the usual Cava blend, but uses Monastrell as the basis for its Rosado and has, promisingly, a little Chardonnay planted too. Over 300,000 cases are made in most years, of which the Gran Tradición Brut Nature is considered the top wine. Other styles include the Extra and Gran Cremant, Brut, Reserva Gran Coupage, Brut Selección, Brut Nature and Brut Gran Tradición. The straight non-vintage has much improved of late and is now a fruity, lime-scented wine. The '79 Monistrol Brut Nature is not a success.

Cavas Masachs   MC   ★
Poniente 20, 08720 Vilafranca del Penedès, Barcelona

The Masachs family made sparkling wine for itself and its friends as early as 1920, although commercial production did not begin until 1940. Since then the annual output has increased to over 160,000 cases care of a big, new plant and Masachs is now a limited company. Grapes from its own 42 ha (104 acres) of vineyards (10 percent of these, encouragingly, is planted to Chardonnay) supply about one-third of the firm's needs. Still, the raw, yeasty, Masachs Brut and the fresh, young, straightforward, appley Gran Reserva Brut are currently both palatable enough. Other Masachs labels include Nature, Rosé, Semi-seco and Seco versions as well as the cheaper Louis de Vernier sparklers, available as Brut Nature Reserva, Brut, Rosé, Seco and Semi-seco. Carolina de Masachs is the firm's new, superior, vintage-dated blend with ten percent Chardonnay in the mix. Josep Masachs Gran Reserva is one of its better standard blends, and Gran Vernier Brut the newest blend.

Mascaró   MC   ★→
Del Casal 9, 08720 Vilafranca del Penedès, Barcelona

Antonio Mascaró's small, traditional family firm, founded in 1946, produces some good white and red still Penedès wines, besides 34,000 cases a year of Mascaró sparklers from 30 ha (74 acres) of its own vines at two different estates. These supply just one-third of its needs. Automatic *remuage* creates a stylish, well-made *blanc de blancs brut* available in *semi-seco* and *seco* styles, and Mascaró also produces a Reservada range in various styles plus Antonio Mascaró Grand Brut and Cava Grapa wines. The firm uses a high proportion of Parellada in its blends, which accounts for their finesse and bouquet, and, encouragingly, is experimenting with Chardonnay. None of the Mascaró wines is vintage-dated.

Masía Vallformosa   MC   ★
La Sala 45, 08735 Vilobí del Penedès, Barcelona

Little known outside Spain, Masía Vallformosa sparkling wines are admittedly not really worth writing home about. With 150 ha (371 acres) devoted to sparkling wine production at three different estates, the firm makes almost 60,000 cases annually. By 1996 Masía Vallformosa hopes its own newly trained vines will supply all its needs. (Chardonnay now makes up a considerable proportion of these vines, but so far this grape has not found its way into the blends.) The Masía Vallformosa Brut, with its raw, appley fruit is no more than acceptable and the Brut Nature, with its soft, ripe, slightly earthy fruit, is drinkable but not special. Gran Reserva, riddled by hand, may be a better bet.

Mestres MC ★★→★★★
Plaza Ayuntamiento 8, 08770 San Sadurní de Noya, Barcelona
Star buy 1312 Brut

Mestres is one of the most historic Cava houses: the Antonio Mestres Sagués house and vineyards date from 1312 – some even say from 1243. Sparkling wine, however, was not produced here until 1928. Today, 80 ha (198 acres) of vines yield all the grapes needed to create 10,000 or so cases of sparkling wine, and production is increasing at a rate of about 800 cases a year. Methods are traditional: all the sparklers are aged for at least three years, with the Clos Nostre Senyor and Clos Damiana enjoying five years plus in the cellar, and the Mas-Via a lengthy, seven-year spell. Mestres' winemaker is keen to make 90 separate *cuvées* every year to supply him with the blending tools he requires, and many young blends are sold to Spain's top restaurants each year under the new Los Cupages de Mestres label. Such detail and care certainly pays off, for the 1312 Brut with its deep gold colour and big, mature, toasty-biscuity, yeast-influenced character is a beautifully made three-star wine. Other sparkling wines produced by Mestres include the Coquet Brut, Brut Nature and Rosado Brut Nature.

Cooperativa de Mollet de Perelada MC ★→
Alt Empordà Perelada, Gerona

This cooperative, with 50 ha (123 acres), was founded in 1975 and is associated with the Castillo de Perelada. It has a French-trained winemaker. This expertise shows in the cooperative's well-made 1,000 cases of sparklers sold under the Rapsodia Brut, Semi-seco and Seco labels. Usually all are made from Macabeo, Xarel-lo and Garnacha Blanco.

Mont Marcal   MC   ★★→
Finca Manlleu, 08732 Castellví de la Marca, Barcelona
Star buy Mont Marcal Brut

Manuel Sancho y Hijas' family is behind this well-designed label.
He founded his company in 1975. Almost two decades later, 42 ha
(104 acres) provide half its needs and produce an impressive annual
crop of over 80,000 cases. Happily, Mont Marcal sparklers are as
impressive as their sales. The straight Mont Marcal Brut has a
lovely, fresh, racy, flowery nose and taste, with only a slight touch
of Cava earthiness on the finish to betray its origins. The Mont
Marcal Nature, with its aggressively clean, young, yeasty taste will
appeal to low-*dosage* lovers when drunk young, but other palates
will want to give it more time. Mont Marcal also produces *semi-
seco*, *seco* and *gran reserva* wines. The most exciting developments at
this firm are in the experiments with Chardonnay, of which only
15 percent has so far found its way into the top Mont Marcal Gran
Reserva Brut *cuvée*. The 1984 base wine was 30 percent
Chardonnay, so we can expect even more distinguished Mont
Marcal sparklers in a few years' time. Spain, the UK and the USA
are the major consumers.

Bodegas Muga   MC   ★→
Barrio de la Estación, 26200 Haro, La Rioja

This well-known but small family *bodega* has one of the best
reputations in Rioja. Just 4,000 cases are made annually of its vintage-dated Conde de Haro (previously sold under the curious
name 'Mugamart') in both *brut* and *brut nature* versions. The firm
uses just one grape, the Viura, for its sparklers. The non-*dosage* Brut
Nature accounts for the majority of production.

Cavas Nadal   MC   →★
08733 El Plá del Penedès, Barcelona

The Nadal family estate dates back to 1510, but Cavas Nadal was
founded as recently as 1943, by Ramón Nadal Giró. Today he is
one of the very few Cava producers whose own grapes supply
almost all his needs. With 121 ha (300 acres), just 54,000 cases of
Cava are made annually and no still wines are produced to add to
this. Due to public demand, Nadal sparkling wine has become
noticeably drier recently. Despite this, neither the current bottlings

of Nadal Brut, nor the premium Brut Especial made, as the name suggests, in special years, are particularly enjoyable. The vintage-dated Macabeo-dominated Brut Salvatge is Nadal's top wine and a new *rosado* was launched in 1993.

Cavas Naveran   MC   ★→
San Martín Sadevesa, Torrelavit, Barcelona
Naveran's Cavas are made under the auspices of a joint venture operation with the Vranken-Lafitte champagne house. Whether this has paid off is hard to tell, as Vranken's quality is not the best the Champagne region can achieve. However, the Vranken Cava does contain an extraordinarily high proportion of Chardonnay in its blend, perhaps as much as 60 percent. The straight Naveran Cavas come in *brut nature* and *brut* styles, amongst others.

Oliveda   MC   ★→
La Roca 3 17750 Campany, Gerona
Freixa Rigau, a family-owned firm situated at Campany near the French border, is still the company responsible for the Oliveda Cavas. With 20 ha (50 acres) of its own vines providing half its needs, Freixa Rigau produces over 20,000 bottles of bubbly annually. Oliveda's style is fruity and uncomplicated, and the wines are made from the usual trio of Cava grapes. The range consists of the Semi-seco, Rosat and Brut d'Oliveda plus the top blend, the non-*dosage* Brut Nature Millessima. Watch out for the new Chardonnay-based Cava. Visitors to Oliveda can admire the wine and Cava cellars plus a collection of 6,000 taps from all over the world.

Parés Baltà   ★→★★
Afueras, Pacs del Penedès, Barcelona
Star buy Brut Nature Privée Cuvée
Parés Baltà is not a name that even the most dedicated Cava drinker comes across regularly. A pity, for although the Brut de Pacs, Cuvée Privée is not special, with its slight, raw fruit and dull finish, the Brut Nature Privée Cuvée is a two-star delight with its clean, refined, flowery bouquet backed up by an elegant, flowery taste and finish. Worth seeking out.

Parxet   MC   ★→★★
Torrente 38, 08391 Tiana, Barcelona

Cavas Parxet was founded in 1920 by the Suñol family at Tiana, just to the northeast of Barcelona. Almost 60,000 cases are produced annually of six different *méthode champenoise* Parxet sparklers from 200 ha (494 acres) of land, some of which is planted to Chardonnay and Chenin Blanc. Most are drunk in Spain but exports go to Germany, the USA and UK. Production is mostly divided between the gold-label, raw, musty, almost rosehip-like Reserva Brut and the infinitely better black-label Brut Nature, which also has a curious though pleasing, flowery, rosehip-like flavour. Seco, Semi-seco and Rosé sparklers are also made. Parxet sparkling wine does not carry vintage dates. Look out for the new 85 percent Chardonnay-based Parxet Extra Brut Chardonnay. Due to the constraints of the small region of Alella, the firm has recently invested heavily in Rioja, so expect to see Cavas from there soon.

Jean Perico   MC   ★→
Can Ferrer del Mas, 08770 San Sadurní de Noya, Barcelona

Jean Perico's label has González y Dubosc firmly stamped at the bottom (a *sous-marque* of González Byass, the sherry people) but this sparkling wine is actually made by SEGURA VIUDAS. Its greeny-gold, full-flavoured, pleasant style does well in blind tastings.

Raimat   MC   ★→
Ctra Nacional 340, 08758 Cervelló, Barcelona

Now owned by CODORNIU, Raimat is situated at Lérida, far inland from Barcelona, almost on the border of Aragón. Here Manuel Raventós from Codorníu has revamped an old operation and set up a spectacular new winery with high tech equipment and extensive new vineyards surrounding the Castle of Raimat. The firm has been making sparklers since 1930. Today they are sold under the Carta Dorada and Rondel labels, and include the premium *cuvée* Rondel Gran Brut, which spends 5–6 years on yeast, and a new 96 percent Chardonnay-based Raimat sparkler with 4 percent Parellada. The last of these is sent out under the Raimat Chardonnay Brut label and 83,000 cases are sold each year. Annual production stands at 1.5M cases, making Raimat Spain's third largest sparkling wine maker after Codorníu and Freixenet.

Cavas Recaredo   MC   ★
Tamarit 7–12, 08770 San Sadurní de Noya, Barcelona
This house, founded in 1924, specializes in the driest of styles,
which it sells under Brut de Brut and Brut Nature labels.

Cavas Rovellats   MC   ★
Finca Rovellats–La Bleda, 08731 San Martí Sarroca
Rovellats owns 210 ha (519 acres) of vines and, with annual production at close to 42,000 cases, no extra grapes or wine are
bought in. With four years' ageing on yeast for its top wines, the
aim is for traditional high-quality sparkling wine. Unfortunately
Rovellats still has some way to go. The Brut Natural Gran Reserva
is soft with an almost rhubarby nose, and the superior Grand Cru
Brut, Gran Reserva Masia sXV, has a pleasant but bland and
vaguely fruity flavour. The latter now has some Chardonnay in its
blend, as does a 500th anniversary wine recently released.

Segura Viudas   MC   ★★★
Ctra Sant Quintin, 08770 San Sadurní de Noya, Barcelona
Star buys Blanc de Blancs Non-Vintage Brut, '78 Brut
The firm was founded in 1954, when Señor Segura Viudas planted
the first vines. The old Segura Viudas house, backed by the magnificent Montserrat Mountain, soon had a modern, handsomely-
designed winery tacked onto it by Rumasa. Now owned by
FREIXENET, Segura Viudas makes sparkling wine for sister firm
CONDE DE CARALT, plus González Byass's Jean Perico and Gerald
Asher's PAUL CHENEAU. Wisely, Segura Viudas has learned to keep
the best for itself: grapes and base wine are received here to be
turned into sparkling wine by winemakers who are clearly well
trained. Visitors to the firm's five levels of subterranean cellars will
note that virtually all the (650,000-case) production is racked by
hand. Segura's three-star sparkling wine currently represents some
of the finest, cheapest and most delicious drinking in Europe. The
Blanc de Blancs non-vintage Brut is big, rich and biscuity and the
truly superb '78 Brut is deep, rich and intense – a wine of real distinction. Segura sparklers use the first 40 percent pressing and spend
2–6 years on specially-chosen yeast, which together determine the
house style. Also in the range are a *seco*, *semi-seco* and *rosado* and the
premium Reserva Heredad in a bizarre, pot-bellied, encrusted bottle.

Torre Oria   MC   ★
Ctra Pontón–Utiel Km 3, 46390 Derramedor-Requena, Valencia

This 110 ha-strong (271 acres) cooperative, owned by six families, was founded in 1977. The cooperative's own grapes supply most of its needs and current production at the modern *bodega* is almost 67,000 cases of *semi-seco*, *brut*, *nature* and a popular *rosado* made from the red Bobal grape.

Celler Trobat   MC   ★
Castelló 5, 17780 Garriguella, Gerona

Celler Trobat's distinctively-bottled sparkling wine hails from the Ampurdán–Costa Brava region. Production amounts to 20,000 cases of *brut*, *seco extra*, *semi-seco* and pink *rosat*, but so far these wines are only available in Spain.

Other Spanish Sparkling Wine Producers

Cavas Blancher, San Sadurní de Noya; Canals y Nubiola, San Sadurní de Noya; C Colomer Bernat, San Sadurní de Noya; J Llopart, San Sadurní de Noya; Taraga Lopez, Vallbona d'Anoia.

Portugal

Wine has been made for 5,000 years on the northwest Iberian peninsula, but Portugal has only been making sparkling wine commercially for just over a century. Its *méthode champenoise* wines are not on a par with those of its neighbour, Spain, despite similarities in climate and some grape varieties. This discrepancy in quality is largely due to Portugal's lack of modern sparkling wine technology and equipment. Most firms use the *méthode champenoise* for want of an alternative; automatic *remuage* and cold-fermentation tanks (necessary given Portugal's high temperatures at vintage time) are relatively rare. However, the quality of still white wines has much improved of late in Portugal and thus at some stage soon a similar improvement in its sparkling wines should take place.

The majority of Portugal's sparkling wines is produced in the Bairrada – a demarcated region that that lies to the north of Coimbra, roughly half way between Lisbon and Porto. Most Bairrada producers buy in neutral, acidic, often oxidized base wines, many from remote areas high up in and around the Douro, to turn into sparklers (further reasons for the quality shortfall, perhaps?). Maria Gomes is the chief grape, followed by Bical, Rabo de Ovelha and, to a lesser extent, Arinto, Sercial and Sercialinho. Encouragingly, plantings of Bairrada Chardonnay appear to be on the increase. The Lamego region, planted with some Chardonnay and Pinot Noir, also produces sparkling wine, as do other areas occasionally, including Setúbal. It is difficult to obtain a wide range of Portuguese sparklers in any other country, but exceptions include Brazil, Angola, Mozambique and other African nations that have historical trade connections with Portugal.

Portuguese Sparkling Wine Labels and the Law

- '*Método Champanhês*' is Portuguese for *méthode champenoise*, and any sparkler with this term on the label has indeed been made by the classic champagne method. Labels printed with 'champagne method' or 'fermented in *this* bottle' are also true *méthode champenoise* wines. Due to the phasing out of *méthode champenoise*, expect instead to see *método tradicional* and *método classico-champanhês*, and eventually simply *método classico*.

- Beware of the words '*Espumante Natural*' as this is a general term that can be attached to any sparkling wine except those made by the carbonated method.

- '*Fermentação em Cuba Fechada*' indicates a sparkler made by the *cuve close* or tank method.

- '*Espumante Método Continuo*' is a legally-approved Portuguese wine term used by Lancers and J M da Fonseca to indicate that their wines are made by the continuous flow method.

- In Portugal (and throughout this section) the following terms are used, listed here with their French equivalent: '*bruto*' for *brut*, '*seco*' for *sec*, '*meio seco*' for *demi-sec* and '*doce*' for *doux*.

Producers

Caves Aliança   **MC**   ★→
PO Box 6, Sangalhos, 3780 Anadia, Aveiro
Unlike most Bairrada firms, Aliança, founded in 1920, has planted Chardonnay alongside its Bical and Maria Gomes, the region's more usual grape varieties. The firm's own grapes supply only a quarter of its sparkling wine requirements, the rest being bought in. Aliança's deliberate change of style a few years ago and its installation in 1986 of a new cold fermentation unit are significant efforts aimed at producing high quality *méthode champenoise* wines – not an easy feat in Portugal. Introducing a winemaker with overseas experience is another step forward in the direction of quality. Five different sparklers are sold annually under the Danúbio, Super Reserva, Extra Reserva, Rosé and Tinto Brut (a red sparkler) labels. Extra Reserva is the best wine.

Caves Altoviso   MC   ★
PO Box 20, Sangalhos, 3780 Anadia, Aveiro
With 30,000 cases produced in most years, and ownership of just
4 ha (9 acres) of mostly Maria Gomes and Bical vines at Sangalhos,
this firm must buy in most of its grape needs. The Reserva Flor
Azul and Altoviso Super Reserva labels are the best here. Requinte
and Memoravel are two more basic Altoviso bubblies.

Caves do Barrocão   MC   ★
Fogueira, Sangalhos, 3780 Anadia, Aveiro
The large Caves do Barrocão is still family-run and, like most
Bairrada producers, uses the *méthode champenoise* to make its
sparkling wines, the most popular brand of which is Diamante
Azul. This goes down well on the home market, accounting for
eight percent of domestic sparkling wine sales, and some is also
exported. Barrocão also makes a pink and red (Tinto) sparkler by
the *méthode champenoise*.

Borges e Irmão   MC   ★
Avenida da Republica 796, 4400 Vila Nova de Gaia, Porto
Borges is better known for its Gatão Vinho Verde than for its
sparkling wines. However, the firm's reasonable, yeasty-fruity
méthode champenoise Fita Azul sells well in Portugal as well as in
Brazil and the other traditional Portuguese export markets.

Caves Borlido   MC   ★
Sangalhos, 3780 Anadia, Aveiro
Founded in 1930 by the Borlido family, Borlido makes three
different sparklers in both *bruto* and *meio seco* versions: Borlido,
Borlido Reserva and – the best of the bunch – Borlido Extra
Reserva. The traditional Bairrada grapes, Maria Gomes and Bical,
are used. Most of the production is sold in Portugal.

Conselheiro Caves Primavera   MC   ★
Aguága de Baixo, 3750 Agueda, Aveiro
This unexciting trio of Sweet, Medium-dry and Brut sparklers is
unlikely to impress any international palates. Of the three, the Brut
is the best – remarkable for its pale golden colour, its curiously rich,
over-ripe, almost cologne-like smell and taste and its aggressive

finish. The Caves also produces Célebre Data Brut, which is an uninspiring wine.

Caves Império   MC   ★
Sangalhos, 3780 Anadia, Aveiro

Founded in 1942 by five families (and joined in 1945 by one more), Caves Império first made sparkling wine in 1943. Today it makes a wide range of wines and brandies with at least five different sparklers, mainly in the *meio seco* category. Distinguishing the Extra from the Super, the Império from the Principe Real and the Principe Perfeito, can be testing, since all are *méthode champenoise* wines made from the usual Bairrada mix of Bical, Maria Gomes, Sercial and (in some cases) the Arinto. Each wine comes in a variety of styles from *bruto* to *meio seco* and there is a rosé version of both Principe Real and Império. The Extra Reserva followed by the Super Reserva are the firm's best. The Principe Real Brut, a lesser wine, is much fancied by locals.

Lancers   CM   →★
Vila Nogueira de Azeitão, 2925 Azeitão, Setúbal

Lancers is a famous brand name in America but is not as well-known elsewhere. IDV (a UK wine firm owned by Grand Metropolitan) together with its Portuguese partner, JM da Fonseca Internacional, are the driving forces behind this big brand and sales of their sparkling non-vintage Lancers Bruto and Lancers Meio Seco, or Extra Dry add up to 71,000 cases annually. This success is due in part to Lancers' continuous method unit, installed in 1984 (bought from Seitz in Germany and modelled on a Russian original) which facilitates high-volume production. The ingenious process enables Lancers to pour base wine continuously into the first tank of a multi-tank unit and 30 days later to remove sparkling wine from the final tank, ready for immediate bottling and shipping. Quality, alas, does not go hand-in-hand with such technology and wine-lovers are unlikely to rave about these sweet sparklers. The base wine is made from local, decolourized black Periquita grapes grown in the Palmela region, south of Lisbon – fine for producing red wine but lacking sufficient steely character to make good sparkling wine.

José Marquês Agostinho Filhos   CC   →★
Rua 5 de Outubro 23, 2331 Entroncamento, Sentarém

About 20,000 cases of sweetish sparkling wine are produced here annually under the Conde d'Arcos, Famoso and Magos labels. The Conde d'Arcos wines, with ten percent Chardonnay in their mix look the best of the bunch. Portugal drinks most of the firm's production, but a little goes to the UK.

Messias   MC   ★
Avenida Marechal Carmona 796, 3050 Mealhada, Aveiro

This traditional Portuguese house, based in the heart of the Bairrada region, has a three percent share of the domestic sparkling wine market and also exports to Portugal's long-standing trade partners in Africa. Some of Messias' sparklers come from grapes grown in its own vineyards but most of the base wine is bought in. Messias produces a curious cologne-like *bruto*. Look out for the new, own vineyard, single-*quinta* fizz, the Quinta de São Miguel.

Caves Montanha   MC   ★
Rua Adriano Henriques 14, 3781 Anadia, Aveiro

Montanha is the winner of gold medals in places such as Bucharest and Bratislava. Caves da Montanha buys in wine every year from the same Bairrada farmers, most of which is made from the familiar blend of grapes – mainly Maria Gomes with a little Bical and Rabo de Ovelha. Five different sparklers are available, but the firm considers the Montanha Real and the gaudily-labelled A Henriques, in *bruto*, *seco* and *meio seco* versions, to be its best. It also makes a Super Reserva, a Reserva and a straight Montanha. Montanha Real Brut's lively, fruity-green, fresh nose shows initial promise but the wine has a disappointingly harsh and rubbery finish.

Caves Monte Crasto   MC   ★→
Justino de Sampaio Alegre Filho, 3780 Anadia, Aveiro

Justino de Sampaio Alegre Filho is the producer of Monte Crasto and, like many other Portuguese sparkling wine houses, it also produces a wide range of table wines and brandies. Second only to RAPOSEIRA in terms of home sales, Monte Crasto has cornered nine percent of the domestic sparkling wine market. Made from the usual Bairrada blend, an aged bottle of Monte Crasto's Paris

1900 Brut, despite its lurid, multi-coloured livery, had a pleasing, mature, buttery, burnt-caramel nose and taste – a good advertisement for the rest of the range.

Luís Pato   MC   ★→
Ois de Bairro, 3780 Anadia, Aveiro

In addition to being the Bairrada region's only sparkling wine operation, Luís Pato produces a range of table wines and brandies. Although this family-owned firm (run by father João and son Luís) has been making wine for more than two centuries at its Quinta do Ribeirinho estate (the house is shown on the sparkling wine label) and more latterly at its Ois de Bairro estate, it has only been producing sparklers since 1982. The distinctly Portuguese grapes, Maria Gomes, Sercial, Bical and Sercialinho, provide the base wine for an annual 7,000 cases of vintage-dated *bruto* and *meio seco* sparklers, with future production likely to contain increased proportions of Sercialinho. Baga is the red Bairrada grape that goes into the unusual and much admired deep pink Luís Pato Bruto, which is well worth looking out for. Currently, the greeny-gold Luís Pato Bruto is a drinkable, ripe, fruity wine with a slightly bitter finish. Portugal takes most of Pato's sparkling wine but a little is exported to the UK.

Caves da Raposeira   MC   ★→★★
5100 Lamego, Viseu

Lamego, at the entrance to the hot Douro region, across the river from Régua is the rather unlikely site of the largest Portuguese sparkling wine producer. Yet in cellars hewn out of the hillside, 600 metres above sea level, this firm (now owned by Seagram) produces Portugal's finest sparkler – the vintage-dated Velha Reserva Brut. Raposeira (the name is Portuguese for 'fox') specializes in sparkling wines, all made by the *méthode champenoise*, but Velha Reserva stands out with its classy fifty-fifty blend of Chardonnay and Pinot Noir. Certainly the '78 Velha Reserva had an almost champagne-like, rich, biscuity nose, let down by a less inspiring, sulphury palate. Raposeira annually produces over 200,000 cases of sparkling wine, made mostly from bought-in grapes such as Malvasia and Sercial as well as Pinot Noir, Chardonnay and Pinot Blanc. The fresh, yeasty Super Reserva and

Super Reserva Rosé, in Brut through to the sweet styles, contain some Pinot Noir, Chardonnay and Pinot Blanc in their mix, and are next in quality to the Velha Reserva. Then follows the Reserva range, which, as the firm's cheapest sparkler, accounts for the vast majority of sales and is produced in both a *bruto* and a *seco* version. In addition to home sales, Raposeira also exports to Angola, Brazil and Venezuela.

Real Companhia
Vinicola do Norte de Portugal   MC   *
314 Rua Azevedo Maglhaes, 4400 Vila Nova de Gaia, Porto
Now owned by mysterious Portuguese dynamo Senhor da Silva Reis, Real Vinicola, as it is known for short, produces a vast range of table wines, brandies and ports. Its sparklers have six percent of the local market and are exported in the main to France.

São Domingos   MC   *→
Caves do Solar, Ferreiros, 3780 Anadia, Aveiro
Another Bairrada sparkling wine, this time from Caves do Solar, which makes a wide range of table wines as well as São Domingos, its sparkling wine. Unlike some other Bairrada sparklers, however, the São Domingos wines are usually clean, lively and well-balanced. The pale golden, straight *meio seco* (half dry for once, rather than half sweet) is, surprisingly, the best in the range, with a bland, fruity nose followed by a pleasingly clean, flowery, fruity palate. The Extra Reserva Brut by comparison has a deeper greeny-gold colour and a mature, vanilla, yeast-influenced bouquet, but a disappointing palate. Rosé fans may not necessarily enjoy the exotic Grande Reserva Rosé with its pale colour and slightly artificial, strawberry flavour. Nevertheless, São Domingos is one of the better Portuguese sparkling wines.

Sogrape   *
Avenida da Boavista, 1163 Porto
Sogrape is the largest Portuguese wine firm, responsible, amongst other more toothsome bottles, for Mateus Rosé. Since the sales of Mateus have slipped, the Guedes family, which owns Sogrape, has turned its attention to other Portuguese wines. This no doubt accounts for its range of Bairrada-based *méthode champenoise*

sparkling wines sold under the Sogrape label. Grapes used mostly include the familiar Bairrada mix of Maria Gomes, Bical and Sercialinho. So far, four different styles have been released, including a *brut*, a *doce* and the top aged Super Reserva Brut. All bar 20 percent of Sogrape's sparklers are drunk in Portugal; a little finds its way to the UK.

Vertice   MC   ★
5070 Alijó, Vila Real

Proof positive that Portugal has sparkling wine potential worth plundering is in the arrival of this joint venture between leading California sparkler, Schramsberg, and Portuguese investors, including the Caves Riba Tua e Pinhão cooperative in the Douro. The Alto Douro has long been a useful producer of bases wines for *méthode champenoise* and Schramsberg hopes that the Vertice blend of four different grapes from the region will provide a premium *méthode champenoise* fizz. The first wine is the '90 Vertice Vintage Reserva, released only in Lisbon and Porto. The '91 vintage and those that follow will be distributed throughout Europe.

J P Vinhos   MC   ★→
Rua Infante d'Henriques 59, 2955 Pinhal Novo, Setúbal

Peter Bright is the wizard Australian winemaker behind the João Pires wines and also the man responsible for churning out the base wines for LANCERS. Over the past decade, Peter Bright has made some of the finest Portuguese white and red wines, so expect good things from his *espumante*, a blend of Fernão Pires white grapes and Periquita red. Aged for three years on yeast, and with with the benefit of the first fermentation in oak casks, the J P Vinhos *espumante* should show the fine flavours of age.

Other Portuguese Sparkling Wine Producers

Vinicola Castelar, Anadia; Ferreira e Santiago, Anadia; Sociedade Vinhos Irmãos Unidos, Anadia; Caves Neto Costa, Anadia; Caves del Rei, Anadia; Caves São João, Anadia; C da Silva, Vila Nova de Gaia.

Italy

Tasting all the Italian *spumanti* could take a lifetime, perhaps even two, for there can be few Italian winemakers who do not produce a sparkling wine. Foreigners note with envy that in addition to drinking over 145M bottles of their own sparkling wines annually, Italians are also keen consumers of champagne. During the past decade Italy has been the leading champagne drinking country on numerous occasions. Italy is clearly *spumante* crazy.

The sweet, grapey, gulpable Asti Spumante can be found world-wide; it accounts for around half of Italy's sparkling wine production and is especially popular in the UK and US. But the finest Italian sparklers can be very elusive: outside the country only a few specialist Italian wine merchants and restaurants sell them.

The *spumante* hunt is a worthwhile one, however, for the quality of these sparkling wines has much improved during the past decade. While the sweet and somewhat simple delights of Asti Spumante may not suit everyone, the drier wines are often as good as much that France can produce. This is a tremendous achievement given Italy's considerably hotter climate (although admittedly over 80 percent is made by the *cuve close* method).

Most of Italy's finest sparkling wines are produced in the most northerly regions – Piedmont, Lombardy, Trentino-Alto Adige and Veneto. Piedmont accounts for the majority. Within this region's borders lies the Asti Spumante zone, with Canelli at its centre, and its southwesterly offshoot, Serralunga d'Alba. Also made here are the low-alcohol, often slightly sparkling, enchantingly fresh and grapey Moscato d'Asti or Moscato d'Asti Naturale. Lombardy, Piedmont's next door neighbour, has two sparkling wine areas, the Oltrepò Pavese zone in its southwest corner and Franciacorta in the centre, close to Lake Iseo. Italy's increasingly fashionable Trentino-Alto Adige region, cool and mountainous, produces some impressive sparklers, as does the Veneto's aromatic Prosecco grape, grown between Valdobbiadene and Conegliano, north of the Piave river.

The sparklers produced in these four regions can conveniently be divided into five different groups. The most important in terms of quality are the *méthode champenoise*, Pinot-based wines made in Serralunga d'Alba, Franciacorta, Oltrepò Pavese and throughout the Trentino–Alto Adige region. 'Pinot-based' could mean either the Pinot Nero (Pinot Noir), the Pinot Bianco (Pinot Blanc) plus Chardonnay and Pinot Grigio (Pinot Gris). Expect these sparklers to range in flavour, just as they do in France, from the fresh, young, fruity and pineapple-like Pinot Bianco- and Chardonnay-dominated wines through to the biscuity, full-bodied and mature Pinot Nero styles.

Many of these Pinot sparklers are produced by members of the Istituto Spumante Metodo Classico Italiano, founded in 1975. Istituto sparklers are well worth seeking out since they must be made from at least 80 percent Pinot-family grapes and have been produced via the *méthode champenoise*. In addition, non-vintage Istituto sparkling wine will have been aged for two years after the harvest, of which 10 months will have been spent on yeast. Vintage Istituto *spumante* is made to even more quality-conscious regulations: the wines age for 28 months, with at least 18 months on yeast.

The most popular Italian sparkler, and probably the country's most famous wine, is Asti Spumante. All Asti boasts the unmistakable, seductive, musky fragrance of the Moscato grape. In the early days, when *méthode champenoise* was the only system Italians had of putting bubbles into wine, preserving the Moscato's distinctive character was difficult. Today, all Asti Spumante is made via the *cuve close* system. The slow cool fermentation is arrested early on before all of the natural sugar in the grape has been turned into alcohol, which accounts both for Asti's low alcohol content and for its luscious, grapey freshness.

The third group consists of the more fragile, *frizzante* (as opposed to fully sparkling or *spumante*) Moscato d'Asti or Moscato d'Asti Naturale wines. This wine in fact provides the base for Asti and is mouthwateringly fresh and fruity with all the youthful charm of the Moscato grape at its very best. But it must be drunk young, when its fruit is at its most vibrant: make sure you drink the youngest vintages available. It can acquire its sparkle from a light secondary fermentation in bottle but more usually, like Asti Spumante, it is fermented slowly in a tank with lower carbon dioxide pressure than the fully *spumante* wines of Asti. Asti lovers who like to watch their alcohol intake will be glad to know that Moscato d'Asti is often as low as five percent alcohol.

The fourth category is the Prosecco-based range of wines. This traditional Italian grape variety is grown chiefly in northern Veneto in the province of Treviso and, to a lesser extent, in Trentino-Alto Adige and Friuli Venezia Giulia. Its strong, aromatic, tutti-frutti quality will not be appreciated by everyone. However, it makes good sparkling wine, mostly via the *cuve close* method in this part of Italy. (Originally the *méthode champenoise* was used.) Prosecco is now the second most popular Italian fizz after Asti Spumante, although this is less obvious to foreigners since Italians drink 50M bottles annually and only 2M bottles are exported. A chic, fashionable glass of a fruity, almond-scented Prosecco is *the* aperitif in the watering holes of Venice both for locals and, increasingly, for tourists. The superior version, Cartizze, from steep, sloping vineyards to the east of Valdobbiadene, when it is the genuine article, is the very best Prosecco you can buy.

The fifth category is usually encountered only in Italy. These sparkling wines are made all over the country from any of Italy's hundreds of grape varieties. Many of them will have been made by small-scale producers who will simply have turned part of their white grape production into sparkling wine. Discovering a good one has increased the enjoyment of many an Italian holiday. Modern Italian winemakers are fond of describing their exciting new wave of good quality wines as the 'renaissance of Italian wine'. Certainly a renaissance has taken place with *spumanti*.

Italian Sparkling Wine Labels and the Law

- Most Italian sparkling wine is made by the *cuve close* or Charmat method. However, *cuve close* bottles do not usually have these words on the label. Occasionally such wines carry the words '*fermentazione naturale*' or '*metodo charmat*'. The production time for *cuve close* sparklers, including ageing, must not be less than six months.

- True *méthode champenoise* wines are denoted by the words '*metodo champenois*', '*metodo classico champenois*', '*metodo tradizionale champenois*', '*champenois d'Italia*' or '*méthode champ-enoise*'. The production time for such wines must be nine months or more. By law, these phrases are now gradually being phased out. The most likely replacements are '*metodo tradizionale classico*', '*metodo classico*' or '*metodo tradizionale*'.

- Artificially carbonated wines will carry the words '*vino addizionato di anidride carbonica*' clearly on the label. Carbonated wines cannot be produced or even stored on the same premises as *cuve close* or *méthode champenoise* wines.

- Sweetness levels range from 'extra *brut*', the driest, followed by '*brut*', 'extra dry', '*secco*' (for *sec*), '*abboccato*' (for *demi-sec*) and finally the sweetest '*dolce*' (for *doux*).

Steep-sloping vineyards around the town of Calamandrana in the Asti Spumante zone

Producers

Anteo   MC/CC   ★ →
Rocca de' Giorgi, 12047 Pavia
With 33 ha (82 acres) of Oltrepò Pavese Chardonnay and Pinot
Nero vines, Anteo's winemaker is well-placed to make good
méthode champenoise wines. So far, apart from Charmat method
spumante, Anteo produces a *méthode champenoise* Brut and Nature.

Antica Cantina Fratta   MC   ★
Via Fontana 7, 25040 Monticelli Brusati, Brescia
The Antica has been closely associated with the BERLUCCHI firm
since 1979. Today, as the labels proudly state, Fratta is under the
direction of Berlucchi's oenologist, Franco Ziliani. Fratta sparkling
wines include Cuvée Antica Fratta Brut, made from early-har-
vested Pinot Bianco and Pinot Nero, and the Pinot Nero-dominant Cuvée Antica Fratta Rosé. The best Fratta wine, the
vintage-dated Cuvée Antica, comes in Brut and non-*dosage* versions.

Arunda   MC   ★
1–39010 Mölten, Bolzano
This firm produces two *méthode champenoise* sparklers: non-*dosage*
Extra Brut and Brut. The grapes used are mostly Chardonnay,
Pinot Bianco and Pinot Nero, grown on hillside vineyards around
Terlan and Girlan in the South Tyrol and vinified in what Arunda
claims is the highest winery in Europe, if not the world, at 1,150
m. Both types are matured for two years in bottle. The Extra Brut
is excessively green and herbaceous.

Villa Banfi   CC/MC   ★ → ★ ★
Montalcino, 53024 Siena
Star buy Brut Pinot Oltrepò Pavese
Villa Banfi must represent the international blueprint for what
every winemaker would like to own if only he or she had the capital: 2,874 ha (7,100 acres) of fine Montalcino land, 95 ha (235
acres) of which are planted to sparkling wine grapes, a vast, com-
puterized, high tech winery, enormous cellars and the handsome
Castello Banfi, dating back to 800 AD. Riunite Lambrusco provided the wherewithal for all this and Banfi's clever winemaker

Dr Ezio Rivella has certainly made the most of the opportunity. The 80,000 cases of Banfi sparklers made annually include Tener Spumante (Sauvignon- and Chardonnay-based) and the red Brachetto d'Acqui Asti Banfi. The firm's excellent, big, biscuity, aged Brut Pinot Oltrepò Pavese (Pinot Nero- and Chardonnay-based) appears not to be made now. Banfi's *méthode champenoise* Brut is its best sparkler, made from Chardonnay and Pinot Nero plus a little Pinot Bianco. The wine's tinny, metallic taste will not appeal to everyone, however. Moscato di Strevi, Banfi Asti Spumante and a tank method Banfi Brut Pinot made from Pinot Nero and Pinot Bianco complete the range.

Barbero   CC/MC   ★
Frazione Valpone, 12043 Canale, Cuneo

The six Barbero brothers all work for the family firm, which must make it rather confusing for the staff. Everyone, however, is kept busy here making 700,000 cases annually of sparkling wine, which is sold under nine different labels. Barbero Asti Spumante accounts for most of this, but the multi-variety Conte di Cavour also sells well as does the Moscato Spumante. The sweet Barbero Gran Dessert is the next best seller, followed by the Pinot Crémant, Chardonnay and the medium-dry Prosecco (made from the grape of the same name). Much smaller quantities are made of Pinot Brut Rosé and Barbero's best sparkler, the vintage-dated *méthode champenoise* Stefano Barbero.

Cantine Bava   CC/MC   ★
Strada Monferrato 2, 14023 Cocconato d'Asti, Asti

For three generations the Bava family has been making sparkling wine at these *cantine* (cellars) situated halfway between Montferrato and Asti. All the grapes for sparkling wine are bought in from local farmers and then turned into Moscato d'Asti, Fior di Moscato, a Moscato Bianco di Canelli, the popular Malvasia di Castelnuovo don Bosco Rosé and the superior *méthode champenoise* Brut Cà Traversa. The Bava family also owns GIULIO COCCHI *spumante*, founded in 1891, which they claim is the oldest surviving *spumante* house in Asti.

Berlucchi Fratelli   MC   ★→
Piazza Duranti 4, 25040 Borgonato di Cortefranca, Brescia
Most unusually this young firm, founded in 1966 by Guido
Berlucchi, only produces sparklers via the *méthode champenoise*.
With the help of Franco Ziliani, fresh from the oenology school at
Alba, Berlucchi's impressive old cellars beneath the Castello di
Borgonato today produce 250,000 cases of sparkling wine a year,
making the firm the leading Italian *méthode champenoise* producer.
Chardonnay and its distant relative Pinot Bianco, plus Pinot Nero
and, intriguingly, Pinot Meunier are the grapes used. The sweet,
peppery Cuvée Imperiale Brut is Berlucchi's most popular
sparkler, made from a blend of all the grapes, from several different
regions. It also comes in a non-*dosage* or *pas dosé* version, which
was previously sold as '*dosage pas opéré*'. A gently sparkling Bianco
Imperiale Berlucchi is also made here as is the Cuvée Imperiale
Max Rosé, a Pinot Nero-dominant rosé. In great years such as
1981 a vintage-dated Cuvée Imperiale Millesimata Brut, aged for
three years on yeast, is also produced. The other wines spend
roughly two years on yeast.

Bersano   MC   ★→
Piazza Dante 21, 14049 Nizza Monferrato, Asti
Three different tank method sparklers, Asti Spumante, Brachetto
Spumante and Pinot Spumante are made here and one *méthode
champenoise* fizz, the Riserva Arturo Bersano. Once part of
Seagram's empire, Bersano is now owned by four Italian share-
holders, and its quality has improved of late. All bar its Asti
Spumanti comes from Oltrepò Pavese grapes and over 100,000
cases of Bersano sparkling wine are made in most years. The
Riserva Arturo Bersano, still hand riddled, is made from the same
Pinot mix as the Pinot Spumante. France and Japan are the two
major export markets.

Desiderio Bisol e Figli   MC/CC   ★
Via Fol 33, 31040 Santo Stéfano di Valdobbiadene, Treviso
Eliseo Bisol's wine estate and distillery, founded in 1875, was
destroyed in the First World War. His son Desiderio started the
business again after the War, buying up vineyard land at Cartizze
and Fol in the heart of the Prosecco region. Today the Bisol

family produces three different *méthode champenoise* bubblies: its top wine, the Riserva Brut, plus a rosé and a *pas dosé*. The rest of the range is tank method fizz bottled under a wide variety of labels, of which most are Prosecco di Valdobbiadene wines from Chardonnay, Pinot Bianco and Pinot Nero. The Bisol Rosé is made from Pinot Nero.

Luigi Bosca e Figli   CC/MC   ★→
2 Via L Bosca, 14053 Canelli, Asti
The Bosca family has owned this firm since it was founded in 1831. Apart from a classic Asti Spumante, it makes a finer *méthode champenoise* Brut Nature and Riserva del Nonno plus a Tosti *spumante*.

Braida-Giacomo Bologna   CC   ★→
Via Roma 94, 14030 Rocchetta Tanaro, Asti
Raffaella Bologna is Braida's clever winemaker. Many regard his Moscato d'Asti as the quintessence of this sparkler, and the family is well regarded in winemaking circles. It also makes a red, fizzy Brachetto d'Acqui.

Bruzzone   CC/MC   ★→
22 Via Vittorio Veneto, 15019 Strevi, Alessandria
Bruzzone is connected with Villa Banfi and also shares Banfi's capable winemaker, Dr Ezio Rivella. Sparkling wine production here consists of Asti Spumante, the red Brachetto d'Acqui and a *méthode champenoise spumante*, of which just 4,000 cases are made annually. Some of these come from Bruzzone's own 40 ha (100 acres) of vines, the rest is made from bought-in grapes.

Ca' del Bosco   MC   ★→
Via Case Sparse 11, 25030 Erbusco, Brescia
Ca' del Bosco, situated in Lombardy's Franciacorta region, rates itself as the most highly-respected producer of Italian *spumanti classici* and it would be hard to disagree. Its prices are outrageous – about the same as for champagne – but Maurizio Zanella is a perfectionist and the combination of his Moët & Chandon–trained winemaker, plus a vast, no-expense-spared, custom-built, temperature-controlled winery and cellars deep underground, is quite formidable. Such attention to detail does not come cheap and

perhaps the eventual Ca' del Bosco bottle price is justified. The 34 ha (86 acres) of vineyards supply almost all the firm's needs and are mostly planted to Chardonnay, Pinot Bianco and Pinot Nero. It buys in an additional 10 ha-worth (26 acres) planted to Pinot Bianco. Older barrel-aged wines make up 15 percent of the Ca' del Bosco *cuvées*. Gentle basket presses are used and all the wines are aged for three years prior to sale. Despite all this, perhaps the most impressive fact about Ca' del Bosco is that the grapes are processed within 30 minutes of being picked. Current production stands at only 14,000 cases per annum and mostly consists of the white grape dominated Dosage Zero and Brut – the latter is big, yeasty, full-bodied and redolent of champagne. The *pelure d'oignon*-coloured rosé, from Pinot Nero, has a yeasty, fruity character. It is made in small quantities, as is a *crémant*. Just 416 cases of Ca' del Bosco's best sparkling wine, a vintage-dated Millesimato, are also produced.

Luigi Calissano   CC/MC   ★→
12051 Alba, Cuneo
Just over 4,000 cases of both *méthode champenoise* and Charmat method sparkling wines are made here annually. Pinot Brut is the tank method sparkler and the Duca d'Alba Brut and Real Brut the two *méthode champenoise* wines.

Casa Vinicola Canella   CC   ★
Via Fiume 7, 30027 San Donà di Piave, Venezia
Luciano Canella runs this sparkling wine firm with his sons and makes 25,000 cases annually. Prosecco di Conegliano Extra Dry is the big seller, but useful quantities of Pinot Chardonnay Brut and Pinot Brut are made too. The latter is a 100 percent Pinot Bianco wine and the former a blend of 70 percent Pinot Bianco and 30 percent Chardonnay. Canella also produces 20 cl nips of Prosecco. Germany receives 10 percent of the production.

Cantina Sociale di Canelli   CC   ★
Via Loazzolo 12, 14053 Canelli, Asti
This cooperative celebrated its 50th anniversary a few years ago. It has 400 members with 500 ha (1,235 acres) between them, planted mostly to Moscato d'Asti but with a little Brachetto. Production is mostly of the Cantina's Asti and stands at 125,000 cases a year.

Moscato Piemonte Spumante and Gran Spumante Riserva Brut (with Riesling and Pinot as the base) are also made.

Carpenè Malvolti   MC/CC
Via a Carpenè 1, 31015 Conegliano, Treviso

Antonio Carpenè, who put Prosecco on the modern wine map and, in particular, introduced the *méthode champenoise* to Conegliano, founded this firm in 1868. He was thus one of the first to bring the *méthode champenoise* to Italy. Today Carpenè Malvolti uses Pinot Nero, Pinot Bianco and Chardonnay grapes grown in the Alto Adige to make *método classico* Malvolti Brut and Brut de Brut. The firm also makes a popular Prosecco di Conegliano. About 300,000 cases are made annually, which makes this family-run firm one of the larger Italian sparkling wine concerns.

Càvit   CC/MC   ★→
Via del Ponte 31, 38100 Trento

This important group of cooperatives is one of the largest in the Alto Adige. It consists of 15 different coops scattered throughout the region, with some 4,500 members. The emphasis here is therefore on quantity (some 125,000 cases of sparkling wine are produced each year), but quality is better than you might suppose. All the sparklers are *cuve close* wines, but the vintage-dated Chardonnay-dominant Graal Ducale, launched in 1984, is a *méthode champenoise* wine, as is the new, 100 percent Chardonnay Firmato. Most of Càvit's members have hillside vineyards planted to Chardonnay and Pinot Bianco, with a little Pinot Nero and Pinot Meunier. Other sparklers from this group include the Chardonnay Brut plus a Pinot (Bianco) Spumante as well as the Chardonnay-dominated Gran Càvit Brut. Case sales add up to roughly 25,000 cases per annum.

Cesarini Sforza Spumante   CC/MC   ★→
38100 Trento

Sforza specializes exclusively in sparklers, made by both the tank method and the *méthode champenoise*. Its everyday sparkling wine is sold under the Riserva dei Conti and Riserva Nature labels. Confusingly, the special occasion *méthode champenoise* non-*dosage* Sforza is also sold under the Riserva dei Conti label, with only the words '*metodo champenois*' to alert consumers to the difference. About 25,000 cases of this are sold annually.

Michele Chiarlo (Duca d'Asti)   CC   ★→★★
Strada Nizza-Canelli, 14042 Calamandrana, Asti
Star buy Gallo d'Oro Moscato d'Asti, Michele Chiarlo Moscato d'Asti

Bottled at Calamandrana, near Asti, Chiarlo's amazingly fresh, fruity DOC Moscati d'Asti shows how glorious these seductive, sweet, grapey wines can be. Most Moscato d'Asti is sweeter and lower in alcohol than Asti Spumante. Other Moscato brand names used here include Rocca della Uccellette.

Cinzano   CC/MC   ★→
Via Gramsci 7, 10121 Torino
Cinzano was set up in the mid-18th century by the Cinzano brothers as a distillery and a bitters producer in line with the best Torino traditions. A century later, Cinzano's vermouth had become popular throughout Europe. In 1893 the firm built a new winery and expanded the rock-hewn cellars at Santa Vittoria d'Alba – still a Cinzano vermouth and *spumante* base today. In 1925 the ever-expanding empire had the perfect logo designed – the famous red, white and blue rectangle. Enterprising Cinzano now has 28 affiliated companies scattered throughout the world pro-ducing and importing vermouth and sparkling wine, amongst other wines, with annual sales adding up to a formidable £240M. In addition to the tank method, soft, frothy Asti Spumante Brut Pinot Nature and Principe di Piemonte Blanc de Blancs, there is a *méthode champenoise* Brut and a non-*dosage* Marone sparkler.

Giulio Cocchi   CC/MC   ★→
17 Via Malta, 14100 Asti
CANTINE BAVA now owns this firm, reputed to be the oldest *spumante* house in Asti. Giulio Cocchi, a Florentine, founded it in 1891 and by 1927 he was exporting to New York, Europe and Venezuela. Today, Cocchi produces Asti Brachetto and Pinot Brut, both by the tank method, a new, superior Primo Secolo Chardonnay Brut by longer tank method fermentation and finally three hand-riddled Giulio Cocchi Classico Champenois, in Rosé,

Riserva and vintage versions. The last two are 70 percent Pinot Noir to 30 percent Chardonnay wines.

Eugenio Collavini Viticoltori   CC/MC   ★→
Via della Ribolla Gialla, 33040 Corno di Rosazzo, Udine
Three generations of Collavinis have looked after this company, now producing 84,000 cases of sparkling wine annually – a third of its total wine production. Short-sighted fans will find it hard to track down Collavini sparklers, for the company's name is usually reproduced in minute lettering on the back label. The appley, perfumed Extra Dry II Grigio in its Beardsley-inspired bottle, a 70 percent Chardonnay, 20 percent Prosecco, 10 percent Pinot Nero blend, is Collavini's biggest seller (54,000 cases). Applause Nature, also partly made from Chardonnay but with 30 percent Pinot Nero, is the firm's only *méthode champenoise* wine. The vintage version of the Applause Nature is Collavini's most expensive fizz.

Conte Loredan-Gasparini   CC/MC   ★→
31040 Volpago del Montello, Treviso
Although better known for the red Venegazzù wines, Conte Loredan-Gasparini does produce some well-made sparklers too. The biscuity *méthode champenoise* Loredan Gasparini Brut is made from 60 percent Chardonnay to 40 percent Pinot Nero, and there is a vintage-dated, 100 percent Pinot Nero version. With 12 hilly hectares (30 acres) of its own vines, planted equally to Pinot Nero and Chardonnay, the firm has all it needs to make about 12,000 cases annually of these two *méthode champenoise* wines. Quality is good due to careful, gentle handling plus a three-year sojourn on yeast. The Loredan-Gasparinis try hard.

Giuseppe Contratto   CC/MC   ★→
Via G B Giuliani 56, 14053 Canelli, Asti
Giuseppe Contratto was established in 1867 and is still a family firm today, with Alberto Contratto now in charge. Annual production stands at 50,000 cases of sparkling wine, mostly made from bought-in grapes, especially Oltrepò Pavese Pinot Nero, although the firm owns 20 ha (50 acres) of Moscato vines at Canelli. Production is large and well-distributed internationally. The range includes the red Freisa d'Asti and Grignolino d'Asti. Asti Spumante

and Brachetto Spumante are the two large quantity tank method Contratto sparklers, 25,000 cases of which are made in most years. The *méthode champenoise* Contratto Brut, Riserva Bacco d'Oro and sweet Imperial Riserva Sabauda are, not surprisingly, more expensive. Riserva Novecento and Reserve for England are other Contratto *méthode champenoise* labels.

Luigi Coppo e Figli   CC/MC   ★
Canelli, Asti
The Coppo family makes a range of sparkling wines at its well-known *spumante* house complete with Asti vineyards. Its best is the *méthode champenoise* Brut Riserva Coppo.

Cora   CC/MC   ★★
14055 Costigliole d'Asti, Canelli, Asti
Star buy Cora Asti Spumante
Cora was founded in 1835, as each bottle of its Asti Spumante tells you three times over. Besides producing vermouth, the firm makes a Pinot del Poggio *spumante* plus the Royal Ambassador Brut *méthode champenoise* from Pinot. The straight Asti is gloriously fresh, floral and grapey: definitely one of the best *spumanti* available.

Corvo   CC   ★
90014 Casteldaccia, Palermo
The Duca di Salaparuta established this firm in 1824. Quality here may not outshine that of other Italian firms but the wines are usually reliable. 12,000 cases of Corvo sparklers are produced annually in a range including the Brut and Demi-sec multi-variety Riserva del Duca di Salaparuta, made by the Charmat method.

Equipe 5   MC   ★→
Viale Vittoria 92b, Rovereto, Trento
Equipe Trentino Spumante is the firm behind Equipe 5, a well-known *méthode champenoise* producer in Trentino. (Five friends founded the firm, in 1964, hence the name.) It buys in Pinot Blanc, Pinot Nero and Chardonnay grapes from the Oltrepò Pavese district in the southwest corner of Lombardy. Five different sparklers are made here (of course) including Brut, Extra Brut, Sec, Brut Rosé and Brut Riserva. Worth seeking out.

Fazi–Battaglia 'Titulus'   CC ★→
Via Clementina 175, 60032 Castelplanio Stazione, Ancona
Fazi-Battaglia produces a clean, refreshing, pepperminty Charmat-method *spumante* Brut.

Ferrari   MC ★→
Via del Ponte di Ravina 15, 38040 Trento
Almost as famous in Italy as the eponymous racing car, Ferrari is now owned by the Lunelli family. Giulio Ferrari, who founded the firm in 1902, is acknowledged as the father of sparkling wine in Trentino and was specifically responsible for cultivating and introducing the Chardonnay grape here. Ferrari owns 40 ha (100 acres) of hillside vineyards in Trento, which provide 20 percent of its needs, with the rest of its Chardonnay being bought in. Production is currently at just over 100,000 cases per annum and the majority is taken up by the Ferrari Brut. Unlike most Italian sparkling wine producers, Ferrari only makes *méthode champenoise* wines and all are riddled by hand. Quality, above all, is obviously what Ferrari is aiming at and the Lunelli family's own Chardonnay always goes into its vintage-dated sparklers. Apart from the Ferrari Brut, the range of non-vintage wines includes a curious, intense, green Pinot Nero-dominated Brut Rosé, a Nature and an Extra Dry sparkler. Ferrari's premium vintage-dated sparklers are worth trying. The incense-redolent '81 Brut de Brut is made in limited quantities, using gentle pressings and grapes from selected vineyards. The '78 Giulio Ferrari Riserva del Fondatore, with seven years on yeast, is also highly thought of.

Fontanafredda   CC/MC ★→
Via Alba 15, 12050 Serralunga d'Alba, Cuneo
One of the largest and best known Piedmont houses, Fontanafredda, as befits its position, makes a wide range of sparkling wines. The firm was founded in 1878 by Conte Emanuele Guerrieri, son of King Vittorio Emanuele II and Contessa Rosa di Mirafiori. Today the 300,000 cases of Fontanafredda sparklers made annually include an Asti as well as the Chardonnay Spumante, Pinot Spumante and Bracchetto Spumante. Fontanafredda's finest sparklers are the non-*dosage* Contessa Rosa Brut Rosé and Extra Brut, *méthode champenoise*

wines made from Pinot and Chardonnay grown at Serralunga d'Alba and also available in Brut and Rosé versions. A 100 percent Pinot Nero-based *méthode champenoise* Brut Gattinera bubbly, from the estate of the same name, is also made. At a recent tasting the Asti was an intense, green, floral wine whereas the Contessa had a perfumed, earthy character.

Nino Franco   CC/MC   ★→
Valdobbiadene, Treviso

The Franco family makes both ancient sweet and modern dry styles of Prosecco, including the elegant, superior Cartizze zone Prosecco and the more old-fashioned, softly sweet sparkler appropriately named Rustic.

Gancia Fratelli   CC/MC   ★→★★
16 Corso Liberta, 14053 Canelli, Asti
Star buy Pinot di Pinot

Gancia, along with Martini, Cinzano and Riccadonna, is one of the world's big *spumante* names. Carlo Gancia founded the firm in 1850 and visited Reims to study the classic method of producing sparkling wine. He was soon convinced that the Moscato grapes from his own region (Asti) could make good sparkling wine and by 1865 the first Gancia sparkler had been launched. (Some sources credit this wine with being the first Moscato-based sparkler. Few would deny however that it was the original ancestor of Asti Spumante.) Carlo and his brother Edoardo were also among the first to turn the Pinot Nero and Bianco grapes grown in the Oltrepò Pavese into sparkling wine. With the firm's sparkling wine and vermouth trades both doing well, Gancia expanded its Canelli winery and set up other branches in Italy, Argentina and France.

Today the Gancia family still owns the company and more than 1M cases of sparkling wine are made every year. Most markets only receive Gancia Asti Spumante, the grapey, muscaty Gran Spumante Demi-Sec, the excellent, zippy, pineapple-like Pinot di Pinot (based on Pinots Nero and Bianco), and the refreshing, elegant and classic Gran Crémant Riserva Vallarino Gancia, made from Trentino Pinot grapes by the *méthode champenoise*. In addition, however, there is the Extra Brut from Pinot Bianco plus the Chardonnay Brut and Sauvignon Brut, both from Veneto grapes.

Look out too for the new, dry Gancia dei Gancia and Castello Gancia sparklers. The USA and UK are the chief export markets.

Kettmeir   CC/MC   ★
Caldaro, Bolzano
The Kettmeir family sold out to SANTA MARGHERITA some time ago, but the family is still in charge here. This augurs well for the quality of its variety of sparkling wines.

Maculan   CC
Breganze, Vicenza
Better-known for its sweet Veneto wines such as the Torcolato, the Maculan family also makes the good, ordinary, tank method Accademia Brut.

Marchese Antinori   MC   ★→
Palazzo Antinori, 3 Piazza Antinori, 50100 Firenze
The current generation of Antinoris, Marchese Piero Antinori and his brother Lodovico, are heirs to 600 years of winemaking and obviously every bit as capable as their ancestors. Indeed, the first Antinori fizz was made in 1905, when the family brought in an Epernay champagne maker to produce it. The Antinoris may well be rather more interested in producing great red wines, but this does not stop them from making a good *méthode champenoise* Brut Nature and superior Extra Brut. The latter is made from 70 percent Oltrepò Pavese Pinot Nero to 30 percent Trentino Chardonnay and is given about two years on yeast. By comparison, the Brut Nature is a fifty-fifty blend of the same varieties from the same regions, with about 18 months on yeast. The first fermentation takes place in stainless steel and the resulting wine has a pleasant, warm, fruity style. Just 21,000 cases of these non-vintage sparklers are made annually, of which the Extra Brut makes up just over 3,000. Antinori is experimenting with automatic *remuage* and yeast capsules, which suggest that production here could increase.

Marchesi de' Frescobaldi   MC   ★→
Via Santo Spirito 11, 50125 Firenze
The distinguished Frescobaldi family only makes one sparkling wine – the biscuity, foamy *méthode champenoise* vintage-dated Brut.

The Chardonnay and Pinot Nero grapes are all bought in from farmers whose vines carpet the Trento hillsides. Given Frescobaldi's giant production of still wines, the 16,000 or so cases of this sparkler seem modest, but it is currently all hand riddled and increased production could be on the way. Ancestor Vittorio degli Albizi, born in France, brought the first Chardonnay and Pinot Noir vines to Italy, in 1855.

Martini & Rossi   CC/MC   ★→
Corso Vittorio Emanuele 42, 10123 Torino
The one Italian sparkling wine firm that everyone has heard of, although better known for its vermouth, Martini & Rossi was founded in 1863. It produces three different sparklers: the lively, grapey Moscato-based Asti, a big seller in Italy, the Riesling Italico-based Riesling Oltrepò Pavese Brut and the Pinot Nero-based Riserva Montelera Brut. Production is huge, as would be expected, and almost 1.5M cases of sparkling wine are produced annually. The majority is sweet Asti, but the yearly 150,000-case sales of the two Bruts are not to be sneered at. The new Riserva Montelera is a *méthode champenoise* sparkler, two-thirds of which is currently riddled by hand and the rest by gyropalette.

Monte Rossa   MC   ★
Via L Marenzio 8, 25040 Bornato, Brescia
This estate winery, with vineyards in the Franciacorta hills, originally made sparkling wine for the family and friends. Three different wines are produced: a Brut, a Rosé and a non-*dosage* sparkler. Pinot and Chardonnay grapes are used.

Montorfano de Filippo   MC   ★→
Coccaglio, Brescia
This estate, complete with the ancient Coccaglio castle cellar, produces fine *méthode champenoise* wines, sold under the Bellavista label, that have a prestigious reputation both in Italy and abroad. Just 5 ha (12 acres) of Pinot Bianco and Chardonnay are used here. The grapes are turned into either the inexpensive and well thought of non-vintage Franciacorta Montorfano de Filippo Brut, the Franciacorta Rosé or the vintage-dated, aged Franciacorta Riserva Luca Marenzio.

Cantine Giacomo Montresor CC ★
Ca di Cozzi 16, 37100 Verona

The Cantine Giacomo Montresor is still owned by the Montresor family, which originally came from France and settled in Italy at the end of the 16th century. The family has been a vineyard owner for several centuries and today its own estates, close to Lake Garda, supply almost all of its grape needs. Chardonnay provides the base wine for more than half of the firm's production, with the local white grapes of Verona accounting for the rest. About 20,000 cases of the Chardonnay Brut Extra, the Pinot Bianco Brut, the multi-variety Bianco di Custoza and the sweet red Recioto della Valpolicella sparkler are produced every year.

Tenute Neirano MC ★→
Via San Michele 39, Mombaruzzo, Asti

Giacomo Sperone and his sons Paolo and Antonio are the forces behind this firm, situated at Mombaruzzo in the Alto Monferrato hills south of Alessandria. The restored cellars with their ultra-modern equipment are capable of ageing about 40,000 cases at any one time. Although the firm produces both still red and white wines, its pride and joy is the *méthode champenoise* Neirano Brut. This sparkler, aged for three years on yeast, is made from a blend of mostly Pinot Nero plus a little Chardonnay. Current production is only 2,500 cases per annum, but the cellars have the capacity to produce about four times as much.

Riccadonna CC/MC ★
Corso Liberta 15, 14053 Canelli, Asti

Ottavia Riccadonna founded this famous Asti firm in 1921. Today its vast Asti plant has a tank capacity of 22M litres and Riccadonna is one of the leading Asti firms (MARTINI & ROSSI, GANCIA and CINZANO are the other three). Annual production of the firm's main sparkling wine labels stands at almost 1M cases and includes the sweet, grapey Asti Spumante, Gran Dessert, the lively, lime-juice-like President Brut and Demi-Sec, Nature de Pupitre, C Balduino and Riserva Privata Angelo Riccadonna. The President Reserve is made from Pinot grapes and enjoys a long cool fermentation. All are *méthode champenoise* wines, as is the vintage-dated Angelo Riccadonna Brut Riserva Privata. The firm exports 25 percent.

Cantine Romagnoli   CC/MC   ★→
29020 Vigolzone, Piacenza

This winery and estate, owned by the Romagnoli family, has some 25 ha (62 acres) of sparkling wine vineyards in the hills of Piacenza surrounding its property. The Romagnoli family produces about 7,500 cases of sparkling wine every year, most of which is taken up by the Romagnoli Brut, whose base wine is made from Pinot Nero and the local Ortugo grape. The rather better Il Pigro Spumante, made from Chardonnay plus a little Pinot Nero, also sells well as does the Charmat method, 100 percent Chardonnay Spumante. A little sweet Malvasia Amabile Spumante is also pro-duced. The firm's finest sparklers are the *méthode champenoise* Pinot Naturale, made from a blend of Pinot Nero and Chardonnay, and the Pinot Nero-dominated Premium and Villa d'Este (the latter is served at the grand Lake Como hotel of the same name). The Premium and Villa d'Este, classy blends, also contain 20 percent Pinot Grigio and 10 percent Chardonnay. Quality will rise here soon due to the installation of a new, cool, fully-equipped cellar.

Rotari   MC   ★
Corso IV Novembre 13, 38016 Mezzocorona, Trento

The Cantine Mezzocorona is the group of wineries behind Rotari sparkling wines. The group made its first sparkling wine in 1976: 520 cases from its own grapes via the *méthode champenoise*. Today, 33,000 cases are made each year, mostly from Chardonnay, but with some Pinot Nero too. Only two sparklers are produced here, the Rotario Brut and Rotario Brut Rosé.

Santa Margherita   CC   ★→
Via I Marzotto 8, 30025 Fossalta di Portogruaro, Venezia

Santa Margherita has some of the most stylish labels in all Italy gracing its bottles of sparkling wine, depicting the Villa Marzotto in Portogruaro. The Marzotto family still owns the firm and Conte Umberto Marzotto is the current president. The original Santa Margherita vineyards have now been ceded to tenant-farmers, from whom the estate buys only the best grapes. About 20,000 cases of non-vintage sparklers are produced here every year. Most are sold under the Prosecco di Conegliano-Valdobbiadene label in Brut and Extra Dry versions. The majority of Santa Margherita fizz is drunk in Italy, but Germany, Belgium and the USA drink reasonable quantities too. Quality is consistent and good.

Cantina Sociale
di Santa Maria della Versa   CC/MC   ★→
15 Via Crispi, 27047 Santa Maria della Versa, Pavia

This cooperative, in the heart of the Oltrepò Pavese region in southwest Lombardy, was founded in 1905. Its members own about 1,000 ha (2,471 acres) planted to Pinot Nero, Pinot Grigio, Riesling Italico (for the Riesling Spumante) and Moscato (for Moscato the Spumante). Production reaches an impressive 50,000 cases per annum of Gran Spumante La Versa Brut *méthode champenoise* and 166,000 cases of Charmat method sparklers. The firm sells very little under its own label. Its Pinot Nero–dominated Pinot Spumante accounts for the majority of production, but La Versa Brut (also Pinot Nero–dominated) deserves its handsome sales too because its quality is good.

I Vignaioli di Santo Stéfano   CC   ★→
Frazione Marini 12, Santo Stéfano Belbo, Cuneo

This recently founded firm specializes in Moscato d'Asti and Asti Spumante, of which it produces 2,000 cases a year. Only 20 percent of its own Moscato d'Asti grapes are used in its vintage-dated sparkler. The rest is bought in, but these grapes come from a small, cool, highly-admired Moscato d'Asti region, high up and to the west of Santo Stéfano Belbo, which is due west of Asti's headquarters at Canelli.

La Scolca   MC
Villa Scolca, 15066 Rovereto di Gavi, Alessandria

Fourth-generation Giorgio Soldati runs La Scolca. Only 3.5 ha (1.5 acres) of a total of 32 ha (79 acres) at this Ligurian Apennine estate (technically within the Piedmont region) are devoted to sparkling wines. The vineyards are entirely planted to the Cortese grape, and La Scolca turns out four different *méthode champenoise* sparklers. With about 2,500 cases a year produced of its most popular wine, La Scolca Brut, and just over 400 cases each of the newly-launched Crémant and Extra Brut versions, Villa Scolca is a small, sparkling wine concern. A vintage-dated Brut completes the range. Quality here is high, with La Scolca using its own yeast strain and all the sparklers being riddled by hand and spending three years on yeast. The wines are very much admired in Italy; the USA forms the main export market. Spumante Pados is another La Scolca label.

Villadoria   CC   →★
65 Via L Bosca, 14053 Canelli, Asti
Villadoria is the Asti Spumante brand name of AZIVISI, an important bottler and shipper of a range of Piedmont wines. The unpleasant Villadoria Brut Spumante is not recommended.

Zardetto Spumante   CC   ★
31015 Scomigo di Conegliano, Treviso
Zardetto, like other quality-minded producers, gives his Charmat method sparklers extended ageing time in tank on the yeast, and as a result the Zardetto Brut has some *méthode champenoise* characteristics. The firm produces 7,500 cases each year. Good Prosecco di Conegliano and Cartizze.

Zonin   CC/MC   ★
Gambellara, Vicenza
The Zonin family's giant Gambellara cellars produce dozens of different sparklers, including Asti Spumante. The top wine is the rather more admired *méthode champenoise* Riserva Domenico Zonin.

Germany

It is hard to love *Sekt*. This is principally because most German sparkling wine is made from tanker-loads of base wine that come from all over Europe but very rarely from Germany's own vineyards. Indeed just ten percent of *Sekt* is likely to be truly German in origin.

Riesling grown in the cool German vineyards can make good sparkling wine, as a few producers prove. But line up 20 of Germany's best-selling sparklers and only five are likely to display any Riesling – or even German – characteristics at all. The rest will reek of whatever wine is going cheap at the time – those low-quality white varieties that are all too familiar components of the EC wine lake and are given a hefty addition of sugar in a usually unsuccessful attempt to cover up their worst characteristics.

Until recently the German wine laws compounded the confusion by allowing these mixtures to be labelled '*Deutscher Sekt*' (German *Sekt*). Now Germany has at least done the decent thing. An EC directive now requires that *Deutscher Sekt* must be made exclusively from German wine or German grapes. Previously, the majority of this wine was only German by virtue of experiencing a second fermentation on German soil. It is to be hoped that this change in the rules will encourage more *Sekt* producers to make fine *Deutscher Sekt* from *Deutscher Wein*, but at the moment about 85 percent of all *Sekt* is cheap, sweet and worth avoiding. Intriguingly, red *Sekt* is becoming more popular (perhaps as a backlash against the ersatz, sweet, white variety?) and now accounts for 12 percent of the total.

At the time of writing, *Deutscher Sekt* amounts to only a tiny proportion of Germany's annual 36M-case production of sparkling wine. Henkell, one of the country's largest *Sekt* producers, is rather coy about revealing which varieties go into which blends, but will nonetheless state which varieties it uses. These are the Riesling, Silvaner, Chardonnay, Sauvignon, Chenin Blanc, Colombard, Folle Blanche, Pinot Noir and Trebbiano. The rest of the industry uses most if not all of these varieties. The Loire supplies the majority of the Chenin Blanc and possibly some Sauvignon, southwest France provides the Colombard and Folle Blanche, Bordeaux gives some more Sauvignon, and northern Italy is probably the source of the Chardonnay, Pinot Noir and Trebbiano. Perhaps there is an excuse for using the more neutral of these varieties, but when *Sekt* smells strongly of the gooseberry-redolent Sauvignon, it is difficult to see the sense in selling it as *Sekt*.

Germany consumes the vast majority of its *Sekt* production, which is perhaps just as well. But in 1991 about 1M cases were exported, mostly by big firms such as Henkell, Deinhard, Fürst von Metternich and Kupferberg. With production so large, it is understandable that the bulk of Germany's sparkling wine is made by the *cuve close* system, with a little also being made by the transfer method and the *méthode champenoise* (four percent of the total).

Contract bottlers put the sparkle into much of Germany's *Sekt* but two new *Sekt* Producers' Associations, or *Sekterzeugergemein-schaft*, in the Mosel and Rheinhessen regions, now turn basic, acidic German white wines into better than average *Deutscher Sekt*. With cheap *Sekt* made from unwanted European bulk wine on sale at little more than cost price, German producers with neutral, high-acid wines needed somewhere of their own to send it – hence the Mosel and Rheinhessen producers' associations. Growers' sparkling wines from organizations such as these will have the word '*winzersekt*' on the label, indicating a Sekt bA, with grape variety and vintage mentioned, whose grapes have been harvested by the producer and which has been made by the *méthode champenoise*. Virtually every firm makes a wide variety of different wines with varying degrees of sweetness. The numerous brand names and styles are an attempt by each *Sekt* house to cater for all tastes.

Encouragingly, *méthode champenoise* appears to be growing in popularity. So too is the production of regional, or even single-vineyard, vintage-dated sparklers, which, as part of the *Qualität-sschaumwein* or the *Sekt bA* categories, account for a tiny yet increasing percentage of the total – five percent at present. For those interested in drinking top-quality sparkling wines, this is one of the most optimistic trends in the German *Sekt* industry.

Riesling vineyards descend to meet the gabled towns along the Rhine

German Sparkling Wine
Labels and the Law

Regulations which took effect from September 1986 mean that there are four categories of German sparkling wine, or *Sekt*.

- The first category, labelled simply '*Schaumwein*', is made from imported wine, usually via the Charmat method, and is the cheapest German sparkler. No vintage date or grape is shown on the label. The alcohol level must be at least 9.5 percent.

- The next level up is '*Qualitätsschaumwein*', or '*Sekt*'. It is made mostly from imported wine but also occasionally from German wine. *Sekt* acquires its sparkle from a second fermentation – usually by the Charmat method. It must be cellared for at least six months prior to sale and have an alcohol level of ten percent or more. Previously, this category of *Sekt* could be sold as *Deutscher Sekt*, although made from imported wine.

- '*Deutscher Sekt*', the third level, is now exactly what it says it is – German sparkling wine made from German grapes. It is therefore on the same German quality level as *Deutscher Tafelwein* (German table wine). Like *Sekt*, it gains its bubbles from a second fermentation, mostly by the Charmat process, and again it must be cellared for six months prior to sale and have an alcohol level of ten percent or more.

- The fourth category, and the finest German *Sekt*, is '*Deutscher Sekt bA*'. It follows the same regulations and is on the same quality level as Germany's still *QbA* wines. That is, the wine must be made entirely from the grapes of one specified region, such as the Mosel or Rheingau. If a more specific area is quoted, such as Bernkastel or Johannisberg, at least 85 percent of the grapes used must come from this area and the remaining 15 percent must be of the same quality. The grape variety may only be stated if 85 percent or more of the *Sekt* is made from that variety. Two grape varieties may appear on the label provided the wine comes exclusively from those varieties. Similarly, a vintage may only be quoted if 85 percent or more of the *Sekt* comes from that vintage. The wine must be cellared for six months before sale and have an alcohol level of ten percent or more.

- *Deutscher Sekt* made by the *méthode champenoise* usually bears these words or the term '*Flaschengärung im champagnerverfahren*'. Both phrases may only appear on the label until 1994. The new term is likely to be '*traditionelle Flaschengärung*'.

- Transfer method sparklers are usually identified by the word '*Flaschengärung*' on the label.

- German sweetness levels correspond roughly to those of French wine and, in fact, the French terms are now more commonly used. They include: *Extra Herb*, for the driest styles; *Herb* or *brut*; *Extra Trocken*, *Extra Brut* or extra dry; *Trocken* or *sec*; *Halbtrocken* or *demi-sec*, and *Mild* or *Doux* for the sweetest.

Producers

Bernard-Massard CC/TM ★→
6–8 Jakobstrasse, Trier (Mosel-Saar-Ruwer)

Bernard-Massard's historic building in the middle of Trier is the headquarters of an operation that produces almost 600,000 cases of sparkling wine a year. The most up-market of these (transfer method and vintage-dated) are the Brut Riesling and Elbling from the Mosel-Saar-Ruwer and the Herrenklasse Riesling Trocken. A new, superior, Riesling Extra Brut Cuvée Zero, a non-*dosage* bubbly in a black bottle, from the single vineyard of Ockfener Bockstein in the Saar, was introduced in 1992. Tank-fermented wines include the silver-labelled Silver Cabinet Extra Dry plus the Graf von Luxemburg Halbtrocken. In addition to these brands, Bernard-Massard has the Royal, Cabinet, Tradition, Diamant and Grand Rouge sparklers – the last of these made from the red Spätburgunder grape. Caves Bernard-Massard in Luxembourg is a sister company. Bernard-Massard also turns some of the fine Friedrich-Wilhelm-Gymnasium estate's base wine into sparkling wine. The firm's '82 Scharzberger Riesling Trocken, with its warm, overripe fruit taste, backed up by some lime-juice-like Riesling character, is a good rather than great *Sekt*.

Black Tower CC ★
57 Mainzerstrasse, Bingen-Rhein (Rheinhessen)

Black Tower is an internationally-famous brand of (still) Liebfraumilch, but the sparkling version – an acceptable, sweet, bland wine – is less well known. This export house was founded in 1947 and is still owned by the Kendermann family.

Brenner'sches Weingut CC ★→
Pfandturmstrasse 20, Bechtheim (Rheinhessen)

A traditional, family-owned estate making a dry Riesling *Sekt* from 24 ha (59 acres), all in Bechtheim.

Brogsitter's zum Dom Herrenhof CC/MC ★
125 Walporzheimerstrasse, Walporzheim im Ahrtal (Ahr)

This historic wine house, complete with its equally historic Sankt Peter restaurant, has vineyards dating back to 1600. The Brogsitter family bought the establishment after the Second World War, and today uses bought-in base wine to make the majority of its annual 25,000 cases. The tank method is used for most of the *Sekt*s, which come in a wide range of styles, but a few are made by the *méthode champenoise*. The vintage-dated red Rotsek Brut and Blauer Spätburgunder are made from Ahr Spätburgunder. The firm also makes Astoria Brut, a Blanc de Blancs *Sekt* from Loire wines and a red *Halbtrocken Sekt*, Sankt Peter. The Dosage Zero Scharzberger Riesling uses Saar grapes, and there is a vintage-dated Riesling.

Burgeff   CC/TM   ★
Geheimrat-Hummel-Platz, Hochheim (Rheingau)
International drinks giant Seagram now owns Burgeff, which was founded in 1836. The leading brands include Schloss Hochheim and Burgeff Grün.

Winzergenossenschaft Burkheim   MC   ★
Winzerstrasse 8, Vogtsburg-Berkheim (Baden)
With 40 ha (100 acres) of vines planted predominantly to Pinot Blanc but with a little Pinot Gris, this Baden-based cooperative produces just 3,000 cases of a *méthode champenoise Sekt* that should be worth trying. Most is a blend of the two grapes sold under the Pinot Burkheimer Schlossgarten label, but a Pinot Blanc Brut and Extra Brut are also made. None is exported.

Deidesheim Sektkellerei   TM/CC
Bennstrasse 37–39, Deidesheim (Rheinpfalz)
Privately-owned, this cellar has 10 ha (25 acres) of Riesling vines at Deidesheim, which provide 10 percent of its 50,000-case needs. The transfer and Charmat methods are used and, although 60 percent of the wines are Riesling-based and 10 percent Chardonnay-based, their low price indicates that quality is not the best available. Royal C59 and the ultra dry Spezial Cuvée, supposedly the driest wine in Germany, are two of this Sektkellerei's sparklers.

Deinhard   CC   ★→★★
Deinhardplatz 3, Koblenz (Mittelrhein)
Star buy '79 Deinhard Lila Imperial Brut
Deinhard is the third largest *Sekt* producer in Germany and likes to

make much of the fact that it is the only *Sekt* firm with vineyard estates in three different areas – Oestrich, Deidesheim and Bernkastel. It is difficult to see the advantage this confers, for apart from a bit of estate wine in the *dosage*, the base wines for most of Deinhard's vast 3M-case production come from the Mittelrhein's 'four valleys' area. But where *Sekt* is concerned, sparkling wine-lovers should be grateful for anything, however small, which betokens quality. Eleven different wines are made at Deinhard's ultra-modern Wallersheim winery, close to Koblenz, which has a capacity of 27M litres. The down-market Cabinet, the main sparkler, is much admired on the local market, where 1.5M cases are downed annually; none is exported. It was introduced in 1888, but Deinhard's first *Sekt* appeared even earlier, in 1843. The non-vintage Lila Riesling is next in line. It has a pleasant, appley freshness and at least 50 percent Mittelrhein Riesling in its mix. One step up in quality and noticeably more 'Riesling' in style, is the vintage-dated Deinhard Tradition, a 100 percent Rhine Riesling *Sekt*. A Cabernet Sauvignon Rosé is also made. The top sparklers are the single-vineyard, vintage-dated Bernkasteler Doctor and Geheimrat 'J' Riesling *Sekt*s from Deinhard's own estates. Look out, too, for the firm's new, export-only, neutral, inoffensive, slightly spicy, baked apple-like Club de Brut and Chardonnay sparklers. All Deinhard sparklers are made by the *cuve close* method and are aged for 6–8 months on yeast.

Deutz & Geldermann   MC/CC/TM   ★→
Muggens-Turmstrasse 26, Breisach (Baden)
This famous champagne house opened a sparkling wine cellar in 1904. By 1925 Deutz & Geldermann's *Sektkellerei* had moved to Breisach. Today the Breisach operation (still owned by the French family, Lallier-Deutz) produces 166,000 cases of *Sekt*, of which most is sold under the Carte Blanche and BOB labels. Its other *méthode champenoise* sparklers include Carte Noire, a Rosé and a widely-admired Brut. Deutz has a cheaper transfer method sparkler which is sold under the Wappen von Breisach Grande Classe (*Extra Trocken*), Privat Cuvée (*Halbtrocken*), and Superb (*Trocken*) labels. Carte Rouge is also made by the transfer method. Somewhat disappointingly perhaps, the base wine for most of Deutz & Geldermann's production comes from the Loire, topped

up with a little Pinot Noir and Chardonnay from Trentino in northern Italy. Deutz & Geldermann claims to be the only *Sekt* house that is using the *méthode champenoise* on such a large scale.

Ewald Theod Drathen   CC   →★
Auf der Hill 4, Alf (Mosel-Saar-Ruwer)

'Cheap and cheerful' is obviously Herr Drathen's motto, for this house's specialities are Liebfraumilch, EC blended wines and the like. The firm was founded in 1860 and is still family owned. The best bet in the Drathen range is the Schloss Avras Halbtrocken, where the extra sweetness covers up what is obviously low-grade base wine to make a sweet and reasonably agreeable *Sekt*. Mosel Trocken is not pleasant, nor is the sweet Deutschherren Cuvée.

Winzergenossenschaft Durbach   TM/CC   ★
Nachtweide 2, Durbach (Baden)

With just over 4,000 cases produced here each year, this Baden coop is obviously more interested in still wines. However, three different Sekts are produced by Durbach, a basic transfer method Durbacher Edelmann plus the superior Durbacher Plauelrain Riesling and the Durbacher Kochberg Pinot Rosé, both made the *méthode champenoise*.

Winzergenossenschaft Ehrenstetten   CC   ★
Kirchbergstrasse 9, Ehrenkirchen (Baden)

Four different *Sekts* are made at this Baden cooperative; Weissburgunder and a pink Spätburgunder are the two priciest in the repertoire, with Gutedel from the Steinberg and Nobling from the Donnerwetter being marginally cheaper. With a little over 4,000 cases made annually, and use of slightly riper Baden grapes, quality should be good.

Faber Sektkellerei   CC   ★
Niederkircherstrasse 27, Trier (Mosel-Saar-Ruwer)

Most German *Sekt* firms use plenty of brands, but Faber, founded in 1952, manages to sell over 4M cases per annum of just two inexpensive wines. Krönung Halbtrocken, made from Trebbiano/ Ugni Blanc, is the biggest seller. The other wine, Rotlese Halbtrocken, is a red sparkler made from Merlot.

Gut Friedburg Sektkellerei   CC   ★
An der Friedburg, Rees
The Müller family make over 800,000 cases of Charmat method sparkling wine here every year in *Trocken* and *Halbtrocken* versions, plus a Riesling Trocken. Mondial Exclusiv is one of the Müllers' labels, but despite the name quality here is not great. Exports are to Germany, the UK, the Netherlands, Denmark and the USA.

Fürstlich Castell'sches Domänenamt   CC   ★
8711 Castell Unterfranken (Franken)
Two princes own this immaculately-kept estate. It is rare to find *Sekt* in Franken, but this castle on a hill makes one: Casteller Herrenberg.

Fürst von Metternich   TM/CC   ★★
Biebricher Allée 142, Wiesbaden (Rheingau)
Star buy Fürst von Metternich Extra Trocken
The Fürst von Metternich sparkling wine, of which over 650,000 cases are produced by Söhnlein Rheingold annually, is one of Germany's best. The Extra Trocken is made from Rheingau Riesling, part of which comes from the Prince von Metternich's Schloss Johannisberg estate. This *Sekt*'s intense, clean, classy, lime-juice-like Riesling character is worth seeking out, for it is one of the very few German sparklers with style.

Ernst Gebhardt Sektkellerei   CC/MC   ★
Hauptstrasse 21–23, Sommerhausen (Franken)
Gebhardt produces 25,000 cases of superior tank method Franken *Sekt* Extra Brut, sold under the varietal labels of Silvaner, Müller-Thurgau, Kerner and Scheurebe plus the more humdrum Rubin Privat and Privat Extra, made mostly from Italian base wine. Discerning drinkers should choose the Franken *Sekt* sparklers or the Privat Edel Brut, made from Elbling. Few exports. Look out for Gebhardt's new *méthode champenoise* Riesling *Sekt*.

Georges Geiling   CC/MC/TM   ★
Mainzerstrasse 18, Bacharach (Mittelrhein)
Georges Geiling has a long and interesting history dealing both with French and with German sparkling wines. In 1890, the firm supplied base wines in cask from Champagne to the German *Sekt*

industry. Today this family-owned company produces 41,000 cases of *Sekt* a year, most of it made by the transfer method, although a few special *cuvées* apparently stem from the *méthode champenoise*. Riesling from the Mittelrhein is the basis for most Geiling *cuvées* but wines from elsewhere, including some based on Chardonnay and Pinot Noir, are also used. Geiling is non-vintage since the firm wishes to produce consistent blends year in, year out. The silver-labelled Austern (oyster) *Sekt* is Rheingau Riesling, as is the Geiling Brut and the up-market Geiling 1890 Chardonnay. There is also a red Spätburgunder sparkler. The cheaper Geiling wines, such as the Hochgewächs, use a mix of Loire wine and Rheinpfalz Riesling. Privat uses Nahe Riesling plus wine from Bordeaux; Krone von Rheinhell is a blend of unspecified German and French wines. Special Cuvée and Cuvée Ultra Brut are two other Geiling brands.

Jakob Gerhardt   CC   ★
PO Box 59, Gerhardtshof, Nierstein (Rheinhessen)
This large Rhine *Sekt* house produces a wide range of sparklers as most big firms do. With 167,000 cases produced in most years, Jakob Gerhardt imports cheap French wine to turn into its most humdrum *Sekts*, reserving the German-grown Riesling, Silvaner, Scheurebe and Morio-Muskat for its classier blends.

Adam Gillot & Söhne   CC   ★
Wormserstrasse 84, Oppenheim (Rheinhessen)
A quarter of the requirements at this medium-sized concern are provided by 6 ha (15 acres) of Riesling and Silvaner vines for 42,000 cases of sparkling wines a year. The tank method sparklers include vintage-dated Riesling, Silvaner, Müller-Thurgau and Spätburgunder. Tastings are held in the firm's 1,000-year-old Huguenot cellar, with receptions in an old ice cellar deep in the Oppenheim hill. Gillot has a sister company in Champagne – Dominic Gillot.

Gräflich von Kageneck'sche
Wein- & Sektkellerei   TM/MC   ★→
Kupfertorstrasse 35, Breisach (Baden)
Owned exclusively by the vast ZBW cooperative cellar at Baden,

the cooperative uses both the transfer method and the *méthode champenoise*. Somewhat confusingly, it has given almost every varietal *Sekt* a separate brand name: Schloss Münzingen is made from Nobling and Weissburgunder, and there is a red *Extra Trocken* from Badische Rotgold. The Brut Badisch Rotgold sparkler is called Freiherr Heinrich and the *méthode champenoise* Müller-Thurgau, Greiffenegg Schlössle. Kageneck is another brand name here, available in Grauer Burgunder, Spätburgunder and Riesling versions. Riesling and Gutedel *Sekt*s are also made. The cooperative considers its Riesling sparkler to be its best and the vineyards will eventually be replanted with this variety. The *Extra Trocken* Riesling Schloss Munzingen has a good mousse and warm, hefty, green taste that many will enjoy.

Friedrich-Wilhelm-Gymnasium
See Bernard-Massard

Sektkellerei Hausen-Mabilon   MC   ★→
Im Staden 114–124, Saarburg (Mosel–Saar–Ruwer)
This 80-year-old firm draws a third of its total needs from 5 ha (12 acres) of vines. Mabilon Brut, Elbling and Extra Dry are the three different sparklers made here via the *méthode champenoise*. With sales of only 12,500 cases, most of the firm's production is drunk in Germany, although ten percent is regularly exported to Texas.

Henkell & Söhnlein Sektkellereien   CC   ★
Biebricher Allee 142, Wiesbaden (Rheingau)
Henkell first started making *Sekt* in 1856. Today it produces an amazing 7M-plus cases a year. Of these, 1M cases are Henkell Trocken – a sparkler that has become so popular throughout the world that many think it is actually the name of a company rather than a brand name. Henkell's early 20th century Henkellsfeld headquarters, with majestic reception rooms above and cellars below, are as impressive as the sales figures. Adam Henkell started it all and in honour of its founder the firm has introduced the smart black-bottled Adam Henkell Extra Brut. With such vast sales it is predictable that Henkell buys in its base wine from Germany, France and Italy. It is somewhat secretive about which wines are used for which blends but is prepared to admit that Riesling,

Silvaner, Chardonnay, Sauvignon, Chenin Blanc, Colombard, Folle Blanche, Pinot Noir and Trebbiano go into its blends. All the wines are made by the tank method, with the new Adam Henkell the most expensive, followed by Henkell Trocken, the red Kardinal plus the white and red Csárdás range. Cheapest of all are the Carstens S C, Ruttgers Club, Caprice and Schloss Biebrich sparklers. Henkell Trocken's ripe, slightly rubbery fruit taste is aggressive but acceptable, as is the sweet, dull, bland Henkell Brut.

Haus Hochheim   CC   ★
Rüdesheimerstrasse 17–19, Hochheim (Rheingau)
Hummel & Co's Hochheim *Sektkellerei* was established in 1884 and produces 83,000 cases of *Sekt* a year. These tank method sparklers are mostly made from bought-in German, French and Italian base wine. The Dry and Extra Dry are the most popular; other brands include Goldlack, Rotlack, Grünlack and Sonder Cuvée.

G C Kessler   TM/CC/MC   ★→
PO Box 150, Markplatz 22, Esslingen (Württemberg)
Kessler, still family run, is Germany's oldest *Sekt* producer, dating from 1826. The original Herr Kessler worked in Champagne for Veuve Clicquot. Kessler sparklers are made by the transfer method, those of subsidiary Gebrüder Weiss, by the tank method.

Kloss & Foerster   CC/MC   ★→
PO Box 31, Kaiserstrasse 4a, Rudesheim (Rheingau)
This family firm began to make sparkling wine in eastern Germany in the 1850s. Four generations later it is in the Rheingau and produces 84,000 cases of *Sekt* a year. The vintage-dated Wappen Trocken, Halbtrocken and red Wappen-Rot wines form the biggest range. Apart from the blended Wappen wines, most Foerster *Sekt* is made from Rheingau Riesling. Brands include Riesling Extra Dry, Bereich Johannisberg Rheingauer Riesling and Traditions-Sekt Halbtrocken. The firm uses the *méthode champenoise* for its Imperator Brut, Rüdesheimer Bischofsberg and red Assmannshäuser Steil sparklers. It makes Prinz von Preussen Brut from Schloss Reinhartshausen grapes, and the red Assmannshäuser Höllenberg from the Staatsweingut's (state cellars') Spätburgunder. Base wines from the Loire and Soave regions are also used.

Christian Adalbert Kupferberg   CC/TM/MC   ★→
Kupferberg-Terrasse 17–19, Mainz (Rheinhessen)

Kupferberg, one of the best-known German sparkling wine names, is somewhat secretive about exactly what goes into its best-selling Kupferberg Gold. Not altogether surprising perhaps, as it sells almost 800,000 cases of the stuff and does not want to give too much away to the competition. Christian Adalbert Kupferberg founded this firm in Mainz in 1850 and two years later was selling Kupferberg Gold, which makes it the oldest *Sekt* brand in Germany. Herr Kupferberg obviously understood the importance of exports, for until 1910 his *Sekt* sold more bottles in Britain than in Germany. Today Kupferberg produces 1M cases annually and makes a sweet red Blauer Spätburgunder besides the Gold. Rosé and transfer method Riesling *Sekt* are made plus the lesser Casino brand. Kupferberg became part of the large Racke wine and spirit group in 1979 and is proud of the fact that it is the only German *Sekt* house to own a champagne firm – Bricout & Koch in Avize. Every year, about 30,000 visitors come to taste the wines and admire the Roman and medieval cellars, the carved wooden casks, the art nouveau pavilion built for the 1900 Paris Exhibition, and the museum.

Langenbach   CC   →★
PO Box 1444, Am Ockenheimer Graben 35, Bingen-Kempten (Rheinhessen)

Julius Langenbach founded this firm in 1852, at Worms. Langenbach makes much of its part ownership of the original Liebfrauenkirche vineyards that surround the Church of our Lady at Worms. It was these vineyards that produced the first *liebfrauenmilc* or 'milk of our lady', better known today as Liebfraumilch (and coming, it seems, from everywhere). Langenbach makes a wide range of tank method *Sekt*. The styles include the vintage-dated Waldracher Riesling and Goldlack Riesling Brut plus the non-vintage Schloss Leutstetten, Sparkling Crown of Crowns, Silver Crown and Weisslack, besides sweet Schloss Dalberg and red Purpur made from the Spätburgunder grape. The silver-labelled Silver Crown, originally launched in 1952 to celebrate the company's centenary, is, sadly, to be avoided. The gold-labelled Crown of Crowns *Sekt* with its curious, sweet, tutti-frutti taste, is just acceptable, showing a family resemblance to Crown of Crowns Liebfraumilch.

Moselland Winzergenossenschaft MC ★→
Bornwiese, Bernkastel-Kues (Mosel–Saar–Ruwer)

The giant Moselland cooperative now has 4,800 members in the Mosel-Saar-Ruwer region but only produces 17,000 cases of *Sekt* annually. Riesling and Elbling are the grapes that go into the *Sekts* and these are sold under four different labels: Nigra, Nigra Imperial, Schloss Lieser and Komturei. Schloss Lieser is a Mosel Riesling Sekt, Komturei a Saar Riesling one, and Nigra Imperial a 'Premium Riesling' Extra Brut looks like being the coop's best sparkler. All are made by the *méthode champenoise* and are thus a cut above the ordinary.

Matheus Müller CC ★
Matheus–Müller–Platz 1, Eltville (Rheingau)

Seagram is obviously happy to keep on expanding its German interests, since this 1836 firm was taken over by it in 1984. 'MM Extra', the firm's best-known sparkler, gets its bubbles via the *cuve clos* method.

Rudolf Müller CC/MC ★→★★
PO Box 20, Küferstrasse 6, Reil (Mosel–Saar–Ruwer)
Star buy '84 Mosel Riesling Extra Dry

Best known for its Bishop or Riesling still wine, this firm also produces a wide range of *Sekt*s. The cheaper versions, based on a blend of Italian, Spanish and German base wines, are sold under the Splendid label in Halbtrocken, Trocken and Cuvée Mild versions. Two fancier, vintage-dated Riesling-based sparklers are also available, the Wwe Dr H Thanisch, Müller Burggraef Brut from the family's own 1 ha (3 acre) single vineyard at Lieserer Niederberg-Helden in the Mosel and the Mosel Riesling Extra Dry. The new Rhein-Cuvée Brut is a less classy blend of Riesling, Silvaner and Müller-Thurgau from the Rhine. For a firm that did not start making sparkling wine until 1956, Müller's current annual *Sekt* production of over 700,000 cases is impressive. Dr Thanisch, Müller's most expensive sparkler, is now a *méthode champenoise* wine. Müller's splendid Halbtrocken is a popular, inoffensive fizz, sweet and fruity, but the real star here is the vintage-dated Mosel Riesling Extra Dry. The '84 vintage was a delicious, ripe, elegant, flowery-appley Riesling, made from fine fruit. As such it is probably Germany's finest *Sekt*.

Weingut Prinz von Hessen   TM/MC   ★
Grund 1, Johannisberg (Rheingau)

Now owned by the Landgrave (Marquis) of Hessen, this Riesling estate produces 4,000 cases of a *Sekt* called Kurhessen. Two transfer method sparklers – an *Extra Trocken* and a Spätburgunder Weissherbst account for most of this, but a magnum version plus the superior Johannisberger Hölle Riesling Qualitätssekt are both made by the *méthode champenoise*.

Ludwig Rilling   CC   ★
Brückenstrasse 2–18, Stuttgart (Württemberg)

Roman remains were found when the Rilling cellar was being built, but there appears to be little that is traditional about Rilling today. The tank method is used to make over 300,000 cases of numerous different sparklers including Schloss Rosenstein, Rilling LR, Resed, Sabinchen, Rosé, Rubin, Moscato and Diadem. Better quality wines are the Bereich Kaiserstuhl from Baden plus the Württemberger Trollinger and Riesling. Finer still are the Brut de Brut and Jubilar plus the other vintage-dated, mostly Riesling-based wines bearing the Hochgewächs stamp. No *Sekt* is exported.

Ritterhof   CC   ★→
Weinstrasse Nord 51, Bad Dürkheim (Rheinpfalz)

The Fitz family has owned the Ritterhof *Sektkellerei*, the third-oldest *Sekt* cellar in Germany, since 1837. The associated Fitz-Ritter estate supplies half of Ritterhof's grapes; Riesling is the main variety. The remainder comes from elsewhere in the Rheinpfalz. Most of the 16,000-case production is Ritterstolz, an ultra-dry sparkler suitable for diabetics. Ritterhof Riesling Trocken and Brut are also on offer, plus red Dürkheimer Feuerberg Halbtrocken Sekt.

Schloss Affaltrach   CC   →★
Am Ordensschloss 15–21, Obersulm (Württemberg)

Over 52,000 cases of tank method wine are made at the Schloss each year. Most is made from imported French and Italian base wine, but Baumann Riesling, in its Extra Dry and Brut versions, is 100 percent Württemberg Riesling. The Franco-Italian wines come in Brillant, Diamant, Smaragd, and a red, or *Rubin*, version. Schloss Affaltrach also produces the Burg Löwenstein sparkler.

Schloss Rheingarten   CC   ★
Geisenheim (Rheingau)
The current Hallgarten Vater & Söhne, whose firm was founded in the Rheingau in 1898 and in London in 1933, must be as well-known today as its ancestors were. Schloss Rheingarten is its bland, sweet, acceptable *cuve close* sparkler.

Schloss Saarfels Sektkellerei   MC   ★→
Domänenstrasse 37, Serrig (Saar)
Schloss Saarfels turns Riesling and Weisserburgunder into almost 11,000 cases of *Sekt* annually, using the *méthode champenoise*. The range includes Trocken, Brut Extra, Edelmarke (Halbtrocken) and a Trocken *Sekt* known as 'Aus dem Felsverlies'. Other *Sekt* brands include Scharzhofberger Trocken, plus the vintage-dated Staadter Maximiner Pralat Brut.

Schloss Vaux   TM/MC   ★
Kiedricher Strasse 18, Eltville (Rheingau)
Founded in Berlin in 1868, the firm bought Château de Vaux near Metz in Alsace Lorraine in 1883, hence its name. Production stands at 30,000 cases of *Sekt* a year, made both by the *méthode champenoise* and by the transfer method. The Riesling-based Schloss Vaux *méthode champenoise* sparklers sold under a variety of regional names are the best. The cheaper transfer method wines are sold under the straight Schloss Vaux label. Schloss Vaux Chardonnay should also be worth trying too.

Schloss Wackerbarth   CC/MC   ★
Sachsisches Staats-Weingut, Radebeul (Sachsen)
Another large German cooperative cellar, whose 167,000 cases of *Sekt* are made by the Charmat method and the *méthode champenoise*. August der Starke is a Charmat method wine; *méthode champenoise* Graf von Wackerbarth is the top fizz. Quality is ordinary.

Hermann Schnaufer   CC   ★
PO Box 27, Althengstett (Württemberg)
Most of the 208,000 cases of *Sekt* made here annually are sold under the Lichtenstein Halbtrocken, Trocken and Riesling Trocken labels. Other tank method *Sekt*s are Württemberg Riesling Trocken and Baden Riesling. Pricky Ananas and Pfirsich Royal are fruit-flavoured sparklers.

Hermann Freiherr von Schorlemer   CC   ★→
Cusanusstrasse 14, Bernkastel-Kues (Mosel-Saar-Ruwer)
This collection of Mosel estates, once owned by the von Schorlemer family, now belongs to Meyer-Horne. The production of *Sekt* is small, but various sparkling Rieslings from the estates are sold.

Sichel Söhne   CC   ★
Werner von Siemenstrasse 14–18, Alzey (Rheinhessen)
It had to happen, of course. Once the famous Blue Nun had visited 81 different countries, Sichel had to come up with something different, so Sparkling Blue Nun was re-launched. Today, the slightly re-styled wine has been made fractionally sweeter to appear closer in style to Blue Nun Liebfraumilch, but its sweet, bland, fruity taste presents little to get worked up about.

Weinbau Sick   MC   ★
Bundesstrasse 3, Emmendingen-Mundingen (Württemberg)
Better known as the producer of cellar machinery, especially the paraphernalia of *Sekt* production, the firm also makes 5,000 bottles of its own sparkling wine every year. The '84 Mundinger Alte Burg is an *Extra Trocken* Riesling *Sekt* made by the *méthode champenoise*.

Söhnlein Rheingold   CC   ★→
Söhnleinstrasse 1–8, Wiesbaden-Schierstein (Rheingau)
The firm that produces the Fürst von Metternich sparkling wine also makes sparklers of its own. Söhnlein Brillant is the best known, but Söhnlein Rheingold, launched in 1876 by Richard Wagner, a friend of the Söhnlein family, is still going strong.

Otto Treis   CC/MC   ★→
Haupstrasse 58, Zell-Merl (Mosel-Saar-Ruwer)

Theodor Treis founded this firm in 1810 and today it is still a family-run business. The tank method and bottle-fermented sparklers are 100 percent Riesling, which is alas still something of a rarity in Germany today. As usual, numerous different sparkling wine brands are made. Apart from the Kongressmarke Schaumwein, the *Sekt*s include Cabinet plus Möselchen and Moselgold, Tradition, Rotlack and a Saar-Riesling.

Verband Deutscher Sektkellereien
Sonnenbergerstrasse 46, Wiesbaden (Rheingau)

Members of this giant association of German sparkling wine producers account for about 98 percent of the country's total sparkling wine production.

Vereinigung Sektguter Rheinpfalz   MC/CC   ★
Siebeldingen (Rheinpfalz)

These *Sekt*s appear in distinctive black bottles complete with stylish, red and white VSR labels. Two different types are made: the tank method, pink Blauer Spätburgunder and Weisserburgunder made from Chardonnay and Riesling repectively, plus the same grapes turned into fizz by the obviously superior *méthode champenoise*. Like most producers associations, VSR also makes a dozen different *Sekt*s under its growers' own labels.

Verwaltung der
Staatlichen Weinbaudomänen   CC/MC   ★→
Niederhausen-Schlossböckelheim, 6551 Oberhausen (Mosel-Saar-Ruwer)

The King of Prussia founded this estate in 1896. Today, its vast vaulted cellars produce not quite 6,000 cases of five different Riesling-based *Sekt*s of which three, including Domäne Ockfen plus the Saar-Riesling Sekt in both Trocken and Brut, styles are made by the *méthode champenoise*. The other two, the Ockfener Bockstein and Serriger Vogelsang *Sekt*s are tank method sparklers. The distinctive black eagle on all the labels is impossible to miss.

Other German Sparkling Wine Producers:

Peter Herres, Trier (Mosel-Saar-Ruwer); G H Mumm (Rheingau); Schloss Böchingen, Böchingen (Rheingau); Schloss Wachenheim Sektkellerei (Rheinpfalz); Sektkellerei Spicka (Mosel-Saar-Ruwer); Winzersekt, Sprendlingen (Rheinhessen).

Note: The the new German post codes, effective from 1 July 1993, were not available at the time of going to press, and for this reason the addresses in this section appear without codes.

Austria

Even if one makes allowances for the Austrian wine industry's tragic problems during the past decade, it is hard to explain the disappointingly low standards in sparkling wine production.

Austria's chief obstacle to producing first class sparkling wine is a lack of suitable grape varieties. Austria's climate should not be a drawback for if Alsace, on a similar latitude, can produce good sparkling wines, then so can Austria. Yet the grape most widely used is the Welschriesling (alias the Italian Riesling), which with its low acidity and dull flavours is not the ideal sparkling wine base. Nor is Austria's earthy, peppery Grüner Veltliner much better. Things are looking up however, for at least one Austrian *Sekt* house is using Pinot Blanc, a relative of Chardonnay, and Riesling *Sekt* is on the increase too.

As if to add to their problems, to create the 21M bottles of *Sekt* produced annually, most Austrian *Sekt* houses buy in base wine rather than make their own, thereby losing control over quality at a vital stage. Few firms, apart from the small-scale producers, use any method other than *cuve close*. If the *méthode champenoise* is too time consuming and expensive, what about the transfer method?

Vienna is the sparkling wine capital of Austria, partly perhaps because there are plenty of festive occasions here at which to drink it. Falkenstein and Poysdorf, a district to the north of Vienna, produces most of Austria's sparklers. Vienna, unlike other cities, where vineyards have been grubbed up in favour of urban sprawl, was sensible enough to allow vineyards within the city limits – and to keep many of them. *Heurigen*, or wine inns, were the logical result of these Viennese vineyards. Most deal in youthful, still wines although several have their own sparklers too.

With such keen local customers and enthusiastic export markets, Austria's *Sekt* firms should do better in the future.

Austrian Sparkling Wine Labels and the Law

The Austrian wine law of November 1985 introduced stringent new legislation, part of which relates to *Sekt*. (In Austria the term '*Schaumwein*' is interchangeable with *Sekt*.)

- Sparkling wine sold as Osterreichischer *Sekt* must be made exclusively from Austrian wine.

- If any Austrian *Sekt* specifies a vintage or region it must come entirely from that vintage or region.

- Apart from the basic Osterreichischer *Sekt* there is a superior category of Austrian sparkling wine known as *Qualitätssekt* or *Qualitätsschaumwein*. This must contain ten percent alcohol and gain its sparkle via the tank method or *méthode champenoise* and not by the carbonated method. *Qualitätsschaumwein* must be kept on yeast for an extended period and be cellared for nine months prior to sale.

- At the other end of the quality scale, all carbonated Austrian wine must bear the following words prominently on the label '*mit Kohlensäure versetzt*' ('carbon dioxide has been added').

- Most Austrian *Sekt* (some 66 percent in 1993) is made by the tank method but the words '*méthode classique champenoise*' or '*nach traditioneller Champagnermethode*' on a bottle denote a genuine *méthode champenoise* wine.

- Austria usually uses the French terms for sweetness levels, but also expect to see '*Trocken*' for *sec*, '*Halbtrocken*' or '*Halbsüss*' for *demi-sec*. However, the amount of sweetness allowed is significantly lower in Austria than in the EC.

Producers

Karl Inführ   CC   ★→
Albrechtstrasse 127, A-3402 Klosterneuburg

Königssekt or King's Sekt is the most famous sparkling wine of this firm, which was founded in 1949 and today makes 167,000 cases a year, besides contract bottling for many others. Königssekt is made by the cooperative at Gumpoldskirchen using Spätrot Rotgipfler grapes. Similarly, the coop at Dürnstein in the Wachau supplies the Rhine Riesling that goes into Ritter von Dürnstein, the firm's oldest and most expensive sparkler. 'Darling Sekt' made from the Grüner Veltliner and Welschriesling, complete with a Queen of Hearts label, does well pre-Christmas and on Valentine's Day. Poste de Vienne, made from the Samling '88 grape is another famous Inführ wine, while *Sekts* such as Le Grand Rouge, Excellent, Pinot Blanc and the fruit-based sparklers, including the strawberry variety, are perhaps less well known. Karl Inführ also makes a bone-dry sparkling wine that is suitable for consumption by diabetics.

Johann Kattus   TM/CC   ★
Am Hof 8, A-1010 Vienna

Since 1857, four generations of the Kattus family have been involved in wine. Johann Kattus II founded the Kattus *Sekt* cellar and established the Hochriegel brand name. The name means 'high hill' and refers to a vineyard owned by the family before the Second World War. Johann Kattus's heyday was probably during the Austro-Hungarian empire, when Hochriegel was served at both the imperial and the royal court. Today it is unlikely that even humble palates will greatly enjoy the curious, sherbety Hochriegel Grosser Jahrgang Brut or the similarly sweetshop-like bouquet of the Alte Reserve. However, Hochriegel's gold foil Trocken Sekt, with its big, somewhat oily taste is worth trying. New here are the *frizzante* wines in white and rosé. Kattus is the second largest *Sekt* producer in Austria.

Hans Kirchmayr   CC/MC   ★
A-3351 Weistrach 123

Producers of *Sekt* and still wine as the name suggests, this house was founded in 1936. With only ten percent of Hans Kirchmayr's production devoted to sparkling wines, the annual turn out of *Sekt* here is just 5,000 cases. The firm's most basic fizz, Mostviertler Obstschaumwein is a *cuve close* wine made from pears and only sold in a *demi-sec* version. More interesting is the Abteisekt Brut and Extra Dry, and the Die Erfüllung Extra Dry *Sekts* based on Grüner Veltliner and made by the *méthode champenoise*. Rieslingsekt is the cellar's best bubbly.

Brüder Kleinoscheg   MC   ★→
Anton Kleinoschegstrasse 66, A–8051 Graz
One of a handful of *méthode champenoise* producers in Austria, this firm sells its wines made by this method under three different labels: Herzogmantel, Goldmark and Derby.

Chorherren Klosterneuburg
Stiftsweingut   CC   ★→★★
Am Renninger 2, A–3400 Klosterneuburg
The Augustine monastery of Klosterneuburg was founded in 1108 by Duke Leopold. Close by is the majestic baroque palace built in 1730 by the devout Emperor Karl VI. Its vast cellars date from this period too. Like many monasteries, Klosterneuburg cultivated vines and made wine from the time of its foundation. Today Klosterneuburg owns 100 ha (247 acres) of vines in four different regions, but only 30 percent of its own grapes are used in the annual production of 33,000 cases of Klostersekt. Grüner Veltliner backed up by a little Riesling, make up the Klostersekt *Trocken* and *Halbsüss Sekts* (complete with gold and silver foils). The Trocken version enjoys a good although slightly simplistic Grüner Veltliner taste, and is clean, peppery and drinkable, whereas the bronze-labelled Rosé made from the St-Laurent grape has a worrying blue-pink colour but a pleasant, albeit unexciting, sweet, fruity taste. The real Klosterneuburg treat, however, is the '83 Grand Reserve Brut made from the Pinot Blanc. Ignore its ridiculous label and concentrate instead on the rich, full-bodied, pineappley Pinot Blanc flavour coupled with that traditional, spicy, peppery Austrian finish.

Krems Winzergenossenschaft   CC   ★
Sandgrube 13, A-3500 Krems

Historic Krems with its onion-tower churches and pretty houses overlooking the Danube is one of the most attractive parts of the Wachau. The cooperative or Winzergenossenschaft, founded in 1938, is efficiently run and uses just five percent of its 1,900 members' 900 ha (2,224 acres) at Krems for its sparkling wine production. Since 1977 it has produced about 17,000 cases every year of Haus Osterreich sparkling wine made from Rhine Riesling and Grüner Veltliner grapes in *Trocken*, *Halbtrocken* and *Extra Brut* versions. All are made by the *cuve close* method. Champion is a new medium-dry Grüner Veltliner-based Krems fizz. Haus Osterreich's Extra Brut, a 100 percent Rhine Riesling blend, is probably the coop's best cuvée.

Gerald Malat   MC   ★
Lingengasse 27, A-3511 Palt

Just 5 ha (12 acres) of Gerald and Wilma Malat's vines are turned into *Sekt* each year but quality is high. Based on Chardonnay, Pinot Blanc and Pinot Noir, there are three styles, all made via the *méthode champenoise*: Brut de Brut (a non-*dosage* wine), Rosé (made entirely from Pinot Noir), and the Prestige edition – as the name suggests, probably the best of the trio.

Lenz Moser Weinkellerei   CC   ★
Lenz Moser Strasse 1, A-3495 Rohrendorf bei Krems

This firm's pretty, ornately-gabled Imperial Yellow winery has been the leading Austrian *Weingut* (wine-producing estate) since the firm's foundation in 1849. The original cellars date back apparently to 970–980 AD and the Moser family, now no longer the owner, seems to have been involved in wine almost as long. The 25,000 cases of Moser sparkling wine are made from Grüner Veltliner and Welschriesling grapes grown mainly at the Schlossweingut Malteser Ritterorden, the estate of the Knights of Malta, and are sold under the Malteser Brut label. In addition there is the cheaper, probably more Welschriesling-based, Lenz Moser Brut Sekt which accounts for the majority of sparkling wine production here. All Moser sparklers are now consumed in Austria.

P M Mounier   MC   ★→
Heiligenstädter Strasse 35–43, A-1031 Vienna

Mounier is one of the very few Austrian *Sekt* firms still to use the old-fashioned *méthode champenoise*. Four different styles, Brut, Sec, Demi-sec and Rouge, are made of the straight Mounier bubbly, mostly from Welschriesling topped up with a little Grüner Veltliner. The vintage-dated Cuvée 262, made from the nobler Rhine Riesling, is rather more stylish. With 18 months minimum on yeast and available in a wide range of sizes, up to a Balthasar (16-bottle capacity), Mounier sparklers are worth seeking out and should have better distribution now they are owned by SCHLUMBERGER. Look out for the Pinot Noir-based wines here.

Ritter   CM   ★
Schloss Raggendorf, A-2215 Raggendorf

The Schlosskellerei Erwin Klenkhart is in the small print at the bottom of most Ritter labels. Half a million cases are produced in most years, including the young, fresh Ritter Trocken, Halbtrocken and Rosé wines, and the superior Extra Cuvée Brut and Extra Cuvée Trocken. The Klenkhart family also produces the grander-sounding Château Raggendorf Classic Brut – a reminder that the family has been at Schloss Raggendorf since 1870. Grüner Veltliner, Welschriesling and Chardonnay are the varieties used. A range of fruit-flavoured fizz is also produced.

Schlumberger   MC   ★→★★
Heiligenstädter Strasse 35–43, A-1190 Vienna

In 1842 Robert Schlumberger gave up his job in a leading champagne house to live and work in his Austrian wife's country. He quickly acquired vineyards in Bad Vöslau, south of Vienna, and began to make *méthode champenoise* wines. Today Schlumberger's *méthode champenoise* sparklers spend about 18–30 months on yeast in the firm's extensive cellars in Vienna before being disgorged. Schlumberger does not actually own vineyards but buys in base wine from about 100 contract growers in the Poysdorf region of the Weinviertel, just as it has done for the last 60 years. Welschriesling is the basis of all Schlumberger sparklers, but a little Grüner Veltliner is used too. Underberg, the giant German drinks company, bought out Schlumberger in 1973 and sales went up from 125,000 cases in 1986 to 417,000 in 1993, with enlarged cellars and automatic *remuage* part of the new regime. While this sounds encouraging, many feel that Austria's oldest sparkling wine producer should concentrate more on quality rather than quantity. Recently Schlumberger's non-vintage Brut made from Welschriesling, has had an earthy, perfumed, lemony character that is not really good enough for Austria's most important and prestigious *Sekt* house. The Goldeck Trocken with its fine, fruity taste, a blend of Grüner Veltliner and Welschriesling is surprisingly sweeter (and spends one rather than two years on yeast). But again, worryingly, it has a slightly dank finish that should not be there. Schlumberger makes a vintage-dated Ultra Brut and a Rosé, the Goldeck Privat and Halbsüss and red Don Giovanni sparklers, as well as producing an Austrian version of the French wine Blanc Foussy under licence for the home market only. Its finest blend must be the Weissburgunder (Pinot Blanc) based Cuvée Victoria. To celebrate the firm's 150th anniversary, Schlumberger launched Jubiläums-Cuvée in a bottle similar to the one the house used first, in 1842.

Siegendorf   CC   ★→
Rathausplatz 12, A–7011 Siegendorf
Siegendorf, founded in 1860 and owned by the Patzenhofer family, enjoys a good reputation both for its still and for its few sparkling wines. Siegendorf's *Sekt* is made by the *cuve close* method and sold under the Imperial label.

Winzerhaus Weinvertriebsges Niederösterreich MC ★
Simmeringer Hauptstrasse 54, A–1110 Vienna
The Winzerhaus cooperative's distinctive emblem graces a wide range of Lower Austria sparklers. Founded in 1898, with 6,000 growers and 400 ha (988 acres), some devoted to the production of sparklers, Winzerhaus is now an important Austrian sparkling wine concern. Its vineyards are planted around Poysdorf in the Weinviertel, principally to Welschriesling and Grüner Veltliner, but now, encouragingly, with 10 percent Chardonnay too. Winzersekt Brut is the biggest brand, but there are reasonable quantities of the Marsoner & Gutmann Cuvée No 87 and Winzerhaus Frizzante Furioso. The last of these is a 40 percent

Chardonnay, 60 percent Welschriesling blend. Production stands at 8,000 cases of *Sekt* per annum.

R Zimmermann   CC   ★
Agnesstrasse 46b, A–3400 Klosterneuburg

Zimmermann makes three sparkling wines: Zimmermann Extra Dry (made from Welschriesling), Charpentier Blaufränkisch Rosé and the vintage-dated Charpentier Brut made from Pinot Blanc. Zimmermann has *heurigen* at Grinzing and Klosterneuburg. It makes just over 9,000 cases per annum of *cuve close* Osterreichischer *Sekt*. Charpentier Brut is Zimmermann's finest sparkling wine.

California

The USA is afloat on a sea of bubbles, consuming about 140M bottles of California sparkling wine a year, to say nothing of the annual tidal waves from Italy (38M bottles), France (18M bottles, of which more than two-thirds is champagne), and Spain (16M bottles). All over the country, despite the troublesome economy of the 1990s, corks have been popping with increasing frequency at functions from modest brunches and pool-side barbecues to grand banquets.

Americans, it seems, despite the anti-alcohol lobby and prohibitively high sparkling wine sales tax, need little excuse to crack open a bottle of bubbly, whether it be the rarefied heights of DPR – Dom Pérignon Rosé – or the distinctly ordinary yet phenomenally successful André from E & J Gallo.

The rate of growth may have slowed down slightly in the last few years but sales are still healthy, for production of California's own sparklers has doubled during the last decade and imports of champagne have trebled in the same period.

American sparklers (of which the vast majority is produced in California) can be divided into two camps: The original 'American champagnes' are typified by the sweet, tutti-frutti Korbel wines and the full-flavoured, hefty Hanns Kornells. The second camp comprises firms aiming to imitate French champagne. Many are succeeding. The arrival in California of seven *grandes marques* champagne houses confirms, and at the same time pays the highest compliment to, the starry goals of the second group. Other champagne firms such as Laurent-Perrier are on the way, it is rumoured, either joining forces with American firms, as Piper-Heidsieck did in founding Piper Sonoma, or else going it alone like Domaine Chandon and Roederer. The latest arrival is Taittinger, which has linked with the American Kobrand group to form Domaine Carneros. Spanish *cava* expertise has also arrived with Freixenet, which now has almost a decade of Gloria Ferrer sparklers under its belt, and Codorniu Napa producing the first few vintages.

Some California *méthode champenoise* concerns have had time to build up experience: Schramsberg was founded in 1965 and Domaine Chandon in 1973. But most California winemakers are still puzzling over the intricacies of the *méthode champenoise* process.

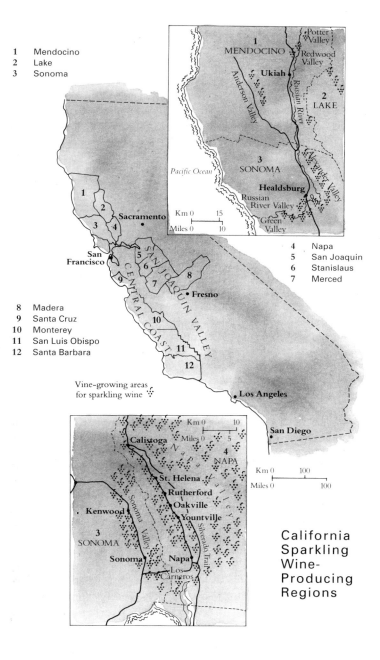

1 Mendocino
2 Lake
3 Sonoma

4 Napa
5 San Joaquin
6 Stanislaus
7 Merced

8 Madera
9 Santa Cruz
10 Monterey
11 San Luis Obispo
12 Santa Barbara

Vine-growing areas
for sparkling wine

California
Sparkling
Wine-
Producing
Regions

Selecting suitable grape varieties is still a problem: the big, bouncy character of most California Chardonnay gives excessively strong fruit-salad flavours. Pinot Noir is much more successful, albeit giving a rosy-tinted product, but is not always easy to find – California is thought to have three different grape varieties masquerading as the authentic Pinot Noir. Attempts to tone down excessive varietal flavour with bland, high-acid varieties such as Pinot Blanc (in California, alas, often confused with the humble Muscadet grape, the Melon de Bourgogne) have also not always worked.

The ideal places for growing sparkling wine grapes have not yet been entirely sorted out. Napa and Sonoma have had their successes, especially in their shared region, Carneros. Chardonnay, and especially Pinot Noir, grown in the Carneros district are much sought after by California's top winemakers, who are also prepared to pay a heavy premium for these grapes. Taittinger's arrival here was yet another demonstration of this district's superiority. The cool Anderson, Redwood and Potter valleys of Mendocino, farther north, where newcomer Roederer is situated, could turn out to be the finest areas of all.

Comparative work on first- and second-fermentation yeast strains has not yet been completed by the experiment-crazy Californians, although at least half the industry uses an efficient Moët & Chandon yeast generously supplied by Domaine Chandon to its competitors. The time spent *en tirage* (on yeast) also varies, from about 12–18 months to as long as seven years for Reserve wines. *Dosage* trials are also still in the early stages, with most firms using half the accepted French *dosage* levels. There is concern too about the use of brandy in the *dosage*. Important firms such as Schramsberg and Chateau St-Jean are in favour of brandy, whilst others such as Iron Horse are opposed to any *dosage* at all, although they occasionally allow a little 'polishing' of the wine to take place by blending back some of the same wine.

The use of reserve wines in blending is contentious. Domaine Chandon is perhaps the chief protagonist, blending up to 15 percent of older reserves into its non-vintage wine. It is thought that Roederer has followed suit. USA wine laws, unlike the French equivalent, can hardly be said to help the reserve wine devotee, for any sparkler with more than five percent of wine from another vintage in its blend cannot be sold as a vintage product. At least the use of gyropalettes for automatic *remuage* seems to be meeting with universal approval, with Domaine Chandon using the aptly-named VLMs, or Very Large Machines, and Piper-Sonoma conventional gyropalettes.

It is been difficult in this section to recommend specific vintages, for, like most New World countries, California has only released a handful of sparkling wine vintages and their supremacy, or staying power, is in many cases as yet unproved. To have come so far so quickly does however mean that whatever else may happen California, and indeed America, look set for a sparkling future.

USA Sparkling Wine Labels and the Law

- Although any sparkling wine in California and elsewhere can still be called 'champagne', new, welcome regulations from 1993 now mean that all USA tank and transfer method sparklers must specify their production method on the label. Terms such as 'Charmat method', 'bulk process', 'fermented outside the bottle' and 'not fermented in the bottle', plus 'secondary fermentation outside the bottle' or 'secondary fermentation before bottling', indicate these styles of wine.

- Genuine *méthode champenoise* sparkling wines need not specify their production method on the label, but in practice often

Wente Bros' restored, 19th century property, Cresta Blanca

do. These wines will increasingly carry the new 'traditional method' or '*méthode traditionnelle*' tag.

- The words 'sparkling wine' or 'sparkling white wine', standing alone on the label, indicate that the wine has been made by one of the lesser methods, such as the bulk method or the transfer method. This process will be specified on the label.

- 'Crackling wine', '*perlant* wine' and '*frizzante* wine' denote a sparkling wine usually with less effervescence than 'champagne' or other sparkling wines.

- 'Carbonated wine' indicates a sparkling wine that has gained its bubbles from artificial carbonation rather than a natural second fermentation.

- The sweetness levels – *brut*, *sec* and *demi-sec* – tend to vary from brand to brand. Any wine designated 'natural', however, should have no *dosage*.

Producers

Adler Fels   MC   ★
5325 Corrick Road, Santa Rosa, CA 95409
This small, family-run winery, on a steep Mayacamas Mountain slope, with a bird's eye view of the Sonoma Valley, is obviously keen to stress its international connections. The tiny amounts of bone-dry Gewürztraminer/Rhine Riesling *méthode champenoise* wine produced here are sold under the Melange à Deux label. The winery name is derived from the German for Eagle Rock – a nearby landmark.

Almaden Vineyards   TM   ★
1530 Blossom Hill Road, San Jos
Founded in 1852, Almaden today produces more than half a million cases of basic transfer method wine from thousands of hectares in San Benito and Monterey. Pink-toned Eye of the Partridge, Le

Domaine, Golden Champagne and other Almaden sparklers have their devotees in the home market. European palates, however, much prefer the still California Chardonnay produced as a joint venture with Laurent-Perrier of France and sold as Caves Laurent-Perrier Chardonnay. Sadly, this has been discontinued due, no doubt, to the new joint venture Sonoma vineyard enterprise between Laurent-Perrier and IRON HORSE.

S Anderson Vineyard   MC   ★★
1473 Yountville Cross Road, Yountville, CA 94599
California determination and grit enable Los Angeles dentist Stanley Anderson and his Davis-trained wife Carol to work at weekends at their small Napa winery. They have now been joined by son John and his wife Tracy, who run the business. Production, which stands at under 7,000 cases annually, is still tiny compared with other wineries. But quality is high due to the family's insistence on only the first pressings of grapes from Carneros and Stags Leap districts being used, plus lengthy yeast-ageing (3–7 years) and hand riddling and disgorging. Impressive rock-hewn cellars here are surrounded by 16 ha (40 acres) of mostly Chardonnay plus some Pinot Noir and Pinot Blanc. Of their released vintages the fresh, yeasty-smoky Blanc de Noirs, a 100 percent Pinot Noir wine, is worthwhile, but eventually production will concentrate on a 60 percent Pinot Noir, 40 percent Chardonnay vintage *brut* blend. Tivoli Brut Noir, 85 percent Pinot Noir, 15 percent Chardonnay, is a lesser Anderson fizz.

André
See E & J Gallo

Beaulieu Vineyard   MC   ★★
1960 St Helena Highway, Rutherford, CA 94573
Grand old California wineman André Tchelistcheff supervised the first BV sparkling blend in 1952 and since then these wines have been served by every American President from Roosevelt to Reagan. European palates, however, are likely to have found past BV sparklers agreeable rather than exceptional. Quality, however, should have stepped up here due to BV's new 8 ha-vineyard (20 acres) for sparkling wine in Carneros, planted to 60 percent Pinot

Noir and 40 percent Chardonnay. Just over 1,000 cases of Domaine Beaulieu Cuvée de Carneros are made each year by hand. Encouragingly, this new release spends five years on yeast before being disgorged and part of the base wine is aged in small French oak barrels to create a dry, more full-bodied style.

Jacques Bonet   CC →★
Italian Swiss Colony, 490 Second Street, San Francisco
This ordinary, inexpensive, bulk method sparkler from Italian Swiss Colony is probably the closest competitor to GALLO's André. It is a mass-market wine with no finesse and the sweet and somewhat flabby Lejon Brut is similar. A range of flavoured 'champagnes' is also sold under the Jacques Bonet label.

J F J Bronco Winery   CC   →★
PO Box 789, 6342 Bystrum Road, Ceres, CA 95307
Cheap but not very enjoyable sweet Modesto sparklers made by the bulk method are sold under the J F J Winery label. The firm is best known for its ubiquitous (in California at any rate) jug and carafe wines. Extra Dry and Naturel are the two styles available. Sales amount to half a million cases annually.

California Cellar Masters   CC/TM   →★
212 West Pine Street, Lodi
Don't let the name confuse you. California Cellars does not grow its own grapes, nor in the case of its Coloma Cellars brand, ferment or bottle its own wine. All that is done for it by Weibel.

Chateau St-Jean   MC 81   ★★
PO Box 293, 8555 Sonoma Highway, Kenwood, CA 95452
Star buy '81 Chateau St-Jean Blanc de Blancs
Since 1980 unglamorous Graton has been the headquarters of Chateau St-Jean's sparkling-wine empire. Apart from the firm's dry, stylish, vintage sparklers, made from bought-in Russian River grapes, accomplished winemaker Pete Downs also makes and bottles wine under contract for several firms; any California fizz with Graton on the label will have been made here. The superb silver-labelled '81 Chateau St-Jean Blanc de Blancs (mostly Chardonnay) with its biscuity nose and rich, full, creamy taste is

the finest wine here, but the elegant, similarly biscuity '82 Blanc de Blancs and the lively and flowery Pinot Noir–dominated '81 Brut are good alternatives. St-Jean's recent '82 Grande Cuvée (65 percent Pinot Noir, 35 percent Chardonnay) with six years plus on the yeast instead of the usual three has plenty of toasty-smoky, aged scents on the nose but a disappointing lime-juice-like palate. In 1984 Chateau St-Jean was bought for $40M (£25M) by Suntory International. The Gold Label non-vintage Brut, a Pinot Noir wine, with 11 percent Pinot Blanc and 6 percent Chardonnay, had an unexciting, deep, exotic, lychee scent and taste.

The Christian Brothers   CC   ★
1991 St Helena Highway, Rutherford, CA 94573
Big and bulky does not, alas, always mean beautiful too. This lay Catholic teaching order came to the USA from Reims in 1848 and by 1887 was making wine commercially. Their sparkling wine with its musk-melon taste is not recommended. Winemaker Brother Timothy's unobtainable birthday bubbly is their best effort yet.

Codorniu Napa   MC   ★→
1345 Henry Road, Napa, CA 94558
Yet another showplace Napa Valley winery, this one rather like a grassed-over, flattened pyramid complete with minimalist interior, smoky-glass windows, waterfalls and pools. Codorníu's California outpost, run by Davis-trained Janet Pagano who combines the roles of general manager and winemaker, is clearly going to be big business, for by the year 2,000, it hopes to produce some 75,000 cases of *méthode champenoise* fizz annually. Given the vast quantities of bubbly Codorníu produces in Spain, this should not prove too difficult. At the moment, Codorniu Napa produces about a third of this target figure, all from its own 101 ha (250 acres), which are not completely planted yet. These are situated in Carneros and Napa Valley and are divided equally between Chardonnay and Pinot Noir. To take advantage of the superior Carneros sparkling wine grapes, Codorniu sells limited quantities of a Carneros Cuvée Blanc de Noir, which should be worth trying. The big seller is the non-vintage Napa Valley Brut, an equal blend of Pinot Noir and Chardonnay, a third of which comes from Carneros and whose production currently tops 16,000 cases.

Cook's   CC/TM/IM   →★
Guild Wineries and Distilleries, 1 Winemasters Way, Lodi

Isaac Cook established this firm in 1859 (known then as the Missouri Wine Company) specifically to produce an American bubbly worthy of christening Clipper ships.

Cook's weird, oily California Brut and its equally unusual-tasting pink sister, Cook's Rosé, accounts for the bulk of the 1M-case annual sales of Guild Wineries and Distilleries, the huge California growers' cooperative. The sweet Cribari, the even sweeter Roma and the Cresta Blanca range (including a dry, citrusy, burnt-toast Chardonnay) account for the rest. Predominantly non-classic varieties are used and all non-vintage Guild sparklers are made by the *cuve close* method, except Cresta Blanca (transfer method) and J Pierrot (injection method). Cook's also makes orange-, almond-, and blackcurrant-flavoured fizz, plus Cook's Sparkling White Zinfandel. The latest innovation here is the ersatz, smoky, over ripe fruit- and lime-juice-like Chase Limogère Brut.

Crystal Valley   CC   →★
415 Hosmer, Modesto

Crystal Valley's Blanc de Noirs is not to my taste. The nose is curious and the colour unappealing. Crystal Valley also makes the Spumante d'Franseca brand.

John Culbertson Winery   MC   ★
32575 Rancho California Road, Temecula, CA 92930

This medium-sized family-owned firm, founded in 1981, makes a wide range of reasonable, albeit unusually flavoured, sparkling wine from bought-in grapes, including a Cuvée de Frontignan. Half its production undergoes automatic *remuage*. The aniseed-nosed '83 Blanc de Noirs is the best wine.

Domaine Carneros   MC   ★→
1240 Duhig road, Carneros

Clever Eileen Crane (ex-Davis, DOMAINE CHANDON and GLORIA FERRER) took another step up the California sparkling wine hierarchy when she moved here in 1987 as winemaker and managing director. Domaine Carneros is the joint venture between Taittinger champagne and the Kobrand Corporation, so now Crane is in the big bubbles league. With 48 ha (120 acres) of prime Carneros vineyards planted to two-thirds Chardonnay, one-third Pinot Noir with a dash each of Pinot Meunier and Pinot Blanc, Crane has all but a quarter of her requirements for a 40,000-case annual production. The Domaine's first release was the Pinot Noir-dominated (but also with 40 percent Chardonnay) non-vintage Domaine Carneros Brut. The second (release date autumn 1993) is the premium '88 Domaine Carneros Blanc de Blancs. With such fine, creamy, delicate fruit at her disposal, Crane does everything in her power to let its quality shine through unmasked, and to do that she avoids oak, oxidization and the use of brandy in the *dosage*. Indeed, Crane maintains that Domaine Carneros is the only California fizz to use Carneros grapes exclusively. The handsome winery building has been rather successfully modelled on Taittinger's own grand Château Marquetterie in Champagne. Quality should be high here, but sadly most of Domaine Carneros's output is consumed in the USA.

Domaine Chandon   MC   ★★→★★★
PO Box 2470 California Drive, Yountville, CA 94599
Star buys Chandon Reserve, Chandon Napa Valley Brut
If Schramsberg is the Krug of Napa Valley, then Domaine Chandon is of course, the Moët & Chandon. And at times Moët's California outpost, founded in 1973, has managed to outshine its Moët-Hennessy owners, consistently providing from the 1984 vintage onwards both quantity and quality. Its own Napa vineyards provide 30 percent of the Domaine's Pinot Noir, Chardonnay, Pinot Meunier and Pinot Blanc grapes (the last of these advocated by the now-retired consulting oenologist Edmond Maudière of Moët & Chandon, Epernay). The remainder is supplied by numerous growers including nearby Trefethen. Annual production (utilizing the Domaine's own Moët yeast strain plus 4,032 enormous Chandon-designed gyropalettes) now stands at almost 388,000 cases per annum.

This is mostly accounted for by the fine Pinot Noir-dominated Napa Valley Brut – a fresh, fruity and smoky-nosed wine. Then follows the gulpable, pale salmon-pink Blanc de Noirs (100 percent Pinot Noir) and the elegant, four-star Reserve (100 percent Pinot Noir and four years on yeast). The fragrant and flowery

Reserve has, since 1987, once again become available (in magnums only). So far all Domaine Chandon bubbly has been non-vintage due to the high proportion (12–15 percent) of reserve wines used in the blends. The Domaine has its own excellent *haute cuisine* restaurant. Rumours of a new *blanc de blancs*-dominant deluxe *cuvée* (called Dom Chandon perhaps?) have not yet come to anything. *See also* Shadow Creek.

Domaine Montreaux   MC   ★→
4101 Big Ranch Road, Napa, CA 94558

This new Monticello Cellars offshoot is now owned entirely by the Corley family with Jim Kakacek the new winemaker. Since 1983 Montreaux has made minute quantities of a Pinot Noir-dominated *brut* vintage wine, partly fermented and aged in barrel. Its first sparkling wine, '83 Domaine Montreaux, was released in late 1987 and now, with 8 ha (20 acres) of vines planted to 60 per-cent Pinot Noir and 40 percent Chardonnay, just 2,000 cases of an aged, full-bodied vintage *brut* are sold each year. The three new Montreaux releases are the '85, '86 and '87 and expect to see a *brut* rosé here by the mid-1990s. Montreaux's distinctive style is partly achieved by the use of Pinot Meunier and by including barrel-aged reserve wines in the *dosage*.

Fetzer Vineyards   MC   ★→
PO Box 227, Redwood Valley, CA 95470

Fetzer is definitely a family-run affair with ten brothers and sisters hard at work. It has only recently become involved in sparkling wine: Fetzer's earliest attempts were experimental rather than commercial and fewer than 2,000 cases of a Pinot Noir-dominated *brut*, rounded off with a little Chardonnay, were sold in California in 1985 and 1986. The nationwide launch was in 1987. So far Hopland grapes have gone into Fetzer sparklers, but future *cuvées* are likely to be made from fine Anderson and Redwood Valley fruit. Look out for a Fetzer Reserve with five years on yeast.

Franzia   CC   ★
17000 East Highway 120, Ripon, CA 95366

Vast amounts of tank method, flavoured Franzia fizz, rejoicing in such non-vinous names as Bavarian Blackberry and Roman

Raspberry, are sold alongside the pink-hued White Zinfandel Champagne. The low-alcohol Franzia California Champagne Brut, sweet and berry, is the firm's best wine.

E & J Gallo Winery   CC   →★
PO Box 1130, 600 Yosemite Boulevard, Modesto, CA 95353

The gigantic Gallo winery, situated at the northern end of the Central Valley – the 'fruit bowl' of America – produces more sparkling wine than any other North American winery: a cool 1M cases per annum minimum of the ubiquitous André and others. Clever advertising, hard-working salesmen and a low price have since the early 1970s made André (and to a lesser extent Ballatore) a staggering success story. Unfortunately, the taste is less impressive than the sales figures.

Geyser Peak Winery   MC   ★
PO Box 25, 22281 Chianti Road, Geyserville, CA 95441

This winery, dating back to 1880, is situated north of Geyserville on a hill overlooking Alexander Valley. It was extensively modernized and expanded almost two decades ago. Production is large and mostly of jug wines, but Geyser Peak's vintage-dated *brut*, made from Sonoma County grapes, is a notch up in quality.

Glen Ellen Vineyards & Winery   MC   ★
1883 London Ranch Road, Glen Ellen, CA 95442

The Benziger family is behind these sparkling wines. Just 5,000 cases are produced annually of two exclusively Carneros Chardonnay-based wines, of which the '87 vintage was the first release. The '88 Carneros Blanc de Blancs accounts for most of the production, but there is also an '89 Carneros Blanc de Blancs Imagery Series sparkler. The latter uses base wines that have been partly barrel-fermented in new French oak.

Gloria Ferrer   MC   ★★
PO Box 1427, 23555 Highway 121, Sonoma, CA 95476

Dubbed the 'First Lady of Sonoma' and named after the Freixenet president's wife, this firm was founded in 1982. Two early Gloria Ferrer Cuvée Emerald Brut non-vintage releases were fragrant and yeasty. These were made at CHATEAU ST-JEAN (Graton) and PIPER

SONOMA, but from late 1986 the wine was made at Freixenet, Sonoma's handsome new winery, complete with underground cellars, near San Francisco. Most of the grapes needed to produce 63,000 cases annually are provided by 81 ha (200 acres) of Freixenet's own fine, full-flavoured Carneros 70 percent Pinot Noir and 30 percent Chardonnay. These grapes are turned into three wines: a Pinot Noir-dominated Royal Cuvée and a *brut*, plus the superior hand-riddled Carneros Cuvée, a 60 percent Pinot Noir to 40 percent Chardonnay fizz with three years on yeast. The Brut is a pleasant, soft, ripe, citrusy, biscuity wine. Visitors will not find the Gloria Ferrer 'Champagne Caves' hard to track down, it is one of the first wineries you see when driving north of San Francisco. The winery is now run by Gloria Ferrer's son, Pedro.

Handley Cellars   MC   ★
PO Box 66, Philo, CA 95466

This minute family firm has chosen a first-class location just down the road from Roederer in the cool Anderson Valley. With their own 4 ha-plot (10 acres) of Chardonnay and Pinot Noir vines now yielding fully, the Handleys make just 1,500 cases a year almost all from their own vines. The first wine, a Pinot Noir-dominated *brut* was released in late 1986, and a Pinot Noir dominated rosé followed soon after. The latest vintage-dated edition is the Handley Cellars Blanc de Blancs, only made in top Chardonnay years.

Hop Kiln Winery   MC   ★
6050 Westside Road, Healdsburg, CA 95448

Anyone who develops a taste for Hop Kiln's *méthode champenoise* Brut Verveux, made from Rhine Riesling grapes, will have no alternative but to keep going back to the winery housed in an hop-drying barn erected in 1905, for it is only sold there. Just 200 cases are made annually, entirely from the owner Dr Martin Griffin's 8 ha (19 acres) of Riesling grapes.

Robert Hunter   MC   ★→
3027 Silverado Trail, St Helena

This Sonoma Valley sparkler stems from a joint venture with Duckhorn Cellars in the Napa Valley. Grapes come mostly from Robert Hunter's vineyard to the west of Sonoma; winemaking expertise comes from Duckhorn. The first release was 5,000 cases of the Pinot Noir-dominated '80 Brut de Noirs, topped up with Chardonnay, followed by the crisp, clean slatey '81 Brut de Noirs. Production is now approximately 8,000 cases per annum.

Iron Horse Vineyards   MC '81 '82   ★★→★★★
9786 Ross Station Road, Sebastopol, CA 95472
Star buys '87 Brut, '81 Blanc de Noirs
This remote hilltop winery grows Pinot Noir and Chardonnay in Green Valley and picks the grapes early. Since 1980 Forrest Tancer's winemaking expertise, enhanced early on with a stint by Reims-trained Claude Thibaut, has made an impressive clutch of lean, elegant, low-*dosage* vintage wines. The Pinot Noir-dominated sparklers are the most stylish, especially the intense, rich, toasty, waxy '87 Brut and the fresh, racy Blanc de Noirs. Reagan and Gorbachev are among those who have enjoyed the soft, smoky '82 Blanc de Blancs. Labels carry disgorge dates. Future plans include the introduction of an Iron Horse Brut Reserve and Rosé. The firm's great strength is the ability to marry first class cool-climate Green Valley grapes with top *méthode champenoise* techniques. The results are some of the most impressive sparklers California makes. No wonder first class champagne house Laurent-Perrier has invested jointly with Iron Horse in vineyards in Sonoma. A new top flight joint venture sparkling wine must surely be the result.

Jordan Vineyards & Winery   MC   ★→★★
PO Box 878, Healdsburg, CA 95448
There is much pomp and circumstance attached to the launch of any Jordan wine, so it is a shame to report that even the top, first '87 vintage of 'J' still has a very long way to go before it becomes the American Dom Pérignon the Jordan family is hoping for. However, its soft, biscuity, herbaceous scent and rather too austere, tart, lemony-herbaceous palate may smooth out with age. The '88 'J' has a rather better, waxy, brioche-like character, but here the Jordans have swung the other way and given the wine a palate that is rather too soft and flabby and could do with a little of the '87's crispness and severity.

Champenois Claude Thibaut, ex-IRON HORSE consultant wine-maker, made the first few vintages here and hopefully the 'J' style, given the experience of a few more California harvests, will settle down. Certainly, Jordan has all the gadgets and gismos to achieve its aims, including a new Coquard press. 'J' is a fifty-fifty blend of Chardonnay and Pinot Noir that comes from as far away as Mendocino and Monterey, but mostly from Russian River Sonoma country. Jordan's own 44 ha (110 acres) of 'J' ranch land began to come into action in 1992, and will eventually produce about half of the firm's grapes. To emphasize the 'J' point, the wine is presented in a distinctive, sea-green, ultra violet-resistant bottle with a painted yellow 'J' fired onto the surface.

Founded in 1986, Tom Jordan and his daughter Judy now run this sparkling wine offshoot of the family firm and expect to produce 20,000 cases in most years.

Kalin Cellars   MC   ★
61 Galli Drive, Novato, CA 94949

Professor Terrance Leighton is the man behind this Novato winery label. He is probably better known for his still Chardonnays than for his unusual, pink *méthode champenoise* Cuvée Rosé Reservée. Europeans will find this wine's boiled red jam-like fruit curious. But, made from a blend of 60 percent Pinot Noir to 40 percent Chardonnay and fermented first in small, used, oak barrels, no one could accuse this professor of anything other than European ideals.

F Korbel & Bros   MC   ★
13250 River Road, Guerneville, CA 95446

Century-old Korbel's range of seven sweet, bland, inoffensive sparklers have recently notched up annual sales of over 1M cases, making it the biggest selling California *méthode champenoise* range in the USA. The redwood forest backdrop plus its gardens, museum and ultra-efficient automation, merit a detour to Korbel. The best wine here is the simple, fruity 100 percent Chardonnay Blanc de Blancs. Korbel Natural with its weird, sweet, perfumed style and Korbel Brut, a blend of Chenin Blanc, Colombard and Chardonnay, with a strange peachy, musky taste are other Korbel experiences. The last of these is one of the biggest USA sparklers, with annual sales of 750,000 cases.

Hanns Kornell Champagne Cellars   MC   ★
1091 Larkmead Lane, St Helena, CA 94574
Four generations of Kornells have made sparkling wine, first in Germany and now in the USA. The firm buys finished wine and adds bubbles via the *méthode champenoise* including hand riddling. The wines sell well, but their strong flavours will not be appreciated by everyone and, like Korbel, are now an old-fashioned California sparkling wine style. The Chenin Blanc-based '80 Blanc de Blancs, soft and peachy, is the best sparkling wine here. Sadly, the Kornell family is no longer involved here and the future of the firm looks uncertain.

Thomas Kruse Winery   MC   ★→
4390 Hecker Pass Road, Gilroy, CA 95020
Situated south of Saratoga, in the Hecker Pass district of the Santa Cruz mountains, Thomas Kruse makes minute amounts of a Naturel-style *méthode champenoise* wine under the Pinot Noir-dominated Insouciance label as well as the new Blanc de Blancs.

Maison Deutz Winery   MC   ★→
453 Deutz Drive, Arroyo Grande, CA 93420
French tradition, from the Deutz champagne house, and California know-how join forces here in San Luis Obispo County. With the firm's own Pinot Blanc, Pinot Noir and Chardonnay grapes on stream and supplying two-thirds of its 28,000-case needs, much less fruit from nearby Santa Maria Valley is being used. Maison Deutz Brut Cuvée, a non-vintage blend of one-third Pinot Blanc, Pinot Noir and Chardonnay, as well as a proportion of reserve wines, is the big seller here. Deutz is aiming for a full-flavoured old-style sparkling wine – principally non-vintage, but vintage too if quality merits it as it did with the '87 Brut Reserve. This wine is always Pinot Noir-dominated and spends three years on yeast. A non-vintage rosé is also made. Sparkling wine whizz-kid Harold Osborne, who also made New Zealand's new, superlative Pelorus, was once in charge but has now gone to Kendall Jackson, who will perhaps release Osborne's sparkling wines soon.

Mark West Vineyards   MC   ★★→★★★
7000 Trenton-Healdsburg Road, Forestville, CA 95436
Star buy '81 Blanc de Noirs
First-time fluke it may have been, but Joan and Bob Ellis's only
sparkling wine to date, the '81 Blanc de Noirs made exclusively
from their own Russian River Pinot Noir grapes, is excellent: its
slightly pink colour and fresh *fraise de bois* bouquet and taste augur
well for future releases.

Paul Masson Vineyards   TM   ★→★★
PO Box 1852, 14831 Pierce Road, Saratoga, CA 95070
Now that Taylor California Cellars has been absorbed into Paul
Masson, this mighty Seagram name is even mightier than before.
Paul Masson's fresh, green, vintage-dated Brut, from Chardonnay
and Pinot Noir topped up with other less noble varieties, is one of
the better transfer method wines. Similarly the Extra Dry is attrac-
tive, but like the Brut needs a shot more of invigorating acidity.

Mirassou Champagne Cellars   MC   ★★→
300 College Avenue, Los Gatos, CA 95032
This fifth-generation family firm was established in 1854 by French
gold prospector Pierre Pellier (his daughter married a Mirassou).
Today the firm uses a blend of 81 ha-worth (200 acres) of Pinot
Noir, Chardonnay and Pinot Blanc grapes grown in cool
Monterey County to make its fresh and lively *méthode champenoise*
sparklers. This gives Mirassou almost all it needs to make 13,000
cases of fizz in most years. Latest innovations from Mirassou
include a mobile vineyard press. The range includes a Pinot Noir-
dominated Brut and Au Naturel, both rounded off with
Chardonnay and Pinot Blanc. The similarly blended Brut Reserve
spends five years on yeast to gain extra flavour and finesse. The
Blanc de Noirs is, as it sounds, a 100 percent Pinot Noir wine. Try
the well-made, clean, easy-to-drink '82 Monterey Brut with its
smell of lime juice.

Robert Mondavi Winery   MC   ★★
PO Box 106, 7801 St Helena Highway, Oakville, CA 94562
Experimental sparkling wine has gone down well here both with
staff and with visitors since 1978. After a thousand taste, technical

and harvest trials the rich, full '85 Chardonnay Reserve Brut and '85 Brut Reserve sparklers were commercially released but only for sale at the winery – as all future sparkling wine vintages will be. Using Carneros Pinot Noir and Chardonnay fruit, the Chardonnay Reserve is made exclusively from that grape, while the Brut Reserve is a fifty-fifty blend. All *cuvées* have a lengthy four years on yeast and quality is high due, amongst other techniques, to hand harvesting, riddling and disgorgement plus fermentation of up to 15 percent of the base wine in new French oak.

The Monterey Vineyard MC ★→★★
PO Box 780, 800 South Alta Street, Gonzales, CA 93926
Part of the giant Seagram organisation. Grapes for Monterey Vineyard's only sparkling wine – the vintage-dated Brut – come every year from the same 8 ha (20 acres) Salinas Valley vineyard (planted to 60 percent Pinot Noir and 20 percent each of Pinot Blanc and Chardonnay). This must be Seagram's most up-market sparkling wine, as production (involving hand riddling) is tiny (just 3,000 cases a year) and the wine is available virtually only at the winery. The once-mighty Taylor California Cellars was previously associated with Monterey Vineyard; it has now been absorbed by PAUL MASSON.

Mumm Napa Valley MC ★→
8445 Silverado Trail, Napa, CA 94558
Secrecy was all, at Seagram's West Coast outpost while its 1979 'Project Lafayette' was being completed, culminating in a Franco-American winery being built on Sterling's extravagant Napa property. The first Mumm release was the '86, and Greg Fowler, previously Schramsberg's winemaker, made the '87 vintage and those that followed. About half of Mumm's Pinot Noir and Chardonnay grapes come from Carneros and, interestingly, small quantities of Pinot Meunier and Pinot Gris are blended into the 60 percent Pinot Noir, 34 percent Chardonnay Brut. Its soft, light, citrusy, crushed-pineapple taste is good, not great. Mumm's Blanc de Noirs Rosé (Pinot Noir with 15 percent Chardonnay) offers ripe but somewhat neutral fruit. Top of the range is the Vintage Reserve, made only in the best years (1985 and 1987 so far) plus the pricier-still Winery Lake Brut, a rarity in that it comes entirely

from one (Carneros) vineyard. Like the Reserve it is a 60 percent Pinot Noir, 40 percent Chardonnay blend.

Nevada City Winery   MC   →★
321 Spring Street, Nevada City, CA 95959

A recently established winery, situated east of the Central Valley and tucked away in the Sierra Foothills (better known in earlier times as California's Gold Rush country). It was set up by locals keen to revitalize the booming pre-prohibition wine traditions of the region with, amongst other wines, a Brut Naturel and Cuvée des Enfants. Future production will be limited to a Chardonnay/ Pinot Noir blend, the Cuvée des Montagnes.

Nicasio Vineyards   MC   →★
483 Nicasio Way, Soquel, CA 95073

Situated in the Santa Cruz mountains, just east of Santa Cruz, this small enterprise owned by Dan Wheeler produces limited amounts of Naturel *méthode champenoise* from Pinot Noir, Chardonnay and White Riesling grapes.

Novitiate Wines   CC   ★
300 College Avenue, Los Gatos

South of Saratoga and the Bay, Novitiate Wines has an impressive history going back nearly a hundred years. The wines are some-what old-fashioned, including the sweet, bulk method Demi-Sec.

Parsons Creek Winery   MC   ★★→
3001 South State Street, Ukiah, CA 95482

Just down the road from Scharffenberger, Parsons Creek buys its grapes from the cool Anderson and Potter valleys. Winemaker Jesse Tidwell makes just 4,000 cases annually and his first release is the crisp, creamy and very drinkable Pinot Noir-dominated non-vintage Brut, which also has some Chardonnay in the blend. Future releases from Parsons Creek are likely to be in the same mould as this wine.

Piper Sonoma Cellars   MC 81   ★★
11447 Old Redwood Highway, Healdsburg, CA 95448

Piper Sonoma's stylish $8M (£5M) showplace winery in Sonoma

– a joint USA/Piper Heidsieck venture – has since 1980 produced crisp, dry, vintage-dated wine mostly from bought-in Sonoma grapes. It is not a wine that will appeal to lovers of bigger, bouncier styles. Production via automatic *remuage* now stands at almost 75,000 cases a year. Most of this is accounted for by the austere, cinnamon-nosed Pinot Noir-dominated '82 Brut. This is followed by a small proportion of the firm's fruity, somewhat earthy '82 Blanc de Noirs, and even tinier amounts of the '81 Tête de Cuvée, a fuller-flavoured and more complex fifty–fifty blend of Chardonnay and Pinot Noir.

Martin Ray Vineyards MC ★→
2060 Louis Road, Palo Alto, CA 94303
North of Saratoga in the Santa Cruz mountains, this small winery, run by yet a Stanford professor, produces tiny amounts of wildly expensive *méthode champenoise* Naturel.

Roederer Estate MC ★→
4501 Highway 128, Philo, CA 95466
Devotees eagerly awaited the first Roederer USA release. The 141 ha (350 acres) of prime Anderson Valley land at Philo have been planted with equal plots of Pinot Noir and Chardonnay, which yielded their first crop in 1986. The resulting wines to date, from a French winemaker, have been tart, lemony and far too green, so there is still work to be done. The new winery's architecture is in 'French country/rustic California' style, with hillside caves hewn out of an old quarry. Production is likely to be about 85,000 cases a year.

Rosenblum Cellars MC ★
2900 Main Street, Alameda, CA 94801
The Rosenblum family and partners turn out just 300 cases a year of their idiosyncratic, spicy sparkling wines. These are made mostly from the Gewürztraminer grape topped up with White Riesling. The wine was originally sold as Napa Valley Sparkling Gewürztraminer but is now called California Sparkling Brut.

San Pasqual Vineyards   MC   →★
13455 San Pasqual Road, Escondido

Just north of San Diego, San Pasqual must surely be California's most southerly sparkling wine producer. Some curious grape varieties (from its own vineyards) are turned into sparklers: the Blanc de Noirs is predominantly Gamay, with a little Sauvignon Blanc and Chenin Blanc. The '81 vintage (only 750 cases) was the first release, with future production intended to be three times as much.

Scharffenberger Cellars   MC 81   ★★→
PO Box 365, 8501 Highway 128, Philo, CA 95466

Hotly tipped as one of the leading Mendocino County *méthode champenoise* winemakers, Scharffenberger has, since 1981, been making some stylish, sophisticated sparkling wine from its not yet fully planted 57 ha (140 acres) of Pinot Noir and Chardonnay grapes from the, equally admired, cool-climate Anderson and Redwood valleys. *Remuage* is performed mechanically. Most of Scharffenberger's annual 30,000 cases is taken up by the Pinot Noir-dominated Brut. A little 100 percent-Chardonnay *blanc de blancs* is also made, however, together with smaller amounts of *brut* rosé and a *crémant* made from Pinot Noir and Chardonnay. Scharffenberger sparklers spend almost three years on yeast prior to disgorgement. Recently, the champagne house Pommery has taken a share of Scharffenberger, which explains why this handsome redwood grove-set winery now has better distribution. Look out for the delicious, light, lemony Brut with its splendid, waxy, brown bread scented bouquet. Scharffenberger's lean, tart Rosé is less impressive.

Schramsberg Vineyards MC   ★★→★★★
1,400 Schramsberg Road, Calistoga, CA 94515
Star buys '81 Blanc de Blancs, '75 Reserve

Registered Historical Landmark No 561 was founded as a winery by Jacob Schram in 1862, complete with an impressive mountain-top Victorian house and rock-hewn cellars. Schramsberg, which is clearly no ordinary California *méthode champenoise* producer, was bought by Jack and Jamie Davies in 1965. Its big, rich, complex sparklers are, even competitors admit, California's answer to Krug. With part barrel-fermented base wine, long ageing on yeast (five years for the Reserve wines), brandy in the *dosage* and noticeable use of old reserve wines, Schramsberg is probably as Krugesque as any California producer can get. The wines are admired by wine buffs and American presidents (Nixon, Carter and Reagan) alike. About 15 percent of Schramsberg's needs are provided by 16 ha (40 acres) of the firm's own Pinot Noir and Chardonnay, and by a neighbouring 8 ha (20 acres) plot, formerly owned by McEckron. Bought-in grapes supply the rest. Most of the annual 40,000-case production is hand riddled with 20 percent on gyropalettes.

Of the six different Schramsberg wines, the glorious, elegant, full Chardonnay-dominated '81 Blanc de Blancs – smoky, racy and yeasty – accounts for more than half of the total production. This is followed by the '80 Pinot Noir-based Blanc de Noirs (rounded off with Chardonnay and Pinots Meunier and Blanc), with its pinky blush and big, fruity, exotic taste. Limited amounts of a pale, pinky-gold, soft and fruity '81 Cuvée de Pinot are on sale as well as the Schramsberg curio, the sweet, aromatic '82 Crémant Demi-Sec pudding fizz, made from the spicy Flora grape and Pinot Blanc. Schramsberg's most expensive bubblies however are its Reserve wines (avoid the excessively smoky-toasty '79) whose *cépage* varies slightly every year: the big, rich, fragrant '78 was 100 percent Chardonnay and the biscuity, almost overblown '80 mostly Pinot Noir. Schramsberg joined forces with the Portuguese recently to launch Vertice, a Douro wine-based *méthode champenoise* sparkler. The latest Schramsberg arrival is J Schram, a *crème de la crème* Schramsberg sparkler with a price to match, blended from over 40 base wines aged for over four years on yeast and presented in a new dark green glass, pot-bellied bottle. The '87 vintage, an intense, rich, big, biscuity wine, was the first release. Schramsberg's second label is the less expensive Mirabelle non-vintage Brut and Rosé, which spend a shorter time on yeast, are made from cheaper North Coast California Pinot Noir and Chardonnay, and are only sold in the USA.

Sebastiani Vineyards   MC   ★→★★
PO Box AA, 389 Fourth Street East, Sonoma, CA 95476
After eight decades in California, Italian traditions are as strong as ever at this third-generation, family-run winery, right down to using Italian brandy in the *dosage* of its non-vintage *méthode*

champenoise Sebastiani Brut. Sebastiani's base wine, made predominantly from 49 ha (120 acres) of Carneros Chardonnay, is trucked over twice to Chateau St-Jean at Graton, first for its *liqueur de tirage* and finally for riddling and bottling. Despite the journeys, the 500 cases of the '87 Richard Cumeo Cuvée de Chardonnay is well thought of. None is exported.

Shadow Creek MC '81 ★→★★
2195 Corbett Canyon Road, San Luis Obispo

Shadow Creek's new owners (DOMAINE CHANDON), mean that Shadow Creek fizz will be made at Chandon's Yountville headquarters by the Domaine's winemakers. Previous wines, including vintage and non-vintage *bruts*, a *blanc de blancs* and a *blanc de noirs*, all made by CHATEAU ST-JEAN at Graton, have had their ups and downs. Today's version of Shadow Creek is a respectable California sparkling wine and a worthy Domaine Chandon second label.

Sierra Wine CC →★
1887 North Mooney Boulevard, Tulare, CA 93274

This south Central Valley producer makes inexpensive, big-selling bulk method sparkling wine sold under the Valley Mission label in both *brut* and extra dry styles.

Sonoma–Cutrer Vineyards MC ★→
4401 Slusser Road, Windsor, CA 95492

Based over the hill from Mark West, and still in the Russian River Valley. Sonoma Cutrer's winemaker, Bill Bonnetti, is aiming for a high-quality 100 percent-Chardonnay wine from the winery's own grapes. Besides undergoing its first fermentation in cask, the wine spends a very lengthy seven years on the yeast. The first *cuvée* was launched in 1987 and a limited production is planned.

Stony Ridge CC ★→
13862 Ridge Road East, Sutter Creek, CA 95685

Stony Ridge is a medium-sized winery situated east of the Bay in the Livermore Valley. It makes an extra dry bulk method bubbly.

Tijsseling Vineyards MC ★→
2150 McNab Ranch Road, Ukiah, CA 95482

Tijsseling, south of Ukiah, is not the easiest winery to find but its vintage-dated sparkler is becoming increasingly widely available. Unlike other Mendocino, or indeed other California fizz producers, fruit for Tijsseling's 10,000 or so cases come from one site – the Tijsseling farm just north of Hopland. So far the winery has made a toasty '82 Pinot Noir-dominated *brut* and a 100 percent Chardonnay non-*dosage* '82 *blanc de blancs*. A 100 percent Pinot Noir *blanc de noirs* is in the pipeline. All wines are disgorge-dated.

Tonio Conti MC ★→
2170 Adelaida Road, Paso Robles, CA 93446

Named after its major Swiss shareholder and owned by Adelaida Cellars, Tonio Conti hopes to plant vines where it now buys its grapes – in the Paso Robles area. For the moment the wines are made at Estrella River. Emphasis here is on the low-*dosage* vintage 100 percent Chardonnay Blanc de Blancs. Helpfully (for *dosage* devotees perhaps?) back labels give disgorge and *dosage* details.

Van der Kamp Champagne Cellars MC ★→
PO Box 609, Kenwood, CA 95452

Martin and Dixie van der Kamp are the major shareholders in this tiny enterprise, founded in 1981. With 24 ha (60 acres) on Sonoma Mountain planted to 80 percent Pinot Noir and 20 percent Pinot Meunier, the Van de Kamps still need to buy in grapes. The fruity '81 Pinot Noir-dominated Brut (which has a little Chardonnay) has gone down well with discerning palates, but quite why the van der Kamps have labelled it English Cuvée is anyone's guess (likewise the 80 percent Pinot Noir, 20 percent Chardonnay '82 Brut Rosé which is called Midnight Cuvée). In addition, a 50 percent Pinot Noir, 50 percent Chardonnay Brut is produced.

Ventana Vineyards Winery MC ★→★★
PO Box G, Soledad, CA 93960

Suppliers of grapes more than of wine, Ventana originally sold Chardonnay and Pinot Noir to other wineries to turn into sparkling wine. It now produces very limited amounts of its own *méthode champenoise* sparklers. Some of Ventana's own Arroyo Seco grapes from cool Monterey were turned into Naturel Cuvée JDM in 1981 and 1982. The blend was two-thirds Pinot Noir and one-third Chardonnay.

Weibel Vineyards   CCTM   *
PO Box 3398, Mission San Jose, CA 94539

Swiss émigré Fred Weibel and his family now use their European winemaking experience to make vast quantities of distinctly Californian, mainly non-vintage *cuve clos*e sparkling wine from bought-in grapes. These wines appear under numerous labels, including Sparkling White Zinfandel, Sparkling Green Hungarian and Crackling Rosé. Since the '85 vintage, Weibel's premium Mendocino fizz has been made via the *méthode champenoise* and the transfer method sparklers have gradually been phased out.

Wente Bros   MC   *
5565 Tesla Road, Livermore, CA 94550

Established in 1833, this fourth-generation family-owned firm is based east of the Bay in the Livermore Valley. The handsome mission-style Cresta Blanca winery, together with its sandstone caves, was restored in 1981 and became the headquarters of Wente's own sparkling wine unit, complete with conference centre and restaurant. Night-picked and field-crushed Chardonnay, Pinot Noir and Pinot Blanc grapes from its own Arroyo Seco vineyards in Monterey are turned into 5,000 cases of the Wente Bros' three sparkling wines. These include the burnt, honey-buttered toast, non-vintage, Pinot Noir-dominated Grande Brut and the no doubt finer, Chardonnay-dominated Grande Reserve vintage-dated Brut at almost twice the price. Wente feels that the '82 and '83 vintages of this wine were its best yet.

The Rest of the USA

At the last count there were more than 120 American sparkling wine producers: it seems that almost every state has one or two sparklers of its own. California, of course, still accounts for about half of these producers (and for the vast majority of all the USA sparkling wine). However, New York State is in second place with roughly 20 producers, with Michigan and Missouri the next biggest sparkling wine producing states. The chief drawback for American winemakers hoping to produce top quality sparkling wines is not the method they employ, for most firms are using the classic *méthode champenoise*, but the choice of grape variety. Severe winters and late springs mean that in many states outside California, winemakers will always have a limited choice. At best, they can grow French hybrids such as the hardy Seyval Blanc, Aurora and Vidal, and at worst American hybrids, such as the Dutchess and Delaware, with their mild, but still noticeable, foxy *labrusca* taste. The most foxy and *labrusca*-like of all the native American hybrids is Concord. The sparkling wines made from this all-American grape are unlikely ever to be admired internationally, despite their devoted local fans. Nor are the Scuppernong-based sparklers from the deep South with their sweet, musky flavours.

Currently the producers who are making the most stylish American sparklers outside California are those using both the classic champagne method and grapes (Chardonnay and Pinot Noir). A good alternative for those with impossible climates are the robust French hybrids, plantings of which are happily on the increase everywhere. This has meant that during the past decade, as new plantings came on stream, there has been a definite improvement in the quality of American sparkling wine. In New York State this marked improvement in quality is especially noticeable since French hybrids and the milder American hybrids replaced the *labrusca*-dominant grapes, such as Niagara and Catawaba, in most firms' sparkling wine blends many years ago.

Michigan's sparkling wine figures in the 1960s and early 1970s had much to do with that curious, sparkling, pink, party phenomenon Cold Duck. Made mostly from sparkling white and red wine, this sweet *labrusca*-like tipple is an Americanized version of the traditional German sparkling wine Kalte Ente or Cold Duck. The wine is no longer as popular as it once was (although produced in numerous states). Those firms who still make it usually have a similar 'sparkling burgundy' as well.

The sparkling wine region to watch in America, outside California, is the Pacific Northwest. For it is here, especially in the cool, almost Champagne-like climate of Oregon, that the widely planted Pinot Noir and Chardonnay produce what could well prove to be the quintessential West Coast sparkling wine base: elegant, restrained wines with subtle fruit flavours, low alcohol and high acidity. This factor, together with the low price of vineyard land compared to California, has already started to attract winemakers from elsewhere. Brian Croser from Australia, in a joint venture with Cal Knudsen, an Oregon pioneer, has produced one of the most stylish of these wines, the classy Oregon sparkler Argyle.

Arkansas

Post Familie Vineyards   MC   ★→
Route 1, Box 1, Altus, AR 72821
Emily Post herself would no doubt have approved of this tidy Alpine-style winery founded by Jacob Post from Bavaria in 1880. The Post *méthode champenoise* Brut and Naturel are a cut above the other Franco-American hybrid wines here.

Wiederkehr Wine Cellars CC   →★
Wiederkehr Village, Altus, AR 72821
Atop Champagne Drive lies the Wiederkehr family's mini Alpine village comprising winery, restaurant et al. Cousins to the Posts, whose winery lies at the bottom of St Mary's Mountain, the Swiss Wiederkehrs produce extra dry bulk method wines under the Chateau du Monte and Hanns Wiederkehr labels.

Connecticut

Haight Vineyard   MC   ★→★★
29 Chestnut Hill Road, Litchfield, CT 06759

Connecticut's first winery to open since the Repeal is now almost two decades old. It produces just 800 cases annually of Haight Blanc de Blancs, made exclusively from its own Seyval Blanc grapes with a dash of Chardonnay to lighten the hybrid load. The wine is made by the *méthode champenoise* (including hand riddling) and produced in either dry or naturel non-vintage versions.

Hawaii

Tedeschi Vineyard   MC   ★
PO Box 953, Ulupalakua, Maui, HI 96790

Hawaii is not the first place anyone would connect with sparkling wine production, but the Carnelian *vinifera* grape thrives in the Tedeschi's sub-tropical vineyard sited on a dormant volcano. The grape is turned via the *méthode champenoise* into the vintage-dated Erdman-Tedeschi Blanc de Noirs Brut. Still and sparkling Pineapple wine is also on offer.

Idaho

Ste-Chapelle Winery   MC/CC   ★★
14068 Sunny Slope, Caldwell, ID 83605

Idaho is better known for potatoes than wine, but perhaps the well-distributed Ste-Chapelle, with its attractive octagonal chapel of a winery, featured on the label, will change all that. This impressive, almost two decade-old concern deals only with the *vinifera* grape (mainly Pinot Noir and Chardonnay Johannisberg Riesling). It currently sells 15,000 cases a year of Riesling *sec* and *demi-sec*, a Chenin Blanc-based brut and a bulk method *blanc de noirs* made from the Pinot Noir. Ste-Chapelle's best wine is the 70 percent Chardonnay, 30 percent Pinot Noir Brut, of which only 500 cases are made annually. It was served during the State's recent 100th birthday celebrations.

Illinois

Thompson Winery   MC   ★
PO Box 127, Monee, IL 60449

Small quantities of Père Marquette and Père Hennepin white and rosé *méthode champenoise* are made every year at this converted railway station. The grapes used are Franco-American hybrids.

Maine

Bartlett Maine Estate Winery   MC   →★
Box 598, Gouldsboro, ME 04607

Maine's first – and possibly to remain its only – winery is run by Bob, Mary and Kathe Bartlett. They make what they describe as 'classic *méthode champenoise*' wine from pears and apples. Classic winemaking equipment and techniques are certainly much in evidence here, including stainless steel tanks, French oak casks, and ageing the wine for five years on lees, but Bartlett Sparkling Pear/Apple Brut is unlikely to convert lovers of the grape.

Massachusetts

Chicama Vineyards   MC   →★
Stoney Hill Road, West Tisbury, MA 02575

Chicama's peach-coloured Sea Mist Sparkling Wine is predominantly Chenin Blanc, topped up with a little Chardonnay and White Riesling. Only 125 cases are made annually at this Martha's Vineyard winery.

Nashoba Valley Winery   MC   →★
100 Wattaquadoc Hill Road, Bolton, MA 01740
Not to be outdone by Maine, this state also boasts a non-vintage
méthode champenoise sparkling apple wine of which 200 cases are
made every year.

Michigan

Fenn Valley Vineyards   MC   ★→★★
6130 122nd Avenue, Fennville, MI 49408
Fenn Valley makes just 125 cases a year of its dry Blanc de Blancs
Naturel (from its own Seyval grapes backed up by another French
hybrid, the Vidal, plus a little Riesling). This is sold chiefly at the
winery, as is a 100 percent sparkling Riesling.

Lakeside Vineyard   MC   →★
13581 Red Arrow Highway, Harbert, MI 49115
Tourists love this easily accessible place, originally known as the
Molly Pitcher winery. Wine-bibbers are likely to find that name,
plus the sweet *méthode champenoise* wine called Touch of Bubbly, all
rather too much.

Leelanau Wine Cellars   MC   ★→
Box 68, Omena, MI 49674
Just over 15 years old, Leelanau makes everything, it seems, from
fruit wines through to hybrid wines, but more and more are being
made from *vinifera*. Chardonnay and Pinot Noir are planted and
small amounts of extra dry *méthode champenoise* produced.

St-Julian Wine Company   CC/MC   ★→
716 Kalamazoo Street, Paw Paw, MI
The wonderfully-addressed St-Julian winery is named after the
patron saint of the Italian founder's home town. Most of the winery's vast production is made from hybrid grapes. Bulk method
sparkling wine is sold under the Chateau St-Julian label and tiny
amounts of *méthode champenoise* San Giuliano are also made.

Tabor Hill   CC   ★→★★
18J Mount Tabor Hill Road, Buchanan MI 49107
Another Alpine-inspired winery. The emphasis here is on French hybrids and *vinifera* varieties such as Chardonnay and Johannisberg Riesling. A small amount of vintage-dated bulk method wine goes out under the Tabor Hill and Brontë labels.

Warner Vineyards   CC/MC   →★
706 South Kalamazoo Street, Paw Paw MI
Next door to ST-JULIAN, this is the largest Michigan producer, buying in grapes from all over the State. The vintage-dated Warner sparklers sold under curious names such as Very, Very Cranberry, Pol Pereaux and Warner, are the best of an uninspiring range.

Missouri

Hermannhof   MC   ★→★★
330 East First Street, Hermann, MO 65041
An 8 ha (20 acres) plot close to Hermannhof supplies Seyval Blanc, Vidal and Villard Blanc grapes for 2,500 cases of *méthode champenoise* Hermannhof's Hermann Brut Champagne. *Brut*, extra dry and *blanc de blancs* styles are all made.

Mount Pleasant Winery   TM/MC   ★→
5634 High Street, Augusta, MO 63332
The century-old Mount Pleasant winery concentrates on French hybrids and *labrusca*. Since the winery was revitalized, in 1968, small quantities of vintage-dated *méthode champenoise*, bulk and transfer method wine have been made in a variety of styles from *brut* to sweet. Chardonnay, Pinot Noir and Pinot Meunier are now part of the winery's 6 ha (14 acre) plot and almost 2,000 cases of bubbly, including St Vincent Rosé and Pearl of Oman Crémant are made annually.

Rosati Winery   MC   ★→
Route 1, St-James, MO
Hybrid grapes and Italian traditions sum up the Rosati style. The

fruity, heavy *brut*, dry and *demi-sec* non-vintage Rosati Champagne is much liked locally.

St-James Winery   MC   ★→
540 Sidney Street, St-James, MO 65559

The 15-year-old St-James Winery is owned by the Hofherrs, whose Fresno State–trained son will no doubt want to move on from mead, fruit wines and Franco–American hybrids to *vinifera* wines. Pink champagne is popular here and Extra Dry and Naturel versions of *méthode champenoise* sparklers are also produced.

Stone Hill Wine Company   MC   →★
Box 26, Route One, Hermann, MO 65041

Prohibition has a lot to answer for. At the impressive hilltop winery of Stone Hill, founded by a German émigré, mushrooms grew where wine was once cellared. Now, more than a century after the winery's foundation, the Helds and their Fresno State oenology department-educated children keep the local German traditions alive and make wine from the native American hybrid grapes via the *méthode champenoise*. 24 ha (60 acres) of hybrid Vidal Blanc vines are turned into almost 1,000 cases of one fizz, the Stone Hill Vintage Brut.

New Jersey

Gross Highland Winery   CC   ★→
306 Jim Leeds Road, Absecon, NJ

This establishment, north of Atlantic City, turns out tank method sparklers under both the Gross Highland and Bernard D'Arcy labels. The move from *labrusca* to French hybrids and *vinifera*, together with the expertise of a winemaker trained at the University of California at Davis, augurs well for future (possibly *méthode champenoise*?) releases.

Renault Winery   MC   ★→
72 Bremen Avenue, Egg Harbor City, NJ 08215

In 1864, champagne salesman Louis Renault travelled west, liked what he saw and planted vineyards. He was soon selling his own wine rather than that of the firm that had sent him. Today, New Jersey's oldest winery receives thousands of visitors a day and hybrid/*vinifera* plantings are on the increase, which is good news for the firm's Renault, Dumont and St-George's brands.

Tomasello Winery   MC   ★
225 White Horse Pike, Hammonton, NJ 08037
The first farming Tomasello founded this winery just after Prohibition and the family's first sparkling wine was made in the late 1940s. A few French hybrids introduced in the early 1970s are now blended in with the ubiquitous 'foxy' grapes native to the East Coast. Today, third-generation Tomasellos make no less than six different sparklers – two of which are sold under the Kainier label. Sparkling wine production however still only adds up to about 6,000 cases per annum, of which the sweet Spumante and sweet (despite its label) Blanc de Blancs Brut are by far the most popular.

New York

Barrington Champagne Company   MC   ★→★★
2081 Route 230, Dundee, NY 14837
Bought-in Chardonnay grapes (plus a little Pinot Noir) from the Finger Lakes are processed traditionally by hand here and turned into some 400 cases of Barrington Blanc de Blancs.

Batavia Wine Cellars   TM   →★
School Street and Hewitt Place, Batavia, NY 14020
This large wine firm sells non-vintage transfer method sparkling wine under the Capri, Imperator and Royal Seal labels.

Benmarl Wine Company   MC   ★→
PO Box 549, Highland Ave, Marlboro, NY 12542
Once a research station for the Hudson River region, Benmarl is now owned by Mark Fuller. Tiny quantities are vinified here, but diligent New Yorkers should be able to track down the firm's vintage-dated Cuvée du Vigneron Mousseux Brut and Naturel,

although they are only produced once every five years. Both are made predominantly from Seyval Blanc grapes.

Bully Hill Vineyards   MC   →★
Greyton H Taylor Memorial Drive, Hammondsport, NY 14840

Bully by name but bizarre by nature, this quirky firm will soon celebrate three decades of trading. Bully Hill's labels both back and front are extraordinary – the wine within, made mostly from Seyval Blanc, topped up with a little Vidal, is less so. The firm's latest idea is a 'champagne rouge' made from red hybrids and labelled 'Mother Ship over Paris', to commemorate the owner's flight over the 1983 Paris airshow – of course.

Casa Larga Vineyards   MC   ★★
2287 Turk Hill Road, Fairport, NY

Some 500 cases of the 100 percent Chardonnay Casa Larga Naturel are produced annually from this estate's own grapes, grown in the Finger Lakes area.

Clinton Vineyards   MC   ★→★★
Schultzville Road, Clinton Corners, NY 12514

Clinton claims that it was the first to produce a *méthode champenoise* sparkler in the Hudson River Valley, just north of New York City. Called Seyval Naturel, it is made exclusively from that hybrid and total production is just 250 cases per annum. An American President with the same name must surely help current sales?

De May Wine Cellars   MC   →★
Route 88, Hammondsport, NY

This family-owned winery only sells wine at the door, so be prepared to make the trek to the Finger Lakes if you like the idea of purchasing a sweet red, rosé or white sparkler made by the *méthode champenoise*. The De Mays follow the traditions they built up at Vouvray in the Loire Valley before leaving France for the USA.

Domaine Charbaut   MC   ★→
Seneka Lake, NY

As the name infers, Domaine Charbaut is the American arm of

Charbaut, the champagne house. Since 1990 Domaine Charbaut has bought in grapes from the Seneka Lake district in the Finger Lakes region for both still and sparkling wines. The 1992 harvest produced some 16,000 cases of both styles. Quality, given the French connection, must be a cut above the usual Finger Lakes level.

Glenora Wine Cellars   MC   ★★
5435 Route 14, Dundee, NY 14837

Almost two decades old and with case sales to the order of 8,000 per annum, this small, quality-conscious Finger Lakes winery uses the grapes from its own 4 ha (10 acres) of Chardonnay and bought-in Pinot Noir, Pinot Blanc and Chardonnay to create its vintage-dated Chardonnay-dominated Blanc de Blancs Naturel, Brut, Brut Reserve and the new Rosé. The wine is hand riddled and aged on yeast for 18 months to three years prior to release. An ex-Chateau St-Jean Californian winemaker is now in charge here.

Gold Seal Vineyards   TM   ★→
Hammondsport, NY 14840

Founded in 1865 at Hammondsport, in the heart of the Finger Lakes, this historic winery was making 'Imperial Champagne' as early as 1870. A series of Reims-trained winemakers turned *labrusca* grapes into bubbly until an ex-Veuve Clicquot winemaker, Charles Fournier, started to work with the *vinifera* in the late 1950s. Today, this Seagram-owned outfit uses the Charles Fournier signature to denote its finest sparkling wine: the disagreeable, burnt-toffee-like Blanc de Blancs made from Chardonnay, Vidal and Ravat grapes. (Henri Marchant is another label.) Other transfer-method sparklers include Naturel, Brut, Extra Dry, Pink and Sparkling Burgundy, all made principally from the native American hybrid grape, the Catawaba. Every Gold Seal wine is now produced at the more modern Taylor Winery, close by.

Great Western Winery   TM/MC   ★→
Hammondsport, NY 14840

Great Western, founded in 1860, pips its Seagram sister GOLD SEAL at the post by being the oldest Finger Lakes winery by five years. Today, the historic Bonded Winery Number One makes several *méthode champenoise* wines of which the big seller must be the mostly hybrid-based Great Western Naturel New York Champagne, sold in a Dom Pérignon look-alike bottle. Other, finer *méthode champenoise* wines include the Pinot Noir-based Blanc de Noirs and the Chardonnay-based Brut Champagne. Sparkling wine is also made here from hybrid grapes via the transfer method and sold under such labels as Cold Duck, Sparkling Burgundy and the more familiar styles of Brut, Pink and Extra Dry.

Hudson Valley Wine Company   CC   →★
Blue Point Road, Highland, NY

This firm, situated in the centre of the Hudson River region, was founded in 1907 and sells about 5,000 cases of sparkling wine a year, made from a combination of American hybrids and the occasional superior French hybrid. Ultra-commercial labels include, among others, Sparkling Burgundy, Cold Duck, Brut, Extra Dry and Naturel.

Knapp Vineyards   MC   ★→★★
2770 County Road 128, Romulus, NY 14541

Knapp Vineyards Chardonnay Champagne Brut, made from Chardonnay plus a little Pinot Noir, is the best sparkling wine here. Alternatively, for half the price, try Knapp's Champagne made from hybrid grapes.

McGregor Vineyard   MC   ★★
5503 Dutch Street, Dundee, NY 14837

Robert McGregor's 9.3 ha (23 acres) *vinifera* vineyard, which, amongst other noble vines, is planted to Chardonnay and Pinot Noir, produces minute amounts of a promising Chardonnay-dominated *méthode champenoise* Naturel.

Monarch Wine Company   CC   →★
4500 Second Avenue, Brooklyn, NY

Situated across the river from Manhattan, Monarch brings in *labrusca* juice from New York State to produce the kosher Manischewitz sparkling wine and the Gallic-inspired Pol d'Argent, Chateau Laurent and Chateau Imperial in a variety of styles including Spumante, Cold Duck and Sparkling Burgundy. Sales are impressive but the wines are less majestic than they sound.

J Roget   CC   →★
Canandaigua Wine Company, 303 North Bloomfield
Road, Canandaigua, NY 14424

J Roget is a brand name of the Canandaigua Wine Company, situated at the head of the odd-sounding Canandaigua Finger Lake
(Canandaigua means 'Chosen Place' in Seneca Indian). Total sales
of flavoured sparkling wines, a style pioneered by the company, are
now in excess of 1M cases per annum. Its most popular line is
L'Orangerie, a peculiar blend of coloured, low-alcohol fizz, orange
juice, triple sec and 'other natural flavours'. Jacques Bonet in *brut*,
extra dry and *spumante* versions is another tank method
Canandaigua fizz. Together with Cook's and its other West Coast-
produced brands, this mighty sparkling wine concern produces
almost 3M cases of cheap, ordinary, tank method wine annually.

Royal Kedem Wine Corporation   CC   →★
Route 9W, Marlboro, NY

As this corporation's brand names of Kedem and Star of Abraham
suggest, the Herzogs, in the heart of the Hudson River area, produce sizeable amounts of kosher wine. Styles made include Cold
Duck, Sparkling Burgundy, Naturel and Demi-sec among others.

Schapiro's Wine Company   CC   →★
126 Rivington Street, New York, NY 10002

Manhattan's last-remaining winery, founded in 1899 by Samuel
Schapiro, produces kosher-approved sparkling wine under the
ubiquitous Cold Duck, Sparkling Burgundy and Spumante labels,
besides pink and dry fizz.

The Taylor Wine Company   TM   →★
Hammondsport, NY 14840

Seagram's third historic Hammondsport winery was founded in
1880. It bought out its next door neighbour, Great Western, in
1961 only to be bought out in turn by Coca-Cola in 1977 and,
eventually, by Seagram in 1983. Until 1968, Taylor's sparklers
were made by the *méthode champenoise* but phenomenal sales (with
12M bottles ageing at any one time) soon necessitated a switch to
the transfer method. Cold Duck and Sparkling Burgundy are made
principally from the foxy *labrusca* Concord, while the Brut, Extra

Dry and Pink sparklers rely heavily on native American hybrids such as Catawaba, Delaware and Aurore.

Wagner Vineyards   CC   →★
Route 414, Lodi, NY 14860
Celebration Cuvée is a cheap tank method sparkler made here from hybrid grapes.

Widmer's Wine Cellars   CC/MC   →★
West Avenue and Tobey Street, Naples, NY 14512
The Swiss Widmers arrived at Naples in the west Finger Lakes in the 1880s. Today there are over 35 Widmer wines, including some 20,000 cases of bulk method bubbly sold under the Lake Niagara name, plus a little *méthode champenoise*.

Hermann J Wiemer Vineyard   MC   ★→
PO Box 38, Route 14, Dundee, NY 14837
Teutonic traditions continue here, for Wiemer's *méthode champenoise* sparkler, the Naturel Vintage Brut, is made entirely from Riesling. Future plans include the introduction of a Chardonnay/Pinot Noir blend.

Windsor Vineyards & Great River Winery   MC   ★
104 Western Avenue, Marlboro, NY 12542
This winery, situated in the centre of Marlboro, sells sparkling wine under the Great River Winery and Windsor labels. Some time ago it was bought out by Windsor Vineyards, a subsidiary of Sonoma Vineyards, which used to be connected with Piper Sonoma. All rather confusing. Small amounts of non-vintage *méthode champenoise brut* are made.

Woodbury Vineyards   MC   ★→
South Roberts Road, Dunkirk, NY 14048
The Woodburys have tended their vines here on the shores of Lake Erie since 1910. It took another 60 years, however, for the family to become interested in the *vinifera* vine. Small amounts of a Chardonnay Champagne Brut are made.

North Carolina

Biltmore Estate Wine Company   MC   ★★
1 North Pack Square, Asheville NC 28803

The celebrated Biltmore stately pile was built by George Vanderbilt in 1895 and is now owned by the wonderfully-titled William Amherst Vanderbilt Cecil. Chardonnay and Pinot Noir have been planted on the estate for some years now. The new vineyards, an imported French winemaker, and a new no-expense-spared winery, started in 1985, and housed in the old dairy barns, should ensure that the vintage-dated *méthode champenoise* Biltmore Estate and Chateau Biltmore wines are better than most. About 2,000 cases are made in most years. Chateau Biltmore comes entirely from the family's own grapes and is the better wine.

Duplin Wine Cellars   MC   →★
Highway 117, Rose Hill, NC 28458

This group of North Carolina grape growers has joined forces to produce, amongst other wines, vintage-dated *brut* and sweet *méthode champenoise* sparklers. They are made from the curiously flavoured Scuppernong grape, unique to the southeastern states.

Ohio

Cedar Hill Wine Company   MC   ★
2195 Lee Road, Cleveland Heights, OH

A doctor-cum-restaurateur-cum-winemaker, who is nothing if not enterprising, makes a *méthode champenoise* sparkler called Chateau Lagniappe in the restaurant's cellar. The wine is only sold upstairs.

Mantey Vineyards   CC   →★
917 Bardshar Road, Sandusky, OH 44870

Sandusky, on the shores of Lake Erie, is the centre of Ohio's wine industry and this revamped 100-year-old winery now produces bulk method bubbly from French-American hybrids.

Meier's Wine Cellars   CC   →★
6955 Plainfield Pike, Silverton, Cincinnati, OH 45236

At the other end of Ohio from Sandusky and close to Cincinnati, these cellars are under the same ownership as MANTEY and MON AMI. Production of *cuve close blanc de blancs* (made in part from French hybrid grapes grown on a small Lake Erie island) is considerably larger here than at the other two firms.

Mon Ami Champagne Company   MC   →★
3845 East Wine Cellar Road, Port Clinton, OH 43452

As the firm's old West Catawaba address suggested, the foxy *labrusca*-redolent Catawaba grape has much to do with the Mon Ami's *méthode champenoise* sparkler. This wine is produced in century-old cellars above which the Mon Ami restaurant is now housed.

Moyer Vineyards   MC   ★→
3859 US Route 52, Manchester, OH 45144

Wineries-cum-restaurants seem to be the thing in Ohio, for the Moyers run both at No 3859. *Méthode champenoise* wine is made here from French hybrids.

Steuk Wine Company   MC   →★
1001 Fremont Avenue, Sandusky, OH 44870

Labrusca reigns supreme at this small winery, whose Extra Dry, Brut and Naturel *méthode champenoise* wines take some getting used to by palates not attuned to the *labrusca* style.

Stillwater Wineries   MC   ★→
2311 State Route 55, West Troy, OH 45373

Hardly the most appropriate name for a sparkling wine house! Stillwater Wineries' non-vintage *méthode champenoise* Brut comes from French hybrid grapes that are grown close to Stillwater River.

Oregon

Argyle   MC   ★★→
691 Highway 99 West, Dundee, OR

Elegant, toasty, smoky Argyle is proof positive that Oregon is the
right place for a classy Pinot Noir- and Chardonnay-based *méthode
champenoise* fizz. Even the *champenois* occasionally put Argyle ahead
of its high class Australian cousin, Croser. Typically, Rollin Soles,
the man in charge here, together with equally well travelled viticulturist Allen Holstein, believes that the most important aspect of
Oregon sparkling wine is the hint of tall, green fir trees, salmon
slapping up stream and the vineyard view of the Cascades shim-
mering on a summer horizon. The rest of us feel that it has rather
more to do with the right grapes grown in Oregon's cool, late
harvest Champagne-like climate, plus top *méthode champenoise*
skills, acquired no doubt not simply from founding partner Brian
Croser and his Australian winery Petaluma, but also from connections with Bollinger.

Brian Croser founded Argyle jointly in 1987 with Calvert
Knudsen, long-time Oregon pioneer and founder in his turn of
KNUDSEN-ERATH. Although no vineyards are owned by Argyle, its
vineyard management company oversees 120 ha (296 acres) of
closely-spaced, trellis-trained, low-cropped Dundee Hills vineyards planted to 60 percent Pinot Noir and 40 percent Chardonnay.
Most of the Argyle grapes come from here. The firm's toasty,
smoky-bacon-like '88 Argyle Brut (Pinot Noir and Chardonnay)
aged for around 3–5 years on lees is the big seller, accounting for
over half of the total output, which is about 16,000 cases a year. A
vintage-dated *blanc de blancs* (100 percent Chardonnay) and Rosé
(100 percent Pinot Noir) complete the Argyle range. Remarkably,
'87 was Argyle's first vintage – for the second to show world class
quality should frighten the French.

Arterberry   MC   ★★
PO Box 772, 905 East 10th Street, McMinnville, OR 97128

Oregon's first *méthode champenoise* wine was made here, in the heart
of the Willamette River Valley, in a corner of the Eyrie Vineyards
winery by a winemaker trained at the University of California at
Davis. Brut and Naturel wines are produced, both vintage-dated.

Chateau Benoit   MC   ★→
6580 North East Mineral Springs Road, Carlton, OR 97111
The Benoits make limited amounts of the vintage-dated *méthode champenoise* Chateau Benoit Brut, among other wines, from nearly 16 ha (10 acres) of Willamette River Valley grapes, including Chardonnay and Pinot Noir.

Hillcrest Vineyard   MC   ★
240 Vineyard Lane, Roseburg, OR 97470
Hillcrest was one of the first wineries to plant noble vines in Oregon and now grows Chardonnay and Pinot Noir. The Vineyard Lane address is reassuring, even if the extra dry *méthode champenoise* wine is sold under the less elegant name of Oregon Mist.

Knudsen–Erath Winery   MC   ★★
Worden Hill Road, Dundee, OR 97115
This leading Oregon winery, with 28 ha (70 acres) in the Willamette Valley, was started by Richard Erath and C Calvert Knudsen. Every year they make 2,000 cases of a Chardonnay-dominated non-vintage *brut*, mechanically riddled and topped up with Pinot Noir. The prospects look promising.

Laurel Ridge Winery   MC   ★→
PO Box 225, Route 1, Forest Grove, OR 97116
David and Susan Teppola own 14 ha (34 acres) of Yamhill County vines and lease a further 8 ha (20 acres) in Washington County. (The latter is one of the oldest vineyards in the Willamette Valley.) These vineyards provide them with all the grapes they need to make 5,000 cases of sparkling wine annually. Most of this is the White Riesling-based Cuvée Blanc, but a superior, Pinot Noir-dominated Brut and a Brut Reserve are also made. Half of Laurel Ridge's production is now sparkling wine, and this is likely to increase with a new planting of 8 ha (20 acres) of Chardonnay and Pinot Noir in 1993 specifically for sparkling wine production.

St Innocent Winery   MC   ★→
2701 22nd Street NE Salem, OR 97302
This ecclesiastical-sounding place has nothing to do with the church, but was founded in 1988 by nine shareholders. The winemaker

here trained at ARTERBERRY and so far just 300 cases of sparkling wine are made here every year, all from bought-in grapes. Most of this is the vintage-dated Brut, which spends three years on lees, but a finer Reserve Cuvée, which spends six years on lees, is in the pipeline and should be ready in 1998. St Innocent is usually a 60 percent Pinot Noir to 40 percent Chardonnay blend. So far only the '88 vintage has been released, the '89 is due soon.

Pennsylvania

Bucks Country Vineyards   MC   ★
6123 York Road, New Hope, PA 18938

This winery, complete with its own wine museum, is housed in an old barn. It produces, among other wines, a non-vintage *méthode champenoise brut* made mostly from bought-in grapes.

Penn Shore Vineyards   MC   ★→
10225 East Lake Road, North East, PA 16428

Expertise from the University of California at Davis turns what are mostly *labrusca* grapes into wine here, but French hybrids and some *vinifera* have also been planted. About 5,000 cases of non-vintage fizz are sold each year, including a *méthode champenoise* Seyval Blanc.

Texas

La Buena Vida Vineyards   MC   ★→
WSR Box 18–3, Springtown, TX 76082

The Smith family's hybrid-dominated vineyards are situated west of Fort Worth and south of Springtown. A *méthode champenoise* non-vintage La Buena Vida Brut and Naturel are the main concerns here.

Virginia

Ingleside Plantation Vineyards   MC   ★→
PO Box 1038, Oak Grove, VA 22443

Virginia's first *méthode champenoise* sparkler was made here from hybrid grapes by the Flemer family, aided by retired Belgian oenology professor Jacques Recht. The infinitely more classy Chardonnay grape, plus some Pinot Noir and Pinot Meunier, are now being used to create a non-vintage dry and rosé. Chesapeake Sparkler is also available. The firm's grape needs for its 500-case annual production are all supplied by its own 2 ha (5 acres) of Virginian vines.

Oasis Vineyard   TM/MC   ★→
Route 1, Hume, VA 22639

An oasis indeed, for this 36 ha-vineyard (80 acres) close to Washington DC, with a view of the Blue Ridge Mountains, turns part of its production into *méthode champenoise* wines, made mostly from Chardonnay and Pinot Noir and sold in Brut, Extra Dry and the new Royal Pink Cuvée versions. 14,000 cases are made in most years.

Rapidan River Vineyards   MC   ★→
PO Box 199, Route 4, Culpeper, VA 22725

The German owner and the German Geisenheim-trained winemaker obviously make a good team here, for both Riesling and Chardonnay have been planted and their Extra Dry *méthode champenoise* sparkler is going down well with locals.

Washington

Chateau Ste-Michelle   MC   ★★
One Stimson Lane, Woodinville, WA

This 'French chateau' in the Yakima Valley made its first wines in the mid-1960s. Its sizeable vineyards are now planted with both Pinot Noir and Chardonnay. Sparkling wine production concentrates on a vintage-dated *blanc de noirs brut* made by the *méthode champenoise*, which spends four years on yeast. Latest releases include a Chardonnay *blanc de blancs* and a Pinot Noir/Chardonnay *brut* blend.

Hinzerling Winery   MC   ★→
1520 Sheridan Avenue, Prosser, WA 99350
The Wallace family, complete with its own Davis-trained wine-maker, runs this winery on the north side of the Yakima Valley. It grows a wide range of noble grape varieties and makes vintage-dated *brut* and extra dry Hinzerling wines.

Mont Elise Vineyards   MC   ★→
315 West Steuben, Bingen, WA 98605
Local German traditions have not stopped the Henderson family from planting Pinot Noir and Chardonnay in addition to noble German grape varieties in its hilltop vineyard overlooking the Columbia River gorge, which forms the border with Oregon. So far only a vintage-dated *méthode champenoise brut* has been released.

Mountain Dome Winery   MC   ★→
PO Box 199M, Route 2, Spokane, WA 99207
The entire Manz family including the three children help out at this small, 2,000 case winery situated in the foothills of Mount Spokane. The Manzs only make sparkling wine and are clearly aiming for quality above all else and do everything they possibly can to acquire it. This includes building a temperature-controlled winery themselves and using only hand-harvested Pinot Noir, Chardonnay and a little Pinot Meunier, which are grown in the Columbia River Valley. In addition, the *méthode champenoise*-only wines undergo their first fermentation in French oak barrels, are aged for four years on lees and half of the production is riddled by hand. Just three different sparklers are made: the vintage-dated Pinot Noir and Chardonnay Brut, plus the Pinot Noir-based Rosé and Blanc de Noir. The firm's first vintage was the '84. Sensibly, Iron Horse's winemaker in California is used as a consultant here.

Preston Cellars   MC   ★→
502 East Vineyard Drive, Pasco, WA 99301
Powerful Preston is one of the top family-owned Washington

State wineries. The estate's own noble *vinifera* vines (including Chardonnay and Pinot Noir) are planted close to the Columbia and Snake rivers. The firm also buys in grapes. Among the wines produced here by Preston's winemaker (trained at the University of California at Davis) is a non-vintage *méthode champenoise* extra dry, available in two different blends: a white Riesling or a Pinot Noir/Chardonnay.

Other USA Sparkling Wine Producers

Bloomington Winery, Indiana; Conestoga Vineyards, Pennsylvania; Highland Manor, Tennessee; Moore Dupont, Missouri; Moyer, Texas; Winery of the Abbey, Missouri; Wines of St Augustine, Florida.

Australia

Australia is close behind California in the making and drinking of sparkling wine. Indeed, sparkling wine is (together with 'coolers') the big growth area in the Australian drinks business. In 1993, Australians drank an impressive 40M bottles of sparkling wine, or, to put it another way, more than one bottle of wine in three consumed was of sparkling wine. Given such a bullish market it is not surprising that the more internationally-minded French champagne houses should set up joint sparkling wine ventures with Australian firms, just as they have done in California. So far, California appears to be winning the joint venture race with seven *grandes marques* firms to its credit. But Australia has signed up three to date. The ventures involve Roederer and Heemskeerk with Jansz, and Bollinger and Petaluma with Croser. Moët & Chandon has set up shop in Victoria's Yarra Valley at Green Point Vineyards and more such combinations, it is thought, are on the way. Drinks business insiders point out that several of these firms share the same Australian distributor, so there is no need to be clairvoyant to see where the next sparkling wine marriages might take place.

The chief difference between Australia and California when making sparkling wine is the excessive heat that Australian winemakers have to deal with. This is particularly a problem at vintage time, when grapes have been known to reach the winery at temperatures of 35°C (95°F) or more. True, the quest for, and planting of, cool-climate vineyards has helped. But it looks as if many Australian sparkling winemakers will be forced for some years to make do either with neutral, hot, irrigated vineyard fruit or else with the rather too overt, sunny, super-ripe fruit flavours that are the hallmark of much of the rest of the country's vineyards. Apart from the danger of donating too little or too much fruit flavour to the end result, base wines made from these vineyards often suffer from low acid and high alcohol levels, again resulting in less-than-perfect bottles of bubbly. The Australian sparkling wine industry is therefore forced to attempt the impossible: to make silk-purse wines out of sow's ear grapes. And yet, many firms compound their difficulties by choosing indifferent grapes when better ones are available. Sultana (California's Thompson Seedless), from the irrigated Riverland vineyards and elsewhere, is probably the low-est of the low. But neither decolourized Shiraz and Cabernet Sauvignon, Ugni Blanc/Trebbiano, Crouchen and Sémillon from the Hunter Valley, nor Victoria's bizarre Ondenc, provide the ideal sparkling wine base. However, the younger generation of winemakers are convinced that employing the classic Champagne mix of Chardonnay and Pinot Noir, and even Pinot Meunier, is the way forward. And this growing trend, together with the arrival of joint ventures with France, should continue to result in some dramatic improvements in the quality of Australia's sparklers.

One problem that will continue to beset the industry as a whole, however, is that just five brands, owned by only a few firms,

Riddling by hand, a practice now frequently replaced by automatic *remuage* using gyropalettes

dominate Australia's sparkling wine sales. One of these firms, the giant Penfolds, now controls Seaview, Seppelt and Lindemans, leaving Orlando as this group's closest competitor. Many envisage that the cheap Australian sparklers will become the monopoly of Penfolds, Orlando and the like, while the expensive, high-quality, hand-riddled *méthode champenoise* wines made from top quality grapes will become the prerogative of smaller, specialist wineries. It is clear that the medium-sized firms in between are the ones who are likely to suffer.

With so many changes in the air it is hard to predict the eventual style of the still-embryonic Australian sparklers. The late 1960s and 1970s was the era of transfer method and *cuve close* wines. So far, the 1980s and 1990s have proved to be the era of high quality, small-scale producer *méthode champenoise* wines, closer to the understated style of French champagne than ever before. Indeed, top Australian sparklers such as Croser and Green Point are every bit as good as most champagne houses' non-vintage *bruts*. Many Europeans are convinced too that there is no reason why the best Australian bubblies should not match the very best that the Champagne region can offer. In the past, Australia's sparkling wines tended to be sweet, coarse and earthy. It is now likely that the first division sparkling wines of the future will carry on reflecting the quality of fine Australian Chardonnay, Pinot Noir and Pinot Meunier fruit. It will continue to be an exciting evolution to witness.

Australian Sparkling Wine Labels and the Law

Australian sparkling wine laws have thankfully been tidied up.

- The words '*méthode champenoise*' now indicate that the wine has been made by the authentic *méthode champenoise*. The word 'champagne', however, may indicate either a genuine *méthode champenoise* or a transfer method wine. A *méthode champenoise* wine must now be fermented in a bottle and aged on its lees for not less than nine months before disgorging.

- The words 'fermented in *this* bottle' indicate a traditional *méthode champenoise* sparkler, while 'fermented in *the* bottle' denotes a transfer method wine. A bottle without either of these phrases is likely to have been made by the *cuve close* or Charmat method.

- Any sparkling wine that has acquired its bubbles by the carbonated method will carry the words 'carbonated wine' on the label or simply 'carbonated' followed by the brand name.

- Terms such as 'brut de brut', '*ultra brut*' and '*natur*' indicate a non-*dosage* wine.

Producers

Angas Brut
See Yalumba

All Saints Estate   MC   →★
Wahgunyah, Victoria 3687
This imposing red-brick castle of a winery sells a sweet sparkling wine called All Saints' Lyre Bird Champagne that receives its bubbles elsewhere.

Arrowfield   MC   ★
Denman Road, Jerrys Plains, NSW 2330
Only 2,000 cases of Cowra region sparkling wine are made here each year, predominantly from Chardonnay, plus a little Pinot Noir. Two wines are produced: the MC or Méthode Champenoise Chardonnay/Pinot Noir Cuvee plus the red PC, or Pinot Cuvee, made by the same method but exclusively from Pinot Noir.

Baskerville Wines   MC   →★
Haddrill Road, Baskerville, WA
Baskerville, a Swan Valley winery, sends some of its Ugni Blanc grapes away to be turned into *méthode champenoise* sparkling wines.

Berri-Renmano IM →★
Renmark, Riverland, SA

Passion Wine, based on passion fruit juice, is among the products of this giant concern, now part of the BRL Hardy Wine Company. Vast quantities of cheap, carbonated sparkling wines are also made.

Best's MC ★★→
Western Highway, Great Western, Victoria 3377

Best's, like nearby SEPPELT's Great Western Winery, was one of the wine pioneers in Victoria's gold country. It was among the first wineries in Australia to experiment with sparkling wines made from Pinot Noir, Chardonnay and Pinot Meunier, produced mostly from old vines. The first sparkler was made here in 1978 and today just 300 cases of *méthode champenoise* Concongella Cuvée are produced annually in Rosé and Brut de Brut versions. The restrained, low-crop '83 Chardonnay has been much admired as has the robust '87, while the rich, toasty-oaky '88 is a good and successful Australian wine style.

Wolf Blass TM ★
PO Box 396, Nuriootpa, SA 5355

Kellermeister, bow-tie fiend and wine promoter extraordinary, Wolfgang Blass is not easy to ignore. Neither are his best-selling wines. Behind the kitsch labels and marketing hype lie some well-made and skilfully-blended examples, with obvious flavours. The transfer method '83 Chardonnay Cuvée Champagne is no exception. The firm's newest sparkler is the Eaglehawk Brut Cuvée, a full-bodied wine that spends 18 months on lees and whose base wines are matured in oak. Over 50,000 cases are sold in Australia in most years. The '87's full, citric, brown bread-like flavours were good not great.

Bleasdale CC →★
Wellington Road, Langhorne Creek, SA 5255

Bleasdale was the first vineyard to be planted in this area, in 1860. Today, the firm's sparkling wines are made by the *cuve close* process from a blend of grape varieties and sold in *brut*, *demi-sec* and sweet, Muscat-based *spumante* styles.

Bonnonee Wines IM →★
Campbell Avenue, Irymple, Victoria

Bonnonee is a producer of inexpensive, flavoured sparkling wines such as Sparkling Passion (made from passion fruit) and Strawberry Sparkling, as well as the more familiar *spumante* style.

Brown Brothers MC ★→
Milawa, Victoria 3678

Brown Brothers is probably the best known wine firm in Victoria, outside Australia. Given the past decade's sparkling wine boom, it is odd therefore that the firm has not produced a widely-distributed sparkling wine before now. Brown Brothers' first attempt, the non-vintage King Valley Pinot Chardonnay, produced for Christmas 1992, has gone down well in Australia, so hopefully the rest of the world will get a crack at it too.

Cambrai MC ★→
Hamiltons Road, McLaren Flat, SA 5171

Cambrai Vineyards was founded 15 years ago. It offers the contract-bottled Mount Wilson Brut.

Chateau Remy MC ★→★★
Vinoca Road, Avoca, Victoria 3467
Star buy Cuvée Brut

Chateau Remy was originally set up to make brandy as a joint venture between Rémy Martin and a local firm, in 1961. A decade later, it suddenly switched to producing sparkling wine, starting with vineyards still planted with varieties intended for brandy. Chateau Remy's Cuvée Brut is still mostly Ugni Blanc-based with a touch, if any, of Chardonnay. However, the wine has a crisp, positive flavour, a fragrant bouquet and a creamy mousse, an excellent achievement for the Bordeaux-bred and -trained winemaker. If the Cuvée Brut has a fault it lies in the alcohol level, which is slightly too high. Great things are expected once the firm's sparklers are made 100 percent from Chardonnay and Pinot Noir.

Chateau Yaldara CC/IM ★
Gomersal Road, Lyndoch, SA 5351

German traditions live on at this ornate Barossa Valley 'Chateau', founded by Hermann Thumm. Yaldara's vast range of sparkling wines does not, alas, always match up to the splendid surroundings. Take your pick from Champers and Orange, Lambrusco and Spumante, and Chateau Yaldara pink, *brut* and *demi-sec*, or from the more promising *méthode champenoise* 'Champagne' range, of which the best are the Great Barossa Brut and vintage Reserve. Lakewood Brut is another Chateau Yaldara *méthode champenoise* wine. The '90 Yaldara Vintage Brut was soft, light and peachy. Robert, Hermann's son, trained at Geisenheim and is now wine-maker here, so Yaldara's teutonic traditions are likely to continue.

Cinzano IM →★
PO Box 488, Griffith, NSW
This Turin firm, now as famous for its *spumante* sparkling wines as for its vermouth, arrived in Griffith half a century ago. However, Cinzano's inexpensive, carbonated, Australian–made brands are not up to the standards set by its Asti Spumante produced in Italy.

The College Winery MC ★→
Barooma Street, Wagga Wagga, NSW
The wine course at Riverina College, set up more than 15 years ago, soon acquired its own commercial winery, which enabled the students to practise what their teachers had preached. Early releases from this well-equipped establishment, using its own and bought-in grapes, were impressive. However its *méthode champenoise* wine (made from Chardonnay and Pinot Noir) does not thrill.

Croser MC ★★→★★★★
Spring Gully Road, Piccadilly, SA 5131
Wine wizard Brian Croser was paid what is probably his greatest winemaking compliment to date when in 1985 the champagne house Bollinger bought a 20 percent share in Petaluma, the winery that produces Croser wines. In other New World sparkling wine joint ventures, Gallic expertise has usually formed an equal part-nership with the local firm. The difference in this case is that Bollinger has, it appears, merely invested in Petaluma. And it must be well-pleased with this investment now that Petaluma, with sev-eral other Australian wineries under its wing, is a AS$9M (£4M) public company, with Brian Croser and Bollinger still owning not

quite a quarter of its shares each. Despite the winery's new status it would appear that all decisions concerning Petaluma's *méthode champenoise* wines will still be left entirely to Croser and his eminently capable young team. This team will be backed as usual no doubt, by voluble, European-style expertise from Len Evans of ROTHBURY (no longer the chairman or even a shareholder here).

So far, 38 ha (94 acres) of immaculate, closely-spaced Chardonnay and Pinot Noir vineyards have been planted in the cool Adelaide Hills region, overlooked by Mount Bonython. These Piccadilly Valley vineyards are near to the original 4 ha (11 acres) Chardonnay and Pinot Noir home plot, which surrounds the well-equipped Petaluma winery. The first commercial Croser *cuvée*, the '85, mostly Chardonnay backed up by Pinot Noir, went on sale in 1987. Since then, about 12,000 cases each of half a dozen Croser vintages have been produced. (The not quite up to scratch '89 was sold on to ROSEMOUNT.) Of these the best so far have been the big, rich, biscuity, fruity '88 and the even more delicious, elegant, waxy, *brioche*-like '90, a three-star fizz. Proportions vary slightly from year to year, the '88 was 60 percent Pinot Noir to 40 percent Chardonnay, the '90 a 60 percent Chardonnay to 40 percent Pinot mix. New sparklers include the re-release of the aged '87 Croser (five years on lees), plus the '90 Blanc de Blancs and the Bridgewater Mill Rhine Riesling Brut, of which little is sold.

All the Croser wines (and plenty of contract fizz made for other firms) are processed and fermented at Petaluma and then transported to nearby Bridgewater Mill for ageing, riddling and disgorgement. This handsome three-storey mill, built in 1860, with its giant 'Old Rumbler' wheel, has been restored and turned into a restaurant/wine cellar and into a shop/wine museum/concert hall. As if all this were not enough, the dynamic Croser has set up a sparkling wine venture in America's cool Pacific Northwest state of Oregon, called Argyle. This man never stops.

De Bortoli   CC/IM/MC   →★
De Bortoli Road, Bilbul, NSW

The De Bortoli family has achieved miracles with its glorious, sweet, Sauternes-like *botrytis* (noble rot-affected) wines. But as yet its sparkling wines – the sweet Muscat-based *cuve close* Vittorio Spumante and carbonated wines – merit less enthusiasm. However, experiments with a Chardonnay-based *méthode champenoise* wine sound more promising.

Ellendale Estate Wines   IM   →★
18 Ivanhoe Street, Bassendean, WA 6054

Retired army man and trained winemaker Robert Hudson makes just 1,000 cases annually of carbonated Sparkling Moselle from Muscadelle and Muscat of Alexandria. These are sold direct from the winery with 30 other wines, including 'Chateau du Plonque'.

Andrew Garrett   MC   ★→
Kangarilla Road, McLaren Vale, SA 5171

Skilful marketeer Andrew Garrett snapped up *méthode champenoise* supremo Warren Randall, who previously made sparkling wine at Wynn's, SEAVIEW and SEPPELT in the late 1980s. As partner and chief winemaker, Randall is the man responsible for the non-vintage Andrew Garrett Pinot Noir, a pale pink bubbly that Australians rate. Intriguingly, the fruit for this wine comes from the Marlborough region of New Zealand, which you might say is as close as the Australians are likely to come to giving the New Zealanders a compliment. Andrew Garrett also makes a well thought of sparkling burgundy.

Green Point Vineyards   MC   ★★→★★★
Yarra Valley, Victoria

Dr Tony Jordan is the man in charge at Moët & Chandon's Australian outpost, whose Yarra Valley bubbly is sold in Australia under the Domaine Chandon label, but everywhere else in the world as Green Point Vineyards. Jordan came to Green Point in 1985 peculiarly well-equipped to produce a first class Australian *méthode champenoise* wine. A chemist by training, he worked with Brian CROSER on experimental blends (before Bollinger took an interest in Petaluma), which must have been a huge help. In running Oenotec, their wine consultancy, which involved travelling all over the country, making wine, planting vineyards and evaluating blends, he was of even greater use. Jordan thus brought to Green Point and Moët & Chandon (Australia) a unique knowledge of his country's best plots of Chardonnay, Pinot Noir and even Pinot Meunier. Small wonder then that Green Point's first overseas release, the rich, creamy *brioche*- and pineapple-layered '89 Brut, was a winner.

To date, Green Point has 30 ha (74 acres) of Chardonnay, Pinot Noir and Pinot Meunier planted on its impressive Yarra Valley site, whose visitors' centre and winery could perhaps prove to be as spectacular as California's Domaine Chandon operation. Despite Green Point's own excellent grapes, Jordan, like his *champenois* colleagues, firmly believes that richness and complexity is built by blending, which explains why one-third bought-in fruit is flown to Green Point from as far away as Tasmania and Coonawarra. Jordan is also a fan of long yeast ageing and, besides giving vintage bubbly here at least two and a half years on its lees, he intends to introduce an LD or 'late disgorged' style.

Other new Green Point sparklers include a delicious, big, full, buttery '90 Blanc de Noirs Brut, a three-star wine, and the crisp, zesty, streamlined '89 Blanc de Blancs. The latter is not the greatest Green Point wine style yet to appear and is similar to the firm's first Australian release, the somewhat skinny '86 Blanc de Blancs. Green Point's latest vintage is the '90, whose rich, full, creamy, yeasty style is not quite in the same league as the magnificent '89. It is however a very impressive, extraordinarily fine, flowery, Chardonnay-dominated wine. Green Point's sales now stand at over 20,000 cases a year and are likely to rise, which is good news for its many fans.

Thomas Hardy & Sons   TM/MC   ★★
Reynell Road, Reynella, SA 5161
Star buy Sir James Cuvée Brut

Several Hardys still work in this once family-owned firm, which is now part of the BERRI-RENMANO BRL Hardy group. Their top Sir James non-vintage Cuvée Brut accounts for just over 50,000 cases of the 200,000 of sparkling wine produced annually. Made from Chardonnay, Pinot Noir and Sémillon, its elegant, citrusy, fruity-floral style makes it a two-star plus wine. The ripe, fruity, agreeable Grande Reserve, also made by the transfer method but this time with Rhine Riesling and Grenache in the blend, accounts for 16,000 cases. Hardy's two latest releases are the Pinot Noir-dominated Lauriston Brut and the 100 percent Rhine Riesling Leasingham Classic Clare, launched to commemorate Leasingham's centenary (the firm is a leading light in Clare wineries). Lesser quantities of transfer method Brut and Demi-Sec Grande Reserve, with some Chardonnay and Pinot Noir in the blend, are also made. Hardy's finest sparkling wine, the *méthode champenoise* Grande Cuvée, based on Pinot Noir topped up with Chardonnay, is produced in small amounts. It spends about three years on yeast.

Hoffmans   CC   ★
Para Road, North Para, Tanunda, SA 5352
This large Barossa Valley winery sells two types of sparkling wine, the Muscat-based Spumante and the superior Hoffmans Brut.

Hungerford Hill   MC   ★→
Broke Road, Pokolbin, NSW 2321
Hungerford Hill is one of the Hunter Valley's biggest visitor attractions, with its inn, cellar visits and restaurant, although there is now some doubt about the firm's future. The H H Collection Champagne '82 is made partly from Coonawarra grapes and from equal proportions of Chardonnay and Pinot Noir. It is a zippy, flavoury wine and shows high acidity.

Irvine   MC/TM   ★
Roeslers Road, Eden Valley, SA 5235
James and Marjorie Irvine, the folk responsible here, make just three sparklers annually, of which the most popular is the Irvine Brut Royale. This unusual *blanc de blancs* is made from Chardonnay and Meslier grapes and spends a lengthy six years on lees, hence its full-bodied style. Irvine's answer to Australia's popular sparkling burgundy wine style is Irvine Merlot Brut, made from the Merlot grape. The third, and cheapest, Irvine sparkling wine, made by the transfer method not the *méthode champenoise*, is the new Meslier Brut, which was launched in 1992. James Irvine is also a consultant to CHATEAU YALDARA.

Jansz   MC   ★→
Pipers Brook via Lebrina, Tasmania 7254
Champagne house Louis Roederer, it is rumoured, had its eye on several mainland wineries before it plumped for Heemskerk as a joint-venture partner. It is, however, still too early to tell whether

Roederer has made the right choice in opting for cool-climate Tasmania. The island's Pinot Noir and Chardonnay are promising, but as yet their quality is mostly unproven. Jansz '90 is the first release – an extraordinarily tart, acid, lemony-oaky wine that smells of violets and is made by the *méthode champenoise*. So far, Heemskerk, the largest Tasmanian winery, has planted 8.9 ha (22 acres) of Pinot Noir and Chardonnay and, judging by the excess acidity in its first release, must still be busy working on experimental blends.

Katnook Estate   MC   ★
Penola Road, Coonawarra, SA 5263

Katnook is best known for its stylish, classic Sauvignon Blanc still wine, which is one of Australia's best examples from this grape. Only a tiny proportion of the firm's sizeable Coonawarra crop appears under the Katnook label, as most of the wine is sold off to other companies. Not too surprisingly, Katnook, which was once advised by wine consultants Oenotec, keeps back *la crème de la crème* for itself. This should have given its Chardonnay *méthode champenoise* wine a helpful start in terms of quality. The '87 Chardonnay Brut, however, while being gutsy and ripe is also a bit soapy.

Krondorf   MC   ★→
Krondorf Road, Tanunda, SA 5352

This Barossa Valley winery was founded in 1978, although parts of the winery and vineyard are much older. It has swiftly made a name for itself in Australia for its well-made varietal wines. The firm's Chardonnay-based *méthode champenoise* wine is also good.

Peter Lehmann   MC   ★
PO Box 315, Tanunda, SA 5352

Ex-SALTRAM winemaker Peter Lehmann buys in grapes from all over the Barossa Valley to turn into a wide range of wines. His Brut Absolu is made from equal parts of Muscadelle and Rouschette and spends three years on yeast. Future releases may well have some Pinot Noir and Chardonnay in the blend.

Lindemans   MC/CC   ★
McDonald's Road, Pokolbin, NSW 2320

Lindemans made a *méthode champenoise* wine called Sparkling

Empire back in 1944, so it is sad to learn that competition is forcing the group (including the Leo Buring and Rouge Homme subsidiaries) to lease its sparkling wine facilities. It is likely to continue to wind down its sparkling wine operation, and there are now very few Lindemans sparklers, apart from small amounts of an expensive Coonawarra Pinot Noir *méthode champenoise* wine called H J Lindeman, sold at the cellar door. However, if you are quick there is still time to slake your thirst with Lindeman's cheaper, *cuve close* wines, such as Leo Buring's Sparkling Ringolde.

Maglieri Winery   IM   →★
Douglas Gully Road, McLaren Flat, SA 5171

Italian Steve Maglieri sells the style of sparkling wine that his countrymen enjoy, including *lambrusco*, and a sweet Muscat-redolent Gran Spumante and Demi-Sec Spumante.

McWilliam's   IM/CC/MC   →★
Marrowbone Road, Pokolbin, NSW 2320

Occasionally, McWilliam's makes magnificent wines, such as the '78 Mt-Pleasant Maria Riesling, but the general run is dull and occasionally faulty, and the sparkling wines are sound if undistinguished. Among them are the sweet, tank method Bodega Sparkling, the slightly less sweet *méthode champenoise* McWilliam's Champagne, Pink Champagne and Brut Champagne, plus the not so distinguished *cuve close* sparklers: Sparkling Moselle, Burgundy and Rosé. The most stylish is the light, frothy, barley sugar-like Markview Champagne Brut. This is made largely from Sémillon, with 20 percent Chardonnay to lighten the load.

Middlebrook   CC   →★
Sand Road, McLaren Vale, SA 5171

Middlebrook has had its fair share of upheavals over the years but, with the help of Oenotec, the high tech wine consultancy firm, this traditional winery gradually moved into the 21st century in the late 1980s. No doubt improvements have been made to the *cuve close* sparkling wine.

Miranda Wines   TM   →★
57 Jondaryan Avenue, Griffith, NSW 2680

Sam, Lou and Jim Miranda make 250,000 cases of mostly transfer method fizz here every year. Barossa Ridge Louana, a *méthode champenoise brut*, is their best wine. Miranda Golden Gate Brut and Golden Gate Spumante are popular, inexpensive and sweet.

Mitchelton   MC   ★→
PO Box 2, Nagambie, Victoria 3608

This vast winery, overshadowed by its faintly ridiculous witch's hat-shaped look-out tower (an apt observation by Australian winewriter, James Halliday), is almost two decades old. Yet with the early help of wine consultancy Oenotec, its wines, especially the whites, are as crisp, lively and palate-pleasing as anyone could ask for. Prospects look good therefore for Mitchelton's recently-released *méthode champenoise* wine.

Montrose Estate   MC   ★→
Henry Lawson Drive, Mudgee, NSW 2850

This Italian-owned winery is nearly 20 years old, but has only recently started making sparkling wine. Consultants Oenotec helped with the first Pinot Noir *méthode champenoise* releases. Montrose bought out Craigmoor, the historic Mudgee winery, and in turn both wineries have been bought by the large ORLANDO/WYNDHAM group. Craigmoor was best known for its sweet, Muscat-based sparklers.

Mountadam   MC   ★→
High Eden Ridge, Eden Valley, SA 5235

Bordeaux oenology graduate Adam Wynn is the third generation of winemaking Wynns at Mountadam. Together with his father he is the driving force here. As the name suggests, the winery sits atop High Eden Ridge, east of the Barossa Valley. Its *méthode champenoise* wines have used blends of both Pinot Noir and Chardonnay, of which 2.5 ha (5.5 acres) are grown nearby and supply Mountadam with all it needs to make just 1,000 cases a year. The '90 Chardonnay/Pinot Noir delivered weird, ripe, barley sugar-like flavours plus a slightly pink colour. It was barrel-fermented and spent three years on lees. The wine is far too pricey for what it is.

Norman's   MC   ★
Grants Gully Road, Clarendon, SA 5157

Jesse Norman planted the first vines here in 1853, but the Norman family no longer owns the winery, which has expanded considerably since the early days. For those who do not wince at the name, the non-vintage *méthode champenoise* Norman's Conquest Brut is a well-made wine.

Olive Farm   MC   →★
77 Great Eastern Highway, South Guildford, WA 6055

This was one of the earliest estates in the Swan Valley, indeed in Western Australia, and vines as well as olive trees have been grown here from the beginning. Olive Farm Champagne is made with gyropalettes. There is also a wide range of table and fortified wines.

Orlando   TM/CC   ★→
Rowland Flat, SA 5352

This large, well-known Barossa Valley firm was founded in 1847 and is now part of the Orlando/WYNDHAM empire. Orlando pioneered the *cuve close* sparkling wine method in Australia, in 1956, with the launch of its Barossa Pearl. Today, the firm makes a wide range of sparkling wines, mostly from bought-in Chardonnay, Sémillon and Palomino. The vintage-dated Carrington Brut Chardonnay is Orlando's finest wine, but *cuve close* pink, white and Gran Spumante versions of Starwine are also made. The Carrington range of transfer method wines, launched in 1980, includes vintage and non-vintage styles. Together with the new, multi-variety, buttery, lime- and lemon-scented Extra Brut (now with a dash of Pinot Noir in the blend), and its light, ordinary rosé sister, the wines in this range are among Australia's best-selling sparklers.

Penfolds Minchinbury   MC/TM/CC   ★
634–726 Princes Highway, Tempe, NSW

Penfolds makes not only Australia's biggest-selling sparkling wines but, according to some statistics, the country's biggest-selling wines of any sort. Case sales of the transfer method Minchinbury Brut and White Seal and the *méthode champenoise* Chardonnay/ Pinot Noir Special Brut reached into the millions in 1993. Unfortunately the quality of this vast production is not up to the standards set by Penfolds' best still wines. Other sparklers in Penfolds' range, such as the transfer method Kaiser Stuhl Brut or sweet Demi-Sec Special Reserve, also disappoint. The sweet-toothed, however, may find Kaiser Stuhl's popular Muscat-based *cuve close* Summer Wine acceptable, as well as the sparkling April Gold, White Duck, and Cold Duck or even the Stock Spumante range of white, rosé and Gala Gold.

Penley Estate   MC   ★→
McLeans Road, Coonawarra, SA 5263
The base wine for Penley Coonawarra Brut is made at the estate but receives its bubbles at Penfolds. Many small Australian sparkling wine concerns follow a similar practice. Penley's '89 Coonawarra Pinot Noir/Chardonnay Brut, made predominantly from the former grape, with its elegant, toasty scent and big, ripe, citrusy fruit is better than most such wines.

Petaluma
See Croser

Rosemount Estate   MC   ★→★★
Rosemount Road, Denman, NSW 2328
In just 17 years, Rosemount has leapt from nowhere to become an impressive winemaking and marketing force. With such dramatic growth, slight ups and downs in quality are perhaps inevitable. However, Rosemount's fine, buttery-oaky, quick-maturing Chardonnays are easy to appreciate – a factor that augured well for the firm's first sparkling wine release, the '83 Chardonnay Brut. This wine, made at Rosemount's winemaking facility at the delightful-sounding Tumbarumba, has a pale gold colour and youthful, fresh, yeasty-smoky taste, although it is let down by a slightly metallic finish. The '90 Brut, a one-off production by PETALUMA, enjoyed a creamy mousse plus a fresh, fruity palate.

Saltram Estate   MC   ★
Salter's Gully, Angaston Road, Angaston, SA 5353
This firm has had changes of fortune over the years, but since it was sold to Seagram, in 1979, life has been calmer. Saltram's Dry Brut Champagne is a good example of a traditional Barossa Valley

sparkling wine. Despite its name, Saltram's Dry Champagne is sweeter. Saltram's Willowbrook is a new release.

San Bernardino   CC   →★
PO Box 938, Griffith, NSW 2680
San Bernardino is owned by the Pilloni and Aliprandi families. Its *cuve close* Spumante, made principally from a blend of Muscat and Sémillon grapes grown in the hot Murrumbidgee irrigation area, is an inexpensive, sweet sparkling wine.

Schinus Molle   MC   ★→
Mornington Peninsula, Victoria
Garry Crittenden is the winemaker here and he also advises GREEN POINT VINEYARDS, which explains why the Schinus Molle Pinot Noir/Chardonnay sparkler is made at Green Point. Unlike Crittenden's Dromana Estate still table wines, the grapes for this sparkling wine are bought in from all over Victoria and South Australia. Quality is good.

Seaview   MC/CC/TM   ★→★★
Reynell Road, Reynella, SA
Star Buy '89 Edmond Mazure Pinot Noir/Chardonnay Brut
Leading Australian sparkling winemaker Norman Walker and his capable winemaking team are the force behind Seaview's *méthode champenoise* wines. Now that Seaview and its associate company Wynns have been bought out by PENFOLDS, its giant new sparkling wine cellars have been built in the Barossa. The reasonably-priced range of Seaview non-vintage sparklers, based on several grape varieties, includes a soft, frothy Seaview Brut, the better smoky-citrusy '88 Seaview Chardonnay/Pinot Noir and a sweet Demi-Sec Grand Cuvée, all of which spend more than a year on yeast. Other Seaview/Wynns sparkling wines include the '82 Tulloch Brut Champagne, made from 100 percent Hunter Sémillon, the splendid, multi-variety, inexpensive, fruity Killawarra Brut and Rosé, and the Muscat-redolent *cuve close* Wynns Black Label Spumante. Seaview's *pièce de résistance*, however, is the stylish lim-ited edition '89 Edmond Mazure, a *méthode champenoise* wine made mostly from Pinot Noir with a little Chardonnay, which spends four years on yeast. Its full, biscuity flavours are good. Even

competitive winemakers rate this sparkling wine as one of the best cheaper bottles currently available in Australia.

Seppelt Great Western   TM/MC   ★→★★★
Seppelt, 181 Flinders Street, Adelaide, SA
Star buy '72 Great Western Show Champagne

This firm dates from 1851, and today produces vast quantities of many different sparkling wines. Great Western's ripe, pleasant, fruity Imperial and Brut Reserve are the most popular in the range. They account for sales of what must be millions of cases per annum (although Seppelt will not confirm this figure). This means that in terms of sales it takes second place on the market to PENFOLDS MINCHINBURY. The Great Western Brut Reserve, like the over-ripe, pineappley '89 Chardonnay version, is made by the transfer method but from several grape varieties, including the curious Ondenc. Most of Seppelt's other sparkling wines are made by the *méthode champenoise*. These have included the strange, aromatic 100 percent Ondenc Great Western '79 Brut, the '85 Hans Irvine Brut, and the non-vintage Brut, which smells very strongly of lychees. Fleur de Lys is another major Seppelt brand.

It is a relief to know that the aggressive proportion of Ondenc in these and other Seppelt blends is gradually being replaced by Pinot Noir and Chenin Blanc. Seppelt also produces limited quantities of numerous varietal and show sparkling wines from Chardonnay, Pinot Meunier, Pinot Noir, Sémillon and Chenin Blanc, as well as the more classic and well-received '88 Seppelt Chardonnay/Pinot Noir. Great Western's Black Label edition of this last wine adds Pinot Meunier to the mix too. The firm's top sparkler is the *méthode champenoise* Salinger, much admired by Australians since its first vintage in 1983, but not likely to find favour with Europeans. The '89 showed perfumed, sweet and somewhat confected Australian fruit. But the most fascinating of all Seppelt's wines to Europeans are, sadly, being phased out. These form Seppelt's answer to Bollinger's RD and are the Great Western Show Champagnes, which spend ten years or more on yeast in Great Western's long, cool tunnels dug by gold miners in the late 1860s. The '70, made from Ondenc, had real class, with a delicious, smoky, bottle-age character.

Not everyone appreciates the qualities of Great Western's

Shiraz-based red Sparkling Burgundy, but the excellent '44 vintage was still going strong in the late 1980s and the most recent version, a strawberry-, blackberry- and cinnamon-scented, cough drop-like wine, is equally appealing.

Taltarni   MC   ★
Moonambel, Victoria 3478

This well-kept and well-run winery is just down the road from CHATEAU REMY. It is managed by the well-travelled Dominique Portet, whose father was formerly at Château Lafite and whose brother, Bernard, runs the Clos du Val winery in California. Dominique Portet trained at Montpellier and then spent some time at Clos du Val before he came to Taltarni, and his cosmopolitan experience is evident. So far, Taltarni, has been producing about 20,000 cases per annum of four different sparkling wines, none of which however is quite as good as Taltarni's still wines. The best hand riddled sparkling wine is the 100 percent Chardonnay *blanc de blancs*, Clover Hill, followed by the fruity, exotic, bonbon-like Cuvée de Brut and the pale pink, fruity, almost banana-flavoured Brut Taché. Taltarni's Royale is a sparkling variety of kir with a little blackcurrant juice blended in with the Ugni Blanc. The firm's latest offering, launched in 1993, is a 100 percent Tasmanian Chardonnay from 17 ha (43 acres) of the its own vineyards there. Taltarni hopes that this wine, aged for two years on lees, will be of 'great Australian quality'. ˙

Tolley Pedare   CC/MC   ★
30 Barracks Road, Hope Valley, SA 5090

Three brothers run this large, family winery. Apart from their cheap, sweet Hope Valley sparkling white, pink and *spumante*, the brothers make two *méthode champenoise* wines, which are much more up-market: the Crouchen-based Pedare Champagne Brut and the more classy Pedare Champagne Dry Premium based on Riesling.

Tyrrells Wines   MC/TM/IM   ★→★★★
Broke Road, Pokolbin, NSW 2321

This grand old Hunter Valley winery is run by Murray Tyrrell and his son Bruce. They currently produce only the base wines for their sparklers, from 61 ha (150 acres) of vines, sending the wines elsewhere to receive their bubbles. Gold medals at Australian shows prove the success of the system here. The top medal-winning wines include bottles such as Tyrrells' stylish *méthode champenoise* Pinot Noir and Pinot Noir/Chardonnay. Ashman's non-vintage transfer method Brut is a lower quality 100 percent Sémillon sparkling wine. Injection method Sparkling Brut and Spumante are also made.

Vasse Felix — MC — ★
Willyabrup, WA 6284

Vasse Felix, founded in 1967 by the Gregg family, is Margaret River's pioneer winery. The first commercial release of its non-vintage *brut*, a Pinot Noir-dominated wine with some Chardonnay and Pinot Meunier in the blend, was in 1987. This *méthode champenoise* sparkler includes vintages going back as far as 1981 and is made from grapes grown in the Margaret River region about 20 miles (32 km) from Vasse Felix.

Woodley Queen Adelaide — TM — →★
Blyth Street, Glen Osmond, SA

Woodley has had a somewhat chequered albeit colourful past, but the recent construction of a new winery may herald an improvement in its wines. The commercial Queen Adelaide Champagne, also available in a drier, *brut*, style, is a vintage-dated transfer method sparkler made from a blend of mostly bought-in grapes. Woodley is now owned by SEPPELT.

Wyndham Estate — MC — ★
Dalwood, via Branxton, NSW 2335

This Hunter River estate, founded by George Wyndham in 1828, claims to be Australia's oldest operating winery. The strong, sweet, yeasty Sémillon Brut Cuvée, with its greeny-gold colour and citrusy Sémillon character is usually a good although not great wine. Wyndham is now owned by ORLANDO and its top blend is the well thought of '86 Wyndham Estate Louis VI.

Yalumba — TM/MC — ★→★★
Eden Valley Road, Angaston, SA 5353

Yalumba in the Barossa Valley was founded by Samuel Smith,

using the proceeds of a successful 19th century gold strike. Today the Hill-Smith family still owns the winery and produces a wide range of still wines as well as 250,000 cases per annum of sparklers. Most of the latter is accounted for by the simple, fruity, lemon- and lime-scented, Sémillon-based Yalumba Angas Brut. This non-vintage wine, made by the transfer method, has *blancs de noirs* wines from Shiraz and Pinot Noir in the mix too. The pink version, based on Cabernet Sauvignon and Carignan, is soft, dull and vaguely raspberry-scented. Angas Brut Classic, three-quarters Chardonnay to one-quarter Pinot Noir, is a ripe, full, lemony step in the right direction. There is also a non-vintage, yeasty Pinot Noir-dominated Yalumba Cuvée Prestige No 1 and a rather good sparkling Cabernet Cuvée Prestige No 2, whose chunky, bitter-sweet raspberry fruit is worth trying. The firm's most exciting news however is the production (which Deutz the champagne house was involved in early on) of a Chardonnay/Pinot Noir/Pinot Meunier *méthode champenoise* wine, of which the latest vintage is the toasty-smoky '88 – D's best effort yet. Angas Brut is well-distributed in Britain.

Yellowglen   MC   ★→
White's Road, Smythesdale, near Ballarat, Victoria 3551
If anyone in Australia could make the perfect *méthode champenoise* wine it is Dominique Landragin. His family comes from Champagne and he himself worked at Lanson and Deutz before arriving in Australia and working for SEPPELT. Yellowglen, which he set up in 1982, has been bought by Mildara, which is now part of the Mildara-WOLF BLASS group, and Landragin has left to return to Champagne.

Yellowglen now produces 150,000 cases of six different *méthode champenoise* wines a year, including Mildara's Windsor brand. They show future promise rather than current pleasure, despite their popularity. M Landragin's successors certainly know their stuff, even if they are hampered by Victoria fruit. Yellowglen's best sparkling wine, the 100 percent Pinot Noir Cuvée Tradition from its own vineyards, is worth trying. Cuvée Victoria, made from equal parts of Victoria Chardonnay, and Pinots Noir and Meunier, is also worthwhile, as is the overt, strong 100 percent Chardonnay. Until the *cuvées* improve, however, Yellowglen's curious harsh, multi-variety non-vintage wine will find little favour in the Brut, the Crémant or the sweet Rosé form. Yellowglen's vintage Brut was introduced in 1990; the '89 vintage was somewhat rough and ready, but at least a move towards quality. The fresh, invigorating Windsor Brut Chardonnay is better. A sparkling Kir-Royale-in-a-bottle is also made under this label. Yellowglen bottles wine under contract for numerous firms.

Other Australian Sparkling Wine Producers

Jane Brook Estate, WA; Capogreco, NSW; Casella's Wines, NSW; Franco's Wines, NSW; Robinvale Wines, Victoria; St Peter's, NSW; Taranga Estate, SA; Tarawein, SA; Verona, NSW; Wantirna Estate, Victoria; Ward's Gateway Cellars, SA; West End Wines, NSW.

New Zealand

Australian sparkling winemakers must look enviously across the sea to New Zealand. Their neighbours have a temperate, maritime-influenced climate and a plethora of naturally acid, crisp, low-alcohol white wines. The Australians, with their much warmer climate and consequent struggle against overripeness, must wonder why they bother.

New Zealand's cool climate plus its already impressive Chardonnay and Pinot Noir wines have ensured the relatively recent arrival of world class *méthode champenoise* sparklers such as the magnificent Pelorus from Cloudy Bay and impressive Deutz Marlborough Cuvée from Montana. Moët & Chandon is about to release its first Marlborough Brut sparkling wine, but only on the New Zealand market. Others are bound to follow the Marlborough *méthode champenoise* trail: the elegant, lean, lengthy Chardonnay and Pinot Noir wines make the perfect sparkling wine base. But what does seem curious to outsiders is how reluctant the New Zealanders have been to develop their natural sparkling wine potential. Cheap carbonated and Charmat method fizz is much more common here than are classic *méthode champenoise* wines. Scarcely 20 percent of New Zealand's sparkling wines is made by the superior *méthode champenoise*, most of it is still injected or at best tank method. Due to the widespread availability here of inexpensive Australian sparkling wine from producers such as Seaview and Yalumba, this trend is, alas, likely to continue. Few firms seem prepared to spend time and money on *méthode champenoise* equipment and the inevitable riddling experiments, yeast trials et al that go with it. However, Montana has set a good example with its splendid joint-venture Deutz-Marlborough Cuvée. Others have already followed this lead and hopefully more will do so before long.

New Zealand Sparkling Wine Labels and the Law

- The words 'fermented in this bottle', 'bottle fermented' and '*méthode champenoise*' denote a genuine New Zealand *méthode champenoise* sparkler.

- Without the above terms on the label, New Zealand sparkling wine, no matter how French the name sounds, is made by the tank or Charmat method. 'Naturally fermented' specifically indicates a Charmat process wine.

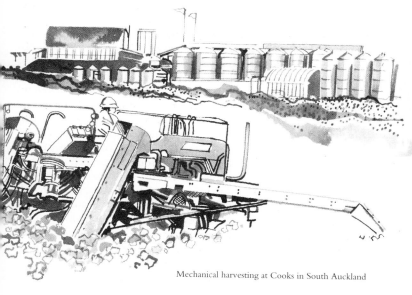

Mechanical harvesting at Cooks in South Auckland

- A great number of carbonated New Zealand sparkling wines are also available. The only clue on the label as to their method of production is that, beyond the brand name, there will simply be the words 'sparkling wine', without the addition of terms such as 'Reserve' or 'Première' to confuse.

- *Spumante* produced in New Zealand is usually made from Muscat grapes.

Producers

Cellier le Brun   MC   ★→
PO Box 33, Terraces Road, Renwick

South Island soil and French expertise came together in the 1980s to make Daniel le Brun *méthode champenoise* sparkling wine. M le Brun, from the champagne family of the same name, acquired vineyard land planted to Chardonnay and Pinot Noir close to Blenheim together with a brand new Coq champagne press. The early still Chardonnay and sparkling Brut and Blanc de Blancs showed future promise rather than current pleasure. To some extent this is still the case with le Brun's rich, golden, toasty, smoky, aged, non-vintage Brut and clumsy, yeasty '89 Blanc de Noirs. Apart from these two sparklers, le Brun's 14,000-case annual production from 13 ha (35 acres) of land, mostly planted to Pinot Noir vines plus a little Chardonnay and Pinot Meunier, currently includes a *blanc de blancs*, a rosé, a vintage wine and the prestige Cuvée Adèle. Le Brun is however a determined man and his future releases should be better.

Cooks   CC   ★
Paddy's Road, Te Kauwhata

Founded in 1969 by a group of Auckland businessmen, Cooks is one of New Zealand's most important wine companies. The firm has had its fair share of financial problems, but this has rarely been reflected in the wine, for the firm has always insisted on quality. Fernhill sparkling Chenin Blanc is its leading brand, and there is also sparkling Chasseur as well as a new product, Casavino, made from Dr Hogg Muscat grapes. Cooks merged with MCWILLIAM'S, New Zealand, some years ago and is now owned by CORBANS.

Corbans   IM   →★
PO Box 21–183, Great North Road, Henderson

This large winery was founded by a Lebanese in 1902 and now has a German winemaker. Grapes from three different production units at Auckland, Gisborne and, more recently, Marlborough are turned into the carbonated Première Cuvée (once a *cuve close* wine), the less toothsome, teutonic-inspired Sparkling Liebestraum, and the Italiano Spumante. The vintage-dated Amadeus is Corbans' top *cuvée*: a rich, Chardonnay/Pinot Noir sparkling wine admired by discerning New Zealanders.

Deutz Marlborough Cuvée   MC   ★★→
Riverlands Winery, Rd 4, 82–099 Blenheim

Strictly speaking this Cuvée is part of the Montana stable, but it is such a shining light to New Zealand's sparkling winemakers – and to the rest of the world's come to think of it – that it deserves an entry of its own. MONTANA launched Lindauer, its first *méthode champenoise* sparkling wine, in 1980. That the firm was able to release the fine, also non-vintage Deutz Marlborough Cuvée just a decade later (a joint venture between Montana and Deutz, the champagne house) says much for the top quality of Marlborough's vines for sparkling wine, and the ability of Montana's personnel to tap into Deutz's considerable *méthode champenoise* expertise.

Canny winemaker and Montana's man at the top, Peter Hubscher, describes the firm's launch of Lindauer in 1980 as the climax of a 'big, long, 13-year learning curve'. The two-year route from signing with Deutz in 1988 to the introduction of the first Deutz Marlborough Cuvée in 1990 sounds more exciting and less arduous. The combination of a New Zealand winemaker with Deutz experience, plus a gentle, giant automatic Coquard press, top, hand-picked Marlborough grapes (in the proportions of 60 percent Pinot Noir to 40 percent Chardonnay) plus two years on yeast, gave Montana the results it was looking for. At the moment, only 30,000 cases of the one Deutz style are released annually and its splendid, usually consistent, rich, ripe, waxy, fruity scent and taste, with some elegant, *brioche*-scented yeastiness is helped along by blending across vintages. Montana's sparkling wine team deserves a medal for achieving that rare wine world phenomenon: quantity and quality.

Glenvale Vineyards   IM   →★
Main Road, Bay View, Napier, Hawkes Bay
Situated in Hawkes Bay, Glenvale is now run by Don and Rob Bird and produces mostly sweet, ordinary sparkling wine under the Bianco, Spumante and Reserve Cuvee labels.

Korepo Wines   MC   ★
Korepo Road, Ruby Bay
No one could be that keen on the name Korepo's Olly's Folly, but this *méthode champenoise* Pinot Meunier and Chardonnay blend from a husband and wife team is popular in New Zealand.

Lintz Estate   MC   ★
PO Box 177, Kitchener Street, Martinborough
Chris Lintz and his family founded this estate in 1987. His 3ha (8 acres) of Martinborough vines as yet produce only tiny quantities of sparkling wine. Under 100 cases were made of the first Lintz releases, in 1991, but the family hopes eventually to produce ten times that amount. So far equal quantities of a *méthode champenoise* Lintz Riesling, Pinot Noir and Chardonnay have been made.

Lombardi Scintilla   IM   ★→
Lombardi, PO Box 8201, Te Mata Road, Havelock North
However scintillating Lombardi Scintilla may be in the eyes of its creators, its sweet, carbonated taste is unlikely to charm international taste buds. The Bianco style is a Müller-Thurgau/Muscatel blend; the Rosato is a cloying, pink Pinotage and Pinot Noir mix.

Matua Valley Wines   MC   ★→
Waikoukou Valley Road, Waimauku
The 'M' here stands for Matua Valley and *méthode champenoise*, the latest brainwave of the Spence brothers, Ross (winemaker) and Bill (viticulturist), who own this winery jointly with the Margan family. Behind the M label, of which 8,000 cases are produced annually, are 15 ha (38 acres) of Pinot Noir and Chardonnay vines in

Auckland and Marlborough. M's blend differs slightly from vintage to vintage but in most years is a 60 percent Pinot Noir to 40 percent Chardonnay blend. A nearby winery puts the bubbles in Matua Valley's M for the Spence brothers.

McWilliam's   CC   →★
Church Road, Taradale, Hawkes Bay

This traditionally-minded firm, founded in 1929, produces wines with flavours that non-New Zealanders can find hard to take. Its popular Charmat method Marque Vue, made from a blend of down-to-earth grape varieties including Chasselas, is sold under Brut, Pink and Medium labels. Marque Vue Gold is the superior version, made from Müller-Thurgau. McWilliam's has merged with COOKS and is now part of the CORBANS group.

Mills Reef Winery   MC   ★
Belk Road, Tauranga

One of New Zealand's tiny, new, *méthode champenoise* producers, in this case making just over 1,000 cases annually. So far, Paddy Preston has produced a handful of vintage-dated Chardonnay-based wines. The 1990 Mills Reef sparkling wine, made from Hawkes Bay Chardonnay, used only barrel-fermented free run juice and boasts a colourful label that will be either loved or loathed. Mills Reef hopes to build a new winery, complete with tasting facilities and restaurant, in the near future.

Montana Lindauer   TM/CC   ★→★★
Riverlands Winery, Rd 4, 82–099 Blenheim
Star buy Montana Lindauer Brut

Pinot Noir and some Chardonnay grown at the Ormond and Riverlands wineries make up two-thirds of the Montana Lindauer Brut Champagne, with the other third made up of Chenin Blanc and lesser grape varieties. The latter proportion has noticeably decreased over the past few years. With about 120,000 cases of Lindauer produced in most years, its style is now one of ripe, bouncy, grapey, almost exotic fruit and the wine is just what it should be: an easy-drinking sparkler. The deep pink, principally Pinot Noir-based version, with its ripe, raspberry fruit is slightly less impressive. Lindauer's top wine is the Special Reserve Brut de

Brut, whose extra ageing on yeast gives the end wine more class and body than the basic version.

Lindauer's quality from about 1989, when DEUTZ arrived, took a big step up. It was the first commercial *méthode champenoise* wine available in New Zealand, but due to the large volume produced is now made by the transfer method. There is also a *sec* version. Fans of the sweeter Muscat grape could try Montana's sweet, successful Bernardino Spumante and Sparkling Muscato Bianco. The firm also produces Mont Royale sparkling wine as well as the pink Pascale, whose blush comes from the addition of a small amount of red wine made from Pinotage, the South African grape.

Morton Estate   MC   ★★
State Highway 2, Aongatete via Katikati

Locals mistook the bizarre, fake Cape Dutch façade of this winery for a mosque or crematorium during its construction in 1982. But don't be put off by appearances – the winemaker here, John Hancock, is one of the best in New Zealand. Now part of the Australia-based Mildara Blass group, Morton Estate has 32 ha (80 acres) of vines, of which nearly 5.5 ha (14 acres) are in Hawkes Bay, 0.5 ha (2 acres) close to the winery and over 20 ha (50 acres) down south in sunny Marlborough. From the '93 vintage, all three Morton Estate styles (13,000 cases in total each year) have been made from the winery's own grapes. Currently, the non-vintage Brut boasts elegant, soft, yeasty, apricotty fruit (three-quarters Chardonnay to one-quarter Pinot Noir) that is bound to go up in quality when it is made entirely from Marlborough fruit. The White Label vintage version is 50 percent Pinot Noir to 25 percent each of Pinot Meunier and Chardonnay, and from the '92 vintage has been made entirely from Hawkes Bay fruit. The Black Label vintage is 100 percent Pinot Noir from Hawkes Bay and Katikati. The latter vintage versions are meaty, barrel-fermented, full-bodied, traditional wines, made specifically to contrast with the fresh, Marlborough fruit-oriented non-vintage, which is the biggest seller by far.

Nautilus Estate   MC   ★
Blicks Road, Renwick

Nautilus Estate, in sunny Marlborough, is Yalumba's New Zealand outpost. Since 1991, the Australian Hill-Smith family has bought in grapes and overseen the making of just one sparkler here, the Nautilus Cuvee Marlborough non-vintage Brut. Just over 1,000 cases are made each vintage and although the blend has been 75 percent Chardonnay to 25 percent Pinot Noir, new releases are likely to be predominantly Pinot Noir, which should tame some of the Nautilus' excess acidity.

Parker   MC   ★→
PO Box 572, 24 Banks Street, Gisborne

Phil Parker makes small quantities of three different *méthode champenoise* sparklers. The range includes the vintage-dated Classical Brut (mostly Pinot Noir with some Chardonnay), plus a well thought of rosé and finally Parkers Dry Flint, a Chenin Blanc-based blend.

Pelorus   MC   ★★★
Cloudy Bay, PO Box 376, Jacksons Road, Blenheim

Already dubbed the 'Krug of New Zealand' by envious antipodean competitors, Pelorus is named after the dolphin Pelorus Jack who guided seafarers safely through Marlborough Sounds a century ago. It does seem entirely appropriate that the man who put New Zealand Sauvignon Blanc on the world wine map with Cloudy Bay should have done the same all over again with the launch of his stunning Marlborough *méthode champenoise* sparkling wine.

David Hohnen would be the first to acknowledge the input into Pelorus of Kevin Judd, Cloudy Bay's winemaker, and of Californian visitor and one-time Schramsberg and Deutz California wine-maker Harold Osborne. The latter's wide experience in the area of sparkling wines and his Fresno State oenology schooling, like Hohnen's, has given Pelorus a full-bodied dimension of flavour that, to date, no other antipodean sparkler can offer.

Strangely, Veuve Clicquot-Ponsardin, which since the early 1990s has controlled Cloudy Bay and its Australian sister Cape Mentelle, has no input in Pelorus whatsoever and indeed the company's majority shareholding in the pair postdates the first Pelorus vintages by several years. If the French have any influence here at all, it will not be seen until the '91 vintage appears.

After an experimental 1986 harvest, the first Pelorus vintage to be released was the '87, followed by the finer '88, whose blend of

55 percent Pinot Noir to 45 percent Chardonnay delivered glorious, rich, golden, hazlenutty complexity. Only 5,000 cases are made each year and about half the grapes used come from the 4 ha (10 acres) of Chardonnay vines that surround the Cloudy Bay winery.

So far, Pelorus has largely met only an antipodean audience, but the '89 vintage is being exported to the UK. Pelorus' extraordinarily, bold, deep, powerful fruit and complexity stems, like Krug, from barrel fermentation and ageing of the base wines, three years' ageing on yeast in bottle for the final blend, plus no doubt the use of mature reserve wine in the mix too. Pelorus is only released when it is four and a half years old. Such an extreme style will probably be loved, or loathed by drinkers. But then, Krug frequently draws the same reaction...

Penfolds Wines   IM/MC   ★
PO Box 18–293 Auckland
Penfolds' New Zealand operation has, since 1986, been owned by MONTANA its most popular sparkler is the carbonated Muscat-scented Demi-Sec Chardon, sweet, low in alcohol, and made in white, pink or Gran Spumante versions, principally from Müller-Thurgau. The carbonated Le Papillon, a mixture of Chenin Blanc and Müller-Thurgau, is thankfully both drier and higher in alcohol. Hyland Brut is Penfolds' most up market *méthode champenoise* wine.

Selaks Wines   MC   ★
PO Box 34, Old North Road, Kumea
Selaks' wines have greatly improved over the past five years and this non-vintage Brut *méthode champenoise* sparkler, made from mostly Pinot Noir plus some Chardonnay, is a notch or two up from Champelle, the wine the firm used to make.

Soljans Wines   IM   →★
263 Lincoln Road, Henderson
This winery, better known for its fortified wines than for its Sparkling Spumante, is run by Frank Soljan's two sons.

Vidal
MC   ★→
PO Box 48, 913 St Aubyns Street East, Hastings
Star buy Vidal Brut
Elise Montgomery is now Vidal's capable winemaker. One of her creations is the 1,000 cases per annum of traditionally-made, vintage–dated Vidal Blanc de Blancs, Blanc de Noirs and the *méthode champenoise* Vidal Brut, a 50 percent Pinot Noir, 50 percent Chardonnay wine made from bought-in Hawkes Bay grapes. All three, alas, are scarce.

Villa Maria Estate
IM   →★
PO Box 43 046, 5 Kirkbride Road, Mangere
Yugoslav descendant George Fistonich owns both Villa Maria and VIDAL but the wineries are run separately. Sparkling wine production here is limited to about 20,000 cases a year of the sweet, carbonated St Aubyns Gold Label, a Müller-Thurgau and Muscat blend, plus the finer, drier Müller-Thurgau-based St Aubyns Black Label.

Seifried Estate
IM   →★
Sunrise Valley Road, Upper Moutere
Hermann and Agnes Seifried make a soft, low–alcohol, carbonated Sparkling Sekt from Rhine Riesling grapes with a dash of Pinot Noir. Just 2,500 cases are made annually.

South Africa

South Africa's sparkling wines took a giant leap forward in quality with the arrival of several new *méthode champenoise* sparklers in the late 1980s. Simonsig's Kaapse Vonkel, launched in 1971, was the Cape's first *méthode champenoise* wine, followed in 1978 by Boschendal's Brut and joined in the 1980s by at least four new brands. Achim von Arnim's Pierre Jourdan looks the most promising of all the newcomers, due to its uncompromisingly classic Chardonnay/Pinot Noir blend. The other producers, too, are gradually working towards this classic *cuvée*, reducing the quota of the Cape's workhorse sparkling wine grapes, such as South African Riesling, Chenin Blanc (known as Steen) and Colombard, year by year and particularly using more of the Cape's true Chardonnay grapes, new plantings of which are beginning to come on stream.

Apart from the intense heat which creates low-acid, high-alcohol wines and higher yields than quality demands, South Africa's sparkling wine producers are hampered chiefly by virus-ridden vineyards and by poor clones and strains of both Chardonnay and Pinot Noir. Resorting to low quality grapes, such as South African Riesling, Chenin Blanc, Colombard and Clairette Blanche, as an alternative does not, alas, produce first-division sparkling wine. The high yields (about three times those of most European vines) that most Cape growers expect do not help either.

And yet, although there are as yet few Cape sparklers to enthuse about, South African winemakers have done extraordinarily well given their viticultural, political and economic problems. Provided the country's sparkling wine momentum is not checked by recent arrivals such as Cold Duck, flavoured fizz and curious Sauvignon Blanc-based sparklers, the expanding sparkling wine market (over 6M bottles per annum) could carry on developing, both in terms of the quantity of wines produced and in the quality of wines available on the market.

To be fair to the Cape's producers the reason why so many Sauvignon Blanc-based sparklers continue to be made here is that from the start this clone was one and the same as the best French Loire Sauvignon Blanc clones. In the early days, the Cape's Chardonnay clones were lacklustre and often not the real thing;

indeed, the first Chardonnay clones in the Cape were Auxerrois and not Chardonnay at all. One of the most encouraging signs of quality in South Africa's sparkling wine production to date is the growing quantity of *méthode champenoise* wines made and the foundation in 1992 of the Méthode Cap Classique Association. Whilst this sounds a somewhat ugly title, one of the MCCA's chief concerns is to make certain the Cape's *méthode champenoise* producers up their quality from vintage to vintage.

A new, more champagne bottle-shaped, Cap Classique bottle launched in 1993 should help to emphasize the MCCA's aims.

South African Sparkling Wine Labels and the Law

- Most South African sparkling wines are made by the *cuve close* or Charmat method. The carbonated method is also used, most commonly for the cheaper wines, but apart from the price there is usually be no indication on the label or elsewhere to tell you which of these methods has been employed.

- However, any sparkler with the words '*perlé*', '*perlant*', or '*pétillant*' on the label will have been made by the carbonated method. These semi-sparkling wines, with less than two atmospheres of pressure, carry a lower rate of tax than fully sparkling wines.

- *Méthode champenoise* wines, of which there are just over a dozen produced in South Africa, are usually designated by the phrase '*cap classique*' and were once distinguished by the words 'fermented in *this* bottle', '*fermenté en bouteille*' and '*méthode champenoise*'. Thankfully, South Africa has agreed with France not to use the word 'champagne' to describe these or any other styles of sparkling wine it produces.

Producers

Ashton Cooperative   CC   →★
PO Box 40, Ashton 6715
In spite of its location in the hot, arid Robertson region, this cooperative still manages to produce a dryish Petillant Blanc glugging wine with slight spritz.

Avontuur Winery   MC   ★→
PO Box 1128, Somerset West 7130
Cordon d'Or is the name of the *méthode champenoise* sparkling wine here, a predominantly Chardonnay blend with a dash of Pinot Noir. Discerning locals deem it to be good, not great.

Backsberg Estate   MC   ★→
PO Box 1, Klapmuts 7625
The Back family has been here for three generations, and its sound, easy-drinking, commercial wines are popular in the Cape. The Pinot Noir- and Chardonnay-based Brut, and the sweeter, pink Pinot Noir-only Sec are not exceptions.

Barrydale Cooperative   MC   ☆☆
PO Box 59, Barrydale 6750
This large coop, situated in the hot Klein Karoo region, has just started to make *méthode champenoise* wines and the first results are awaited with interest.

Graham Beck Winery   MC   ☆→☆☆
PO Box 724, Robertson 6705
Probably the brightest new star in the Cape sparkling wine firmament and, although only founded in 1991, already much admired. Just 10,000 cases of sparkling wine are expected from here annually from 40 ha (99 acres) surrounding the winery in the Madeba Valley. The first release, in spring 1993, was the non-vintage Brut Royale, a 55 percent Chardonnay, 45 percent Pinot Noir blend. Next in line is the Blanc de Blanc Brut Zero, made exclusively from Chardonnay and due out in spring 1995. Wood fermentation for the Beck base wines, plus almost two years' yeast ageing in a high tech, state-of-the-art winery completed in 1990, demonstrate

Graham Beck's keenness on quality. Graham Beck now also controls the DOUGLAS GREEN-Bellingham group.

Bellingham   CC   →★
Franschhoek Road, Franschhoek 7690
Bellingham's Paarl estate, founded in 1693, dates back to the early pioneering days in the Cape. Bellingham once belonged to the Union Wine group, but is now the property of the DOUGLAS GREEN-Bellingham group, owned by Graham Bech. Its distinctively labelled wines, featuring the curvy Bellingham Cape Dutch gable, have been selling well. Bellingham Gold, a sweet Chenin Blanc-based sparkler is as successful as the tank method, Chardonnay-based Brut and the Pinotage-based Rosé.

Bon Courage Estate   MC   ★
PO Box 589, Robertson 6705
André Bruwer is in charge here, and his two new carbonated sparklers − the pink from Pinot Noir and the white from Chardonnay − are intended to slake Cape thirsts whilst they wait for the firm's first *méthode champenoise* vintage, the '92, to mature.

Boschendal Estate   MC   ★★→
Groot Drakenstein 7680
Star buy '82 Boschendal Brut
This 300-year-old estate boasts one of the finest examples of H-plan Cape Dutch farmhouses. Since 1979 it has offered the *méthode champenoise* Boschendal Brut. Once Riesling-based, from the '84 vintage it has contained increasing proportions of Chardonnay and Pinots Blanc and Noir at the expense of the Riesling. Even so, the complex, mature, flowery '82 vintage, with its creamy mousse and steady stream of small bubbles, was the country's finest sparkling wine. Later releases have relied more on Pinot Noir with some Chardonnay − the same blend used in the firm's well thought of Brut Rosé. Boschendal's newest *méthode champenoise* fizz is Le Grand Pavillon, made from Chardonnay, Sémillon and Riesling and consequently less fine, although popular.

Buitenverwachting   MC   ★→
Klein Constantia Road, Constantia 7800

Hard to pronounce but worth the effort, for Buitenverwachting Brut, a *méthode champenoise* sparkler based on Pinot Noir but with a measure each of Pinot Gris and Chardonnay, has gone down well with Cape commentators.

Cinzano Spumante   IM/CC   →★
Gilbey House, Stellentia Road, Stellenbosch 7600

Europeans could be forgiven for imagining Italy to be the source of this best-selling sweet sparkling wine, but it is made and bottled by Gilbey's, South Africa. Gilbey's produces almost 200,000 cases of non-vintage carbonated/tank method sparkling wine here. Labels include the straight carbonated Spumante plus the pink Tiziano and the new, dry, Sauvignon Blanc-based, tank method Vittoria.

Delheim Wines   CC   ★
PO Box 10, Koelenhof 7605

Ebullient 'Spatz' Sperling has made several styles of sparkler so far at his hilltop Stellenbosch Delheim estate, including a dry Pinot Noir-based rosé and a finer Riesling-based *brut*.

Douglas Green Wines   CC   →★
Box 4617, Randberg 2125

Once closely connected with the KWV operation in Paarl, this firm is now part of the DOUGLAS GREEN-Bellingham group and owned by GRAHAM BECK. It buys in wines from elsewhere and simply blends and bottles them. Currently its list of sparkling wines includes the Cuvée Brut Celebré, Demi-Sec and Blanc de Noir.

Eikendal Vineyards   MC/CC   ★
PO Box 2261, Stellenbosch 7600

Swiss traditions and an Australian winemaker no doubt account for the wacky Eikendal approach. Look out here for the Duc de Berry carbonated Demi-sec sparklers, and for tiny quantities of a *méthode champenoise*, Pinot Noir- and Chardonnay-based Eikendal Brut, which is about to be launched. Quality is only average, given that Chenin Blanc accounts for half of both blends.

Fairview Estate   MC
PO Box 583, Suider–Paarl 7625
This winery's great view of the extraordinary Table Mountain is the explanation for the 300-year-old property's name. Fairview's *méthode champenoise* sparkling wine is sold under the Charles Gerard label, as are the other reserve wines made here by the Back family. Son Charles is in charge, and this no doubt accounts for the brand name. The well thought of Pinot Noir-based bubbly is aged for over two years on its lees, and this accounts for its quality.

Fleur du Cap Wines   CC
PO Box 5001, Stellenbosch 7600
This firm, part of the large Oude Meester group, has offered several sparkling wines, including a South African Sauvignon Blanc-based *cuve close* which is somewhat curiously named Premier Grand Cru.

Franschhoek Vineyards Cooperative   IM
PO Box 52, Franschhoek 7690
Nestling beneath the dramatic Franschhoek mountains, this cooperative produces carbonated Sauvignon Blanc-based fizz plus a sweeter blend made from lesser varieties.

Grand Mousseux   MC/IM
SFW, PO Box 46, Stellenbosch 7599
Grand Mousseux is the biggest-selling brand of sparkler in South Africa. It is made by the Stellenbosch Farmers' Winery, which is also responsible for the NEDERBURG sparkling wines. The top sparklers are the *méthode champenoise* Grande Cuvée, based on Pinot Noir and Chardonnay, and the Blanc de Blancs Chardonnay. Lesser carbonated wines include the Spumante Vins Doux and Sec, plus the red Grand Rouge. SFW also makes the popular, sweet, salmon-pink Fifth Avenue Cold Duck.

Here XVII   CC/MC
Oude Meester, Papegaaiberg, Stellenbosch
Oude Meester, with its large Bergkelder cellars, is one of the largest and most powerful South African wine groups and the owner of this brand, of which it sells at least 25,000 cases a year. Here XVII

Souverein is a sweet, sherbety *cuve close* blend of several varieties, dominated by the Sauvignon Blanc. Its posher relative is the Pinot Noir-based Grande Cuvée. Oude Meester also sells small amounts of vintage-dated *cuve close*: the positive, grassy J C Le Roux Sauvignon Blanc, made exclusively from that grape. Best of the bunch is the vintage-dated J C Le Roux Pinot Noir *méthode champenoise*, as yet available only in small quantities. With its earthy, hefty flavour it is not, however, the finest *méthode champenoise* wine that the Cape produces. Other *méthode champenoise* wines include the J C le Roux Chardonnay, heavily Pinot Noir-influenced, Kap Sekt and Pongracz. Carbonated wines include the red La Chanson and the white Muscat-scented Le Domaine.

Pierre Jourdan (Clos Cabrière)   MC   ★→★★
Box 245, Franschhoek 7690
Star buy Pierre Jourdan Brut

Winemaker and *méthode champenoise* enthusiast Achim von Arnim runs the Clos Cabrière business. The Clos Cabrière estate, founded in 1694, has so far released five sparkling wines, all vintage-dated and made via the *méthode champenoise*. The Pierre Jourdan Brut Savage uses the first pressing of partly bought-in Chardonnay and Pinot Noir. It was the first of such *cuvées* to be available commercially in the Cape. With no *dosage*, Brut Savage is the purest example of the von Arnim Signature and from the '92 vintage, like all the Pierre Jourdan bottles, has come almost exclusively from Clos Cabrière's own grapes. Its rich, mature nose and flowery, flavoursome palate is an excellent first effort and amongst the best *méthode champenoise* wines the Cape produces. The standard Pierre Jourdan Brut, like the Savage, is 60 percent Chardonnay to 40 percent Pinot Noir and the limited edition, mature Cuvée Reserve is the same wine with four years on yeast. Apart from the Pierre Jourdan Brut, the two other 'big' wines here are the Blanc de Blancs and the Cuvée Belle Rosé (100 percent Chardonnay and Pinot Noir respectively). The firm produces 10,000 cases in most years, and the quality of the wines is high, due to von Arnim's determination and hands-on style (base wines fermented in oak, riddling by hand). When Clos Cabrière's new, close-spaced, hillside, Pinot Noir-clone vines all come on stream in the near future, it is likely that the estate's sparklers will take another step forward in quality.

Krone Borealis (Twee Jongegezellen Estate) MC ★→
PO Box 16, Tulbagh 6820

Founded in 1710, Twee Jongegezellen is the second oldest family-run estate in the country. T J is known for its pretty, rambling 1719 homestead and gardens, plus the delightful Krone family, which is still at the helm. Today, son Nicky is in charge, but papa N C Krone keeps his eye on T J too. The firm's first *méthode champenoise* vintage wine was the '87, aptly-named Krone Borealis after the Corona Borealis constellation (both Krone and Corona mean 'crown'). What primarily separates the 8,000 cases plus made annually of Krone Borealis from the more humdrum Cape *méthode champenoise* competition is the cool, concentrated excellence of Tulbagh Valley Chardonnay and Pinot Noir; the blend is a fifty-fifty mix of the two. Night harvesting, hand *remuage*, no added sulphur, slightly oaked base wines, plus three and a half years' yeast ageing in splendid underground cellars built specifically for sparkling wine, are other quality controls that few other Cape *méthode champenoise* producers bother with. Nicky Krone is so convinced of the positive forces and life-enhancing negative ions in every bottle of Krone Borealis that this is noted on the label. Expect to see a new Krone Borealis sparkler in 1996. The cellars and vineyard are currently being expanded, which must lead to an increase in production and more of this much-admired sparkling wine to go round.

KWV
(Ko-operatieve Wijnbouwers Vereniging) CC/MC ★
Laborie Estate, Taillefer Street, Paarl

This powerful semi-official cooperative and controlling body was set up in 1918 to help farmers dispose of bulk wine and obtain a fair price for their crop. The coop now has 6,000 members. Few KWV wines are sold in South Africa; most are reserved for export. The Its mediocre *cuve close* Mousseux range, made principally from Chenin Blanc and available in a pear-drop-like *brut* and *demi-sec* accounts for most of the sparkling wine sales. New sparklers here include the Petillant Blanc and Rosé. Small amounts of KWV's Laborie estate transfer method, Pinotage-based Blanc de Noir are on sale in the Cape.

L'Ormarins Estate   MC   ★
Franschhoek, Suider Paarl

Under the Bergkelder's umbrella, L'Ormarins is an old Cape estate, founded by Huguenot Jean Roi, but only recently given a new, high tech lease of life. The first L'Ormarins Jean Roi *méthode champenoise* bubbly, the '87, was made from Pinot Noir and Chardonnay. Future vintages are likely to follow this path.

Nederburg   CC/MC   ★→★★
Meaker Street, Huguenot 7646

Nederburg is part of the large Stellenbosch Farmers' Winery group (*see* Grand Mousseux). Two styles of sparkling wine are made. The South African Riesling–dominated (now with Sauvignon too) silver-labelled Première Cuvée Brut is raw and assertive, and very popular; there is also a Cuvée Doux Muscat-scented version. Dryer still is the Premier Grand Cru, again Sauvignon Blanc-based. The superior German-inspired gold label Kap Sekt has some Rhine Riesling in the blend together with Cape Riesling, and this shows in its attractive lime–juice-like taste. Look out for the new limited edition Blanquette – as the label states, a classy '*méthode champenoise de Chardonnay*', launched to celebrate Nederburg's 200th anniversary.

Rustenberg Estate   MC   ★→
PO Box 33, Stellenbosch 7600

Rustenberg must be the most idyllic Cape estate, with an extraordinarily beautiful setting that few who visit could ever forget. Etienne le Riche is no winemaking slouch either, and has produced a string of fine Rustenberg reds. This augurs well for Centenary, the *méthode champenoise* sparkler that he made especially for Rustenberg's 310th anniversary. The firm's last 100 vintages have been bottled without a break, a record that I doubt any other Cape estate could match.

Simonsig Kaapse Vonkel   MC   ★→
Simonsig Estate, PO Box 6, Koelenhof 7605

Frans Malans, joined now by his three sons, launched Kaapse Vonkel, the Cape's first *méthode champenoise* wine, in 1971. The wine has improved considerably since some Chardonnay and Pinot

Noir was added to its Chenin Blanc base. From 1987, this bone-dry vintage-dated sparkler has been made entirely from Pinot Noir and Chardonnay, with the '90 vintage containing about two-thirds Pinot Noir. Today, there are 7 ha (18 acres) of Simonsig vines used for sparkling wine production, and 5,000 cases are made annually. Expect a Kaapse Vonkel prestige *cuvée* in 1997, possibly with some of the Cape's first Pinot Meunier in the mix.

Tradition Charles de Fère   MC/CC   ★→
Villiera Estate, PO Box 66, Koelenhof 7605

The Villiera Estate in Paarl is owned by the Grier brothers, one of whom worked for a short time in Champagne. Exactly which *champenois* traditions rubbed off on the firm's pleasant, ripe, fruity, biscuity sparkler, made mostly from Pinotage and Pinot Noir plus a little Chenin Blanc, is difficult to judge. However, this inexpensive wine, available in Carte d'Or, Tradition, Grand Cuvée and Rosé versions, has gone down well with locals. Other Villiera labels include the *méthode champenoise* Woolworths wines, plus Blue Ridge Brut and Rosé. Pinot Noir was used increasingly here during the 1980s and Chardonnay has appeared in the blends from 1990. Over 18,000 bottles are made annually. Jean Louis Denois of Charles de Fère in France, whose excellent *méthode champenoise* wines are made just outside the Champagne region, has been a consultant here since the '84 vintage, hence the brand name.

The Rest of the World

Bulgaria

Bulgaria produces some of the finest white and red wines in eastern Europe. Whether this applies to its sparkling wines, known as *Iskra* (or *spark*), is difficult to say, for few are exported. West Germany, however, imports one of the better Bulgarian sparklers, Schwarze Meer, which is made by the modern, efficiently-run plant at Tchirpan. This firm's Balkan Crown sparkling Riesling and sparkling Chardonnay have started to acquire export markets too, and both of these wines should be worth seeking out. Another Bulgarian winery, Targovishte, sells the basic Biliana and Albena sparklers, but the best Bulgarian fizz is Magura, which comes from the town of the same name.

About 2M cases of Bulgarian sparkling wine are produced annually. Now that there is a 'free', no longer exclusively state-controlled wine market here, many Bulgarian producers have begun to export and sell their wines themselves. Given the world's interest in sparkling wine, this could perhaps lead to the arrival soon of several classy, new Bulgarian bubblies.

Canada

Canada's sparkling wine producers appear to concentrate on Cold Duck and the like made from *labrusca*-redolent hybrids rather than anything more serious. André's Baby Duck is probably the country's most successful sparkler in this category, but numerous other firms, including Jordan and Barnes, make similar styles. Bright's, an old Ontario firm, uses French and American hybrids as well as the *labrusca* grapes to make its range of du Barry sparklers; it also now has a 'champagne' made from the Chardonnay grape.

Château des Charmes, which has two 'champagnes', is also based in Ontario as is Château Gai, which uses hybrid vines as the base for its Charmat method sparkling wines. Inniskillin, again an Ontario house, founded in 1974, has a *méthode champenoise* vintage-dated Blanc de Blancs Chardonnay, plus the non-vintage L'Allemand. The latter is apparently a German *Sekt*-style sparkler, still made by the *méthode champenoise* but from Grey Riesling and Gamay Beaujolais grapes. Karl Podamer, a fourth Ontario house, makes *méthode champenoise* wines from a range of grape varieties including Chardonnay. The Summerhill Estate Winery in British Columbia produces a *méthode champenoise* Cipes Brut made from Riesling. Canada clearly has some way to go before it becomes a fine sparkling wine source of the world.

Central and South America

Surprisingly, Mexico is responsible for the foundation of much of South America's wine industry. Spanish missionaries first planted the vine in Mexico around 1524 and gradually it was transported south to Chile, Peru and Argentina. In general, the South American taste, in both its own sparkling wines and in imported champagne, is for the sweeter or *doux* styles. Many champagne houses now produce a *doux* champagne exclusively for this market.

Most of Mexico's wine regions are situated north of Mexico City. Although there are numerous growers, there are very few producers. Several international names are to be found here, but the majority of Mexico's sparkling wines are made by Mexicans. Cavas de San Juan, with its Carte Blanche *méthode champenoise* wine is a well-known producer, as is Bodegas de Santo Tomás. Other firms making sparkling wine include Vinícola de Aguascalientes (with its Champ d'Or brand), Hacienda Alamo and Marqués del Aguayo; Freixenet of Spain is responsible for Sala Vive. The base wines for most of these sparklers comes from a wide range of grapes, including Chenin Blanc, Chardonnay, Ugni Blanc, Colombard, Sémillon and Pinot Noir.

Working south through the countries, Colombia and Venezuela both make sparkling wines, but only on a small scale. Venezuela is one of the few South American countries to restrict the use of the word 'champagne' to genuine, imported French champagne.

Brazil, on the other hand, makes sizeable quantities of sparkling wine – about 417,000 cases annually (the same as Argentina and Chile). Brazilian bubbly is mostly produced in the semi-tropical Rio Grande do Sul region, where the majority of the country's still wine is also made.

The first Brazilian sparkling wine was produced by Armando Peterlongo in 1913 and the firm still makes such wines today. The grapes used for this and other Brazilian sparklers are gradually being switched from *labrusca*-redolent hybrids to more noble varieties including Riesling, Trebbiano, Pinot Noir and Sémillon. Other Brazilian sparkling wine brands include George Aubert, Bernard Taillan, Heublein do Brasil's Bratage plus Companhia Vinicola Riograndense's Moscato Espumante.

International sparkling wine firms are also firmly established in Brazil. Moët & Chandon, together with its partners, Cinzano and Monteiro Aranha, has been the force since 1974 in the south of the country, at Garibaldi, behind Provifin's successful M Chandon label, of which only 15,000 cases are produced each year. Brazil's subtropical climate, and grapes such as Sémillon, Chasselas and Welsch Riesling are not, as even Moët itself admits, ideal sparkling wine components. Martini & Rossi is responsible for the Brazilian Champagne de Greville, plus a locally made *spumante*.

There are fewer Chilean sparkling wine producers but they make roughly the same amount as Brazil. The biggest producer is Alberto Valdivieso, founded in 1887, which uses the *méthode champenoise* to make its top range of sparkling wines, sold under the Nature, Brut and Grand Brut labels and made from Chardonnay and Pinot Noir. Other, sweeter Demi-Sec and Moscato Valdivieso wines, using the lesser Torontel and Sémillon, are produced via the Charmat method. The firm makes half a million cases of sparkling wine annually. Concha y Toro has a range of *cuve close* wines made for the firm by its subsidiary, Subercaseaux. The other major *cuve close* producers are Santa Ana and Santa Carolina, with their Champagne Chileno Santa Carolina. Undurraga, the important table wine producer, also sells sparkling wine, including cheap, carbonated sparklers made by Viña Manquehue.

Perhaps the most exciting news regarding Chilean sparkling wine is that Torres, the leading Spanish wine firm, is now about to make *méthode champenoise* sparkling wine at its Chilean outpost.

Argentina's biggest sparkling wine producer is probably the Casa de Saint Remy, with its Duc de Saint Remy and Marie Boucau *méthode champenoise* wines. Finca Flichman is another big Argentine sparkling wine name. International companies have a foothold here too, the most notable of which is Bodegas Chandon in Mendoza, founded in 1960 and run by Moët & Chandon, which produces 4M bottles of sparkling wine here annually. These include Baron B, Chandon and H Mercier. The grapes used include Ugni Blanc, Sémillon and other similar varieties, but given their obviously humdrum quality, the end result is reputed to be surprisingly simple, fresh and appealing. Also situated in Mendoza is Rémy Cointreau's Henri Piper. This is the second largest brand in Argentina and at the upper, more pricey end of the country's sparkling wine spectrum. It is available in Brut, Demi-Sec and Extreme versions. The last of these is Henri Piper's prestige *cuvée*. Deutz too has sparkling wine interests in Argentina, having been involved since 1985 with the Argentine house of Navarro-Carreas.

The CIS (Former USSR)

Russians are devoted sparkling wine, or *shampanskoye*, drinkers. Before the Revolution, vast quantities of the finest French champagne enlivened the tedium of long, frozen Russian winters, for those who could afford it. The *dosage* levels were high – about three times those of the current *doux* or rich champagnes. Today, Russians appear to have the same sweet tooth. Most of the country's sparkling wines, whether white or red, are very sweet, although there are some dry versions wines available. The introduction of the classic champagne grapes and the possibility of growing exports should encourage production of the drier styles.

Most Russian fizz is produced by the transfer method or the continuous flow method – a system perfected by the Russians (*see* pages 15–16), and one that is both speedy and cheap. The CIS produces about 21M cases of *shampanskoye* annually – the dramatic 45 percent increase in production the late 1980s no doubt came as a result of using the continuous flow system. The CIS hopes to double this figure before too long.

Well known Russian continuous flow method brands include Grand Duchess, a 45 percent Aligoté, 35 percent Sauvignon Blanc and 20 percent Traminer blend, plus the marginally finer St Petersburg, whose blend now apparently includes some Pinot Noir and Chardonnay.

As more commercial, independent systems replace the old Communist structure in Russia's wineries, new finer sparkling wines should come on stream. There has been much interest and investment in sparkling wine production here of late. Moldova, one of the new, independent Russian States on the Black Sea and sandwiched in between Romania and the Ukraine, has good Chardonnay and a tradition of producing sparkling wines (admittedly by the Russian continuous flow system) and could well be the site of some much improved *shampanskoye* in the future.

Western Germany, the old Communist bloc and the CIS itself are the chief consumers of *shampanskoye*. The three main export brands are Krim, Nazdorovya and Rossiya. Quality is mostly sweet, flabby and mediocre, with white Krim a strange, perfumed fizz and the red not unlike an unpleasant, sulphury version of Italian *lambrusco*. Inside the CIS, Abrau-Durso from the Crimea, made by the *méthode champenoise*, is said to be the finest Russian *shampanskoye*, and therefore should be worth seeking out. The red Tzimlianskoe and white Zolotoye are also available. Sovietskoye, in a variety of styles, is the most widely distributed *shampanskoye*.

England

The world's winemakers are amazed that England grows grapes at all in its distinctly cool, marginal climate for vines, let alone makes wines from them, but England has had vineyards since Roman times. The earliest English *méthode champenoise* wine was made by Nigel Godden at Pilton Manor near Shepton Mallet in Somerset. Made from the Müller-Thurgau and Seyval Blanc, it scores points for trying but not for finesse.

In 1985, David Carr Taylor introduced Carr Taylor Dry Sparkling Wine, again made by the *méthode champenoise*, from his vineyards close to Hastings in Sussex. Initially, only limited amounts of the young, green, acidic '85 vintage, made from Kerner, Reichensteiner and Schonburger grapes, was released. More recent blends are attempting to move towards a mix of predominantly Chardonnay, rounded off with Pinots Noir and Meunier. About 4,000 cases are made in most years in a variety of styles including Rosé and a Special Vintage *demi-sec*.

Rock Lodge in Sussex now produces tiny quantities of the Reichensteiner-based *méthode champenoise* Impresario! Brut besides bottling about 20 different sparkling wines for other English vineyards. Thames Valley Vineyards in Berkshire and Lamberhurst in Kent are other English wine producers involved in the sparkling wine industry.

Greece

Unsurprisingly, the hot, arid, Greek landscape does not produce any sparkling wines of note. However, the maritime-influenced climes of the island of Rhodes do produce one Greek sparkler of interest: the *méthode champenoise* Brut and Demi-Sec from CAIR. This is a cooperative, founded in 1943, and the biggest producer by far of Rhodes wines. To date, CAIR is the only *méthode champenoise* sparkling wine producer in Greece; its quality is as you would expect it to be.

Hungary

Hungarian sparkling wine is divided into two categories: *pezsgö*, sparkling wine made by the *méthode champenoise*, and the lesser quality *habzobor*, foaming wine made by the transfer or Charmat method, which is about half the price. The Hungarians, like their eastern European neighbours, enjoy sweet or medium-sweet fizz with distinctive regional flavours. The most famous and traditional *pezsgö* sparkling wine house is Törley in Budafok, close to Budapest. Törley was founded in 1880, and today produces some

83,000 cases of *méthode champenoise* wine annually, as well as using the transfer method for a *sec* and *demi-sec*. Hungarovin, which owns Törley, also has two other big sparkling wine plants in Budafok, whose brands, Hungaria and Francois, made by the Charmat and transfer methods, account for some 242,000 cases annually between them.

Hungarian sparkling wines are produced in a wide range of styles from *brut* to *delicatesse*, the sweetest. Apart from the Hungarovin, leading Hungarian sparkling wine producers include Hosszuhegyi, Kiskunhalas, Villaany-Mecsekaljai, Balatonboglaar, Koezeep-Magyarorszaagi and Szikra. Hungarian sparkling wine is mostly sweet and mediocre in quality. Kiskunhalas does however produce a highly thought of Sparkling Chardonnay, and Balatonboglaar makes a good sparkler from the Muscat grape. Henkell, the German *Sekt* house, is thought to be involved with Balatonboglaar. Charmant and Pompadour are two other Hungarian sparkling wine brand names.

Visitors to Hungary will see vast quantities of cheap Russian sparklers on sale there as well as Hungarian *habzobor*. Hungary, despite its new 'free trade' status, like Bulgaria still exports a great deal of its sparkling wine to the CIS, East Germany, Poland and elsewhere in Eastern Europe. However, the arrival here of several highly skilled western winemaking teams such as Hugh Ryman's from Australia has encouraged new wine skills, and perhaps one day a first class Hungarian *habzobor* will appear.

India

India is probably the last place in the world anyone would look to as the origin of a *méthode champenoise* wine, but since 1983 it has indeed produced one: Royal Mousseux. It is made by the Indage group, originally under advice from Piper-Heidsieck's Champagne Technologie. Ugni Blanc, Pinot Blanc and Chardonnay grapes grown at Narayangaon near Bombay, in the Maharashtra region, are turned into sparkling wine at a £4M winery that is exclusively French-equipped. What is remarkable, given India's hot climate and lack of winemaking expertise, is just how good Royal

Mousseux is. Its pale gold colour is backed up by a flowery bouquet and a soft, flowery, perfumed palate. The wine previously appeared under the Marquise de Pompadour label but is now sold as Omar Khayham. A Royal Mousseux made by the *cuve close* method is produced by the same firm and is available in India.

The latest Indo–French *méthode champenoise* project is between A Charbaut & Fils of Champagne and the Pimpane Cooperative. This joint venture is sited in Maharashtra, in the Jaulke Vani region, which accounts for the name given to this *blanc de blancs* sparkling wine: Princess Jaulke.

Israel

Baron Edmond de Rothschild established the modern Israeli wine industry by founding two wineries to the north and south of Tel Aviv. Today these process more than two-thirds of the country's grapes. The vintage-dated President's Sparkling Wine, under the Carmel label, is made at the southern winery. This *méthode champenoise* sparkler comes in two versions – as a *demi-sec* and as the classier Brut Sambatyon.

Luxembourg

Luxembourg, sandwiched between Belgium and Germany, is overlooked by most wine drinkers. A pity, because its cool, northern vineyards are beginning to produce some good wines from noble grapes and Luxembourg is especially keen to make fine, up-market sparkling wines. Indeed, the industry was given a welcome boost with the launch of Crémant de Luxembourg in 1991, a term intending to put traditional method Luxembourg fizz on the same level, perhaps, as those of France. So far there are only four companies of note involved in the sparkling wine industry: Caves Bernard-Massard at Grevenmacher, run by the Clasen family, is the largest, producing some 167,000 cases of *méthode champenoise* wine annually. Most of this, made from Elbling, Pinot Blanc and

Riesling, is sold as *brut* but the range also includes a classier Pinot Blanc-, Riesling- and Chardonnay-based Cuvée de l'Ecusson sparkling wine. Gales & Cie at Bech-Kleinmacher produces some 67,000 cases of fizz every year. Once again, most of this is sold as the Riesling-based Brut Private Cuvée, but there is a cheaper St-Martin range whose Carte Blanche is the only *cuve close* wine, the rest being made by the *méthode champenoise*.

Two-thirds of Luxembourg's wines are made in cooperatives. The Vinsmoselle Coopérative at Stadtbredimus makes about 17,000 cases of Duc Henry *cuve close* sparkling wine every year. Most of this is made from the lesser quality Elbling and Rivaner grapes. Caves St-Rémy-Desom at Remich also makes *cuve close* sparkling wine, sold under a variety of labels including St-Remy, Desom, Dicks, Albert-Georges, Calvador and Duc de Monclair.

The best place to taste Luxembourg sparkling wine is in Luxembourg itself, but it is exported, mainly to Belgium and the Netherlands.

Romania

Like those of its eastern European neighbours, Romania's *spumos* or sparkling wines, are sweetish and not very exciting. However, Romania has plantings of Chardonnay and Pinot Noir and hopefully it will not be too long before commercial quantities of sparkling wine from these grape varieties are available. Premiat, made by the *méthode champenoise*, is the country's most famous sparkling wine. Romania makes about 1.5M cases of sparkling wine annually.

Switzerland

Swiss sparkling wine is confusing. Most of it is not Swiss at all, simply a blend of local grapes, mixed in with a hefty proportion of (usually) Chenin Blanc from the Loire to create the *blanc de blancs* styles, and with Muscat from northern Italy to make the *spumante* sparklers. Detecting the genuine Swiss sparkling wine from the imported, often blended product is not difficult. The majority of Swiss sparkling wines made from imported wine usually carry the words '*elaboré en Suisse*' or '*imbottigliato in Svizzera*' followed by '*produit de France*', '*spumante d'Italia*' etc. There are, however, true Swiss sparkling wines sold under labels such as Grand Vin Mousseux du Valais, an important Swiss wine–producing region to the east of Lake Geneva, and Grand Vin Mousseux du Vaud, a region just to the north of the Lake. The fruity but dull Chasselas is the white grape used for these and other Swiss sparkling wines.

Switzerland's sparklers are made either by the *méthode champenoise* (which is usually indicated on the label) or by the *cuve close* method. Mauler & Cie at Môtiers, founded in 1829, with its range of *méthode champenoise* wines is thought by many to produce the finest Swiss sparkling wines. About 20 percent of the firm's needs comes from its own Pinot Noir and Chardonnay vines; the rest, generally Pinot Noir, is imported from France.

The Former Yugoslav States

These States are much better known for Laski Riesling than they are for sparkling wine, yet they do make fizz. Sparkling wines here are known as *biser*, or 'pearl'. One of the most familiar is called Fruskogorski Biser and is made by Navip, which also produces a finer sparkler called Milion. Another example is Bakarska Vodica, made by Istravino. Slovenia is the only area to produce *méthode champenoise* wines; Radgona's is called Zlata Radgonska Penina.

Glossary

Appellation Contrôlée/AC Superior French quality wine designation which guarantees the source and production method, but not the quality.

Blanc de Blancs *See* page 19.

Blanc de Noirs *See* pages 19–20.

Bodega A Spanish firm that makes wine. The term also means 'wine cellar'.

Buyer's Own Brand/BOB *See* page 20.

Cantina Italian wine cellar or winery.

Cava Spanish sparkling wines made by the *méthode champenoise*. In the past, also used to describe a sparkling wine establishment or producer.

Carbonated or injection method The cheapest and least lovely method of producing sparkling wine. CO_2 is pumped into a closed tank containing still wine and the wine is then bottled under pressure. *See* page 16.

Charmat method Another name for *cuve close*. *See* page 15.

Chef de cave The cellar manager and winemaker.

Cold settling, clarification or débourbage This usually takes place prior to fermentation, when the cloudy must, or unfermented grape juice, is cleared of its haze and grape particles by being chilled in a tank. Often chemicals are used to encourage this clarification and settling process.

Cold stabilization The modern method of clearing cloudy wine that has just finished fermenting, by chilling it in a tank and allowing the particles to precipitate to the bottom. The old-fashioned method was simply to open the winery doors to let in cold, autumn air.

Continuous or Russian Continuous Flow method A method of producing sparkling wine continuously, where the second, bubble-inducing fermentation takes place in a series of tanks. *See* pages 15–16.

Coteaux Champenois Still red or white wines of the Champagne region.

Crémant Softly sparkling or 'creaming' sparkling wines. *See* page 19.

Cuve close An inexpensive method of producing sparkling wine in which a second, bubble-inducing fermentation takes place in a tank. *See* page 15.

Cuvée The French word for a blend. Hopefully a harmonious mix of wines that have been blended together to produce a sparkling wine that is better than each of its components.

Dégorgement or disgorging *See* page 13.

Dégorgement à la glace *See* page 13.

Dégorgement à la volée Disgorging performed by hand without the sediment being frozen.

Deutscher Sekt bA The finest German *Sekt*, on a par with still QbA wines. *See* page 192.

Deuxième taille Juice from the final pressing of the *méthode champenoise*, now forbidden in Champagne.

Dosage A blend of wine and sugar added to champagne and other sparkling wines before the final cork is put in.

Frizzante *See* Pétillant.

Girasol 'Sunflower' in Spanish. A metal riddling frame containing about 500 bottles. Used in Spain, California and elsewhere.

Grande marque Term applied to a leading champagne house.

Gyropalettes Roughly the same as a *girasol*. *See* page 13.

Hybrids These grapes are usually a cross between noble *vinifera* vines and hardy, lesser vines such as *vitis labrusca* from the USA. French hybrids are themselves often a cross between hybrids and *vitis vinifera*.

Liqueur de tirage *See* page 12.

Malolactic fermentation A secondary fermentation in which harsh, malic acids are converted into gentler, lactic acids.

Méthode champenoise Traditional, costly, time-consuming champagne and sparkling wine production method in which bubbles are produced by a second fermentation in bottle. *See* pages 10–13.

Méthode dioise A refined version of the *méthode rurale*, involving a 3–4 month fermentation before bottling and used exclusively for making Clairette de Die. *See* page 14.

Méthode gaillaçoise A variation on the méthode rurale. *See* page 14.

Méthode traditionnelle Traditional method, or *méthode tradition-nelle*, sparkling wines are, as the name suggests, made by the same sparkling wine process as the *méthode champenoise* (*see* pages 10–13). Due to new EC regulations, the term '*méthode champenoise*' is now being phased out and gradually replaced with the term '*méthode tra-dionnelle*'. *See* pages 16–17.

Micro-billes Porous yeast capsules for *remuage*. *See* page 13.

Mousseux Fully sparkling wines. *See* Crémant, page 19.

Non-vintage *See* page 17.

Perlant Wines with the least sparkle of all. *See* page 21.

Pétillant Slightly sparkling wines. *See* page 21.

Prestige or deluxe *See* page 18.

Pupitres Wooden riddling or *remuage* racks. *See* page 12.

Qualitätswein eines bestimmten Anbaugebietes/QbA German quality wines of defined geographical origin.

Racking The process of running off wine from one cask to another, either to remove it from its yeasty sediment and put it into a clean cask, or to aerate it.

Remuage *See* pages 12–13.

Reserve This is a catch-all wine term that, when it appears on a label, often means nothing at all. It can, however, signify superior sparkling wine. Quality-minded producers of sparkling wine often use a portion of aged reserve wines in the final *dosage* of their blends in order to give the finished wine that extra measure of age, complexity and finesse.

Rosé Pink champagne or sparkling wine usually made from a blend of red and white wine. The finest examples are made by the saignée method, in which red grape skins slightly stain the juice pink, before being removed. *See* page 18.

Schaumwein German for sparkling wine at its cheapest level. *See* page 191.

Sekt German for sparkling wine; a step up from *Schaumwein*. *See* page 191.

Singe-vineyard *See* page 20.

Spumante Italian sparkling wine.

Straight blend Sparkling wine producers make a plethora of wine styles. To simplify the issue, the use of the word 'straight' in this book refers to a standard, non-vintage *brut* blend.

Transfer method Compromise method where a second, bubble-inducing fermentation takes place in bottle and the wine is then transferred to a tank. *See* pages 14–15.

Vin de cuvée Finest quality juice from the first 'free run' pressing of the *méthode champenoise* process.

Vin de taille The second pressing from the *méthode champenoise*.

Vintage *See* page 18.

Vins mousseux de qualité/VMQ French quality sparkling wines.

Vitis labrusca A less noble branch of the vine's family tree. *Labrusca* grapes have a malodorous, almost foxy scent. They are still grown in the wine world, particularly in the USA, outside California.

Vitis vinifera The most noble branch of the vine's family tree. *Vinifera* grapes such as Chardonnay and Pinot Noir produce the world's finest sparkling wines.